Jews on the Move: Modern Cosmopolitanist Thought and its Others

Jewish cosmopolitanism is key to understanding both modern globalization, and the old and new nationalism. Jewish cultures existing in the Western world during the last two centuries have been and continue to be read as hyphenated phenomena within a specific national context, such as German-Jewish or American-Jewish culture. Yet to what extent do such nationalized constructs of Jewish culture and identity still dominate Jewish self-expressions, and the discourses about them, in the rapidly globalizing world of the twenty-first century? In a world in which Diaspora societies have begun to reshape themselves as part of a super- or non-national identity, what has happened to a cosmopolitan Jewish identity?

In a post-Zionist world, where one of the newest and most substantial Diaspora communities is that of Israelis, in the new globalized culture, is "being Jewish" suddenly something that can reach beyond the older models of Diasporic integration or nationalism? Which new paradigms of Jewish self-location, within the evolving and conflicting global discourses, about the nation, race, Genocides, anti-Semitism, colonialism and postcolonialism, gender and sexual identities does the globalization of Jewish cultures open up? To what extent might transnational notions of Jewishness, such as European-Jewish identity, create new discursive margins and centers? Is there a possibility that a "virtual makom (Jewish space)" might constitute itself? Recent studies on cosmopolitanism cite the Jewish experience as a key to the very notion of the movement of people for good or for ill as well as for the resurgence of modern nationalism. These theories reflect newer models of postcolonialism and transnationalism in regard to global Jewish cultures.

The present volume spans the widest reading of Jewish cosmopolitisms to study "Jews on the move."

This book was originally published as a special issue of the *European Review of History*.

Cathy S. Gelbin is a Senior Lecturer in Film and German Studies at Manchester University, UK. She specializes in modern German-Jewish culture, including intellectual history, literature and film.

Sander L. Gilman is a Distinguished Professor of the Liberal Arts and Sciences as well as Professor of Psychiatry at Emory University, Georgia, USA. A cultural and literary historian, he is the author or editor of well over ninety books.

Jews on the Move: Modern Cosmopolitanist Thought and its Others

Edited by
Cathy S. Gelbin and Sander L. Gilman

LONDON AND NEW YORK

First published 2018
by Routledge
2 Park Square, Milton Park, Abingdon, Oxon, OX14 4RN, UK

and by Routledge
711 Third Avenue, New York, NY 10017, USA

Routledge is an imprint of the Taylor & Francis Group, an informa business

© 2018 Taylor & Francis

All rights reserved. No part of this book may be reprinted or reproduced or utilised in any form or by any electronic, mechanical, or other means, now known or hereafter invented, including photocopying and recording, or in any information storage or retrieval system, without permission in writing from the publishers.

Trademark notice: Product or corporate names may be trademarks or registered trademarks, and are used only for identification and explanation without intent to infringe.

British Library Cataloguing in Publication Data
A catalogue record for this book is available from the British Library

ISBN 13: 978-1-138-55530-3

Typeset in Minion Pro
by RefineCatch Limited, Bungay, Suffolk

Publisher's Note
The publisher accepts responsibility for any inconsistencies that may have arisen during the conversion of this book from journal articles to book chapters, namely the possible inclusion of journal terminology.

Disclaimer
Every effort has been made to contact copyright holders for their permission to reprint material in this book. The publishers would be grateful to hear from any copyright holder who is not here acknowledged and will undertake to rectify any errors or omissions in future editions of this book.

Contents

Citation Information   vii
Notes on Contributors   ix

Part I: Jews in modern cosmopolitanist thought

1. Cosmopolitanism and the critique of antisemitism: two faces of universality   1
   Robert D. Fine

2. Aliens vs. predators: cosmopolitan Jews vs. Jewish nomads   16
   Sander L. Gilman

Part II: Jews and cosmopolitanism in interwar Germany

3. Revolutions, wars and the Jewish and Christian contribution to redemptive cosmopolitanism in Franz Rosenzweig and Eugen Rosenstock-Huessy   29
   Wayne Cristaudo

4. Hotel patriots or permanent strangers? Joseph Roth and the Jews of inter-war Central Europe   46
   Ilse Josepha Lazaroms

Part III: Jews, cosmopolitanism and political thought

5. Marxism, cosmopolitanism and 'the' Jews   60
   Philip Spencer

6. New futures, new pasts: Horace M. Kallen and the contribution of Jewishness to the future   79
   Jakob Egholm Feldt

7. Rootless cosmopolitans: German-Jewish writers confront the Stalinist and National Socialist atrocities   95
   Cathy S. Gelbin

Part IV: Jews and the new cosmopolitanism

8. Inviting essential outsiders in: imagining a cosmopolitan nation   112
   Claire Sutherland

9. 'Cosmopolitan from above': a Jewish experience in Hong Kong   129
   Xun Zhou

CONTENTS

10. The possibilities and pitfalls of a Jewish cosmopolitanism: reading Natan Sznaider through Russian-Jewish writer Olga Grjasnowa's German-language novel *Der Russe ist einer, der Birken liebt* (All Russians Love Birch Trees) 144
    Stuart Taberner

11. Cosmopolitan Europeans? Jewish public intellectuals in Germany and Austria and the idea of 'Europe' 163
    Anita Bunyan

12. Drifting towards Cosmopolis 179
    Ruth Novaczek

13. Maximalism as a Cosmopolitan strategy in the art of Ruth Novaczek and Doug Fishbone 193
    Rachel S. Garfield

    Index 211

Citation Information

The chapters in this book were originally published in the *European Review of History*, volume 23, issue 5–6 (October–December 2016). When citing this material, please use the original page numbering for each article, as follows:

Chapter 1
Cosmopolitanism and the critique of antisemitism: two faces of universality
Robert D. Fine
European Review of History, volume 23, issue 5–6 (October–December 2016), pp. 769–783

Chapter 2
Aliens vs. predators: cosmopolitan Jews vs. Jewish nomads
Sander L. Gilman
European Review of History, volume 23, issue 5–6 (October–December 2016), pp. 784–796

Chapter 3
Revolutions, wars and the Jewish and Christian contribution to redemptive cosmopolitanism in Franz Rosenzweig and Eugen Rosenstock-Huessy
Wayne Cristaudo
European Review of History, volume 23, issue 5–6 (October–December 2016), pp. 797–813

Chapter 4
Hotel patriots or permanent strangers? Joseph Roth and the Jews of inter-war Central Europe
Ilse Josepha Lazaroms
European Review of History, volume 23, issue 5–6 (October–December 2016), pp. 814–827

Chapter 5
Marxism, cosmopolitanism and 'the' Jews
Philip Spencer
European Review of History, volume 23, issue 5–6 (October–December 2016), pp. 828–846

Chapter 6
New futures, new pasts: Horace M. Kallen and the contribution of Jewishness to the future
Jakob Egholm Feldt
European Review of History, volume 23, issue 5–6 (October–December 2016), pp. 847–862

Chapter 7
Rootless cosmopolitans: German-Jewish writers confront the Stalinist and National Socialist atrocities
Cathy S. Gelbin
European Review of History, volume 23, issue 5–6 (October–December 2016), pp. 863–879

Chapter 8
Inviting essential outsiders in: imagining a cosmopolitan nation
Claire Sutherland
European Review of History, volume 23, issue 5–6 (October–December 2016), pp. 880–896

Chapter 9
'Cosmopolitan from above': a Jewish experience in Hong Kong
Xun Zhou
European Review of History, volume 23, issue 5–6 (October–December 2016), pp. 897–911

Chapter 10
The possibilities and pitfalls of a Jewish cosmopolitanism: reading Natan Sznaider through Russian-Jewish writer Olga Grjasnowa's German-language novel Der Russe ist einer, der Birken liebt *(All Russians Love Birch Trees)*
Stuart Taberner
European Review of History, volume 23, issue 5–6 (October–December 2016), pp. 912–930

Chapter 11
Cosmopolitan Europeans? Jewish public intellectuals in Germany and Austria and the idea of 'Europe'
Anita Bunyan
European Review of History, volume 23, issue 5–6 (October–December 2016), pp. 931–946

Chapter 12
Drifting towards Cosmopolis
Ruth Novaczek
European Review of History, volume 23, issue 5–6 (October–December 2016), pp. 947–960

Chapter 13
Maximalism as a Cosmopolitan strategy in the art of Ruth Novaczek and Doug Fishbone
Rachel S. Garfield
European Review of History, volume 23, issue 5–6 (October–December 2016), pp. 961–978

For any permission-related enquiries please visit:
http://www.tandfonline.com/page/help/permissions

Notes on Contributors

Anita Bunyan is a Fellow in German and the Director of Studies in Modern Languages at Gonville and Caius College, Cambridge, UK.

Wayne Cristaudo is a Professor of Politics at Charles Darwin University, NT, Australia.

Jakob Egholm Feldt (1972) is an Associate Professor of Transnational and Global History at Roskilde University, Denmark.

Robert D. Fine is an Emeritus Professor of Sociology at the University of Warwick, UK.

Rachel S. Garfield is an artist and an Associate Professor in Fine Art at the University of Reading, UK, who also writes on contemporary and modern art.

Cathy S. Gelbin is a Senior Lecturer in Film and German Studies at Manchester University, UK.

Sander L. Gilman is a Distinguished Professor of the Liberal Arts and Sciences as well as Professor of Psychiatry at Emory University, USA.

Ilse Josepha Lazaroms is a Prins Foundation Fellow at the Center for Jewish History in New York, USA.

Ruth Novaczek is a Visiting Research Fellow at CREAM, University of Westminster, UK.

Philip Spencer is an Emeritus Professor in Holocaust and Genocide Studies at Kingston University, UK.

Claire Sutherland is a Senior Lecturer in Politics at Durham University, UK.

Stuart Taberner has been Professor of Contemporary German Literature, Culture and Society at the University of Leeds since 2005, and is a Research Associate in the Department of Afrikaans and Dutch, German and French at the University of the Free State, South Africa.

Xun Zhou is Reader in Modern History at University of Essex, UK.

Cosmopolitanism and the critique of antisemitism: two faces of universality

Robert D. Fine

ABSTRACT
The antisemitic imagination sometimes derides Jews as 'rootless cosmopolitans', and sometimes as the particularistic enemy of cosmopolitanism. The seemingly contradictory character of these antisemitic representations is not new but needs unpacking. In this article the author argues that Enlightenment cosmopolitanism has shown two faces to Jews: an emancipatory face manifest in movements for legal recognition of Jews as equal citizens and for social recognition of Jews as equal human beings; and a repressive face that has been expressed in the form of the so-called 'Jewish question'. The former holds that Jews are human beings and treats this sense of common humanity as a practical imperative; the latter turns 'the Jews' into an imagined collectivity incapable of meeting the universal standards of humankind. The Jewish question is *in nuce* the question of what is to be done about the harm Jews inflict on humanity at large; it appears and reappears in the modern world in a variety of forms; and it is always at odds with the emancipatory face of cosmopolitanism. The author illustrates this conflict within cosmopolitanism at three key moments of Western European history: the eighteenth-century Enlightenment, nineteenth-century revolutionary thought, and the 'new cosmopolitanism' of our own time. He addresses in a historical fashion some of the difficulties the ambivalence of cosmopolitanism poses for our understanding of antisemitism and conversely some of the difficulties the study of antisemitism poses for the further development of cosmopolitan ways of thinking.

Prejudices, like odorous bodies, have a double existence both solid and subtle — solid as the pyramids, subtle as the twentieth echo of an echo, or as the memory of hyacinths which once scented the darkness.

– George Eliot, *Middlemarch* (1874)

Two faces of universalism

Under the register of the 'rootless cosmopolitan Jew', Jews have been conceived on one hand as lacking in roots in the nations that granted them 'hospitality', and on the other as acting as an international network loyal only to themselves. This pejorative reference to Jews, which was favoured by Stalinist regimes after 1945 and paved the way for the trials and tribulations Jews endured in Eastern Europe in the post-war and Cold War periods, had connotations of disloyalty, lack of patriotism, foreignness and worldwide conspiracy. It was first cousin to cognate terms like 'enemy of the people' or 'enemy of the human species', which began their modern lives as markers of terror in the French Revolution, and signified what we might call a 'bad universalism'.[1] It was contrasted with the 'good universalism' associated with the idea of a universal nation, a nation whose particular interests corresponded with the interests of humanity as a whole, and more especially with Communist conceptions of 'proletarian internationalism', which identified Russia as the 'universal nation' par excellence.[2]

Pejorative uses of the term 'cosmopolitanism' endure today within contemporary Sociology, including 'Marxist' Sociology, although with less fateful consequences. Radical critics of cosmopolitanism have lined up to demean it as the 'class consciousness of frequent travellers', as the ideology of corporate managers and intergovernmental bureaucrats, tax dodgers and jet-setting academics – anyone with expensive tastes and a globetrotting lifestyle.[3] The once noble term 'cosmopolitan', proudly and at vast personal expense embraced by Jewish writers like Stephan Zweig and Joseph Roth to confront the allure of nationalism and Fascism in the inter-war period, has been decried as the idealized expression of those who renounce the normal obligations of national citizenship, such as paying one's share of taxes and contributing to democratic social life. Before one can say Amazon or Starbucks, the cosmopolitan is turned into the 'cosmocrat' who runs the City or the 'cosmoprat' who floats ethereally above the world with a false sense of moral superiority. These sceptical currents contrast markedly with positive uses of the term 'cosmopolitan' among the classical figures of sociology, including Marx and Durkheim.[4]

Antisemitism is a versatile beast and Jews have been vilified not only for being 'rootless cosmopolitans', but also for a failure to be cosmopolitan at all. Kant, one of the 'founding fathers' of modern cosmopolitan philosophy, echoed a well-established prejudice when he wrote that in the case of the Jews 'all estimation of other men, who are not Jews, is totally lost, and goodwill is reduced merely to love of their own tribe'.[5] Kant showed in this passage that it is possible to turn cosmopolitanism into a weapon against Jews, though Kant himself went on in later life to challenge the misuse of cosmopolitanism as a weapon against colonized peoples supposedly less civilized than the Europeans who conquered and occupied their countries. He began to destabilize the racial stereotypes perceptible in his own Anthropology by looking back to the monogenetic origins of the human species and forward to our future moral unity.[6] The main point is not how far Kant was able to rid himself of the prejudice that the Jews were in some substantial sense locked in 'love of their own tribe' and bereft of 'all estimation of other men', but to acknowledge the possibility that even among the most cosmopolitan of thinkers, universal categories can, if adopted unreflectively, metamorphose into means of reproducing old racial and antisemitic typifications.

The Janus-faced capacity of cosmopolitanism both to pursue a policy of radical inclusion on the basis of common humanity and to pathologize one or other category of people as the enemy of humanity[7] has manifested itself in its relation to Jews through a dialectic of emancipation and prejudice – in its emancipatory aspect treating Jews as fellow human beings and drawing practical conclusions from a sense of common humanity, while in its prejudicial aspect deeming Jews incapable of acting as universal human beings – at least as long as they remained Jews. The two faces of cosmopolitanism have not only represented a problem for Jews but for all categories of people to whom the labels 'not-yet human', 'inhuman' or even 'anti-human' are attached. Yet what is specific to the Jewish experience in Western Europe is the way in which the property of 'particularism' has been projected onto them. A temptation that long preceded the constitution of antisemitism has been to treat conflicts between Jews and non-Jews not as ordinary human conflicts but as the symbolic expression of a metaphysical conflict between the Particular and the Universal – Judaism on the side of the particular and Christianity on the side of the universal. While Jewish emancipation movements have been oriented to the legal, political and social recognition of Jews, at least in the West, the Jewish question has typically been based on how to understand the harm 'the Jews' as a category inflicted on humanity as a whole, what to do about it and how to bring it to an end.

I shall seek to illustrate my argument by addressing the two faces of cosmopolitanism at three pivotal moments in Western history: the eighteenth-century Enlightenment, the revolutionary tradition of the nineteenth and twentieth centuries, and the 'new cosmopolitanism' of our own day. I shall argue that at every stage there has been a struggle waged over the spirit of cosmopolitanism between forces of Jewish emancipation and of the 'Jewish question' that are not always easy to distinguish.

I should say as an aside that this task leads me to question some dominant modes of historical consciousness within my own field of Sociology. For example, some of the leading sociological advocates of the 'new cosmopolitanism', while acknowledging the dual character of cosmopolitanism, have placed it in a rigid time frame. Thus in *Cosmopolitan Vision* the sociologist Ulrich Beck wrote that universalism is two-faced, with 'respect' on one side and 'terror' on the other.[8] Beck argued that Enlightenment universalism was based on the 'elimination of plurality' and 'sacrifice of particularity' and that it universalized 'Western' values in order to pathologized the values of others. He maintained that the 'humanist universalism' of the eighteenth-century Enlightenment was deeply flawed in not recognising rights of particularity, but that at least it put human universality on the agenda. He then maintained that Enlightenment cosmopolitanism was succeeded by the rise of 'methodological nationalism' in the nineteenth century in which there was no universal moment at all. This appeared to Beck as the age in which nationalism, imperialism and racism became supreme. In the current period, according to Beck, what has finally arisen is 'post-universalism' that leans toward both a universal conception of humanity and toward the recognition of difference and rejection of all homogenising claims. Situating the cosmopolitan synthesis of the universal and the particular in the here and now has allowed Beck to label as 'obsolete' both the humanist universalism of the Enlightenment because of its readiness to sacrifice rights of subjective freedom to the universal, and the methodological nationalism of the nineteenth and twentieth centuries that sacrificed any idea of the universal. This enabled Beck to present the new cosmopolitanism of our own age as 'post-universal' in the sense that it is finally capable of reconciling our universal humanity and our particular differences.

The central problem with this approach to history that I want to consider here is that it rules out the possibility that recognition of difference and suspicion of homogenising claims were already present within the Enlightenment or the alternative possibility that the elimination of plurality and sacrifice of particularity remain temptations within the new cosmopolitanism. I would suggest that it is an illusion of progress to lock the past in the past as if it contained no alternative possibilities, and to idealize the present in the present as if we have definitively learned the lessons of history and now know exactly what is to be done. I would further suggest that we can problematize the limitations of this historical consciousness by reconfiguring cosmopolitanism not so much as a stage of history that renders obsolete the properties of a previous stage, but as a repeated struggle for emancipation that constantly has to confront its own demons. I shall endeavour to support this argument by exploring how that in all three of the cosmopolitan moments we survey in the history of the West – the eighteenth-century Enlightenment, the nineteenth-century revolutionary tradition and 'new cosmopolitanism' of our own times – a struggle has been waged over the spirit of cosmopolitanism between the perspectives of Jewish emancipation and the Jewish question.

Universalism and the Jewish Question: the experience of Enlightenment

One of the richest sociological accounts of relations between Jewish emancipation and the Jewish question is to be found in Jeffrey Alexander's *The Civil Sphere*.[9] Alexander is especially skilful in revealing the extent to which the sacrifice of particularity was present in the Enlightenment and how this shaped its relation to Jews and Judaism. He offers various examples of the 'endemic inferiority' projected onto Jews even among supporters of Jewish emancipation. He observes how often Jews were labelled incapable of participating in the civic life of Christian societies, irredeemably egotistic and self-oriented, loyal only to their own and not to the host nation, and narrowly tribal in their orientation. Alexander cites approvingly a comment made by Arthur Hertzberg in his important study of *The French Enlightenment and the Jews*: that 'modern, secular anti-Semitism was fashioned not as a reaction to the Enlightenment and the Revolution, but within the Enlightenment and Revolution themselves'.[10]

Alexander maintains quite rightly that leading supporters of Jewish emancipation, like Christian von Dohm in Prussia, represented Jews as incapable of manifesting the universal solidarity required for civil life. Dohm endorsed the belief that the political harmfulness of Jews is the 'general experience of our states' because of the Jews' 'clannish religious opinions', 'bitter hatred of all who do not belong to the tribe' and inability to look at others as 'members of a common civil society'. It is true that Dohm was tempted to justify Jewish emancipation in terms of 'solving the Jewish question'. He formulated the 'Jewish question' in terms of the corruption of Jews, understood in terms of conspiracy, usury and self-interest, and explained the corruption of Jews in terms of the restrictive circumstances in which they were forced to live. His great hope was that better circumstances would make Jews better people. Dohm argued that 'the hard and oppressive conditions under which the Jews live almost everywhere' explained their corruption, even if he added that fortunately 'the Jew is more a man than a Jew'.[11] Similarly, the revolutionary French emancipationist, Clermont-Tonnerre, attributed the corruption of Jews to the unjust laws of the old order and saw the abolition of these laws as the condition of Jewish improvement.

> Usury ... so justly censured is the effect of our own laws. Men who have nothing but money can only work with money: that is the evil. Let them have land and a country and they will loan no longer: that is the remedy ...
>
> The Jews have their own judges and laws ... that is your fault and you should not allow it. We must refuse everything to the Jews as a nation and accord everything to Jews as individuals ... It is repugnant to have in the state an association of non-citizens and a nation within the nation.[12]

In both cases, that of the Prussian reformer and French revolutionary, the harmfulness of the Jews was presupposed, explained by reference to the conditions Jews were subjected to, and translated into the credo that the overcoming of these conditions would permit Jews to become full, productive members of civil society. According to this concept of emancipation, improvement in the civic status of Jews would lead to improvement in the Jews themselves.

In an essay on 'Enlightenment and the Jewish Question' (1930) Hannah Arendt perceptively commented that the idea of a 'solution to the Jewish question', which the Enlightenment deployed to support political emancipation, was later to become the conceptual ground on which modern political antisemitism would be built: 'The classic form in which the Jewish question was posed in the Enlightenment provides classic antisemitism its theoretical basis.'[13]

We should, however, be cautious about overstating the negativity of Enlightenment. We should not lose sight of the extraordinary achievement it prefigured, the treatment of Jews as equal citizens with the same rights as other citizens. It prepared the ground intellectually for the supersession of the old order in which Jews were designated a separate 'nation' within their various host societies, permitted to profess their own religious and legal institutions, but subjected to all manner of occupational, fiscal and residential restrictions that left most Jews poor, vulnerable to persecution and in thrall to their own rabbinical and financial elites. Emancipation meant the construction of a society of equal citizens in which Jews would be integrated as autonomous human beings of a certain faith, or no faith at all, rather than as a separate 'nation within the nation'.

We should also recognize that the Enlightenment was not confined to one voice.[14] It was a magnificent international movement in which voices could be heard, which attended less to the harm Jews caused to humanity than on the harm the host society caused to Jews. Most notably, perhaps, the Jewish Enlightenment philosopher, Moses Mendelssohn, the man who solicited Dohm's text on *Civic Improvement of the Jews*, registered his approval of a development that meant that 'the Rights of Man are beginning to be taken to heart' but was very critical of Dohm's way of arguing for the rights of man. Mendelssohn looked forward to 'that happy time when attention will be given to human rights in all their proper compass', but his premonition was rather of a barbarism to come: 'Reason and Humanity raise their voices in vain; for hoary Prejudice has completely lost its hearing.'[15] In the conviction that Enlightenment had 'not trodden down all the tracks of barbarism in history', Mendelssohn sought to radicalize the basis of Dohm's conclusions. Observing how 'prejudice assumes the forms of all ages, on purpose to oppress us, and puts obstacles in the way of our civil admission'[16], he took exception to Dohm's assumption that Jews needed moral regeneration. He saw parallels between the prejudices of those who in the past sought to transform Jews into Christians and those who wished now to transform Jews into useful citizens. Whilst Dohm maintained that improvement in the civic status of Jews would improve the Jews, Mendelssohn maintained that all special restrictions on Jews must be ended without demanding any changes in the behaviour of Jews in return. If abandonment of the Jewish way of life were either the condition or outcome of civil union, Mendelssohn added: 'We must rather do without civil union.' He called on Jews to remain 'stiff-necked' in the face of a Faustian pact that was demanded of them, that they abandon 'harmful' Jewish habits in return for equal rights. Mendelssohn was a universalist. His God was not the exclusive God of the Jews but the God of all humankind. When he defended the usefulness of 'Jewish' usury, he also rejected the notion that a society could 'without serious injury to itself dispense with … the seemingly most useless of its inhabitants'.[17] He protested against the persecution of Jews but also against torture and religious fanaticism in general, against wrongs done to Jews but also against wrongs done by Jews. On the one hand, he held that Jews did not need lessons in universalism from those who brought them the Inquisition; on the other, he opposed Dohm's plan to continue to grant Rabbis licence to persecute those who defied their authority.

Dohm was not the villain of the piece nor was Mendelssohn the hero, but we glimpse here the extent to which Enlightenment cosmopolitanism was a field of struggle as far as attitudes to Jews were concerned – not just between its more and less 'tolerant' representatives, but between two aspects of Enlightenment consciousness. For example, Voltaire has the reputation of being one of the less sympathetic of the *illuminati* to Jews, but he authored in 1761 a ringing protest against the Inquisition he put in the mouth of a fictional Rabbi of Smyrna. The Rabbi called on everyone to regard everyone else as fellow human beings and condemned an auto-da-fé in Portugal in which (according to Voltaire) a Jesuit, two monks, two Muslims and 32 Jews were burned to death. Concerning the murdered Jews Voltaire's Rabbi said:

> What was their crime? Nothing other than that of being born [Jews] ... Can you believe that while the flames devoured these innocent victims, the Inquisitors and the other savages chanted our own prayers? ... these pitiless monsters invoked the God of mercy and kindness, the forgiving God, while committing the most atrocious and barbarous crimes ... Thus by a contradiction as absurd as their fury is abominable, they offer to God our *makibs*, they borrow our religion itself, while punishing us for having been brought up in our own religion.[18]

The paradox to which Voltaire's Rabbi gave expression was that the Christian victimizers considered their Jewish victims incapable of acting as universal human beings, while they usurped for themselves the claim to universal humanity.[19]

The revolutionary tradition

Jeffrey Alexander demonstrates that many of the prejudices against Jews we find in Enlightenment cosmopolitanism were reproduced in the West in the revolutionary socialism of the mid-nineteenth century.[20] He maintains that there were 'striking parallels' between representations of Jews in Enlightenment thought and those to be found in radical critiques of capitalist society. According to Alexander, Marx himself built on 'anti-Jewish stereotypes to develop an anti-capitalist critique', convinced himself that 'Jewish qualities must be abolished for a good society to be established', and paved the way for Marxist movements after Marx to carry 'powerful antisemitic overtones'.[21] He concluded that the inability of Marxism to face up to the rise of antisemitic movements in the last quarter of the nineteenth century and its own dabbling with antisemitism reveal a broader 'failure of universalism'.

Again this judgement seems to me overly negative. Opposition to Jewish emancipation in the name of a renewed 'Jewish question' was articulated within socialist, anarchist and other revolutionary circles, but what we also find is that the synthesis of Jewish emancipation and the Jewish question characteristic of the Enlightenment broke into mutually antagonistic extremes. Within revolutionary circles opposition to Jewish emancipation was now expressed in the name of the Jewish question and support for Jewish emancipation was now predicated on rejection of the Jewish question. This split was personified in the debate in 1843–4 between Karl Marx, a critic of the Jewish question who was firmly on the side of Jewish emancipation, and the radical Young Hegelian Bruno Bauer, a critic of Jewish emancipation who was firmly on the side of the Jewish question.[22]

The problem with Judaism, as Bauer saw it, was that it was fundamentally hostile to any idea of universal humanity. According to Bauer, while history is a process of development, the Jews refuse to change and serve as an exception to its universal laws. They do not care for universal human interests; they do not evolve morally or spiritually as human beings; they show excessive pride in considering themselves the 'chosen people'; they claim discrimination at the hands of European society but actually possess prodigious influence over the destiny of Europe – not least through financial manipulation. Bauer's re-instatement of the Jewish question led him to declare that the Jews should be emancipated only if they rid themselves of their Judaism. Otherwise emancipation would serve as a licence to inflict harm on the world.[23]

Bit by bit Marx unravelled the anti-Judaic prejudice contained in his former colleague's false radicalism. He sought to demonstrate how irrelevant the Jewish question was to Jewish emancipation. The main issue for Marx was not whether flesh and blood Jews actually fitted the image of Judaism Bauer drew – there were others who showed how far from the truth it was[24] – but rather how to rid socialism of the whole way of thinking associated with the Jewish question. The grammar of Marx's argument in favour of Jewish emancipation was quite simple. Since the rights of man include the right to be religious or not in any way one wishes, what grounds could there be for excluding Jews because of the alleged self-centredness of their religion? Since the rights of man include rights to pursue particular interests, what grounds could there be for denying civil rights to Jews because of their alleged particularism? Since the rights of citizens abstract political man from society, what grounds could there be for excluding Jews because of their alleged role in society? Since money in modern society is the supreme world power, what grounds could there be for denouncing Jews for allegedly turning money into their God? Marx revealed that Bauer's opposition to Jewish emancipation was the sign of a general inability to understand the modern world or the role of rights, law and the state within it. The real question was not the Jewish question, but whether a backward state like Germany could catch up with progressive states like the United States and France that had already granted equal rights to Jews.[25]

Marx recognized that mainstream representatives of the revolutionary tradition made frequent use of anti-Judaic motifs in their critique of capitalism. For example, he and Engels expressed their contempt for the 'foul and enervating literature' of 'true German socialism' capable only of 'hurling the traditional anathemas against liberalism' and of presenting Jews as 'a secret world power which makes and unmakes governments'.[26] Marx and Engels between them developed the most biting critiques of leading Left intellectuals who waded in the murky waters of antisemitism – including Dühring, Proudhon, Fourier and Bakunin. Marx is wrongly accused of sharing the anti-Judaic prejudices of his age, a judgement that does not begin to capture the thrust of his argument in favour of emancipation. True, there are passages in Marx's second essay of *On the Jewish Question* that appear to deploy anti-Judaic economic motifs, but read in the context of Marx's first essay, written very shortly before, and in the context of Marx and Engels' critique of Bauer in *The Holy Family*, written very soon after, it may make more sense to read them in a severe style, that is, as ironic formulations of the anti-Judaism he was attacking.[27] The radicalism of Marx's critique of Bauer lay in the fact that he was one of the first to dissociate Jewish emancipation from the Jewish question.

The difficulty encountered by Marxists after Marx is that although they tended to see themselves as heirs to Marx's revolutionary critique of capitalism, they could be as tempted by the legacy of Bauer as by that of Marx himself.[28] By the last quarter of the nineteenth century the political emancipation of Jews was being accomplished in most countries of Western Europe, but it was accompanied by the growth of multiple social resentments collected under the label of 'antisemitism' and directed both at Jews and at the states that granted them equality. In this context Marxists generally rejected the antisemitic contention that the harm caused by Jews derived from an unalterable 'Jewishness'[29], but they were still tempted to admit the corruption of Jews and look for improvement in the behaviour of Jews as a crucial first step in overcoming antisemitism. August Bebel is celebrated for having described antisemitism as the 'socialism of fools', but even this critical depiction could be read as a claim that antisemitism was a form of socialism, albeit a foolish form. Interpreted in this way, the inference was at times drawn, as Lars Fischer has argued in *The Socialist Response to Antisemitism in Imperial Germany*, that antisemitism contained a kernel of truth that was a matter of concern for socialists as well as for antisemites.[30]

A tendency grew within Marxism to re-read Marx's *critique* of the Jewish question as if it were a defence and as if Marx were Bauer. Lars Fischer recounts that leading Marxist opponents of antisemitism, some of whom were Jewish, re-presented Marx's essays *On the Jewish Question* as an argument for the postponement of the emancipation of Jews until the socialist revolution, that is, until such time as Jews could appear on the world stage as human beings rather than as Jews. In the Second International's republication of Marx's writings, it omitted the first essay that offers explicit support for the political emancipation of Jews, included the second essay that contains the most problematic statements about money being the God of the Jews, and retitled the whole as 'A World without Jews'.[31] Mainstream Marxism was tempted to read Marx through the distorting lens of the Jewish question, even if within Marxism there were those like Rosa Luxemburg who understood the dangers present within this reading.

I do not wish to deny that the roots of Marxism's misreading of Marx's critique of the Jewish question can be found in certain ambiguities present in Marx's own 'real humanism'. If the conception of human emancipation developed in *The Communist Manifesto* signified, as Karl Löwith put it, 'emancipation from every kind of particularity in human life as a whole; from the specialisation of occupations just as much as from religion and privatisation'[32], then it is hard to imagine what place there could be for Judaism in this nihilistic vista of a future Communism in which the particular was so emphatically subsumed to the universal. Be this as it may, the prevailing conception of human emancipation Marx put forward was not aimed at excluding the Jews for supposedly failing the test of human universality, as it was for Bauer, but rather with overcoming the dominance of abstractions over real human beings epitomized by very abstractions of 'the Jews'. The real humanism Marx reached out for was not about excluding Jews from civic life because of their alleged particularism, but about recognising that the right of Jews to have rights was like the right of all human beings to have rights[33]; it was a starting point for a long and uncharted journey of human emancipation.

The struggles waged between advocates of Jewish emancipation and those of the Jewish question were more urgent within the nineteenth-century revolutionary tradition than they had been within the eighteenth-century Enlightenment because of the rise of antisemitism. Marx's emphasis on the need to construct within the revolutionary tradition a culture of self-criticism as well as criticism of existing conditions, and to build on rather than trash Enlightenment conceptions of rights of particular freedom, was never more needed than when antisemitism became the sign under which the so-called 'final solution of the Jewish question' was given priority over all other economic and political imperatives. The problem was that echoes of the Jewish question could still be heard within Marxism itself. The battles fought between the critique of the Jewish question and its radical reinstatement turned out to be far from a marginal issue.

Contemporary cosmopolitanism

Let me now move on to the third 'period': the post-war turn to the 'new cosmopolitanism' in the West. Again I shall bounce off the work of Jeffrey Alexander. His case is that in American society today, or at least at the time of his writing, Jews are finally being accepted both in their universality as human beings and in their particularity as Jews. To use Ulrich Beck's striking contrast, the 'either-or' of human universality *or* Jewish particularity has at last yielded to the 'both-and' of human universality and Jewish particularity. Alexander refers, for instance, to the popularity of Woody Allen films to make the case that it is now the non-Jew, not the Jew, who must give up an earlier identity to make the 'transition from provincialism to cosmopolitanism, from particularity to universalism'. According to this history, Jewish particularity has gained the recognition it deserved as a positive identification and source of admiration.[34] Alexander gives to history of the Jews, in the United States at least, a happy ending.

It appears that after the Holocaust the idea of the 'Jewish question' was marginalized and delegitimized in mainstream Western society. As the horror of the Holocaust became a more familiar theme in popular culture, public commemoration and laws criminalising Holocaust denial, working through Europe's antisemitic past became an integral part of the larger European project to reconstruct Europe as a pluralistic, postnational political community. A cosmopolitan *Weltanschauung* developed which emphasized European responsibility to reflect generation after generation on its agency in the genocide of Jews. This normative stance called for an embodied and iterated European self-criticism of its own murderous history. There is, however, an ambiguous relation between facts and norms, as the critical theorist Jürgen Habermas has put it, which opens up a space to conceive of Europe as having learnt the lessons of history and rid itself of its longest hatred. In recent years there has been a subtle shift from a critical cosmopolitanism that demand of Europe an on-going engagement with its history of antisemitism, to a more complacent and Eurocentric form of cosmopolitanism that prides Europe on having the cultural resources to reflect on its history. The displacement of European self-criticism by sense of European self-satisfaction has been expressed in the new cosmopolitan confidence that history is on its side.

One of the normative concerns of contemporary cosmopolitanism has been that collective memory of the Holocaust should not become methodologically or politically nationalistic – it should not privilege the suffering of Jews at the expense of other sufferings, it should not crowd out other injustices, it should not neglect other forms of racism, it should not stigmatize whole categories of people as antisemitic, and it should not turn the cry 'Never Again' into the injunction never again only *to Jews*:,in short it should not isolate Jewish emancipation from the emancipation of others. This appears to be the stuff of universalism. However, a reversal manifestly occurs when universalism is turned into the accusation that the Jews have turned collective memory of the Holocaust into everything the cosmopolitan says it should not be, and when the agents of this collective memory are treated as a unitary group characterized by their exclusivity. The sociologist Raymond Aron raised an analogous issue in a discussion of racism and antisemitism, when he wrote of the temptation to treat racists and antisemites in as totalising a way as the racist depicts Black people or the antisemite depicts Jews.[35]

The realisation of this reversal may be exemplified in the authorship of the contemporary Marxist philosopher, Alain Badiou. He condemns what he describes as an exceedingly powerful and reactionary current in contemporary political life that speaks in the name of the 'Jew' and claims to see antisemitism everywhere (*antisémitisme partout* is the sarcastic French title of a book he co-authored).[36] According to Badiou, this political current has constructed a 'victim ideology' that refers exclusively to its own Jewish victimhood, renders other forms of victimisation invisible, demands that Israel's crimes be tolerated, and accuses those who do not tolerate them of antisemitism. He declares that these 'purveyors of antisemitism' are not just on the side of Israel against Palestinians, but also on the side of all repressive power against popular resistance. Badiou writes in the name of a tradition of universalism he traces back to St Paul's disconnection of Christianity from established Judaism. Affirming the cosmopolitan credo that the state must be universal and non-identitarian, he sets it against the Jewish state by presenting Israel as placeholder for all that is hostile to the cosmopolitan vision. He imposes the matrix of a struggle between universalism and particularism onto the national conflict between Palestine and Israel. Badiou is in fact far closer to Bauer than Marx, when he singles out Israel as a uniquely illegitimate state, Zionism as a uniquely harmful nationalism, supporters of Israel as a uniquely powerful lobby, and memory of the Holocaust as a uniquely self-serving reference to the past.

This repressive aspect of cosmopolitanism brings the Jewish question right back into circulation, albeit in the form of antizionism. It turns cosmopolitanism into an ideology that accuses its 'other' of ideology. It converts cosmopolitanism from a demand for critical reflection on Europe's past into an uncritical resource to label 'others' as barbaric and idealize oneself as civilized. It takes the premise of the old Jewish question, that 'we must refuse everything to the Jews as a nation and accord everything to Jews as individuals', as a justification for constructing Zionism as its other.[37] Echoes of the old prejudices connected with the Jewish question are still to be heard in the new cosmopolitanism, but so too is the struggle between prejudice and emancipation. From a cosmopolitan point of view it is not of course wrong to criticize Israel: the many malpractices of the Israeli state *must* be criticized. Israel is no more exempt from criticism than any other state. What is wrong is to deploy the sign of cosmopolitanism to impose the perspective of the Jewish question onto a national conflict.[38]

The development of a cosmopolitan self-consciousness in the proper sense of the term is the endeavour to supersede nationalism, that is, the turning of the nation into an 'ism', not the endeavour to heap onto *Jewish* nationalism all the defects of nationalism in general. It confronts racism and antisemitism from a universal rather than national perspective, but understands that nothing may appear more 'natural' than that if you are attacked as a Jew, Muslim, African or Black, you fight back as a Jew, Moslem, African or Black. While criticism of exclusive forms of resistance to racism and antisemitism is a hallmark of cosmopolitan thinking, the cosmopolitan recognizes that exclusivity is a temptation facing all antiracist movements and does not single out resistance to antisemitism as if exclusivity were its distinctive attribute. In its emancipatory aspect the cosmopolitan consciousness is not content to reconstruct old moral divisions of the world between 'us' and 'them', in which idealisation of the self as 'universal' and stigmatisation of the other as 'particular' are achieved through mechanisms of denial and projection.[39] It recognizes rather the unity of our universal lives as human beings, our particular lives as Jews, Christians, Muslims and so on, and indeed our singular lives as unique thinking individuals.[40]

In conclusion

The emancipation of Jews in Western Europe did not solve the Jewish question in part because support for Jewish emancipation was in large measure premised on the prejudices of the Jewish question, in part because the prejudices of the Jewish question were reinforced, reified and racialized once Jewish emancipation was accomplished, and in part because of the abstraction of political emancipation from the social emancipation of Jews. The legal recognition of Jews as equal citizens contained within itself the developmental possibility of encouraging the social recognition of Jews as fellow human beings, but it also contained within itself the regressive potential to breed resentment against the treatment of seemingly inferior and alien beings as if they were equal members of the same community. *Ressentiment* is the passion aroused by the treatment of the unequal as equal.[41] If the allocation of equal rights to Jews was viewed by some as a merited reward for their contributions to the community, it could by the same logic also be viewed as an undeserved privilege that renders invisible the harm they do to the community and that makes sense only in terms of a conspiracy between 'the Jews' on the one hand and those political forces of the state that granted them rights on the other. It was not accidental that Jewish emancipation and the growth of antisemitism were coeval Western Europe in the last half of the nineteenth century, just as it was not accidental, as Alexis de Tocqueville acutely observed in *Democracy in America*, that the emancipation of slaves in the United States and the growth of anti-Black racism were coeval. The greatness of the emancipatory tradition represented by Mendelssohn, Marx and modern critical theory is that it not only challenged the negative representations of Jews expressed in terms of the Jewish question but also severed the justification of universal rights from any notion of communal worth or worthlessness.

The 'Jewish question' is no less the product of modernity than Jewish emancipation. We have seen that it assumes different forms in different periods – theological anti-Judaism, secular discrimination, genocidal antisemitism, demonisation of the Jewish nation, or some admixture of these elements. What seems to characterize the Jewish question in the West is the abstraction of the category of 'the Jews', the assumption that this category is the cause of harm to humanity, the projection onto 'the Jews' of the quality of either particularism or false universalism, practical attempts to find a 'solution' to the Jewish question, and not least resistance to all empirical criticism. In *Antisemite and Jew* Jean-Paul Sartre described antisemitism as a 'passion' that is neither caused nor refutable by experience: 'The essential thing here is not a "historical fact" but the idea that the agents of history formed for themselves of the Jew.'[42] There is a sense in which the antisemite can never lose the argument. If it is pointed out that most Jews are not powerful financiers, or that most powerful financiers are not Jews, the antisemitic imagination remains no less fixed on the Jewish financier. Similarly, if it is pointed out that most Israelis are not supporters of ethnic cleansing and that most supporters of ethnic cleansing are not Israelis, the antizionist imagination remains no less fixed on the Israeli who supports ethnic cleansing. In this sense the Jewish question provides a template for misrecognising the world.

The temptation of the contemporary cosmopolitan consciousness is to situate the Jewish question in the past, as if it were an outmoded prejudice inexorably coming to an end. The allure of this time-consciousness is apparent when modernists treat antisemitism as the product of pre-modernity, postmodernists treat antisemitism as the product of high modernity, postnationalists treat antisemitism as the product of national modernity, and cosmopolitans treat antisemitism as the product of a bygone age of methodological nationalism. The assumption behind these forms of historicisation is to regard antisemitism as a residue of the past and close our eyes to new forms and new conditions of emergence. While the strength of this approach is to challenge naturalistic conceptions to antisemitism that treat it as a permanent feature of relations between Jews and non-Jews, its answer is merely to turn this time consciousness on its head and confine antisemitism to the past. It is never able to explain how things turn out so badly.

If cosmopolitanism is not reflective about its own capacity for reversal, it can simply end up reproducing all the old dichotomies. Cosmopolitanism is revealed here not so much as a stage of history that makes 'obsolete' what came before, but as a way of thinking that repeatedly has to struggle for its own existence. The cosmopolitan outlook is not a quietism that looks back on the past with the contented smile of one safely ensconced in the future, but a critical theory that pits itself against regenerated forms of domination and superstition – even against those that appear under the aegis of cosmopolitanism itself.[43] The potential for the Jewish question to slip back into our cosmopolitan consciousness and to re-present 'the Jew' as the personification of the particular, is a compelling case in point.

Notes

1. See especially Edelstein, *Terror of Natural Right*, 26–42.
2. See, for example, Figes, *The Whisperers*, 454 and Gruner, "Russia's Battle Against the Foreign."
3. See Calhoun, "The Class Consciousness of Frequent Travellers."
4. See Gilbert Achcar, *Marxism, Orientalism, Cosmopolitanism*.
5. Kant, *Anthropology from a Pragmatic Point of View*, 100.
6. See Kleingeld, "Kant's Second Thoughts on Race" and Robert Bernasconi's critique of Kleingeld in "Kant's Third Thoughts on Race."
7. See Habermas, *Inclusion of the Other*, for the inclusive face of cosmopolitanism and Benhabib, "Nous et les autres" in *Claims of Culture* for the exclusive face.
8. Beck and Cronin, *Cosmopolitan Vision*, 30.
9. Alexander, *The Civil Sphere*, 459–548.
10. Hertzberg, *The French Enlightenment and the Jews*, 7.
11. von Dohm, "Concerning the Amelioration of the Civil Status of the Jews" (1781). See Rose, *Revolutionary Antisemitism in Germany* and Traverso, *The Jews and Germany*.
12. Cited in Hunt, *Inventing Human Rights*, 155–8.
13. Arendt, "Enlightenment and the Jewish Question" in Arendt, *The Jewish Writings*, 54–5.
14. See especially Muthu, *Enlightenment against Empire*, ch. 1.
15. Feiner, *Mendelssohn*, 144.
16. Cited in Feiner, *Moses Mendelssohn*, 139, from Mendelssohn's Preface to his translation of Ben Israel's *Vindiciae Judaeorum*. Republished in Micah Gottlieb (ed.), *Moses Mendelssohn: Writings on Judaism, Christianity, and the Bible*, Curtis Bowman, Elias Sacks, and Allan Arkush (trs.).
17. Feiner, *Mendelssohn*, 143.

18. These quotations are drawn from Voltaire, "The Sermon of Rabbi Akib" and are cited in Paul Berman "Jews, Muslims, Liberals, PEN Boycotters Beware: Voltaire is Laughing at You: Is the Enlightenment Philosopher Having a Moment?" *Tablet*, 1 May 2015, http://tabletmag.com/jewish-arts-and-culture/books/190669/pen-boycotters-voltaire Voltaire's text is available in Noyer, *Voltaire's Revolution: Writings from His Campaign to Free Laws from Religion*.
19. See also Hegel's comment on Fries where he argued that it is a matter of 'infinite importance' that 'a human being counts as such because he is a human being, not because he is a Jew, Catholic, Protestant, German, Italian, etc.' and that when we speak of Jews as human beings 'this is not just a neutral and abstract quality … for its consequence is that the granting of civil rights gives those who receive them a self-awareness as recognized legal persons in civil society'. Hegel repudiated those who sought to deny civil and political rights to Jews on the pretext that the Jews were a foreign nation and not an integral part of the people: 'If they had not been granted civil rights, the Jews would have remained in that isolation with which they have been reproached, and this would rightly have brought reproach upon the state which excluded them'. See Hegel, *Philosophy of Right, Preface*, 15–16.
20. Alexander, *Civil Sphere*, 465–8.
21. Alexander, *Civil Sphere*, 486–8.
22. Marx, "On the Jewish Question," in Colletti's *Marx's Early Writings*.
23. For the history of anti-Judaism see the monumental work of David Nirenberg, *Anti-Judaism*, 433–9. As will become apparent, I do not share his interpretation of Marx or his premature placement of Marx in this Western tradition.
24. See for example the discussions of Moses Hess and Heinrich Heine in Hal Draper's *Karl Marx's Theory of Revolution*.
25. For an elaboration of this argument see Fine "Rereading Marx on the 'Jewish Question'" in Stoetzler, *Antisemitism and the Constitution of Sociology*, 137–59.
26. Marx and Engels, "Communist Manifesto," 57.
27. See Marx and Engels, *The Holy Family*, 112–43.
28. See Spencer, "Marxism, Cosmopolitanism and the Jews" in this volume.
29. On the essentialist roots of the idea of "Jewishness" see Arendt, *Origins of Totalitarianism*, 80–8.
30. See in particular Fischer, *The Socialist Response to Antisemitism in Imperial Germany*.
31. This is well documented in Fischer, *The Socialist Response to Antisemitism*.
32. Löwith, *Max Weber and Karl Marx*, 106.
33. See Arendt, *Origins of Totalitarianism*, ix.
34. See also the work of Beller, Antisemitism, ch. 8. "After Auschwitz" and Sznaider, *Jewish Memory And the Cosmopolitan Order*, ch. 1.
35. Aron 1969: 87–88,
36. See Badiou and Hazan, Antisémitisme Partout, and Badiou "The uses of the word 'Jew'". Badiou's real target is probably the "new antisemitism theory," which is in fact a diverse body of thought expressing concern over and analysing the development of new forms of antisemitism in the global age. See Judaken, "So What's New: Rethinking the 'New Antisemitism' in the Global Age."
37. For an emphatically reductive reading of the manipulative functions of the charge of antisemitism, see Butler, "The Charge of Anti-Semitism," 101–27.
38. See for example Harrison, "Anti-Zionism, anti-Semitism and the rhetorical manipulation of reality", ch. 1.
39. For elaboration of this argument see Fine, "Nationalism, Postnationalism, Antisemitism: Thoughts on the Politics of Jürgen Habermas," ÖZP, 409–20. I also draw on a reading of two conceptions of justice in Sen, *The Idea of Justice*, 106–15.
40. Glynis Cousin emphasizes the unity of the universal, the particular and the singular in "Rethinking the Concept of Western."
41. Regarding the relation of modern antisemitism to other modern forms of racism see the insightful article by Christine Achinger "Threats to modernity".

42. Jean-Paul Sartre, *Antisemite and Jew*, 15.
43. The idea of universalism as a "regulative idea" is helpfully discussed and defended in Chernilo, *The Natural Law Foundations of Modern Social Theory*. See also Fine, *Cosmopolitanism*, chs. 1 and 2.

Disclosure statement

No potential conflict of interest was reported by the author.

References

Achcar, Gilbert. *Marxism, Orientalism, Cosmopolitanism*. Chicago, IL: Haymarket Books, 2013.
Achinger, Christine. "Threats to Modernity, Threats of Modernity: Racism and Antisemitism through the Lens of Literature." *European Societies* 14, no. 2 (2012): 240–258.
Alexander, Jeffrey. *The Civil Sphere*. Oxford: Oxford University Press, 2006.
Arendt, Hannah. *The Origins of Totalitarianism*. New York, NY: Harcourt Brace, 1979.
Arendt, Hannah. *The Jewish Writings*. New York, NY: Schocken, 2007.
Aron, Raymond. *Paix et Guerre entre les Nations*. Paris: Calmann-Levy, 1969.
Badiou, Alain. "The Uses of the Word 'Jew'." http://www.lacan.com/badword.htm (Accessed October 2012).
Badiou, Alain, and Eric Hazan. *L'Antisémitisme partout: Aujourd'hui en France*. Paris: La Fabrique Edition, 2011.
Beck, Ulrich, and Ciaran Cronin. *Cosmopolitan Vision*. Cambridge: Polity, 2006.
Beller, Steven. *Antisemitism: A Very Short Introduction*. Oxford: Oxford University Press, 2007.
Benhabib, Seyla. *The Claims of Culture: Equality and Diversity in the Global Era*. Princeton: Princeton University Press, 2002.
Berman, Paul. "Jews, Muslims, Liberals, PEN Boycotters Beware: Voltaire is Laughing at You: Is the Enlightenment Philosopher Having a Moment?" *Tablet*, 1 May 2015 (Accessed May 2015) at http://tabletmag.com/jewish-arts-and-culture/books/190669/pen-boycotters-voltaire.
Bernasconi, Robert. "Kant's Third Thoughts on Race." In *Reading Kant's Geography,* edited by S. Elden and E. Mendietta, 291–316. Albany: SUNY Press.
Butler, Judith. *Precarious Life: The Powers of Mourning and Violence*. London: Verso, 2004.
Calhoun, Craig. "The Class Consciousness of Frequent Travelers: Toward a Critique of Actually Existing Cosmopolitanism." *South Atlantic Quarterly* 101, no. 4 (2002): 869–897.
Chernilo, Daniel. *The Natural Law Foundations of Modern Social Theory: A Quest for Universalism*. Cambridge: Cambridge University Press, 2014.
Cousin, Glynis. "Rethinking the Concept of Western." *Journal of Higher Education Research and Development* 30, no. 5 (2011): 585–594.
von Dohm, C. "Concerning the Amelioration of the Civil Status of the Jews" (1781). In *The Jew in the Modern World: A Documentary History*, edited by Paul Mendez-Flohr and Jehuda Reinharz. New York, NY: Oxford University Press, 1995.
Draper, Harold. *Karl Marx's Theory of Revolution*. New York, NY: Monthly Review Press, vol. 1 (1977), 109–129; vol. 2 (1978), 300–302, 548; vol. 4 (1981), 291–303.

Edelstein, Daniel. *The Terror of Natural Right: Republicanism, the Cult of Nature, and the French Revolution*. Chicago, IL: University of Chicago Press, 2011.

Feiner, Shmuel. *Moses Mendelssohn: Sage of Modernity*. New Haven and London: Yale University Press, 2010.

Figes, Orlando. *The Whisperers: Private Life in Stalin's Russia*. Harmondsworth: Penguin, 2008.

Fine, Robert. *Cosmopolitanism*. London: Routledge, 2007.

Fine, Robert. "Rereading Marx on the 'Jewish Question': Marx as Critic of Antisemitism?" In *Antisemitism and the Constitution of Sociology*, edited by Marcel Stoetzler, 137–159. Lincoln, OR: University of Nebraska Press, 2014.

Fine, Robert. "Nationalism, Postnationalism, Antisemitism: Thoughts on the Politics of Jürgen Habermas." *ÖsterreichischeZeitschriftfürPolitikwissenschaft* 39, no. 4 (2009): 409–420.

Fischer, Lars. *The Socialist Response to Antisemitism in Imperial Germany*. Cambridge: Cambridge University Press, 2007.

Grüner, Frank. "'Russia's Battle Against the Foreign': the Anti-Cosmopolitanism Paradigm in Russian and Soviet Ideology." *European Review of History: Revue europeenne d'histoire* 17, no. 3 (2010): 445–472.

Habermas, Jürgen. *The Inclusion of the Other: Studies in Political Theory*. Cambridge: Polity Press, 1998.

Harrison, Bernard. "Antizionism, Antisemitism and the Rhetorical Manipulation of Reality." In *Resurgent Antisemitism: Global Perspectives*, edited by Alvin H. Rosenfeld. Bloomington, IN: Indiana University Press, 2013.

Hegel, Willhelm. *Elements of the Philosophy of Right*. Cambridge: Cambridge University Press, 1991.

Hertzberg, Arthur. *The French Enlightenment and the Jews: The Origins of Modern Anti-Semitism*. New York, NY: Columbia University Press, 1990.

Hunt, Lynn. *Inventing Human Rights: A History*. New York, NY: W. W. Norton, 2007.

Judaken, Jonathan. "So What's New: Rethinking the 'New Antisemitism' in a Global Age." *Patterns of Prejudice* 42, nos. 4–5 (2008): 531–560.

Kant, Immanuel. *Anthropology from a Pragmatic Point of View*. Cambridge: Cambridge University Press, 2009.

Kleingeld, Pauline. "Kant's Second Thoughts on Race." *Philosophical Quarterly* 57 (2007): 573–592.

Löwith, Karl. *Max Weber and Karl Marx*. London: Routledge, 1993.

Marx, Karl. "On the Jewish Question." In *Marx's Early Writings*, edited by Lucio Colletti. Harmondsworth: Penguin, 1992.

Marx, Karl, and Friedrich Engels. "The Manifesto of the Communist Party." In Karl Marx, *Selected Works*. London: Lawrence and Wishart, 1970.

Marx, Karl, and Friedrich Engels. *The Holy Family or Critique of Critical Criticism: Against Bruno Bauer and Company*. Moscow: Progress, 1980.

Muthu, Sankar. *Enlightenment against Empire*. Princeton: Princeton University Press, 2003.

Nirenberg, David. *Anti-Judaism: the Western Tradition*. New York, NY: W. W. Norton & Company, 2013.

Noyer, G. K. (ed.). *Voltaire's Revolution: Writings from His Campaign to Free Laws from Religion*. London: Prometheus Books, 2015.

Rose, Paul Lawrence. *Revolutionary Antisemitism in Germany: From Kant to Wagner*. Princeton: Princeton University Press, 1990.

Sartre, Jean-Paul. *Antisemite and Jew*. New York, NY: Schocken, 1965.

Sen, Amartya. *The Idea of Justice*. London: Allen Lane, 2009.

Spencer, Philip. "Marxism, Cosmopolitanism and the Jews." *European Review of History* 23, nos. 5–6 (2016).

Sznaider, Natan. *Jewish Memory And the Cosmopolitan Order*. Cambridge: Polity, 2013.

Traverso, Enzo. *The Jews and Germany*. Nebraska: University of Nebraska Press, 1995.

Aliens vs. predators: cosmopolitan Jews vs. Jewish nomads

Sander L. Gilman

ABSTRACT
Certainly the question of Jewish rootlessness or rootedness has been a major topic of German-Jewish historiography from the *Wissenschaft des Judentums* to the present day. That this concept as articulated in the paired notions of cosmopolitanism and nomadism is actually shaped by the Jews of Central Europe as the litmus test for that which is considered (positively or negatively) cosmopolitan and/or nomadic has not been examined in any detail. The present article is the beginning of a conversation on the contested meanings and conflicted perceptions attached to the vagaries of the image of the 'rooted' or 'rootless' Jew in German culture as the touchstone for any understanding of cosmopolitanism since the Enlightenment.

The history of cosmopolitanism from the Enlightenment to the twentieth century focused on the double strand of a positive or a negative image of mobility.[1] The Jews were the litmus test for this in German-speaking Central Europe: were they 'aliens', a beneficent or at least a malleable population because they were mobile, or were they 'predators', a threat to established or evolving national identity because of their mobility? This discourse, with all of the ambiguities on both sides of the issue, was reflected in the idea of a cosmopolitan versus a nomadic people. And the Jews, from the Old Testament to the present, were taken as the exemplary cases for each position.

From the Baroque idea that the Jew was the original Gypsy to the Enlightenment discourse about the movement of peoples through the debates within Zionism in the nineteenth and twentieth centuries about the rootedness of the Jew, the antithetical idea of the movement of the Jews as an indicator of potential integration or isolation from the national state remains a factor in defining the cosmopolitan.[2]

Over and over again cosmopolitanism and its sister concept nomadism have taken on quite different meanings when their referent is the Jews. Once this litmus test is applied, both cosmopolitanism and nomadism are clearly revealed as symbolic manifestations of the antisemitic stereotype, which associates Jews with capital. Such a history of the cosmopolitan points toward the ambivalence of these very concepts when applied in the present day to specific categories of social and geographic mobility, whether these refer to the Jew, the asylum seeker, the migrant or,the undocumented immigrant. The marginal and excluded of Enlightenment Germany may have transmuted into the global citizen of the twenty-first century in some instances, but the aura of the corrupt and corrupting, of the rootless and the transitory, of the foreign and the unhoused always remains beneath the surface and shapes the sense of what it means to be cosmopolitan and global. And as such it impacts upon the self-image of those so defined.

The universal claim of globalisation and its surrogate cosmopolitanism is that all human beings share certain innate human rights, including the free movement of peoples across what are seen as the superficial boundaries of nation, class, race, caste and perhaps even gender and sexuality.[3] The tension between the universal and local meanings of cosmopolitanism, however, originally arose in the Enlightenment, as did the common use of the term itself. Standard etymologies in various European languages note that it is a Greek term, its modern use having been borrowed from the French into English as early as the sixteenth century by the necromancer John Dee to denote a person who is 'A Citizen [...] of the [...] one Mysticall City Vniuersall'.[4] However, it only became common usage in English in the early nineteenth century. In German the term *Weltbürger* (world citizen) was likewise generated in the early sixteenth century to provide an alternative to the French *cosmopolitisme* and *cosmopolite*. The French Academy documents *cosmopolitisme* in its dictionary of 1762, but that is the first 'official' recognition of a much older usage. As in English, the earlier German usages are sporadic. Erasmus seems to have been the first to use it in the early sixteenth century in a letter to Zwingli referring to Socrates who, when asked of what city he was a citizen, replied that he was a 'Weltbürger' (κοσμοπολίτην sive mundanum).[5] The term only came into wider use in the German Enlightenment, thus earlier than in English. It seems to have been Jakob Friedrich Lamprecht who popularized the term in German with his periodical entitled *Der Weltbürger* (1741–1742). G.E. Lessing used the term cosmopolitan (rather than *Weltbürger*) in 1747 but a wide range of Enlightenment figures quickly followed suit. Functioning as the litmus test for the cosmopolitan in the German Enlightenment in all of these cases is the status of the Jews.

One of the major Enlightenment thinkers, the Abbé Grégoire, who attacked the facile use of a universal claim of cosmopolitanism before the National Assembly during the French Revolution, wrote:

> A writer of the last Century [Fénelon] said: I love my family better than my self: I love my country better than my family but I love mankind better than my country. Reason has criticized both those extravagant people who talked about a universal republic and those false people who made a profession out of loving people who lived in a distance of two thousand years or two thousand leagues in order to avoid being just and good towards their neighbours: systematic, de facto cosmopolitanism is nothing but moral or physical vagabondage.[6]

For the Abbé the local case was the question of the universal emancipation of French Jewry as French citizens, trumping their specifically Jewish identity, an idea of which he was a powerful advocate.[7] For the Enlightenment, and it is with the Enlightenment that this tale begins, it is the Jews in Paris, not in the distant past nor in far away Palestine, that are the litmus test for true French cosmopolitanism. Anything else is merely 'vagabondage': moral or physical nomadism. It was the attention to the immediate and the proximate that defined true cosmopolitanism, a topic much debated at the time. But it is immediately contrasted with the merely nomadic.

The first major German literary advocate of cosmopolitanism, Christoph Martin Wieland, who devoted several essays to cosmopolitanism in the 1780s, most famously 'The Secret of Cosmopolitan Order' in 1788: 'Cosmopolitans [...] regard all the peoples of the earth as so many branches of a single family, and the universe as a state, of which they, with innumerable other rational beings, are citizens, promoting together under the general laws of nature the perfection of the whole, while each in his own fashion is busy with his own well-being' (xiv–v). Wieland, like the *philosophes*, sees this as a transcendental category, trumping the local. Wieland is himself paraphrasing Friedrich II's oft-cited note of June 1740 concerning Huguenot and Catholic toleration, but not emancipation: 'Each should be blessed in their own manner' ('Jeder soll nach seiner Façon selig werden') a toleration grudgingly extended in 1750 to Prussian Jewry.[8] Wieland's own Enlightenment views on the Jews are clear: he mocks, in his *Private History of Peregrinus Proteus* (1781), the pagan whose grandfather 'had a boundless aversion for Jews and Judaism; his prejudices against them, were, perhaps, partly unjust, but they were incurable;' yet equally detested Christians, who '[…] passed for a Jewish sect'.[9] (II: 32) Enlightenment thought more generally promoted a rooted cosmopolitanism, a universalist sensibility rooted in the nation. Religious affiliation, particularly that of the Jews, was rejected for its particularity. Wieland's cosmopolitanism thus contests the religious exclusivity of both Christians and Jews over the universal.

Jewish cosmopolitanism is contested when it is defined in terms of capital; when it is uncontested any discussion of capital is avoided. Indeed, any discussion of the fantasies about some type of unitary definition of Jewish cosmopolitanism necessarily hangs on the very meaning associated with capital and its function within the new nation-state. The fantasy of the Jews is that of a people or nation or race driven solely by their own economic motivation. It is Shylock's curse that the historian Derek Penslar so elegantly presents as a core reference for Jewish identity in modernity.[10]

The Jews as an abstraction and as a social reality come to be the litmus test in the Enlightenment through which these notions' potential and difficulties can be analysed.[11] When cosmopolitanism is examined under this lens we have a double focus: firstly, the role that the abstraction, 'the Jews' played in formulating theories of the acceptability of, or dangers in, the movement of peoples beyond and across national boundaries and, secondly, the response of actual individuals who define themselves as Jews to such attitudes and meanings. This is a forerunner of what the British scholar of geography, Ulrike Vieten, calls the 'novel form of *regional cosmopolitanism* [that] is underway in Europe'.[12] But it has deeper historical roots. As the meanings of all of these concepts (cosmopolitanism, boundary, Jews, as well as capital) shift and evolve, so too do the responses of those generating them and seeing them as applicable or inapplicable to their particular circumstances as these change.

If we are to examine the debates about the Jews as the touchstone of cosmopolitanism in the Enlightenment, and specifically within the German-language Enlightenment, then two conflicting definitions of the Jews must first be separated. Firstly, the Jews are a people who ascribe to a particular religious belief and practice and who are at least potentially able to freely follow their beliefs in the new, Enlightened world of the European national state. Secondly, the Jews are seen as the concrete manifestation of the exploitative force of capital, whose rise parallels the very establishment of such states, at least in the eyes of these commentators.

J. G. Herder (1744–1803) is thus torn between these two poles. In his *Ideas for A Philosophy of the History of Mankind* (1784–1791) he defines the nation as 'a group of people having a common origin and common institutions, including language'; the nation-state represents the union of the individual with the national community; each people is unique; polyglot entities are 'absurd monsters contrary to nature'.[13] The Jews must join the body politic by integrating their linguistic practice into that of the naturally occurring nation-state. But can they? According to Herder:, 'The Jews of Moses are properly of Palestine, outside of Palestine there can be no Jew' (351). Yet 'a time will come when no person in Europe will inquire whether a man be a Jew or a Christian. Jews will live according to European laws and contribute to the state' (486).

Nevertheless, 'each nation has its center of happiness in itself, like every sphere its center of gravity', he writes in *Also a History of Mankind* (1774). In his *Theological Letters* (1780–1781) he too approvingly quotes the remark made by François de Salignac de La Mothe Fénelon, Archbishop of Cambrai, that was later evoked by the Abbé Gregoire (and virtually every other Enlightened commentator on cosmopolitanism): 'I love my family more than myself; more than my family my fatherland; more than my fatherland humankind.' Yet for Herder it is the status of the nation, of the fatherland, that is at the core of any and all questions of individual identity and thus individual happiness.

The 'nation' in question is not racial entity, but rather a linguistic and cultural one (indeed, in the *Ideas* and elsewhere Herder rejects the very concept of a biologically defined race). Herder's views reflect those of the time, as expressed by Johann Georg Schlosser, in the critical poem 'Der Kosmopolit' (1777): 'It is better to be proud of one's nation than to have none.' Are the Jews a nation or merely wandering cosmopolitans?[14] If a nation, can or should they become part of another nation? Or are they, as Johann Gottlieb Fichte notoriously stated in his 1793 pamphlet 'A Contribution to Correcting Judgments about the French Revolution', a threat: 'In nearly all the nations of Europe, a powerful, hostile government is growing, and is at war with all the others, and sometimes oppresses the people in dreadful ways: It is Jewry!' The Jews are a 'state within the state', incapable of any integration and thus damned to wander the world.[15] Truly vagabondage.

According to Herder, writing in the *Ideas for A Philosophy of the History of Mankind*, even if the Jews had stayed 'in the land of their fathers, and in the midst of other nations, [...] they would have remained as they were; for and even when mixed with other people they may be distinguished for some generations downward' (36). The 'more secluded they live, nay frequently the more they were oppressed, the more their character was confirmed' (36). In fact, he suggests that, ideally, 'if every one of these nations had remained in its place, the Earth might have been considered as a garden, where in one spot one human national plant, in another, another, bloomed in its proper figure and nature' (36). The movement of peoples interferes with the natural function of language in defining people. But the reality of history is that almost every people on earth, as Herder points out, 'has migrated at least once, sooner or later, to a greater distance, or less' (36). The impact of this migration is shaped by the 'time when the migration took place, the circumstances by which it was occasioned, the length of the way, the previous state of civilization of the people, the reception they met with in their new country, and the like' (36).

And yet, Herder sees the very origin of 'the coining of money' as one of the contributions of the 'many little wandering hordes' in the Middle East, 'according to the Hebrews' (317). As the Jews spread across Europe 'in the manner that they spread abroad as a people' they held its nations in thrall thanks to their command of money. They did not invent usury, Herder states, but 'they brought it to perfection' (335). The Jews move among and across the nations like everyone else, yet Herder is happy to quote from Kant's lectures on practical philosophy: 'Every coward is a liar; Jews, for example, not only in business, but also in common life.'[16] On this point, Herder and Kant agree.

Yet the Enlightenment had an alternative manner of speaking about the Jews as a people that offers a different history of the concept of cosmopolitanism. For Christian Enlightenment thinkers, cosmopolitanism was the hallmark of the Enlightened subject rooted in a particularist universality. Jews, confined to their backward particularity, could not by definition achieve this status. Herder in his *Ideas for A Philosophy of the History of Mankind* (1784–1791) provided a rather standard Protestant reading of the Hebrew Bible (*Tanakh*) that presented the Jews as a nomadic people. Whether this was ever historically true or not, it is clear that the texts assembled into what came in Christianity to be called the Old Testament are the product of city-states. Whether the Jews were or were not just one of 'many little wandering hordes' (51) as Herder describes them, is the question but it is clear that the Old Testament, at least in Genesis, represents a nostalgia for a simpler time and space which came to be defined in the Enlightenment as 'nomadic'. Herder lists all of the innovations of these nomads; among them is the invention of 'trade by weight and measure', capitalism.(52)

Herder, for whom the nomad represented not only earlier stages of Jewish development, also described the Jews as still existing in the present in what he saw as a throw-back to their nomadic past. This is found in the overlapping history of the Sinti and Roma and the Jews. It should be noted that some early German commentators, such as W. E. Tentzel at the close of the seventeenth century, correctly argued that the 'Gypsies' had come from South Asia even if they were uncertain of their exact origins (Tenzel's guess was Ceylon).[17] However, those theologians who were focused on converting the Jews looked closer to home. The Christian Hebraist Johann Christoph Wagenseil claimed in 1705 in his *Benachrichtigungen Wegen Einiger die Gemeine Jüdischheit Betreffenden Sachen* that the first Gypsies (*Zigeuner*) were indeed Jews who fled into the forests after having been accused in the fourteenth century of poisoning wells. Claiming that they had come from Egypt, they cheated the peasants there by claiming to be able to effect wondrous cures, tell the future and prevent fires. Eventually they returned to the cities and again became sedentary and declared themselves Jews. But vagabonds, thieves and beggars had joined them and they continued their nomadic ways. As proof, he claims that the Gypsies were unknown before the fourteenth century and that the language of today's Gypsies is full of Hebrew words and that their amulets use Kabbalistic formulas.[18] In Johann Jakob Schudt's infamous *Jüdische Merckwürdigkeiten* (1714) there is a long chapter that claims that Wagenseil was simply wrong and that the Jews were condemned to their wanderings in Egypt for having rejected Jesus and Mary on their flight to Egypt.[19] He follows this with a long digression on the Eternal Jew, the shoemaker Ahasverus, or Cartaphilus, condemned to wander the world because of his rejection of Christ. Learning the language of each country he visits (502), he must wander, as Christ condemned him to do so, until the Second Coming. The Jews, according to Schudt are, like the Turks, 'sanctimonious cheats' because of their usury (504). In both cases the economic role of the Jews as pseudo-nomads is integral to these contradictory images. Whether authentic or not, the Jews are nomadic in the same way as the Sinti and Roma, even if they are not 'Gypsies' *per se*.

The Enlightenment saw nomads as not using their given space productively. As early as the mid-eighteenth century, Goethe would see the nomad through the lens of the colonist in his explanation of why it is seductive for Germans to seek adventures abroad in *Wilhelm Meister*. The novel's protagonist Lenardo speaks of the enticement of 'immeasurable spaces [that] lie open to action' and of 'great stretches of country roamed by nomads'.[20] In the present, nomads have no value and must be replaced by those who do, but this is a false promise that may lead to the corrosion of the Europeans' national identity.

In this Enlightenment view, nomads add no value to the land today and thus seem to need to be replaced by members of a national community. But it is these self-same nomads in the past that were the starting point for the national state and its most egregious exploitative feature, capital. Karl Marx in *Capital* wrote that 'nomad races are the first to develop the money form, because all their worldly goods consist of moveable objects and are therefore directly alienable; and because their mode of life, by continually bringing them into contact with foreign communities, solicits the exchange of products' (I: 2).[21] The nomad is implicitly cast as the *Urcapitalist*, the Jew, whose drive in the modern world is shaped by his inheritance from the desert (this is also analogous to the explanation for the rise of monotheism among the Jews: the need for a portable God after the destruction of the Temple).[22]

In contrast to Marx, George Simmel in the *Philosophy of Money* (1907) explains that 'as a rule, nomadic peoples hold land as common property of the tribe and assign it only for the use of individual families; but livestock is always the private property of these families. As far as we know, the nomadic tribe has never been communistic with regard to cattle as property. In many other societies too movables were already private property while land remained common property for a long period thereafter' (353).[23] Not so much *Urcapitalists* as *Urcommunists*, perhaps?

Two decades before, the Russian Zionist Leon Pinsker had argued in his German-language pamphlet *Auto-Emancipation* (1882) that the statelessness of the Jew in the age of nationalism condemns him to be a nomad. For the Jewish people

> produces in accordance with its nature, vagrant nomads; so long as it cannot give a satisfactory account of whence it comes and whither it goes; so long as the Jews themselves prefer not to speak in Aryan society of their Semitic descent and prefer not to be reminded of it; so long as they are persecuted, tolerated, protected or emancipated, the stigma attached to this people, which forces it into an undesirable isolation from all nations, cannot be removed by any sort of legal emancipation.[24]

For Pinsker, these are nomads living as 'Jew peddlers' because they refuse to acknowledge their own rootedness in the desert as true nomads.

If the nation-state has its roots in a nomadic world before capital, and if the cosmopolitan symbolically represents the dangers (and advantages) of capital, we can turn to a major Jewish thinker of the late nineteenth century for a sense of the linkage between the two concepts. The detailed 1876 study of the constitution of Jewish mythology by the great Jewish Hungarian scholar of Islam, Ignaz Goldziher, adds a further nuance to our sense of the ambivalent image of the cosmopolitan hovering between advantage and danger.[25] For Goldziher (1850–1921): 'The national level [of Jewish mythopoeia] can be sorted out of the mix. It was Abraham, not yet rethinking these tales in national terms, who was not yet a cosmopolitan figure, but as an individual [who formed these tales]' (our translation, 59). In this portrayal of the Biblical Abraham, individuality – the particular – and cosmopolitanism – the universal – are portrayed as dichotomous. Abraham is an individual, not a cosmopolitan, for he is part of 'the nomadic level that found its element in a continual wandering from grazing pasture to grazing pasture, in the continual changing of their abode, before it was historically grounded in the completion of its movement to agriculture' (64). Like the Arabs, whom Goldziher idealizes, the Jews (here he cites Philo) 'glorify their nomadic life' (103). The Jews detest artisan labour (*Handwerk*), no matter how intense 'their desire for money', as below their status as nomads (105). They are thus inherently different in their storytelling from the ancient Greeks and the Aryan inhabitants of South Asia:

> The Hellenes and the Indians have their primary figures of myth being of a cosmopolitan character, for Zeus and Indira have no specific national character, even though now and then they are specifically local. The figures of Hebrew myth in this period become the national ancestors of the Hebrew people, where myth is raised to become the national prehistory of the Hebrew people before its settlement in the land of Canaan. (306)

Here, the national and the cosmopolitan appear as diametrically opposed. Jewish tales are restrictedly national and local, rather than cosmopolitan and global. They are the product of the world of the nomad, at least as imagined from the point of view of the Biblical national Jewish state, which remained local, unlike the transcendental worlds of Greece and India.

Nomadism is also pressed into service to explain the origin of the Jews' 'natural' relationship to cosmopolitanism and to capital. The German economist Werner Sombart, in his classic response to Max Weber's *The Protestant Ethic and the Spirit of Capitalism* (1905) wrote in *The Jews and Modern Capitalism* (1911) of the 'restless wandering Bedouins [who] were the Hebrews' who established in 'this promised land' an 'economic organization' where 'the powerful and mighty among them after having conquered large tracts of land instituted a sort of feudal society. Part of the produce of the land they took for themselves, either by way of rent in kind, by farming it out to tax-collectors, or by means of the credit nexus' (325).[26] In other words, proto-capitalists, but of a particularly nasty kind – the origin of the stereotyped Jewish banker in the world of the nomad. For Sombart the contemporary Jew is an extension of the earlier nomad as far as the Jews' character and relationship to capital is concerned.

Max Weber responds in *Ancient Judaism* (1920–1921), where he argues against such a view.[27] He accepts that there is a narrative (but not historical) succession of 'the stages of the three Patriarchs from the "nomad" Abraham to the "peasant" Jacob' (438). However, he refutes the idea that the nature of Jewish usury stems from any Biblical claims to divine approbation in Deuteronomy 28: 43–44:[28] 'The medieval and modern money and pawn usury of the Jews, the caricature in which this promise was fulfilled, was certainly not intended by the holy promise.' Rather, Weber reads this as being symbolic of the triumph of city over countryside 'which prevailed in every typical polis throughout early Antiquity from Sumerian-Accadian times' (69). While a particular quality of the Jews, it is one no different from the cosmopolitan world of the ancient city with its myth of agrarian settlement.

The Jews are nomads: Herder and his reading of the Bible say so and the essence of the Jew is captured by his nomadism in the present-day world of the nineteenth-century pan-European anti-Semite. In the seminal anti-Semitic work of Richard Wagner's son-in-law Houston Stewart Chamberlain's *Foundations of the 19th Century* (1912), the history of the Jew in the distant past is again the history of the Jew today: 'Of all the histories of the ancient world there is none that is more convincing, none more easily to be realized, than that of the wanderings of the patriarch Abraham. It is a story of four thousand years ago, it is a story of yesterday, it is a story of today.' But it is the history of a degenerate people, Chamberlain argues, for

> any change in the manner of living is said to have a very bad effect on the high qualities of the genuine and purely Semitic nomads. The learned [A.H.] Sayce, one of the greatest advocates of the Jews at the present day, writes: 'If the Bedouin of the desert chooses a settled life, he, as

a rule, unites in himself all the vices of the nomad and of the peasant. Lazy, deceitful, cruel, greedy, cowardly, he is rightly regarded by all nations as the scum of mankind.'[29]

And it is the history of an impure race as well: 'As a matter of fact the current opinion is that the Semite and even that purest Bedouin type are the most absolute mongrels imaginable, the product of a cross between negro and white man!'[30] Mixed races, Chamberlain suggests, have no spaces left for them so they simply wander.

As early as 1887, the Austrian-German Orientalist Adolf Wahrmund had cast the Jew-as-nomad as the essential capitalist:

> Thus we have the typical image of the private enterprise of the nomad, that continues until today, in the form of the wandering merchants and dealers who cross the land selling junk, stocks, and [...] thus rob our peasants and return on the Sabbath with their plunder home to wife and children [...].[31]

The very nature of capitalism is that of the 'parasitic' nomad and is the essential nature of the Jew.

However, the Jews are not very good nomads insofar as they violate one version of the Enlightenment's underlying assumptions concerning the claims of cosmopolitanism, namely the Greek concept of ξενία, *xenía*. As the German journalist Otto Gildemeister noted in 1921: 'Even the highest law regarding the safety of the stranger (*Gastfreundschaft*) is not recognized by these nomads. Thus Jewess Jael murders Sisera after having been tempted into a tent and served milk. Trusting her he goes to sleep. Then Jael drives a stake into his temple and mocks his mother when she comes to seek her son.'[32] 'True nomads' are ideals against which the Jews are often set from the Enlightenment onwards.[33]

The ancient Jews violate the rules of many of the nomads described in the *Lebensraum* theorist Friedrich Ratzel's *History of Mankind* (1896), where the Jews are seen as originally

> nomads like their kinsmen in Arabia and Syria [...]. Their oldest books know nothing of fixed altars and their sacrifices are always of cattle. They took to a settled life on conquering and dividing the land of Canaan. But the promised land was only an oasis [...]. The misfortunes of the national ruin, however, brought about a purification which in a race aesthetically deficient, but spiritually proud and austere, tended to strengthen the conception of a deity all powerful and all-knowing, and at the same time jealous and severe.[34]

It is only through 'contact with the Greeks, fundamentally Aryan, yet touched by a Semitic spirit, who, independently of the Jews, had gone through a process of spiritual refinement in the direction of truth, knowledge, and beauty, [that] Christianity developed into a power capable of transforming races'. Any value that the Jews have comes only through their being filtered through Greek sensibility and the resultant creation of a modern consciousness. For Ratzel, the Jews' initial contribution to Western culture may have been a sort of primitive monotheism (as opposed to Christianity) but their long-term impact is on 'above all the economic life of other nations' (548).

In the nineteenth century, the philosopher Ernest Renan saw in the Jews the survival of 'nomadic instincts' and the 'nomadic nomos' of the Jews into modern times, while René Guenon would write of the 'perverse nomadism of the Jews'.[35] It is the character of the Jews as nomads in the present day that defines Renan and Guenon's claim. And, one can here quote Felix Delitzsch, of *Babel und Bibel* infamy, when in 1920 he notes concerning the continuity of Jewish nomadic character from the Biblical period that: 'It is obvious that such a people, which is deliberately landless or an international people, presents a great, a frightening danger for all other peoples of the earth.'³⁶ Jews were aggressive nomads and remain so today.

However, the Jews are also terrible at being nomads because, well, they are Jews. Adolf Hitler states this baldly in *Mein Kampf*, echoing his reading of Houston Stewart Chamberlain:

> Since the Jew never possessed a state with definite territorial limits and therefore never called a culture his own, the conception arose that this was a people that should be reckoned among the ranks of the nomads. This is a fallacy as great as it is dangerous. The nomad does possess a definitely limited living space; only he does not cultivate it like a sedentary peasant, but lives from the yield of his herds with which he wanders about in his territory. The outward reason for this is to be found in the small fertility of a soil that simply does not permit of settlement. The deeper cause, however, lies in the disparity between the technical culture of an age or people and the natural poverty of a living space.³⁷

The Jews are only symbolic nomads in the modern world. That the Jews are nomads in this pejorative sense means that they are, in the present world, parasites on settled, non-nomadic national peoples. Echoing Wagner's claim that the Jews lack the ability to create original art, the psychologist C. G. Jung stated in 1934 in a lecture in Hitler's Berlin that

> the Jew who is something of a nomad, has never yet created a cultural form of his own, and as far as we can see never will, since all his instincts and talents require a more or less civilized nation to act as a host for their development. Aside from certain creative individuals, the average Jew is already much too conscious and differentiated to be pregnant with the tensions of the unborn future. The Aryan unconscious has a higher potential than the Jewish; that is the advantage and the disadvantage of a youthfulness not yet fully estranged from barbarism.³⁸

It is not what one does but who one is that defines the nomad, defines the cosmopolitan, symbolising the role that identity is seen as playing in the world one inhabits.

Martin Heidegger in a lecture in 1937 said more or less the same thing: 'A Slavic people would experience the essence of our German space certainly differently as we do. Semitic NOMADS would most probably not experience it at all.'³⁹ This was echoed in his so-called *Black Notebooks* when he wrote that: 'The question of the role of World Jewry is not a racial but rather a metaphysical one about the type of human specificity, that in all cases can be extrapolated as a world-historical "goal" from the ROOTLESSNESS of the Becoming from Being.'⁴⁰ For such thinkers Jewish Nomadism is a permanent stain on Jewish character in contrast to the stability of the German (or even the Slav). Jewish thinkers about Nomadism, on the other hand, saw it as a transitional phase to some further (and improved) state.

And the image of the Jew makes this concrete, impacting upon how Jews themselves understand their own function in the society they inhabit. It is no wonder that Max Brod, writing in Martin Buber's periodical *The Jew* (*Der Jude*) in 1916, complained: 'One should not inject us with being a centrifugal force in society and then marvel at the findings of "nomadism" and "critical destruction" in our corpse.'⁴¹ It is this internalisation of the cosmopolitan and the nomad that has come to define the Jew in the post-Enlightenment world, indeed even into the twenty-first century.

Modern Jewish historians, such as Jacob Neusner in *Self-Fulfilling Prophecy: Exile and Return in the History of Judaism*, have argued for a material understanding of diaspora.⁴² For Neusner, it is the model of wilderness and land, the dialectic between tent and house, nomadism and agriculture, wilderness and Canaan, wandering and settlement, diaspora and state. The Welsh Congregationalist W. D. Davies has argued, in *The Territorial Dimension in Judaism*, that this dichotomy is well balanced in the Bible, that for every quote praising wilderness as the decisive factor in Judaism, there could be found a counterpart in praise of the Land of Zion.[43]

Galut, on the other hand, is often understood as the experienced reality of being in exile, albeit structured, however, by the internalisation of the textual notion of the diaspora and tempered by the daily experience (good or bad) of life in the world. The Jew experiences the daily life of exile through the mirror of the biblical model of expulsion, whether it be the expulsion from the Garden of Eden or freedom from slavery in Egypt. Galut has formed the Jewish self-understanding of exile. The voluntary dispersion of the Jews ('Galut' or 'Golah') is articulated as being inherently different from the involuntary exile of the Jews ('Diaspora'). These two models exist simultaneously in Jewish history in the image of uprooted and powerless Jews on the one hand, and rooted and empowered Jews on the other. It is possible to have a firm, meaningful cultural experience as a Jew in the Diaspora or to feel alone and abandoned in the Galut (as well as vice-versa): two people can live in the very same space and time and can experience that space and time in antithetical ways. Indeed, the same person can find his or her existence bounded conceptually by such models at different times and in different contexts.

In the on-going tension between the cosmopolitan and the nomad, the alien and the predator in German culture, we are confronted with the core of the idea of the mundivagant Jew. Whether understood as a racial or a cultural factor in the age of evolving nationalism, the view is that Jews transcend the 'natural' order of the evolving idea of the national state as homogenous and settled. Whether that homogeneity is sought in language or geographic borders or both, the Jews were excluded from that invented community by the widely held views of their nature or their practices. Such views in the late nineteenth century shaped the evolving idea of Zionism as a state ideology to embrace the Jews as a national people as well as the rising antisemitic parties of Germany and the Austrian Empire that advocated the removal the Jews from the body politic. These tensions have not vanished in the twenty-first century.

Notes

1. See, for example, Beck and Sznaider, "Unpacking Cosmopolitanism for the Social Sciences," 1–23, as well as their "A Literature on Cosmopolitanism: An Overview," 153–64. Recently Nirenberg, *Anti-Judaism: The Western Tradition*, has raised the question of the projection of such spectral qualities into the stereotype of the Jew.
2. The most salient literature remains Sznaider, *Jewish Memory and the Cosmopolitan Order*; Beck and Sznaider, "Unpacking Cosmopolitanism for the Social Sciences: A Research Agenda," 1–23; Appiah, *Cosmopolitanism: Ethics in a World of Strangers (Issues of Our Time)*. Peter L. Berger and Charles Taylor have respectively framed and contested this basic debate within cosmopolitanist theory from the mid-twentieth century. See Berger, *The Sacred Canopy*; Taylor, *A Secular Age*.
3. Brennan, *At Home in the World*.
4. Dee, *General and Rare Memorials*, 54.
5. "Mitteilungen: Weltbürger," *Neuphilologische Mitteilungen* 27 (1926): 13.
6. Lallement, *Choix de rapports, opinions et discours prononcés à la tribune nationale depuis 1789 jusqu'à ce jour* (1818–1823).
7. Berkovitz, Rites and Passages, 152.
8. Actually he wrote "Die Religionen Müsen alle Tolleriret werden und Mus der fiscal nuhr das auge darauf haben, das keine der andern abruch Tuhe, den hier mus ein jeder nach Seiner Fasson Selich werden!" Cited by Raab, *Kirche und Staat*, 194.
9. Wieland, *Private History of Peregrinus Proteus the Philosopher*, 2: 32.

10. Penslar, *Shylock's Children*.
11. Gilman, *Multiculturalism and the Jews*.
12. Vieten, *Gender and Cosmopolitanism in Europe*, 7.
13. Herder, *Outlines of a Philosophy of the History of Man*, 658.
14. Wirtz, *Patriotismus und Weltbürgertum*.
15. *Johann Gottlieb Fichtes sämmtliche Werke*, Abt. 3: 149.
16. Mack, *German Idealism and the Jew*, 5.
17. Tentzel, *Monatliche Unterredungen Einiger Guten Freunde von Allerhand Büchern und andern annehmlichen Geschichten*, 833.
18. Wagenseil, Benachrichtigung wegen einiger die gemeine Jüdischheit betreffenden wichtigen Sachen, 473–88.
19. Schudt, *Judische Merckwürdigkeiten*, 470–512.
20. All references are from Noyes, "Goethe On Cosmopolitanism and Colonialism: Bildung and the Dialectic of Critical Mobility," 443–62.
21. Marx, *Capital*, 182–3.
22. Sidra DeKoven Ezrahi, "Considering the Apocalypse," 138–9.
23. Simmel, *Philosophy of Money*.
24. Simmel, *Philosophy of Money*.
25. Goldziher, *Der Mythos bei den Hebraern: Und Seine Geschichtliche Entwickelung*.
26. Sombart, *The Jews and Modern Capitalism*, 325.
27. Weber, *Ancient Judaism*.
28. "The stranger that is within thee shall get up above thee very high; and thou shalt come down very low. He shall lend to thee, and thou shalt not lend to him: he shall be the head, and thou shalt be the tail."
29. The Hittite scholar Archibald H. Sayce was indeed philosemitic. In his 1903 Gifford Lectures he wrote that: "It is usually the fashion to ascribe this concentration of religion upon the present world, with its repellent views of Hades and limitation of divine rewards and punishments to this life, to the inherent peculiarities of the Semitic mind. But for this there is no justification. There is nothing in the Semitic mind, which would necessitate such a theological system. It is true that the sun-god was the central object of the Semitic Babylonian faith, and that to the nomads of Arabia the satisfaction of their daily wants was the practical end of existence. But it is not among the nomads of Arabia that we find anything corresponding with the Babylonian idea of Hades and the conceptions associated with it. The idea was, in fact, of Babylonian origin. If the Hebrew Sheol resembles the Hades of Babylonia, or the Hebrew conception of rewards and punishments is like that of the Assyrians and Babylonians, it is because the Hebrew beliefs were derived from the civilisation of the Euphrates." *The Religions of Ancient Egypt and Babylonia*, 295.
30. Chamberlain, *The Foundations of the 19th Century*, 369.
31. Wahrmund, *Das Gesetz des Nomadentums und die heutige Judenherrschaft*, 91; our translation.
32. Otto Gildemeister, *Judas Werdegang*, 15.
33. For an example, see the German philosopher Christoph Meiners, "Kurze Geschichte der Hirtenvölker in den verschiedenen Theilen der Erde," 654–85.
34. Ratzel, *The History of Mankind*, 83ff., 547ff.
35. Cited by Rossman, Russian Intellectual Antisemitism in the Post-Communist Era, 8.
36. Delitzsch, Die grosse Täuschung, 1: 105.
37. Hitler, *Mein Kampf*, 300–11, 324–7.
38. C. G. Jung, *Interviews and Encounters*, 193.
39. Heidegger, "Über Wesen und Begriff von Natur, Geschichte und Staat," 82.
40. Heidegger: *Überlegungen* XIV, 121. I am indebted to Trawny, *Heidegger und der Mythos der jüdischen Weltverschwörung*.
41. Brod, "Der Erfahrung in ostjüdischen Schulwerk," 1: 35: "Man soll uns nicht eine Zentifugalkraft einimpfen und hintenach wundern, 'Nomadentum' und 'kritische Zersetzung' an unserm Leichnam konstatiren!"
42. Neusner, *Self-Fulfilling Prophecy: Exile and Return in the History of Judaism*.
43. Davies, *The Territorial Dimension in Judaism*.

Bibliography

Appiah, Kwame Anthony. *Cosmopolitanism: Ethics in a World of Strangers (Issues of Our Time)*. New York: W. W. Norton & Company, 2007.

Beck, Ulrich, and Natan Sznaider. "Unpacking Cosmopolitanism for the Social Sciences: A Research Agenda." *British Journal of Sociology* 57 (2006): 1–23.

Beck, Ulrich, and Natan Sznaider. "A Literature on Cosmopolitanism: An Overview." *The British Journal of Sociology* 57 (2006): 153–164.

Berger, Peter L. *The Sacred Canopy: The Social Construction of Reality. Elements of a Sociological Theory of Religion*. New York: Anchor, 1967.

Berkovitz, Jay R. *Rites and Passages: The Beginnings of Modern Jewish Culture in France, 1650–1860*. Philadelphia, PA: University of Pennsylvania Press, 2004.

Brennan, Tim. *At Home in the World. Cosmopolitanism Today*. Cambridge, Mass.: Harvard University Press, 1997.

Brod, Max. "Der Erfahrung in ostjüdischen Schulwerk." *Der Jude* 1 (1916–1917).

Chamberlain, Houston Stewart. *The Foundations of the 19th Century*. 2nd ed. London: John Lane, The Bodley Head, 1912.

Davies, W. D. *The Territorial Dimension in Judaism*. Minneapolis: Fortress Press, 1991 (1982).

Dee, John. *General and Rare Memorials pertayning to the Perfect Arte of Navigation*. London: John Daye, 1577.

Delitzsch, Felix. *Die grosse Täuschung, kritische Betrachtungen zu den alttestamentlichen Berichten über Israels Eindringen in Kanaan*. Stuttgart: Deutsche Verlags-Anstalt, 1920–1921.

Ezrahi, Sidra DeKoven. "Considering the Apocalypse: Is the Writing on the Wall Only Grafitti?" In *Writing and the Holocaust*, edited by Berel Lang, 137–159. New York: Holmes and Meier, 1988.

Gildemeister, Otto. *Judas Werdegang: in vier Jahrtausenden*. Leipzig: Weicher, 1921.

Gilman, Sander L. *Multiculturalism and the Jews*. New York: Routledge, 2006.

Goldziher, Ignaz. *Der Mythos bei den Hebraern: Und Seine Geschichtliche Entwickelung*. Leipzig: F.A. Brockhaus, 1876.

Heidegger, Martin. "Über Wesen und Begriff von Natur, Geschichte und Staat." Übung aus dem Wintersemester 1933/34. In *Heidegger und der Nationalsozialismus. Dokumente*, edited by Alfred Denker und Holger Zaborowski. Heidegger-Jahrbuch 4. Karl Alber Verlag: Freiburg u. München, 2009.

Heidegger, Martin. *Überlegungen XIV, 121*. In *Überlegungen XII–XV*, edited by Peter Trawny. Gesamt-Ausgabe 96. Frankfurt am Main: Vittorio Klostermann, 2014.

Hitler, Adolf. *Mein Kampf (1927)*. Trans. Ralph Manheim. Boston: Houghton Mifflin, 1943.

Herder, Johann Gottfried. *Outlines of a Philosophy of the History of Man*. Trans. T. Churchill. London, 1800.

Jung, C. G. *Interviews and Encounters*. Ed. William McGuire and R. F. C. Hull. Princeton: Princeton University Press, 1977.

Johann Gottlieb Fichtes sämmtliche Werke. Ed. I.H. Fichte. Berlin: Veit und comp., 1845–1846.

Lallement. *Choix de rapports, opinions et discours prononcés à la tribune nationale depuis 1789 jusqu'à ce jour* (1818–1823).
Mack, Michael. *German Idealism and the Jew: The Inner Anti-Semitism of Philosophy and German Jewish Responses*. Chicago, IL: University of Chicago Press, 2003.
Marx, Karl. *Capital*. Harmondsworth: Penguin, 1976.
Meiners, Christoph. "Kurze Geschichte der Hirtenvölker in den verschiedenen Theilen der Erde." *Neues Göttingisches historisches Magazin* 2 (1793): 654–685.
"Mitteilungen: Weltbürger." *Neuphilologische Mitteilungen* 27 (1926): 13.
Neusner, Jacob. *Self-Fulfilling Prophecy: Exile and Return in the History of Judaism*. Atlanta: Scholars Press, 1990 (1987).
Nirenberg, David. *Anti-Judaism: The Western Tradition*. W.W: Norton, 2013.
Noyes, John K. "Goethe On Cosmopolitanism and Colonialism: Bildung and the Dialectic of Critical Mobility." *Eighteenth-Century Studies* 39, no. 4 (2006): 443–462.
Penslar, Derek. *Shylock's Children: Economics and Jewish Identity in Modern Europe*. Berkeley: University of California Press, 2001.
Raab, Heribert (ed.). *Kirche und Staat: Von der Mitte des 15. Jahrhunderts bis zur Gegenwart*. Munich: Deutscher Taschenbuch Verlag, 1966.
Ratzel, Friedrich. *The History of Mankind*. London: MacMillan and Ltd, 1896.
Rossman, Vadim. *Joseph*. Russian Intellectual Antisemitism in the Post-Communist Era Lincoln, NE: University of Nebraska Press, 2002.
Sayce, Archibald H. *The Religions of Ancient Egypt and Babylonia*. Edinburgh: Clark, 1903.
Schudt, Johann Jakob. *Judische Merckwürdigkeiten: vorstellende was sich curieuses und denckwürdiges in den neuern Zeiten bey einigen Jahrhunderten mit denen in alle IV. Theile der Welt, sonderlich durch Teutschland, zerstreuten Juden zugetragen: sammt einer vollständigen Franckfurter Juden-Chronick, darinnen der zu Franckfurt am Mayn wohnenden Juden, von einigen Jahr-hunderten, biss auff unsere Zeiten, merckwürdigste Begebenheiten enthalten: benebst einigen, zur Erläuterung beygefügten Kupffern und Figuren*. Frankfurt: [s.n.], 1714.
Simmel, George. *Philosophy of Money*. Trans. Tom Bottomore and David Frisby. London: Routledge and Kegan Paul, 1978.
Sombart, Werner. *The Jews and Modern Capitalism*. Trans. M. Epstein. New York: E. P. Dutton, 1913.
Sznaider, Natan. *Jewish Memory and the Cosmopolitan Order*. Cambridge: Polity Press, 2011.
Taylor, Charles. *A Secular Age*. Cambridge: Belknap Press of Harvard University Press, 2007.
Tentzel, W. E. *Monatliche Unterredungen Einiger Guten Freunde von Allerhand Büchern und andern annehmlichen Geschichten. Allen Liebhabern Der Curiositäten Zur Ergetzligkeit und Nachsinnen heraus gegeben* 1 (1689).
Trawny, Peter. *Heidegger und der Mythos der jüdischen Weltverschwörung*. Frankfurt am Main: Vittorio Klostermann, 2014.
Vieten, Ulrike M. *Gender and Cosmopolitanism in Europe: A Feminist Perspective*. Farnham: Ashgate, 2012.
Wagenseil, Johann Christof. *Benachrichtigung wegen einiger die gemeine Jüdischheit betreffenden wichtigen Sachen : worinnen-I. Die Hoffnung der Erlösung Israelis. II. Wiederlegung der Unwahrheit als ob die Jüden Christen-Blut brauchten. III. Anzeigung wie die Jüden von schinden und wuchern abzubringen. IV. Bericht von dem Jüdischen Gebeth Alenu. V. Denunciatio Christiana, wegen der Jüden Lästerungen. Diesen sind beygefügt - Rabbi Mose Stendels, in Jüdisch-Teutsche Reimen gebrachte Psalmen Davids*. Leipzig: Johann Heiniche Witwe, 1705.
Wahrmund, Adolf. *Das Gesetz des Nomadentums und die heutige Judenherrschaft*. Karlsruhe und Leipzig: H. Reuther, 1887.
Weber, Max. *Ancient Judaism*. Trans. Hans H. Gerth and Don Albert Martindale. New York: Free Press, 1967.
Wieland, C. M. *Private History of Peregrinus Proteus the Philosopher*. London: Printed for J. Johnson, in St. Paul's Churchyard, 1796.
Wirtz, Michaela. *Patriotismus und Weltbürgertum. Eine begriffsgeschichtliche Studie zur deutsch-jüdischen Literatur 1750–1850*. Tübingen: M. Niemeyer, 2006.

Revolutions, wars and the Jewish and Christian contribution to redemptive cosmopolitanism in Franz Rosenzweig and Eugen Rosenstock-Huessy

Wayne Cristaudo

ABSTRACT
This article addresses the important contribution of Judaism and Christianity to cosmopolitanism through the works of Franz Rosenzweig and Eugen Rosenstock-Huessy. It argues that while the usual approach to cosmopolitanism is to consider its philosophical origins, the European roots of cosmopolitanism as an actual process are deeply indebted to the central importance of redemption within the Jewish and Christian faiths. Whereas Rosenzweig explores the mutual interdependence and respective social significance of Jews and Christians (in spite of the fundamental inimicalness between these two faiths), Eugen Rosenstock-Huessy argues that the messianic logic inherent in the redemptive tradition also spawned the messianic aspirations behind the great European revolutions, including the anti-Christian and atheistic French and Russian. The article concludes by looking at the United States after the Second World War as continuing the 'mission' of redemptive cosmopolitanism.

Introduction

Typically, works on cosmopolitanism emphasize the contribution of Cynic, Stoic and Kantian philosophy to cosmopolitanism.[1] Most philosophical treatments of cosmopolitanism also tend to explore cosmopolitanism as a normative project in which moral agency, rights and duties, and law are the essential 'mediators' for achieving the desired cosmopolitan outcome. Thus, for example, Seyla Benhabib, taking her philosophical orientation from Jürgen Habermas, speaks of cosmopolitanism as 'a philosophical project of mediations, not of reductions or of totalizations'[2], and mediations are accomplished by 'individuals as moral and legal persons in a worldwide civil society'[3] rationally conversing with each other as they each justify their moral concerns.[4] Sometimes, as in Gerard Delanty's *The Cosmopolitan Imagination: The Renewal of Critical Social Theory*, the philosopher or theorist investigates the 'critical and transformative nature of cosmopolitanism'.[5] But ultimately, even such an imminent critique is beholden to a cluster of emancipative political 'ideas' which direct the analysis; in spite of its ostensible materialism, critical theory has always displayed an idealist revolutionary disposition which measures what is wrong with what by judging it against what might be were we not misled by bourgeois self-interest. There are noticeable exceptions to this approach, such as Ulrich Beck's seminal sociological study *The Cosmopolitan Vision*, which takes its cue from 'global crises and [the] dangers produced by civilization'. It argues that 'a new cosmopolitan realism [is] … essential to survival.'[6] Then there is Robert Fine's Hegelian supplementary corrective to a natural-rights-based cosmopolitanism intent on 'drawing cosmopolitanism firmly into the terrain of history, politics and the social'.[7] Broadly, I think the approach of Beck and Fine is helpful. However, neither addresses the fact that the roots of European values are religious. And while modern appeals to and arguments about the value of cosmopolitanism are invariably secular, the actual sentiments and feelings of Europeans were the result of close on two millennia of religious cultivation. Moreover, while it is true that cosmopolitanism is a Greek term to describe a philosophical aspiration of a small number of dreamers, it is a mistake to see this as an important source of Christian universalism, as Delanty, for example, does.[8] When Paul mentions philosophy he is unequivocally negative (for example, Colossians 2:8; cf. 1 Timothy 6:20). As Acts 17 illustrates, the philosophers could make neither head nor tail of what Paul was on about. Paul's universalism is not grounded in a philosophical idea – nor is it the result of philosophical deliberation, but it is a response to what Paul holds as a divine command. The actual *culture* of redemption in Europe received its original impetus as a reality not from a small number of philosophers, but the experience of Jews in the diaspora, and Germanic peoples renouncing tribal differences and gods to enter into a common faith in the suffering Son of God.

Both Jews and Christians grasped that in order to build a community certain energies had to be sacrificed. Redemption required the negation of certain creations, and the rebinding of those creations under the direction, not of a pantheon of discordant (divine) energies, but of One God who commanded us to love Him and each other. This drive for concordance is also conspicuous amongst the philosophers of Antiquity and their dream of cosmopolitanism. But the difference between the Jewish and Christian faiths and the philosophers of Antiquity was that religious faith commands every aspect of every creature, and from the outset fosters scepticism in our intelligence or reason (*nous*) to grasp life's meaning and mystery.

In contrast to the writings on cosmopolitanism mentioned above, Franz Rosenzweig (1886–1929) and Eugen Rosenstock-Huessy (1888–1973) in different, but complementary, ways addressed how the redemptive faiths of the Jewish and Christian peoples help create and better see the conditions in which the world becomes one and we become better neighbours. They did not call this process cosmopolitanism, because they saw the word itself as bearing too much questionable philosophical freight. Where possible they deliberately avoided philosophical 'names' in order to draw their readers into the more primordial semantic fields of religious world-making, the better to help them understand the fecundity of the pre-philosophical, and hence less idealistic, way of naming. But, as we shall see, what Rosenzweig is talking about when he speaks of the redemption of the world, and Rosenstock-Huessy's providential (redemptive) reading of war and revolution, and universal history, with its 'metanomics' of what Rosenstock-Huessy will eventually call a 'planetary society', provides us with invaluable insights for thinking about a cosmopolitan future.[9] The trope of political redemption is, of course, also to be found in Benjamin (who admired Rosenzweig), Adorno, Taubes and Agamben. And Adorno had provided a much quoted formulation which captures the religious or theological longing and stance behind their thinking: 'The only philosophy that can be responsibly practised in the face of despair is the attempt to contemplate all things as they would present themselves from the standpoint of redemption.'[10] But the calls of Adorno, Benjamin and others for a new society are all symptomatic of what Rosenzweig saw as a chief defect in Marxism: its desire to storm heaven by overleaping the immediate neighbour in favour of the neighbours of the future.[11] In the final section of the article I apply their insights, and argue that since the end of the Second World War the United States has, not always for the better, continued to orientate itself geopolitically by way of this redemptive mission, with little recognition that it is doing so, and asking much of peoples whose own historicity is not driven by the desire or need for redemption.

The Star of Redemption

In 1916, Rosenzweig and his former teacher, Rosenstock-Huessy, while stationed to different fronts of the Great War, engaged in what may well be the most important Jewish-Christian exchange ever undertaken.[12] Both were very vocal in the fact that each saw the other as his most important teacher.[13] Rosenstock-Huessy even described his own system at one point in a letter to his wife and Rosenzweig's one time beloved, Gritli, as 'the popularized version of the *Star*, translated into Christian German, just as Franz's own translation of Jehuda Halevi was the *Star* translated into Jewish'.[14] For all their inimicality, they concurred that the Jewish and Christian peoples both lived under a God who commanded them to love their neighbour, and that the two faiths were assigned to express that love in different ways: the Jew to live in eternity and to celebrate annually the 'stations' of eternity; the Christian to ever be on the way in the world and to bring all peoples into one history and one world. Jews and Christians thus were both responding to God's revelation that 'love is as strong as death', and that God commands us to redeem the world. This letter exchange would be the most important creative spur in the intellectual lives of the two men, spawning Rosenzweig's *Star of Redemption,* Rosenstock-Huessy's *In the Cross of Reality: A Sociology in Two Parts: Volume 1 The Hegemony of Spaces* and *Volume 2 The Full Count of the Times*.[15]

Whereas, as we shall see later, Eugen Rosenstock-Huessy's (post-) Christianized vision of the 'planetary society' is easily identifiable as a kind of (non-philosophically driven) cosmopolitanism, the relevance of Franz Rosenzweig's *Star of Redemption* to a more apt framing of cosmopolitanism is somewhat less obvious. This is largely because the *Star* is primarily devoted to demonstrating how Judaism and Christianity are both rooted in revelation and redemption, but Christianity is: (1) nothing without Judaism;,and (2) ever in danger of lapsing into the pagan or natural, that is, non-redemptive (which is most definitely not to say 'non-mystical' or 'non-spiritual') ways of being in the world. However, the case that the *Star* makes for the inimical alliance between Judaism and Christianity is an argument for a vision of and response to life which wishes to redeem it.

From the outset of the *Star* philosophy as such is deprived of any royal road to what he calls 'the All'. Thus while the *Star* contains a critique of philosophy generally, and specifically of its traditional totalising 'claims' about God, world and 'man', it sets out a new kind of philosophy which is forced into a more humble role in its attempt to help make sense of our personal, communal and historical existence. Thus in Rosenzweig philosophy ends up as a team member alongside history, sociology and anthropology, and, most of all, theology, because theology has devoted itself to exploring life as an act of creation, revelation and redemption. Concomitantly, the *Star* negates any notion that a particular form of life or approach to social existence – as cosmopolitan theorists have traditionally done – should or could take their ultimate direction from philosophy. This feature of the *Star* is all too often ignored by more academic readers, for whom philosophising is their primary *raison d'être*. Hence, for example, because the *Star* is concerned with redemption and love of the neighbour, it is commonly misrepresented as primarily an ethical work, and in the last 20 or so years it tends to be (mis)read as more or less consistent with what Levinas is wanting to do. The problem with such interpretations as provided by Richard Cohen, Robert Gibbs, Bruce Rosenstock and even the magisterial work on Messianism in twentieth-century Jewish philosophy by Pierre Bouretz is that they all downplay or completely ignore election and 'blood', two central concepts in Rosenzweig's apologetics of Judaism which retain a distinctly 'tribal' (non-universalist) view of Judaism.[16] Further, Rosenzweig was politically very conservative, and given what democracy opened up in Germany (including its own extinction) I think insensitivity to Rosenzweig's very specific battles renders fusing his 'problems' with those on the contemporary academic ethico-political agenda very problematic. Finally, I think that the unassailable reason for not treating the *Star* primarily as a contribution to ethics is that at its heart it is not providing a teaching that it wants all to live by. What most academically trained philosophical readers of the *Star* completely ignore is that whereas books on ethics wish to 'convert' people to a common point of view (in the manner of the very idealism Rosenzweig is critiquing) from which they then derive some sense of how to act ethically, Rosenzweig neither thinks this is possible, nor even desirable. This should be obvious in so far as Rosenzweig is emphatic in his identification of the elect as being bound by blood. That this is so consistently overlooked, or else seen as something verging on Fascism, is symptomatic of how deeply the modern (and post-modern) mind is steeped in voluntarism: how it wants the world to surrender to its will – whether the will is primarily construed in terms of sheer power or conatus (Hobbes, Spinoza, Leibniz, Nietzsche), or morality and politics is beside the point. It is against such catastrophic moves of modernity – with its voluntaristic faiths in science, commerce, morals, politics and the nation, which culminated in the Great War – that Rosenzweig appeals to a 'new thinking'.

For his part, Rosenzweig only discusses ethics as such in the context of the Jewish and Christian faiths as part of a greater exploration of revelation and redemption. For peoples not overtly seeking redemption (which for him is everyone else) he is not offering anything, except an insight into how Jews and Christians think. But in so far as he sees Christianity as driven by the mission of historically converting the peoples of the world into their faith (in the same God as the non-missionising Jews), and into the world that their faith has made, he does see that all peoples are swept up in the redemption of the world, even if a more detailed depiction of the conditions and processes of this sweeping up is not his major concern.

It is worth pausing upon some other features of the *Star*, to convey some of the power that this work has in providing an alternative to what I think can fairly be labelled as the more typical academic philosophical approach to reality in general and thinking about cosmopolitanism in particular: the more typical philosophical approach which frequently invokes 'difference' in the abstract only to surreptitiously slide all really decisive differences under some greater unity or identity of philosophy's devising. The identity then reintroduces difference into moral-political binaries such as oppressor/ oppressed, persecutor/ victim and so on. This ultimately creates the false impression that we all more or less want the same important things (whether it be goodness, love, justice, respect, whatever). Unlike Derrida,

Deleuze, Foucault and Lyotard who all brushed up against this problem, only to fall back into the identity of emancipation, and what to them was an unquestioned and unassailable form of political voluntarism, Rosenzweig does not proceed thus. The eschewal of such seductive suppressions of difference is one reason why I hold Rosenzweig and Rosenstock-Huessy as far more innovative thinkers than the poststructuralists, and the radical liberal ethico-political social theorists who are now so academically ubiquitous.

Rosenzweig draws out how different peoples are, and how their differences are developed through their different supplications: different modes of the sacred channel; different flows and forms of desire; different forms of action and appeal; and ultimately different communities. To be sure, the interaction and intermixing of communities creates all manner of hybrid appeals – and there is a reasonable argument to be made that Rosenzweig is in danger of essentialising different peoples. Though I think this misses the point that Rosenzweig was drawing attention to a very important dimension of community formation that had tended to be overlooked or downplayed in Philosophy and Sociology. Hence his exploration is of the different motivations and orientations provided by different faiths rather than working within *a priori* moral conditions.

Rosenzweig insisted the *Star* was not a book on the Philosophy of Religion.[17] It is a book on redemption, what redemption is, why it is significant and how it is *not* an ideal philosophical end, but a lived disposition. Its methodological starting point of inquiry is the nature of what powers command communities and peoples. To undertake that examination, Rosenzweig has to dismantle the idealistic legacy of philosophy which has so blinded Western thinking about itself and its past. It is a polemical book, and much of the polemic is directed against those that find in religion a common spiritual or mystical core, especially the kind of perennial philosophy that is frequently invoked today in interfaith dialogues as the common centre of all religious experience. Rosenzweig is not interested in any core other than redemption itself. Thus *The Star's* polemical engagement with Taoism, Eastern folklore, Hinduism, Buddhism and especially Islam invariably proves an embarrassment to scholars who see Rosenzweig as an ethicist[18], for if by ethics we are appealing to some kind of unity of common spiritual ends, Rosenzweig falls well short – but this is because he has no interest in an ethics which appeals to such a tacit unity of spirits. He does not believe that all peoples have surrendered to the same spirits and are seeking the same spiritual ends. Instead, Rosenzweig argues that some peoples elevate the Tao, others nirvana, others the eternal play of creation, others an immortal soul that is completely free from 'the prison of the body', and others (for Rosenzweig this is intrinsic to Islam) the energies and powers of creation, which Jews and Christians require to be sacrificed for redemption of the self, world and even God. There is no common appeal between these peoples – which is not to deny (but of no major interest to Rosenzweig) that we might find some sub-groups who share a common set of mystical longings and practices.

The central thread running through the Star is that the Jews were unique amongst peoples in the pre-Christian Ancient world in believing in the existence of the following triad of thought: (1) that a *loving relationship* existed between God, man and world; (2) that the Jews had a revelation – a revelation which took them beyond the creative dimension of the natural – that 'love was as strong as death;' and (3) that by living under this revelation and by following the commandment to love the neighbour the Jewish people, God and the world would be all redeemed. For Rosenzweig, the Davidic symbol was based around the faith and task provided by connecting these six poles of existence: God, Man and World, on the natural plane, and then upon the overlapping 'higher' plane, accessible through theology, Creation, Revelation and Redemption. He argued that while it was natural, hence commonplace and widespread to divide reality into human beings, (the) God(s) and the world, the Jewish people saw an intrinsic relationship among all three. And that insight opened them up to another triadic plane of the real.[19] Note that, for Rosenzweig, even God Himself is in search of redemption. And this suggests a God of lack as well as plenitude, and it becomes one of the key distinctions he discerns between what Jews and, later, Christians mean by 'God' and what Muslims mean by Allah, who is a God of plenitude, and, according to Rosenzweig, has servants but not relationships. A redeemed world was a world which had been drawn from a negation of those features of life not worthy of participating in 'an infinite life'. It was a world that is 'fully alive', a world in what has been created has now been deemed divinely worthy of infinitude because it is infinitely lovable.[20] Rosenzweig argued Jewish existence requires living ever in anticipation of this yet-to-come. That is to say, the Jews are required to be an eternal people living ever in anticipation of eternity.[21] And much of the first book of the third part of *The Star* is devoted to showing how the Jewish calendar is an expression of an eternal people triumphing over time: 'Temporal life is denied to this people for the sake of eternal life ... it is always somehow between a worldly and a holy life.'[22]

For Rosenzweig, the Jews are the living embodiment of the Davidic Star, 'the coal in God's fire', dwellers in anticipation of eternity, whose blood connection is not tied to the land, as with other peoples (hence Rosenzweig's difference from Zionists), and (in this argument that predates modern Israel and now is only relevant to Jews not living in Israel) whose everyday mother tongue is ever alien to its 'holy language'.[23] Christians, on the other hand, are defined by their historical becoming. The Jews dwell in the heavenly light – while Christians pursue that heavenly light as they seek ever to draw others into their faith, and thus attempt to make one vast concordance of times and peoples, drawing all into one historical calendar and a world of common ends. This is why, for Rosenzweig, Christianity could not simply be understood as consisting of the two great historical branches – Catholic and Protestant – which he identifies as the Petrine Age, in which the Mother Church tied the life of the individual human's destiny to the 'destiny of the world' through love[24], and the Pauline Age, with its emphasis upon the 'unconditional[ity]' of 'faith alone' which freed the soul of 'all fences and walls'.[25] But it also has to take into account that hope in which 'faith and love adapt themselves'[26] for a better future that characterizes modern Christian(ized) peoples who not only have lost or 'outgrown' any use for or loyalty toward the outward features of their Christian faith, but are largely ignorant of it. (It was this ignorance, rather than any desire for conversion itself, that was central to why Rosenstock-Huessy devoted so much of his life to instructing people of the West about their Christian heritage).

For Rosenzweig (following Schelling's insight in his *Philosophy of Revelation*) this 'shapeless, necessarily unorganized, and hence always dependent on the organized Churches' is the Third or Johannine Age of the Church.[27] But Rosenzweig takes this much further with his insight that the peculiar Johannine character of modernity is to be found in Goethe's prayer 'Hope': 'Give, oh labor of my hands, the great happiness that I can finish it!'[28] Rosenzweig observes that Goethe thought of himself as 'the only Christian of his time such as Christ wanted one to be'[29], and he saw himself as drawing upon 'all the power flowing from Christ'. The peculiarly modern Johannine consciousness, for Rosenzweig, thus consists in conceiving of the uniqueness of one's life and destiny, and the entire fate of the world as interdependent. According to Rosenzweig, this faith in the power and destiny of human potential – a faith that is as visible in the Nietzschean superman as in Marx's faith in the proletariat (both of which for Rosenzweig fall into a zealotry not found in Goethe)[30] – is the prayer that is common to 'the peoples' and 'secular orders of Christianity'.[31] Of course, Nietzsche had argued that Kantianism was but one more Christian 'trope' as were the various modern radical and democratic social movements, which were the secular means for continuing Christianity. Rosenzweig takes this much further, even arguing that Nietzsche and Schopenhauer were 'Christian' thinkers. Thus in a letter to Rudolf Ehrenberg he wrote:

> Previously the philosopher was a Greek, who discovered Christianity; in the cases of Schopenhauer and Nietzsche, the philosopher is a Christian, who knows as little of Christianity as – most Christians, but is stuck up to the ears and beyond in Christian concepts: conversion, overcoming, change of will, the holy, rebirth, compassion, hardness.[32]

In sum, then, for Rosenzweig, through their historicity the inhabitants of the modern Western world embody a Johannine Christian form of life – responding as they do to the command that the 'Christian must directly convert the pagan in himself.'[33] Because of their lack of historical self-consciousness, what Rosenzweig identifies as Johannine hope is rarely grasped as the result of Christian cultivation, as the modern soul invariably sees itself as 'natural', or rational, or moral, or 'typical'.

We can sum up thus: without Christianity, the effect of Judaism remains tribal; without Judaism, Christianity is severed from the embodiment and testimony to the truth of God's covenant and promise of election. The value of the Jew to the Christian is that the Jewish life and cycles embodies 'eternity'; the value of Christianity is that it potentially builds a world more in conformity to revelation, redeeming pagan creations as it moves through the times, reviving and reconstituting institutions and works that had long been thought dead by 'raising' them to 'the plane' in which creation links up with revelation and redemption: for example, the Christianisation of tribes and empires, the revival of the university, and the arts. This line of argument suggests that the Renaissance of humanism, for example, with its revival of pagan literature and taste is an example of historical redemption, i.e. Christianisation. For Rosenzweig, the pagan is creativity itself: redemption is not of nothing, but of the creative achievements of the peoples of the whole world, which is to say paganism.

Applying Rosenzweig's perspective to cosmopolitanism, we can say it is meaningless without it negating the communal bonds of solidarity which obstruct the redemption of the world. Moreover, the Greco-Roman philosophical roots of cosmopolitanism remain idealistic, and hence one more delusionary attempt to flee social death, if they are not drawn into the revelation that 'love is as strong as death' and the redemptive command 'to love the neighbour'. For both Rosenzweig and Rosenstock-Huessy, whose excavation of redemptive history (*Heilsgeschichte*), with all its blood and gore is far more detailed than Rosenzweig's historical sketches, European history is a confirmation that it was the universalistic aspirations of the Christian peoples that made Greek and Roman cosmopolitan ideals more than mere ideals felt by a small number of insightful men. It is not the case that eventually these philosophical insights would be transmitted to the people of Europe and that they would act accordingly. Nor was it the case that Christian peoples needed cosmopolitan ideals to extend their aspirations of solidarity beyond their tribes and empires. Rather the historical reality of Christian peoples incorporated a great deal of the historicity of the Greeks and Romans, as well as Jews, and Germanic tribes: that reality had been one in which all manner of different groups had become neighbours drawn into a common faith and common form of life (albeit with various social distinctions). Without this very real commonality, the cosmopolitan aspirations of the enlightened philosophers would not have counted for anything. Neither the traditional appeals of empires nor tribes could adequately assist in the new bonds of solidarity that were required if such collective existential, social and 'spiritual' alterities were not simply to become sources of endless conflict. Given the propensity for conflict that is potentially ubiquitous even within collectives that have been founded on common appeals and life-directions, the capacity to establish ever new dwellings of spiritual solidarity is intrinsic to us having any flourishing shared future. In the language of cosmopolitanism, and to borrow a term from Eric Voegelin: there can be no *social/political cosmion* unless some sufficiently sturdy common sources of appeal can be widely shared and defended.

Rosenstock-Huessy on Christianity, revolution and moving toward a metanomic world

What overwhelmed Rosenzweig so much about Rosenstock-Huessy's thought, when he first encountered it, was the realisation that it was not the philosophical coherence of a set of ideas that made the world (this he believed was the central defect of idealism), but rather the world is made by the faiths that inspire the actions of its makers. That faith had been expressed in every seal of every great event in Europe up until the French Revolution: later, in the great correspondence that took place between them in 1916, Rosenzweig would provide insights that would also lead Rosenstock to thoroughly modify his own insight. First, the faith did not really stop with the French and Russian revolutions; rather those events in spite of their ostensible anti-Christian and, in the case of the Russian Revolution, unreservedly atheistic orientations, were, nevertheless, utterly impossible without the Jewish/Christian messianic promise that propelled them. That is to say the post-Christian must not be confused with the non-Christian. Secondly, any Christian innovation could never completely escape its Jewish dependency.

Rosenstock-Huessy eventually addressed the question of the role of Christianity and its relationship to Jews, in *In the Cross of Reality*. His examination of how the times have moved towards a concordance, of how history becomes a universal history and why that is important is the central feature of a corpus that was enormous in its scope and scale.

In his *Out of Revolution* and *Die Europäischen Nationen* (two works that treat of the same events in different sequence, with the German version providing a far more elaborate theoretical framework) he argues how the Great War was the event that eventually drew the entire planet into a common history, and ultimately forces us into what philosophers christen a 'cosmopolitan' condition. In his books on revolution the Great War was the culmination of all of European history, or, more precisely, the culmination of the 'total revolutions' that spanned the millennium from the reforms at Cluny, and Pope Gregory VII's subsequent undertaking to clean out the corruption of the Church, through to the French Revolution, which unleashed the forces of nationalism that would bring not only the nations and empires of Europe, but the peoples of the world, into a great collision. Out of that great collision and catastrophe would come the last of the millennium's European 'total revolutions' – the Russian Revolution, which would play a decisive role in the anti-colonial struggles of the twentieth century. The 'marriage of War and Revolution' (as he named an earlier book), in spite of its massive suffering, had forced the species into an inescapable planetary unity that we know all dwelt within. That unity, or cosmopolitan condition, could, argued Rosenstock-Huessy, only be fruitful and sustainable were it to be based upon the peaceful, yet fecund, tensionality that came from people preserving their spiritual differences and sharing the potencies accumulated by their tradition (thus the times as Rosenstock-Huessy argues in *Full Count of the Times*)[34] so that we could survive and grow beyond our common suffering. Rosenstock-Huessy presented his study of revolutions as a metanomic reading of history and society, with its joyous exultation of the overcoming of suffering, and the 'synchronization of mutually exclusive social patterns of behaviour'.[35] It is precisely this synchronisation that is most powerfully exhibited by different peoples and contrary heritages that is the cosmopolitan problem and condition.

Whereas, as we suggested earlier, cosmopolitan theorists generally look for and defend some normative dimension of our common humanity, for Rosenstock-Huessy, catastrophe, suffering and love are the core concepts of social transformation and relative concordance. In this respect, Rosenstock-Huessy also argues that if we can speak of 'progress' in the West, in so far as Western technological, economic and administrative systems spread globally, it is not because of any kind of moral superiority, or higher ideals as such, but horrors and crises – loves and hates – that have triggered a series or sequence of fanatical commitments to rid the world completely of its corruption. Gregory VII's totalising claims on behalf of the Church against the Holy Roman Emperor, Henry IV, which Rosenstock-Huessy saw as the first spark in the combustive sequence of European revolutions, was not historically momentous because of its moral character or utopian vision, but because it provided a novel and peculiarly redemptive form for the violent energies of war and rebellion. Unlike rebellion, *revolution* was no longer simply a cyclical process of ruler or dynastic replacement or bloodshed followed by relative peace and prosperity, but a cumulative sequence of totalising aspirations attacking the social roots and political forces that impeded those aspirations. Further, the revolutionary achievements circulated in Western Europe far beyond their territorial place of origin, as each great new revolution built upon freedoms already won in earlier revolutions, whilst powering on in order to rectify what the preceding revolution had left untransformed. Rosenstock-Huessy analysed the major revolutions that he saw as being traceable back to the Papal revolution:[36] the Italian revolution (the Renaissance), the German revolution (the Reformation), the English revolution, the French revolution and the Russian revolution. He also identified the peculiar achievements and legacies bequeathed to subsequent generations that are literally the 'fall-out' (not merely as 'ideas' but as instantiations) of revolutions. That legacy includes the elevation of a previously repressed, subordinate or disposed type. Working chronologically backwards and to take a very small and rather erratic samples of the countless examples that are scattered throughout Rosenstock-Huessy's two studies on revolution, the following examples from his chapters on the Russian, French and English revolutions well illustrate what he is doing.

> The Russian revolution, which disposes of the prior inimical type by making 'every proletarian a capitalist', has left a legacy of: the social welfare of the worker, an approach to social life governed by totality and reproduction, statistics and economy, and permanent revolution. It left a deep and enduring sceptical impression about the limits and hypocrisy of bourgeois society. It demanded that in aesthetic matters we consider materiality and solidarity and not simply genius and art for art's sake. It pushed the world much more in the direction of an atheistic society, and, for much of the twentieth century, gave people hope in a world revolution.
>
> The French revolution made 'every man of talent an aristocrat' and left a legacy of: nationalism and national revolutions, the citizen, and literature as the cipher of the character of a nation. It ensconced secular society, and did away with Christendom by 'inventing' faith in Europe. It

appealed to a society and government based upon 'reason' and merit, elevated the genius above the man of birth, created 'the revolutionary' as a type, and emancipated the Jews. It introduced the decimal system, elevated the importance of novelty in everyday life, devoted our attention to the 'organization of discovery', took art out of the church and home and placed it and other 'discoveries' in the exhibition.

The English revolution made 'every gentleman a king' by restoring the common law and power to the parliament, making private property a right which could not be overturned by the prerogative power of the monarch, and by constitutionally limiting the powers of the crown. In place of the haphazard practices of wealth extraction required for governing, it set up a system in which economic information and the budget would be accessible to ministers of the parliament. It took the 'waves of all seas and oceans' as 'a single water', and the 'Western World' replaced the Western Church and Roman empire. It established a 'commonwealth', and enabled the parliamentary invasion of the Church.

Other formulae which Rosenstock-Huessy suggest provide a key to the revolutionary motivation are: for the German Revolution (Reformation) – 'every Christian a priest'; the Gregorian revolution which reaches into the Renaissance and finds its most elaborate artistic defence in the great paintings of the revolutionary mother church and in Dante's judgments in the *Comedy* – 'every soul a member of the Church'; and the Cluniac reform which founded All Soul's Day – 'every human creature a soul'.

In his *The Full Count of the Times*, Rosenstock-Huessy adopts a similar methodological approach toward the respective legacies of the social formations of Antiquity. He argues that the four identifiably distinctive social modalities of Antiquity were the tribe, the empire, the polis and the Jewish nation. Each one, he argued, provided legacies which were fundamental to human flourishing – and as in the works of revolution he lays out their respective 'creations'. He then argues that each of these formations experienced crises which led from tribe to empire, and to the respective escape-routes of Greeks and Jews out of empire. Christianity not only formed at the intersection of these social modalities, but was able to provide a framework in which features of all these formations were able to survive. It would take me too far afield to go into the intricacies of his historical and sociological arguments; here I just wish to draw attention to a key difference between Rosenstock-Huessy and Rosenzweig. Whereas Rosenzweig's brief was to locate precisely the source and character of redemption, Rosenstock-Huessy's was to identify what is redeemable. Like Rosenzweig (though in far more historical detail) he credits Christianity for its universalising mission. But eventually he came to argue – in the two volumes of his *In the Cross of Reality* and *The Christian Future and the Modern Mind Outrun* – that Christianity, Judaism, Buddhism and Taoism each provide unique and invaluable resources for assisting modern human beings in their fight against spiritual and social asphyxiation. Also, unlike Rosenzweig, while he sees Islam as having to respond to the challenge of equality between the sexes, he argues that Islam had an important part to play in bringing warring tribes largely untouched by the presence of Christianity into a common history.

I have given the briefest of sketches of what is a highly elaborate socio-historical argument. While Rosenstock-Huessy's attempt to look for the redeemable and valuable potencies across different traditions has now become a more widely held point of view, there is no denying that Rosenstock-Huessy's real achievement is his analysis of the European revolutions, Christianity as a social and historical force, and those features of Antiquity which would feed into European history.

The continuing process of redemptive cosmopolitanism

The vastness of Rosenstock-Huessy's ambition (much as in Marx), not to mention the terrain to be covered, meant that his work is much more a 'methodological example' than a completed system. It thus leaves open to others a 'research project' where they can continue building on his efforts. In the last section I want to pick up on this method as I touch upon 'the continuing process of redemptive cosmopolitanism' in the aftermath of the Second World War, and the acceleration of cosmopolitanisation.

At the end of the Second World War the heirs of two revolutionary traditions (the American and the Russian) found themselves occupying hegemonic positions enabling them to attempt to fashion the world in their image. For his part, Rosenstock-Huessy saw the American Revolution as a semi-revolution rather than a totalising revolution in its own right. That was because its rationale was not so much in making the world anew in its own image, but in establishing its independence. For Rosenstock-Huessy, it is a kind of half-way house between the French Revolution which it inspires, and the English and German revolutions which it is pushed by. The English influence is manifest in its appeals to property, as well as the fact that the English revolution was essentially a Puritan revolution. Puritanism itself was part of the circulatory fall-out, from the German revolution, in its spread from Germany to Geneva to Scotland to England to North America.[37] Of course, Luther is the flashpoint of reform, but it is Calvin and his followers who irrevocably transformed the nature of political life. For while the commercial Italian city-states were the birthplace of modern European politics – the *Machiavellian Moment* as Pocock argues[38] – Calvin's Geneva 'purified' the politicisation of urban spaces both through its community-styled participation, and its civil religion. Without the belief in salvation and election, the perseverance of the saints, and civic commitment requiring close-knit communities based on shared faith and moral education in scripture, it is hard to imagine the transformation from the violent *virtù* of the Italian republics to the austerely virtuous and 'transparent' republican literate communities that reach from Geneva, to America, to Paris. To be sure, the Rousseauian and Robespierrian fusion of freedom with moral purity, and the decision to make moral freedom the necessary source of the subjection of natural laws certainly played its part in preparing the new scale and type of violence that was carried out in the Terror, and reproduced in Communist revolutions. I leave aside completely the matter of the revolution's role in the incipience of the modernist ideological amalgam that will differentiate into the three-way ideological struggle for modern supremacy in the next century, and simply make note that it was Enlightened principles that shaped the Declaration of Independence and the Declaration of the Rights of Man and that are the conspicuous antecedents of Wilson's 14-point plan after the First World War, and the United Nations with its Universal Declaration of Human Rights. But the French Enlightenment itself, as Rosenstock-Huessy argues in both his volumes of revolution, is deeply impacted by the experience of the French Calvinists, the Huguenots. The St Bartholomew massacre of the Huguenots in Paris would be a major spectre that would come back, in a more general philosophical anti-Christian form, to haunt the Catholic Church for its role in that slaughter.

In the aftermath of the Second World War, with the Old World crippled spiritually, financially and militarily, the United States was conscious of its 'manifest destiny' (a Calvinist term and one which was central to the nineteenth-century Monroe doctrine) as it took upon itself the role of saving the 'community of nations'. If Wilson represents the moment when the United States first enters the stage as a major player in world affairs, by the end of the Second World War there were only two main players left, and one of them was, from this perspective, a 'godless' 'evil empire'. Ironically, though, both superpowers were enmeshed in the same dynamic of revolt intent on changing the entire world, but separated by different foundational times and locations, and the different historically charged narrative elements and energies that constituted and emanated from them.

What is common to the entire revolutionary impetus from Gregory VII to Voltaire and Jefferson to Lenin and Stalin is the faith in the redeemed nature of the world to come, a world in which justice and peace will rule. Those regions of the world which neither the French Revolution nor, in the immediate aftermath of the Second World War, the American Revolution, could draw into the underlying messianic logic of the European revolutions, were, by and large, swept along historically by the Russian Revolution, as they smashed more archaic class relationships, formed planned economies and, in so far as they were able, an educational underpinning for the new societies they were creating. Though even where it drew people further into a global totality, the immense emanating force of nationalism from the French Revolution also impacted irrevocably. That the Russian Revolution would survive, as in China, only where it compromised with the earlier revolutionary 'achievements' of nationalism (the French Revolution) and private property (the English and American revolutions) confirms Rosenstock-Huessy's insights about the circulatory and cumulative manner of revolutions.

The converse of this is that revolutions which occur in environments completely lacking in the antecedent conditions whose tensions produced mass revolt will generate versions of the antecedent conditions they lacked – or else come into a dead end. This is also why the vastness of the gap between the revolutionary dream and reality to be transformed is in inverse proportion to the accumulated revolutionary stock or heritage. Thus, for example, the success the Catholics and Jesuits had in France against the Huguenots spared France the Reformation – but at the cost of a far more savage anti-clericalism. Enlightenment in Germany, on the other hand, was not an anti-clerical affair precisely because the excesses of the Church had been curbed earlier by the Reformation, and in the non-Protestant South, by the reforms largely taken on board in the Counter-Reformation. Another side to this can be observed in the reason that the United States was better able to represent the interests of the Puritan revolution and the rights of property against the Communist revolutions. The French revolution was a commercial and professionally led revolution, but it was also a revolution of the nation. When the nation is plagued by poverty on the scale of that experienced within France at the time of the Revolution, the commercial side of the revolution had to be balanced by anti-commercial forces, which is exactly how the revolution played itself out in class terms. By comparison, the English and American revolutions were not predicated upon the masses and their poverty. To put it another way, capital had a 'purer conscience' when the Puritans revolted to entrench their right to property and their right to follow their calling through the use of their property free from prerogative abuse. The United States for all its talk of the nation is still not a nation in the sense of that defended by the French Revolution. This is nowhere more evident in the way that race, and the legacy of slavery, still plagues the United States in a political manner far more *intransigent* than in Europe, even allowing for the various political polarisations within Europe, that in the case of former Yugoslavia has led to mass killing and the defining of nations along ethnic lines. But the problem of race in the United States admits of no such territorial demarcation for a resolution.

I am suggesting here that the qualities that contributed to the United States' hegemonic position at the end of the Second World War pertain to the logic of revolution itself – and that logic plays itself out historically. Thus it was because what would become the United States was so remote from Europe and its indigenous inhabitants relatively (in purely power terms) disadvantaged administratively, militarily and technologically, thus conquerable, that the Puritans could build a world there. The United States' relative geographic isolation from Europe enabled it to sit out much of the world wars, then 'clean up' when it entered, and finally take on the hegemonic role it did. But, ironically, its social memory was in many important respects less historically 'advanced' than the European nations it was reconstructing. Consider for example how a European responds to the anachronistic arguments coming out of the United States for gun ownership, or to conservative arguments for not having public health care.

In assuming its hegemonic role, the United States could not help but impress itself upon those parts of the world it sought to rebuild. The United States, as we have said, was both Puritan and Enlightened. Much of the world it found was not. But it is also the case that much of the world has a very different social subconscious. This is also true of the United States. The Enlightenment and Puritan narrative appeals which function in official reflexive domains are far from concurring with the multiple appeals and their congruent identities which really constitute the United States. The outcome of the interplay between a stringent cluster of official narrative appeals, with their underlying Enlightened/ Puritan 'value-triggers', and the relative narrative chaos that occurs within different 'communities' that occurs domestically within the United States, is very similar to the international situation that the United States has to operate within. That is, just as in the United States there is a great gulf between the 'purity' of its public narrative and public institutions, and the actual vast chaotic 'impurity' of lived practices of US 'citizens', internationally there is a chasm between the kind of rights'-based rhetoric of US-led international diplomacy and the international behaviour of states (including, as all its critics point out, the behaviour of the United States itself, a fact all too conspicuous in the choice of its allies, and the behaviour of its soldiers).

The world is also being swept onto a common path by the technologies that themselves originally emerged as important components of the revolutionary responses to unbearable conditions. Technologies are techniques as much as things, and as techniques they are alignments of social practices. Thus, Marx, perhaps better than anyone, saw that the deployment of a technology requires certain social conformities. Thus to the extent that any part of the world becomes implicated in global commerce and trade, it becomes implicated in a range of technologies and administrative processes that are needed to facilitate these ends. This does not mean cultures do not matter, but their materialisations are profoundly changed by technological adaptations. To the extent that nations want to modernize, they enter into the revolutionary processes of modernity.

I have emphasized that the United States is an important expression of that revolutionary process – but it is not the only one. And, to repeat, it is caught in its own historicity. Europe, on the other hand, for all its troubles, is no longer dwelling in 1945, and it draws upon its revolutionary heritage which predates and postdates the American Revolution. But now, neither Europe nor the United States are world leaders, even if they are the most economically advanced areas, and the United States the most militaristically advanced: for we are endlessly reminded that outside of the American-European-Australasian alliance, the humanitarian ideals of the United States and the accompanying vision of an international order and international law have no geopolitical support. And while, for example, the economic emergence of China and India, to take two of the more conspicuous, is not possible without the revolutionary logics embedded in the processes they absorb, neither is developing under the tutelage of the United States or Europe. Unlike those helped by the United States in the process of post-War reconstruction, the Chinese and Indians neither talk nor think like Puritans or Enlightened *philosophes*. Nor have the post-Second World War Japanese or South Koreans, even with having democracy (which immediately and resiliently failed to emulate the US or European models), Coca-Cola, the rebuilding of universities, and so on.

There are also many nations and regions, groups and regimes which want little truck with the messianic ends that we have tracked here. In the post-Cold War period, Russia is concerned with preserving any imperial presence it can still manage, but it has ceased to play any role in a greater messianic logic. But, the biggest challenge to the messianic Western logic of nations has been the rise of Islamism, a rise first made manifest in Western eyes with the Iranian Revolution, which caught the West completely off guard. (The irony of it being a Shia state should not be overlooked). It is a rise that can reasonably be interpreted (as it is from within the ranks of Al Qaeda and Islamic State) as part of an on-going global struggle, a World War. What is notable, though, is how that the overwhelming majority of Muslims, living in Western democracies, reject the Islamist calls to overthrow the *kafir* and their institutions. The challenge to the West is how it will be able to affirm and maintain the freedoms and openings to other traditions that it had momentarily gained since the Second World War as tribalistic reactions and moral panic break out. On the other hand, Muslim nations are also caught between those drawing upon the nationalist legacies that were part of the European traditions and enabled democracy to exist in countries such as Malaysia, Indonesia, Pakistan and Turkey (precarious as some of these democracies are), and those who see such boundaries as a means of Islamic weakness, division and corruption.

The amount of what Rosenzweig identified as that core Johannine virtue – *hope* – is palpable in the kinds of narratives issuing from Western intellectuals, journalists, teachers and the like, as well as Muslims who emphasize the compatible features of Islam and Western secular democracies (which we have characterized here as Johannine – and which could also more generally be classified as post-Christian). The extent of this hope is a matter of no small importance in a world in which US hegemony is finding itself increasingly less supported, and in which the West and what it stood for in its revolutionary traditions and anti-totalitarian 'victories' simply cannot be taken for granted. This hope has also emerged at a time when the West has become increasingly conscious and largely ashamed of its colonialist and imperialist past – without which any redemption of the world, any true 'great society', would be impossible. For the redemptivist view of history, what the Germans have called a *Heilsgeschichte*, differs from the realist view of international politics, not, as with the idealist, in positing an ideal as such and seeking to deploy legislatively expansive international public institutions for ensconcing the ideal, but in discovering how the real is transcended by a new reality, a more lovable reality, and identifying the processes that are making that reality possible. This too is ultimately the difference between a view of cosmopolitanism that focuses more on the norms we need to share to become members of one greater society than, as Rosenstock-Huessy's metanomic analysis does, the contradictory historical processes that are at work in the world that are making us become neighbours.

The redemption of the world was always conceived as one of struggle – the struggle between the continuity of sheer creation and the negation involved in judging specific aspects of creation as redeemable or irredeemable. The struggle continues, but everywhere there is an increasing consciousness of the neighbour, and thus, in spite of the great chaos of global geo-politics, ever greater hope that there may one day be peace and we all be members of one great '*cosmopolitis*'. That is where Greek not only means Jew thanks to the hybrid of Christianisation, but where all peoples with all their heritages find the best, that most worthy of love, that is one great gift to a future, whilst bidding farewell to what is so shameful that it deserves to die. That we cannot have one without the other, a shared future without certain sacrifices, is the lesson of Western and subsequent global revolutions, and the inescapable condition of any real and flourishing cosmopolitanism.

Notes

1. Cf. Nussbaum, "Kant and Stoic Consciousness;" Brown, *Grounding Cosmopolitanism: From Kant to the Idea of a Cosmopolitan Culture*; and Kleingeld, *Kant and Cosmopolitanism*.
2. Benhabib, *Another Cosmopolitanism*, 20.
3. Benhabib, 16.
4. Behabib, *Another Cosmopolitanism*, 16, also 18.
5. Delanty, *The Cosmopolitan Imagination: The Renewal of Critical Social Theory*, 6.
6. Beck, *The Cosmopolitan Vision*, 14.
7. Fine, *Cosmopolitanism*.
8. Delanty, *The Cosmopolitan Imagination: The Renewal of Critical Social Theory*, 28.
9. Rosenstock-Huessy, *Out of Revolution: Autobiography of Western Man*, 755–8, and *Speech and Reality*, 40–2, and *Planetary Service: A Way into the Third Millennium*.
10. Adorno, *Minima Moralia: Reflections from Damaged Life*, 247.
11. Rosenzweig, *The Star of Redemption*, 292–3.
12. Rosenstock-Huessy, *Judaism Despite Christianity: The 1916 Wartime Correspondence between Eugen Rosenstock-Huessy and Franz Rosenzweig*.
13. See Cristaudo, *Religion, Redemption and Revolution: The New Speech Thinking of Franz Rosenzweig and Eugen Rosenstock-Huessy*, and Stahmer, "Franz Rosenzweig's Letters to Margrit Rosenstock-Huessy, 1917–1922."
14. Letter from Eugen to Gritli [Margrit] Huessy, 1.11.24, available in the Rosenstock-Huessy Collection at Dartmouth College.
15. Rosenstock-Huessy, *Im Kreuz der Wirklichkeit: Eine nach-goethische Soziologie*, 3 vols. Volume 1 has now been translated by Jurgen Lawrenz, with Frances Huessy and myself, and is to appear with Transaction in Spring/Summer 2017.
16. Bouretz, *Witnesses for the Future: Philosophy and Messianism*; Cohen, *Elevations: The Height of the Good in Rosenzweig and Levinas*; Gibbs, *Correlations in Rosenzweig and Levinas*; Rosenstock, *Philosophy and the Jewish Question: Mendelssohn, Rosenzweig and Beyond*; Simon, *Art and Responsibility: A Phenomenology of the Diverging Paths of Rosenzweig and Heidegger*.
17. Rosenzweig, *The New Thinking*, 69.
18. E.g. Putman, "Introduction," to Rosenzweig, *Understanding the Sick and The Healthy: A View of World, Man and God*, 18, and Palmer and Schwartz in Rosenzweig, *"Innerlich bleibt die Welt eine". Ausgewählte Texte von Franz Rosenzweig über den Islam*, 7–32 and 111–47.
19. This is behind Pollock's argument about Rosenzweig replacing one All with another. See Pollock, Benjamin. *Franz Rosenzweig and the Systematic Task of Philosophy* (Cambridge: Cambridge University Press, 2009).
20. Rosenzweig, *The Star of Redemption*, 239–40.

21. Rosenzweig, *The Star of Redemption*, 241.
22. Rosenzweig, *The Star of Redemption*, 323.
23. Rosenzweig, *The Star of Redemption*, 320–1.
24. Rosenzweig, *The Star of Redemption*, 297.
25. Rosenzweig, *The Star of Redemption*, 299.
26. Rosenzweig, *The Star of Redemption*, 302.
27. Rosenzweig, *The Star of Redemption*, 302–3.
28. Rosenzweig, *The Star of Redemption*, 293.
29. Rosenzweig, *The Star of Redemption*, 295.
30. Rosenzweig, *The Star of Redemption*, 292–3, 304–5.
31. Rosenzweig, *The Star of Redemption*, 301.
32. See footnote 11, Rosenzweig, *Philosophical and Theological Writings*, 52.
33. Rosenzweig, *The Star of Redemption*, 303.
34. The importance of this formulation was conveyed to me in personal correspondence by Michael Gormann-Thelen.
35. Rosenstock-Huessy, *Speech and Reality*, 40.
36. Thanks to Rosenstock-Huessy's student, Harold Berman, Rosenstock-Huessy's term "Papal Revolution" has become a reasonably widely used term for the event that used to generally be classified as the Gregorian Reform or Investiture conflict. Berman, *Law and Revolution: The Formation of the Western legal Tradition*, vol. 1.
37. Important contributions on this vast topic on Geneva's impact upon the North American founding include: Miller, *The New England Mind: The Seventeenth Century*; M. Kingdon, *Calvin and Calvinism: Sources of Democracy*; Walzer, *The Revolution of the Saints: A Study in the Origins of Radical Politics*; Wolin, *Politics and Vision*; Cuddihy, *No Offense: Civil Religion and Protestant Taste*; Kuyper, *Lectures on Calvinism*.
38. Pocock, *The Machiavellian Moment: Florentine Political Thought and the Atlantic Republican Tradition*.

References

Adorno, Theodore. *Minima Moralia: Reflections from Damaged Life*. Translated by E.M. Jephcott. London: Verso, 1974.
Beck, Ulrich. *The Cosmopolitan Vision*. Translated by Ciaran Cronin. Polity: Cambridge, 2006.
Benhabib, Selya. *Another Cosmopolitanism*. Oxford: Oxford University Press, 2008.
Berman, Harold. *Law and Revolution: The Formation of the Western Legal Tradition: Volume 1*. Cambridge, Mass.: Harvard University Press, 1983.
Bouretz, Pierre. *Witnesses for the Future: Philosophy and Messianism*. Translated by Michael B. Smith. Baltimore: John Hopkins University, 2010.
Brown, Garrett. *Grounding Cosmopolitanism: From Kant to the Idea of a Cosmopolitan Culture*. Edinburgh: Edinburgh University Press, 2009.
Cohen, Richard A. *Elevations: The Height of the Good in Rosenzweig and Levinas*. Chicago: University of Chicago Press, 1994.

Cristaudo, Wayne. *Religion, Redemption and Revolution: The New Speech Thinking of Franz Rosenzweig and Eugen Rosenstock-Huessy*. Toronto: University of Toronto Press, 2012.

Cuddihy, John. *No Offense: Civil Religion and Protestant Taste*. New York: Seabury Press, 1978.

Delanty, Gerard. *The Cosmopolitan Imagination: The Renewal of Critical Social Theory*. Cambridge: Cambridge University Press, 2009.

Fine, Robert. *Cosmopolitanism*. London: Routledge, 2007.

Robert, Gibbs. *Correlations in Rosenzweig and Levinas*. Princeton: Princeton University Press, 1994.

Kingdon, Robert M. *Calvin and Calvinism: Sources of Democracy*. D.C. Heath: Lexington, 1970.

Kleingeld, Pauline. *Kant and Cosmopolitanism*. Cambridge: Cambridge University Press, 2012.

Kuyper, Abraham. *Lectures on Calvinism*. Grand Rapids: Eerdmans, 1999 (1931).

Miller, Perry. *The New England Mind: The Seventeenth Century*. Cambridge, Mass.: Harvard University Press, 1954.

Nussbaum, Martha. "Kant and Stoic Consciousness." *The Journal of Political Philosophy* 5, no. 1 (1997): 1–25.

Pocock, J. G. A. *The Machiavellian Moment: Florentine Political Thought and the Atlantic Republican Tradition*. Princeton: Princeton University Press, 1975.

Rosenstock, Bruce. *Philosophy and the Jewish Question: Mendelssohn, Rosenzweig and Beyond*. New York: Fordham University Press, 2010.

Rosenstock-Huessy, Eugen. Letter from Eugen to Gritli [Margrit] Huessy, 1.11.24, available in the Rosenstock-Huessy Collection at Dartmouth College.

Rosenstock-Huessy, Eugen. *Speech and Reality*. Norwich, Vt.: Argo, 1970.

Rosenstock-Huessy, Eugen. *Planetary Service: A Way into the Third Millennium*. Translated by Mark Huessy and Freya von Moltke. Norwich, Vt.: Argo, 1978.

Rosenstock-Huessy, Eugen. *Out of Revolution: Autobiography of Western Man*. Providence, RI: Berg Publishers, 1993.

Rosenstock-Huessy, Eugen. *Im Kreuz der Wirklichkeit: Eine nach-goethische Soziologie*, 3 vols. (Volume 1 Die Übermacht der Räume; Volume 2/3 Die Vollzahl der Zeiten). Mit einem Vorwort von Irene Scherer und einem Nachwort von Michael Gormann-Thelen, Edited by Michael Gormann-Thelen, Ruth Mautner and Lise van der Molen. Mössingen-Talheim: Talheimer, 2008–2009.

Rosenstock-Huessy, Eugen. *Judaism Despite Christianity: The 1916 Wartime Correspondence between Eugen Rosenstock-Huessy and Franz Rosenzweig*. With a new foreword by Paul Mendes-Flohr, a new preface by Harold Stahmer, and a new chronology by Michael Gormann-Thelen. Chicago: University of Chicago Press, 2011.

Rosenzweig, Franz. *The New Thinking*. Edited and translated by Alan Udoff and Barbara Galli. Syracuse: Syracuse University Press, 1999.

Rosenzweig, Franz. *Understanding the Sick and The Healthy: A View of World, Man and God*. Translated by Nahum Glatzer and Introduced by Hilary Putnam. Harvard: Harvard University Press, 1999.

Rosenzweig, Franz. *Philosophical and Theological Writings*. Translated and edited, with notes and commentary by Paul W. Franks and Michael I. Morgan. Indianapolis, IN: Hackett, 2000.

Rosenzweig, Franz. *"Innerlich bleibt die Welt eine". Ausgewählte Texte von Franz Rosenzweig über den Islam*. Edited and introduced with afterword by Gesine Palmer and Yossef Schwartz. Bodenheim: Philo Verlag, 2002.

Rosenzweig, Franz. *The Star of Redemption*. Translated by Barbara Galli. Wisconsin: University Of Wisconsin Press, 2005.

Simon, Jules. *Art and Responsibility: A Phenomenology of the Diverging Paths of Rosenzweig and Heidegger*. New York: Continuum, 2011.

Stahmer, Harold. "Franz Rosenzweig's Letters to Margrit Rosenstock-Huessy, 1917–1922." *Leo Baeck Institute Yearbook* 34 (1989): 385–409.

Walzer, Michael. *The Revolution of the Saints: A Study in the Origins of Radical Politics*. Cambridge: Massachusetts, 1982.

Wolin, Sheldon. *Politics and Vision: Continuity and Innovation in Western Political Thought*. Princeton: Princeton University Press, 2004.

Hotel patriots or permanent strangers? Joseph Roth and the Jews of inter-war Central Europe

Ilse Josepha Lazaroms

ABSTRACT

This article examines the connection between cosmopolitanism and the Jews by taking a close look at the intricacies that made up the life world and thought of one of the most celebrated Jewish 'cosmopolitans' of the twentieth century, Galician-born journalist and author Joseph Roth (1894–1939). By approaching the question of non-belonging versus being at home everywhere – the two extremes of a cosmopolitan life – from a micro-historical, biographical perspective, this article investigates the darker side of Jewish existence in the decidedly ambiguous and increasingly threatening political climate of inter-war Europe. It traces the unravelling cosmopolitan dream of a single individual as he finds himself engulfed by the political and social narrowing of the European Jewish life worlds. In this process, the significance of a Jewish past or heritage is examined as one of the factors that fuels and complements, as well as contradicts, the cosmopolitan worldview.

Introduction: life on the tip of a pen

In this article, I would like to approach the connection between cosmopolitanism and the Jews from inside the life world of an author who has more often than not been characterized as a quintessential Jewish cosmopolitan. After decades of relative obscurity in the 1950s and 1960s, Joseph Roth re-emerged on the literary scene as someone perpetually in mourning for the lost world of the Habsburg Empire. He was a journalist and writer who had voluntarily uprooted himself from his humble Jewish origins in Galicia, and subsequently roamed the war-torn continent with a raging pen: someone who felt himself at home in the capital cities of inter-war Europe – Vienna, Berlin, Paris, Amsterdam – and who left behind precious few material traces of his biographical existence. In the titles of his works – named, for instance, for a despairing Job or the many nameless wandering Jews that he encountered in person and in spirit – we can feel echoes of the emotional dimensions of his uprooted life.

The idea of cosmopolitanism that is implicitly connected to his life is perhaps based most of all on Roth's own sense of internal homelessness, which surfaced in his manic, itinerant lifestyle. For scholars and admirers of Roth and his generation, many of whom emerged from the fallen European empires without a clear sense of belonging, this is a kind of cosmopolitanism that places the fact of not having a home – national, metaphorical, ideological – on equal footing with the notion of being at home everywhere in the world. The attraction of this rather straightforward interpretation of inter-war Jewish cosmopolitanism is clear. It has the potential to explain some of the posthumous interest that has befallen Roth's persona and fiction, enticing readers to delve into the phantasmagorias of life worlds now lost to us. Also, this approach to cosmopolitanism prompts readers who are also scholars, such as this author, to try to understand Roth's predicament as an uprooted, and later, after 1933, an exiled, Jew in inter-war Europe.

One of the paradoxes of Roth's life, however – and perhaps by extension of the idea of cosmopolitanism – is that Roth was at home in very *few* places in the world, and that the places where he did feel at home or encountered a sense of belonging were often temporary or out of reach. His travels, in the mid-1920s, to the harbour of Marseille and other cities in the south of France, where he felt 'happy and at home, and not the least bit romantic'[1], were cut short by his obligations to the *Frankfurter Zeitung*, which called him back to Berlin. His efforts to remain in Paris were frustrated by the same newspaper, as it decided against making him their Paris correspondent, a position he desperately wanted. The French language, which Roth admired partly because it was everything that German was not, remained out of reach as an instrument of his profession due to his imperfect command of it (some of his correspondence, however, is written in French). And finally, moving upward along the scale of abstraction, there is Roth's dependency on alcohol and the intoxication it brought: a sphere of reversed clarity where Roth felt at ease – at home, if you may – and which required a dedicated and destructive repetition in order to maintain this state of mind. In other words, the moments that Roth experienced a sense of belonging were rare; the moments that he felt happiness, even rarer.

Perhaps the life of Joseph Roth entices readers and historians alike because it encapsulates, on the one hand, a case of extreme private – existential – restlessness, and, on the other, presents an acute example of how the persecution of European Jewry carved itself out on the psyche of a singular individual. Roth dedicated himself to being a witness to the crime of the Nazi persecution of the Jews, as well as the many other crimes and injustices, both small and large, that he witnessed along the way. The fact that he did so through the lens of the 'uprooted outsider' is undeniable; but does this make him, or any of his contemporaries who were haunted by the same historical events, a cosmopolitan?

In order to understand Roth's hold over the intellectual imagination, it does not suffice to emphasize the ambivalence and the non-conformity, indeed the unclassifiable nature, of his persona – traits that resonate deeply with postmodern theories about the self and the modern world. Nor can it just be the tragic ending of his life that has created sustained interest in his writings. While these issues certainly matter, it seems to me more honest to aim at an understanding that places Roth's profound and oftentimes self-inflicted sense of non-belonging in the context of the virulent intellectual and political sways and misfortunes of inter-war Europe; indeed, to grasp his convoluted itinerary along the lines of his private, yet increasingly exposed and vulnerable, stature as a famous journalist of Galician-Jewish origin in German and in Central European society.

If anything, Joseph Roth was a man who was at home on the tip of his pen. According to his friends, Roth lived in a state of constant panic and 'mental high tension'[2], churning out books and feuilletons with increasingly feverish speed as the political situation in Europe worsened. In a self-defeating exercise that was typical of his individualist stance, Roth's attempt at creating order in the inter-war world was perpetually undermined by his deeply pessimistic vision of modernity. In the mid-1930s, for instance, he became convinced that he had recognized the hand of the Antichrist in the European crisis, diagnosing the latter as the work of the devil. Roth invested the book he wrote on the subject, *The Antichrist* (1934), with hopes that bordered on the messianic.[3] We can only imagine the disappointment, quickly brushed off with excuses about the 'ill tempo' in which the book was written, when his words fell on deaf ears and were relegated to the domain of the unsound.

Roth himself realized that 'living on the tip of his pen' was not a condition that could be sustained for very long – and it seems that it was a question of pride to fully embrace this risk. Three months before the outbreak of the Second World War, in May 1939, Roth collapsed in café Le Tournon in Paris, and died a few days later in a hospital for the poor. As the translator Michael Hofmann observed, the old world had used him up. At the time of his death, however, it was not just the individual Roth who perished; an entire patchwork of dreams and ideas that had sustained intellectuals throughout the inter-war years also vanished, including that of Jewish cosmopolitanism. In this sense, Roth is a writer who in many ways embodies our intellectual fascination with the 'outsider' and the implied critical perspective this position stands for. I would like to turn the concept of cosmopolitanism upside down by looking at it 'from below', in other words, from the very particular circumstances of a single man. By exploring the many intricacies that make up the existential universe that Joseph Roth constructed for himself and that resonated across his generation, I aim to expose the tragic side of European Jewish cosmopolitanism in the 1920s and 1930s, so that we can nuance our understanding of the concept itself, as well as the Jewish involvement with it.

In search of a borderless Europe

So, one way to begin is by looking at how the story ended. In January 1939, a few months before his death, Roth received a letter from the PEN Club inviting him to be a special guest at the World Congress of Writers, to be held in New York in May of the same year. At a time when, the letter stated, the four basic freedoms – the right to speak, the right to publish, the right to worship and the right to assemble – 'are being denied and threatened over an increasingly large part of the world, it seems to us particularly urgent that writers from all countries should gather to consider ways and means of defending free expression under difficult circumstances'.[4] This Congress, as was also known at the time, was an indirect means of getting Jewish intellectuals out of Europe before it would be too late. For Roth, however, even London, where Stefan Zweig had taken refuge in 1934, was too far, both geographically and mentally, to consider it as a new home. It is unsure whether Roth responded to this letter. It was found among his belongings after his death.

Taking this into account, it seems unlikely that Roth ever gave a serious thought to this 'escape route' to the United States that was offered to him. He felt duty bound to remain on European shores. This was partly due to the fact that he belonged to a group of European intelligentsia whose humanism was deeply rooted in the culture that surrounded them. Yet he was atypical in the sense that he was not able to pick up his dreams and transport them to a place outside of Europe. All around him, persecuted intellectuals began their exodus as soon as peace had been declared in Versailles. It began with the flight of Hungarian Jews identified as Communist or otherwise left wing after the failed revolutions of 1918–19, when waves of anti-Jewish sentiment and pogroms, tacitly encouraged by the regime of Admiral Miklós Horthy, swept through the country. Many of them went to Vienna and Berlin, where, due to the German education they had received in Hungary, they felt at home. They hoped that their exile would be temporary, and that, as soon as the revolutionary chaos and waves of antisemitism had subsided, they would return to Hungary. While some did, many others no longer saw a future for themselves in Hungary and continued their emigration, often to the United States. This trajectory, which Tibor Frank has called 'double exile', was made significantly more difficult after the restrictive Immigration Act of 1924.[5] Yet despite this, many people continued to try to obtain visas – not only Jews who left Hungary, but in general those who felt that Jewish life on the continent had taken an irreversible turn for the worse. This trend continued after January 1933, when Hitler came to power. Seen in this light, an exilic itinerant who, despite being clearheaded about the prospects of a Jewish future in Europe, chose to stay rather than crossing over into relative safety abroad, was an exception.[6]

Despite the fact that the war had officially ended and arms had been laid down – although especially in East Central Europe the 'long great war' continued into the early 1920s[7] – the European world, it seemed, had changed for the worse. After 1918, two powerful myths emerged that gravely distorted the image of European Jewry. On the one hand, the early post-war years saw the rise of the so-called 'Judeo-Bolshevik myth', which conflated Jews with Communists and Communists with Jews. On the other hand, Jews were suspected of undermining the order of the newly established nation-states with their desire for world domination, based on the assumed power of Jewish finance.[8] These contradictory yet persistent ideas (Jews are Communists; Jews are capitalists) led to suspicion towards assimilated Jews in Western Europe, who were increasingly seen as an 'enigma'. As a people without a state, Jews had become an anomaly in a world divided up primarily into mono-ethnic nation-states. These stereotypes reinforced the image of the Jew as a rootless and potentially revolutionary person, a dangerous and unsettling element in the new European order.

This, however, is only one side of the coin. On the other side, and based on similar notions of existential rootlessness, we find the much-romanticized notion of the Jew as a cosmopolitan and boundless thinker who transcends traditional borders and who is at home in the entire world. Needless to say, both images are cultivated extremes, put to work in antisemitic as well as philosemitic representations.

In addition to these volatile post-war stereotypes, another condition that greatly affected the lives of European Jews was the rearrangement of the national borderlines. Displacement both forced and voluntary, especially during the early years, became a reality for many Europeans, including Jews. One of the legacies of the inter-war period is exactly this notion of uprootedness. However, one should be careful in the application of this concept, especially where it touches upon, or is conflated with, the concept of exile, which has been described in critical theory as a (post)modern representation of the modern condition in general. While it may yield insights on a theoretical level, this becomes problematic when the notion of exile is applied to universal conditions – for instance, to the plight of refugees, Europe's incessant migrations or postmodern subjectivity – and romanticized to the point where it advocates a nomadic, cosmopolitan existence for everyone. The way, for instance, in which Jewish narratives of displacement are sometimes used as a paradigm for the displacement of contemporary refugees naively glosses over the particularities of each of these situations. Furthermore, the glorification of cosmopolitanism, considered one of the most valuable legacies of the Jewish experience, is detrimental to any understanding of the realities of a past life – indeed, the pain and the wounds of exile. The whole point of nomadism, in the end, I would argue, is to be able to stay somewhere, to plant roots against the odds, and to feel the growing pains of having a home. To romanticize homelessness, or, in its current wording, cosmopolitanism, as a twenty-first century attribute available to, or at least desirable for, all modern subjects is both immoral and an insensitive representation of those people who were left homeless as a result of war, famine, or persecution.

When we look in more detail at the uses and abuses of exile, or the memory of exile, in contemporary academic discourse, we find that the idea of the exilic experience as a model for an intellectual ethics is especially fashionable. What this means is that exile, as a position of social exclusion, is considered as a morally superior vantage point for intellectual reflection. The outsider, stripped of her socio-political status and turned into a universal subject, is believed to possess a more original, and therefore intellectually more transgressive, view on the inner workings of the societal life on which she reflects. What is problematic about such a disembodied view of exile are the ways in which it minimizes or masks the extent to which exile involves 'concessions, contaminations, complicities, negotiations and, in general, institutional dependency'.[9] In the case of exiled writers, it ignores the material circumstances of a writing life in exile. It does not address issues of employment, legal status, housing or access to means of intellectual production, such as publishers and media outlets. Instead of a morally superior position from which to reflect critically upon the world, exile is (also) a condition that entails loss, contamination and the sacrifice of ethical principles for the sake of survival. The reasons underlying the exiled writer's intellectual 'unclassifiability' are very often practical and pragmatic, not (only) the result of an unstable or genius mind. As such, one needs to be cautious about the extent to which we derive an ethical example from any type of suffering. In other words, the concepts of displacement and exile, and by extension, cosmopolitanism, are in dire need of historicisation.[10]

One of the issues at stake here is that in telling Joseph Roth's life story, his 'cosmopolitan' legacy – as a man of letters at home in hotel rooms and in possession of very few material belongings – was deeply intertwined with his exile. And his exile, in turn, was a decidedly European predicament. It originated in a course of events that sprang from the midst of European civilisation. Roth dedicated most of his writing life to understanding what went wrong in Europe, despite the ever-narrowing prospects of Jewish life, for him and for others, on the continent. His day-to-day life was plagued by questions of income and readership. How, then, did the idea of home express itself in the wider scope of his imagination? How did he reshape his own existence in the absence of a clear sense of national, religious or ideological belonging? Within the boundaries of his geographical life world, delineated clearly by his recalcitrant intellect, what did his commitment to Europe (and this refusal to leave its shores) mean?

Internal homelessness and political exile

As Tony Judt has observed – speaking also of his own life – to consider someone a 'rootless cosmopolitan' is to gloss over the variety of contrasting heritages in which any person is inevitably rooted.[11] Here as elsewhere, the question of Jewish heritage is crucial. It was in a centrifugal movement away from this heritage, in the predominantly Jewish town of Brody, Galicia (in present-day Ukraine), that Roth attempted to assimilate into Viennese society.[12] And it was by a drastic leap of faith – into misery and pain – fuelled by his wife Friederike

Reichler's deteriorating mental health during the late 1920s, that he returned to it. To what extent Roth's childhood in Brody contributed to a life of wandering is impossible to assess. He grew up an only child in a home that was composed of an absent father and an overbearing mother. One of the main characteristics of Brody was that it was a border town, and as such home to a large variety of languages that could be heard on a daily basis. John Hughes has argued that the fact that Roth grew up surrounded by a multiplicity of languages left a mark on his ideas about identity as something that was always, by necessity, rooted in multiplicity.[13] This notion of linguistic multiplicity is echoed in Roth's literary oeuvre, where characters make multiple appearances, jump onto the stage in distant and strange incarnations, from novel to novel, and speak to each other across the stories, creating the image of Roth as a puppet-master skilfully controlling his literary universe.

From the beginnings of his career as a journalist, Roth was part of a generation of inter-war intelligentsia for whom adherence to opposing ideologies and political parties, resulting in temporary but not necessarily tangential identifications, was more the rule than the exception. It entailed an intellectual swaying back and forth against a background of instability, mobility and persecution, especially for the Jews of Europe. Feeling the aftershocks of one world war, and faced with the threat of another, shifts in the private and public self-understandings of Jewish intellectuals often had a desperate, existential air to them, something which after 1933 turned into an urgent, at times mortal concern. The fact of a 'Jewish birth' – or 'accident', as Roth called it – remained an important question on the minds of assimilated Jews in Western Europe. For many of the inter-war Jewish intelligentsia, the loss of the Jewish tradition as a predominantly positive attribute influenced them in ways that went beyond the ambivalence, or so-called 'split identity', of their personae and words. The eccentric and individualist stance for which Roth is currently celebrated should thus be understood as part of an intellectual mind-set that was not atypical of the inter-war years in Europe. During Weimar, many intellectuals changed their politics in 'a bewildering fashion' from a position on the extreme Left – the Republic meant a new beginning – to an apolitical or strongly anti-Communist position towards the late 1920s.[14] In this political spectrum, an explicit focus on Jewishness was contrary to the beliefs of many intellectuals, who saw themselves first and foremost as Europeans. As Malachi Hacohen observed, the utopian visions of many Central European Jewish intellectuals – such as the idea of a Republic of Letters, for instance, or Karl Popper's 'Open Society' – were inspired by the dilemmas of national integration. 'Assimilated Central European Jews,' Hacohen writes, 'rejected Jewish identity but failed to gain acceptance into their nations. They could assimilate only into an imagined cosmopolitan community.'[15] This notion of a shared humanity, however, became increasingly difficult to uphold in a society where 'Jewishness', as a racial category, was actively forced upon the lives and the self-identification of Jewish intellectuals. And, since no such community based on the shared humanity of European intellectuals actually existed, many felt themselves 'homeless' in an ideological sense. Furthermore, the times were too violent and unpredictable to allow writers to remain uncommitted and exist primarily in an abstract, imagined reality.[16]

While Roth shared the universal, cosmopolitan elements of the idea of a European intellectual community, he was original in the sense that nothing could sway him permanently, and he remained detached from all official parties or ideologies. To remain unattached in a social climate that was dominated by the pull of ideologies claiming to offer existential and political stability in the post-war chaos included a certain risk. In this context, the dislocation caused by Roth's break with his Jewish heritage contributed greatly to the cultivation of his own societal marginality, and, more importantly, it became the undercurrent to his seemingly effortless and charming cosmopolitan lifestyle.

The reality, however, was more complicated. In exile, Roth suffered the loss of his German readership and his ties to German publisher Kiepenheuer & Witsch. His response to these challenges was to develop a kind of ethical probity: his loyalties were consciously blurred as a result of shifting identifications and a pressing need to make a living. The pragmatic demands of life in exile often exceeded the desire for intellectual purity, a concept that, in any case, for Roth was a sign of aloofness. Even if his convictions swayed, Roth's involvement with newspapers of different political persuasions was often caused by a desperate need for paid employment. His choices were purely pragmatic. Indeed, he had a family to feed, which included, besides his wife and the costs for her institutionalisation, from 1933 onwards his lover Andrea Manga Bell and her two young children. 'The children can't live on fresh air. Nor can I stick the whole caboodle in a pokey 1½-room flat either. […] In my case, love goes through the conscience, the way with others it goes through their stomachs.'[17] When it came to work, he could not be picky.

It was this predilection for a particular kind of cosmopolitanism – one that was rooted in everyday concerns, as opposed to floating comfortably above them – that caused a rift in his lifelong friendship with Stefan Zweig. Zweig's apolitical attitude in regards to Nazi Germany irritated him, and Roth accused his mentor of being naïve as to the dangers of Hitler's Third Reich. Zweig was a writer who had come to intellectual maturity in the age of reason, and his belief in progress and the underlying humanism of mankind was profound. Roth was angered by what he saw as a denial of responsibility on the part of intellectuals who had come face to face with the European crisis. In July 1934, while exiled in Nice, Roth wrote to Zweig: 'You are clever. I am not. But I see what you cannot see because your cleverness exempts you from seeing. You have the grace of reason, I the grace of misery.'[18] In typical fashion, Zweig responded by showering Roth with fatherly advice and money (and it was the latter that Roth wanted, quickly discarding the former). This, however, is not just an example of a generational or temperamental difference between the two men. It demonstrates a sense of marginality felt by Roth that was absent in Zweig's perception of himself as a 'German writer of the Mosaic faith'. It was this marginality that prompted Roth to cultivate the 'grace of misery', the conscious effort to isolate himself and to identify with the suffering of the thousands of unnamed poor, unemployed and marginalized. He did so not out of a sense of eccentric withdrawal, but for the sake of historical clarity and understanding.[19]

During the years of Roth's political exile, from 1933 to 1939, his focus on wandering as a human fate intensified. Prior to 1933, Roth had lived an uprooted life. He was, in his own words, a 'hotel patriot'.[20] Now, this was a kind of cosmopolitanism that required ample money, a privileged position reserved for successful journalists and writers. Yet at the same time, it was a cosmopolitanism based on a lack, on the impossibility of return. In light of the instability of the inter-war decades, out of sheer necessity Roth turned to wandering as an idealized fate. His inquiry started with the Jews. While remaining comfortably stationed in the West, in his writings Roth increasingly turned to the East in order to find a more 'authentic' form of Judaism. Already in 1927, he lamented the fact that Western Jews had forgotten 'how to wander, how to suffer, and how to pray'.[21] Whereas wandering had also been the lot of his non-Jewish characters of the post-war generation – in novels such as

The Spider's Web (1923), *Hotel Savoy* (1924) and *Rebellion* (1924) – it became a specifically Jewish theme in the long essay *The Wandering Jews* from 1927. This loving and at times troubled account of the complexities of East European Jewish life in the inter-war years was written with the hope 'to persuade the Jews and non-Jews of Western Europe to grasp the tragedy of the Eastern Jews'. Roth, who had a deep sympathy for the refugees and displaced persons who were flooding the capital cities of Europe after the Great War, took it upon himself, at least in writing and spirit, to ameliorate their fates. The tragedy of Eastern Jewry was on his mind constantly, and it served as an example, a kind of lightning rod, for his critique of post-war nationalism. He fought against the new borders that the post-war European order imposed upon people's sense of belonging and their ethnic, moral and national identifications.

Yet there were moments of lightness, too. The pinnacle of Roth's personal experience of living on a borderless continent came in 1925, when he arrived in Paris. At the time, he was still a young man whose journalistic career had brought him great success. His spell at a press encampment on the Eastern Front in 1917 was a distant memory, and he was relieved to leave behind the war veterans that were crowding the streets of Vienna and Berlin – places where, anyway, he felt, modernisation was taking an increasingly gloomy turn. Soon after his arrival in Paris, he wrote an elated letter to Benno Reifenberg, his editor at the *Frankfurter Zeitung*. Paris, he wrote, was the 'capital of the world', and whoever had not been there was only 'half a European'. It was 'free, intellectual in the best sense'. Moreover – and this remains one of the most enigmatic sentences Roth uttered – 'Paris is Catholic in the most urbane sense of the word, but it's also a European expression of universal Judaism' ('You must come here!' he added).[22] A few letters later he insisted that Reifenberg's young son must learn French. 'It will make a European of him.'[23]

Roth was not alone in his attraction to Paris, with its legacy of revolutionary France. Many intellectuals exiled from pre-Nazi Germany also felt at home there, as well as the many artists, painters and bohemians who assembled in the cafés of the picturesque Latin Quarter. One of the attractions of Paris was that it promised an escape from the increasingly nationalized atmosphere that was quickly developing elsewhere in Europe. In particular, the marker of Jewishness as an ethnic category that was forced upon the Jews of Germany, Austria and Hungary, in Paris could still fade against the background of humanist values and dreams in France. Roth, too, was attracted, in the words of Derek Penslar, by the 'national myth of France as the birthplace of revolution'.[24] Yet the irony is that Roth, who had since a very early age tried to unshackle himself from the constraints he felt the Jewish tradition placed on him, once in Paris felt compelled to stress the existence of a 'universal Judaism' as the epitome of a free, unburdened, and, yes, cosmopolitan belonging. This realisation, sparked by his elation at being able to be a 'free man' in Paris, formed the beginnings of his return to his own version of humanist and secular Judaism.

Limits of the cosmopolitan imagination

But there were limits to what could be imagined. Or, in reverse, it became apparent that the imagination ran into certain boundaries as it stretched itself further and further beyond the real. For instance, Roth's mental wellbeing in the spiritual realm of French humanism could never be translated into linguistic belonging. It never materialized into a self-identification as a French writer, shackled as he was by his (German) mother tongue. While at work in

Marseille, he complained that it was impossible to write about humans in a language that had only brought forth 'geniuses and murderers, the outcomes of a barbaric people'.[25] For Roth this observation quickly morphed into a much larger question, and became a dichotomy between two worldviews: between Paris (humanism) and Berlin (Fascism), between France and Germany. This dichotomy played itself out in Roth's literary universe as the axis between which his plots unfolded – light and darkness, good and evil. But whereas his novels may have offered a 'way out' of the schism, and presented both writer and reader with an artistic means of coming to terms with it, on the personal level it could not be overcome. 'I feel terribly sad because there are no bridges between certain races,' Roth wrote in 1925 from Paris to Reifenberg. 'There will never be a connection between Prussia and France.'[26] He believed that the only way Europe could reach its full potential as a civilisational force was by expelling Germany from its midst, the country he described in no unclear terms as a 'depository of hell on earth'.[27] Already in 1925, he noted that 'the air has become fairly unbreathable in Germany', and he refused to return to Berlin.[28]

While he mourned the loss of the multinational empires and the relatively peaceful co-existence of the different nationalities within its borders, Roth could not imagine this same constellation to work equally well in post-war Europe, no matter how much his intellect urged him towards a borderless world. The nation-states as they emerged after 1918 had carved out boundaries not only on the map of Europe but also in the psyches of those inhabiting them, and Roth felt less and less at home in the language of the nation that was to cause the greatest chasm of his time. He distanced himself from literary circles in Germany, and from German writers living in exile in France. He had no wish to be part of the 'Gruppe 1925', a Marxist discussion group led by Alfred Döblin. 'I don't want any ties to German writers,' he confided to a friend. 'None of them feels as radically as I do. [...] Between ourselves, it's no advantage to belong to such a club. There are people in it I despise.'[29] He was equally reluctant to move too much in what he called 'Jewish circles', and French writers, while admiring their tradition, were almost without exception 'too bourgeois' for his taste. His cosmopolitan existence, despite the many friends, colleagues and publishers that joined him for drinks and late-night conversations at this café table, seems to have been an increasingly solitary one.

Perhaps, then, there is some truth to Malachi Hacohen's observation that Roth may not have been a proponent of cosmopolitanism at all, but instead an advocate of an idiosyncratic form of 'illiberal multiculturalism'. Roth's hope to return to a supranational form of imperial governance, expressed in novels dealing with the Habsburg experience such as *The Radetzky March* (1932) and *The Emperor's Tomb* (1938), was based on the idea of enabling a mosaic of indigenous ethnocultural communities. It envisioned a peaceful coexistence of Christian, Jewish and other groups, which nevertheless remained closed off to each other – something that in the nineteenth century was regulated by, or in the hands of, the king or emperor.[30] It is this notion of ethnic separateness that distinguishes Roth from the more common notion of cosmopolitism that proposes a way of life based on the evaporation, or at least the blurring, of boundaries. Despite his itinerant lifestyle and a mind that accepted very few limitations on his imagination or his manners, it appears that some bridges remained difficult to cross – in particular those between continents, nationalities and nations.

As the 1920s gave way to a threatening and sorrowful new decade, Roth continued to lead a wildly itinerant life inside a patchwork of increasingly narrow realms of belonging – geographical, mental, linguistic. He never owned an apartment. The only time he lived in one was in Berlin with his young wife – he lasted about six months. A house 'with pictures on the walls' seemed odd, even romantic (in a sentimental sense) to him.[31] He was proud to call himself a patriot not of nations but of temporary residences – hotels – and he dedicated many of his feuilletons to the subject of life coming through its revolving doors. 'Nothing ties me,' he wrote in the summer of 1925. 'I am not sufficiently sentimental to believe in categories like future, family, etc. etc.' He did, however, feel sufficiently sentimental to devote himself to an entire string of publishing houses, and to their newspapers, which to Roth were 'the last vestiges of the old humanistic culture'.[32] But, as suited his character, he immediately undermined these expressions of belonging by observing that for a writer, true independence meant being able to live without having to submit to the censorship of newspapers, as pre-war novelists had done.[33] 'The feeling of not belonging anywhere,' he wrote in 1927, 'which has always been with me, has borne out.'[34] A year later, while applying for Austrian citizenship, Roth was forced to prove, or at least state, his nationality, which from a legal point of view proved difficult. It confronted him with the fact that he had been living a fantasy, that he had, in his lonesome and at times erratic mind, cultivated a fictional self that had no real echoes in the world of politics and borders. 'For the past 25 years,' he observed, 'I've been living as a sort of fantastic figment.'[35] This propensity for self-invention was evident in Roth's masked autobiographies, which, despite the surreal twists or 'untruths' they contained, are beautiful to read:

> I have covered many miles. Between the place where I was born, and the towns and villages I have lived in in the last ten years – and lived in only, apparently, to leave them again – lies my life, amenable more readily to spatial than to chronological measurement. The years I have put behind me are the roads I have travelled. Nowhere, in no parish register or cadastre is there a record of my name or date of birth. I have no home, aside from being at home in myself. Wherever I am unhappy is my home. I am only ever happy abroad. If I leave myself even once, I will lose myself. Therefore, I take great care to remain within myself.[36]

What mattered to Roth was to remain within himself in what was essentially a condition of perpetual homelessness. In this way, Roth undermined the mythology of an ultimate return that often accompanies notions of exile. Nor did he appreciate those things a traditional home entails. Towards the end of his life, he said: 'I have never – long before the catastrophe – [the disillusion of Austria-Hungary] had any understanding of furniture and the like. I shit on furniture. I hate houses.'[37] But even if Roth developed a notion of homelessness that was oriented more towards the present than the past – in other words, a positive assessment about staying put in his exilic day-to-day life – this does not mean that he discounted the costs. His vision of non-belonging sharpened with the years, and it was formulated from within the tensions between real and metaphorical displacement, between exile as a reality and exile as a metaphorical or ideological concept.

What can be said about Roth's so-called 'inner exile' or estrangement was that it was to a large degree self-inflicted, the result of a personal, intellectual disposition, despite the historical forces that would later meet him halfway. His preference for hotel rooms, lobbies, and cafés, based on an abhorrence of domesticity, materialized long before the enforced political exile of 1933. It was a form of voluntary detachment from the 'normal' day-to-day life in which most people choose to anchor themselves. Yet it is important to note that Roth did not consider his itinerant lifestyle to be anything out of the ordinary. 'I haven't lived in a house since my eighteenth year,' he wrote to Zweig in 1929, 'aside from the odd week staying with friends. Everything I own fits into three suitcases. It doesn't strike me as at all odd, either. What is odd to me, though, and even romantic, is a house, with pictures on the walls, and so on and so forth.'[38] But as Israeli novelist David Grossman has noted, living in a house with 'mobile walls' is an extremely vulnerable and at times terrifying predicament.[39]

Conclusion

As the years went by, Roth's solitude grew, and his inclination to remain within himself became more and more acute. His letters chronicle this increasingly mournful plight. In the early 1930s, Roth's inner estrangement reached a peak. His drinking spiralled out of control, despite claims from the drinker himself that the toxins kept his mind sharp and prevented his immediate death. 'Don't worry about my drinking, please,' he wrote to a concerned Stefan Zweig in November 1935. 'It's much more likely to preserve me than destroy me. I mean to say, yes, alcohol has the effect of shortening one's life, but it staves off *immediate death*. And it's the *staving off of immediate death* that concerns me, not the *lengthening of my life*.'[40] He realized he could not count on too many years ahead of him. His wife had been locked up in mental institutions for more than five years, fuelling him with guilt for her condition. As Irmgard Keun, the German novelist and Roth's lover during the late 1930s, said: 'He was so vulnerable, that he felt he needed to wear a mask also in my company.'[41] The few occasions, at which Roth felt he could do without pretence, was when he was writing. In exile, while seemingly enjoying his lavish and free cosmopolitan lifestyle, Roth's self-narration became a survival strategy, and the nostalgia that sometimes accompanied it could therefore be considered a 'romance with [his] own fantasy'.[42]

Roth dealt his characters a similar fate, whether it came in the form of sudden and abrupt departures, or in leaving them stranded in unnamed border towns.[43] He became increasingly idiosyncratic in his responses to the danger of Nazi Germany, throwing out words as though they were bombs. Perhaps, as Judith Butler has argued, there is a certain poetics in non-belonging and the impossibility of arrival. It is, as she writes, certainly true that departure and arrival were constant issues for European Jews, 'who were considering leaving Europe for Palestine, but also for other sites of emigration.'[44] Yet the tragedy inherent in Joseph Roth's fate – in other words, the darker side of non-belonging – was clear to Roth himself, and evident in his conscious decision not to leave the distressed continent. His endless flight fuelled his pen, but it cost him his life. There was a thin line between his private sense of restlessness and the persecution that resulted from being an eastern European Jew in inter-war Europe. In other words, Roth's now much celebrated uprootedness, indeed his cosmopolitanism, resulted from his historical times as much as it did from his person. The relative ease with which he conducted his non-committal lifestyle and pursued the supranational dream that flowed from it was perpetually undermined by the existence of actual, real borders.

In a letter to Zweig, Roth commented upon the fate of Lieutenant Franz Tunda, the hero of *Flight Without End* (1927), who escaped from a Russian POW camp during the First World War and tried to make his way home to Vienna. Roth said: 'I have qualms about that "tragic" component, I think our postwar man no longer has that "classical" capacity for tragedy, which is no longer a component of character but is still present in the "historical view." Which means there is perhaps tragedy in the way we view the fate of someone like Tunda, even though he himself won't see or feel it.'[45]

So, let the fact that Roth recognized the tragedy inherent in his own fate be a humble signpost to all those committed to the 'historical view', historians and readers alike, so as to nuance our understanding of cosmopolitanism through the lens of how it was lived and experienced, but almost never named, by one of its most unhappy proponents.

Notes

1. Roth, *A Life in Letters*, 131 (26 January 1929). All quotations are from this edition.
2. According to Dutch art historian Frans Hannema, who knew Roth in Paris, Roth lived in a constant state of *"geistige Hochspannung."* Collection Joseph Roth/David Bronsen, Interview Bronsen–Frans Hannema, on 27 October 1960, 1: JR/DB 10/94/19.2/13. Dokumentationsstelle fuïr neuere österreichische Literatur, Vienna.
3. Roth, *The Antichrist*. Originally published as *Der Antichrist* in 1934.
4. *A Life in Letters*, 530–1 (21 January 1939).
5. Frank, *Double Exile*.
6. For the emigration of Hungarian intellectuals, see Congdon, *Exile and Social Thought*.
7. Böhler, Borodziej, and von Puttkamer, *Legacies of Violence*, 2.
8. Ablovatski, "The 1919 Central European Revolutions and the Judeo-Bolshevik Myth."
9. Faber, "The Privilege of Pain."
10. See, for instance, Kaplan, *Questions of Travel*; and Evelein, *Exiles Traveling*.
11. Judt, *The Memory Chalet*.
12. For a history of Brody, see Kuzmany, *Brody*.
13. See also Hughes, *Facing Modernity*; and Tonkin, *Joseph Roth's March into History*.
14. Déak, *Weimar Germany's Left-Wing Intellectuals*, 18.
15. Hacohen, "Dilemmas of Cosmopolitanism," 106, 139.
16. As Déak argued: "'Homelessness' might become an advantage if it allowed the individual the freedom of unemotional and uncommitted observation. But these intellectuals were neither unemotional nor uncommitted; nor were they allowed to be impartial observers. On the contrary, they were urged to alternately identify themselves as Jews and as Germans – being alternately chided, when they tried, for clannishness or for 'infiltration.'" Déak, *Weimar Germany's Left-Wing Intellectuals*, 25–6.
17. *A Life in Letters*, 421 (1 September 1935).
18. This translation (by the author) is from the German edition of Roth's correspondence. See Kesten, *Joseph Roth: Briefe 1911–1939*, 353. For Hofmann's translation (who rendered the original "Unglück" as "unhappiness"), see *A Life in Letters*, 348 (13 July 1934).
19. This is the main premise of my study Roth, *The Grace of Misery*.
20. See also Snick, *Hotelmens: Reportages and Brieven – Joseph Roth*.
21. Roth, *The Wandering Jews*. Originally published as *Juden auf Wanderschaft* in 1927.
22. *A Life in Letters*, 38–39 (16 May 1025).
23. Ibid., 44 (25 July 1925).
24. Penslar, *Jews and the Military*, 154.
25. *A Life in Letters*, 47 (22 August 1925).
26. Ibid., 39 (16 May 1925).
27. *Pariser Tagblatt*, 6 July 1934.
28. *A Life in Letters*, 46 (18 August 1925). Roth did travel to Germany a few more times prior to January 1933, but it was always to his greatest chagrin.
29. Ibid., 67, 71 (undated, and 11 February 1926). Other writers who belonged to this group were Bertold Brecht, Kurt Tucholsky, and Egon Erwin Kisch.
30. Hacohen, "Kosmopoliten in einer ethnonationalen Zeit?"
31. *A Life in Letters*, 133 (27 February 1929).
32. Ibid., 55 (30 August 1925). And in 1928: "It's my only home soil, and must do for me as fatherland and exchequer" (111, 8 January 1928).
33. Ibid., 107 (27 December 1927).

34. Ibid., 105 (21 December 1927).
35. Ibid., 124 (30 July 1928).
36. Ibid., 150 (10 June 1930). This is a fragment of the famous letter to publisher Gustav Kiepenheuer on the occasion of his fiftieth birthday. Michael Hofmann commented that "the one big falsehood of this letter is made up of what are actually lots of tiny truths" (154).
37. Ibid., 527 (10 October 1938).
38. Ibid., 133 (27 February 1929). As mentioned, this is not entirely the case. During the early 1920s, Roth lived for six months in an apartment in Berlin with his wife Friederike.
39. David Grossman, in an interview with Dutch journalist Gideon Levi for the documentary series *Israel, Tussen Droom en Werkelijkheid* (2009).
40. *A Life in Letters*, 429 (12 November 1935).
41. "Er war so verletzbar, daß er sich auch mit gegenüber einer Maske bedienen mußte." Irmgard Keun, quoted from Bronsen, *Joseph Roth*, 476. Translation by the author.
42. Boym, *The Future of Nostalgia*, xiii.
43. Lazaroms, "Borderlands: Joseph Roth's Dystopian Imagination," 220, 236.
44. Butler, "Who Owns Kafka?"
45. *A Life in Letters*, 115–116 (24 January 1928).

Bibliography

Archives
Joseph Roth/David Bronsen Collection. Dokumentationsstelle für neuere österreichische Literatur, Vienna, Austria. Handschriftensammlung.
Primary sources
Israel, Tussen Droom en Werkelijkheid [Israel, between dream and reality]. Dutch documentary series by journalist Gideon Levi, 2009.
Pariser Tagblatt.
Roth, Joseph. *A Life in Letters*. Translated and edited by Michael Hofmann. London: Granta, 2012.
Roth, Joseph. *The Antichrist*. Translated by Richard Panchyk. London: Peter Owen Ltd., 2010.
Roth, Joseph. *The Wandering Jews*. Translated by Michael Hofmann. New York and London: W. W. Norton & Company, 2001.

Secondary literature

Ablovatski, Eliza. "The 1919 Central European Revolutions and the Judeo-Bolshevik Myth." *European Review of History/Revue européenne d'histoire* 17, no. 3, thematic issue "Cosmopolitanism, Nationalism and the Jews of East Central Europe," edited by Michael L. Miller and Scott Ury (June 2010): 473–489.

Böhler, Jochen, Włodimierz Borodziej, and Joachim von Puttkamer, eds. *Legacies of Violence: Eastern Europe's First World War*. Munich: De Gruyter Oldenbourg, 2014.

Boym, Svetlana. *The Future of Nostalgia*. New York, NY: Basic Books, 2001.

Bronsen, David. *Joseph Roth: Eine Biographie*. Cologne: Kiepenheuer & Witch, 1974.

Butler, Judith. "Who Owns Kafka?" *London Review of Books* 33, no. 5 (3 March 2011): 3–8.

Congdon, Lee. *Exile and Social Thought: Hungarian Intellectuals in Germany and Austria 1919–1933*. Princeton, N.J.: Princeton University Press, 1991.

Déak, István. *Weimar Germany's Left-wing Intellectuals: A Political History of the Weltbühne and Its Circle*. Berkeley: University of California Press, 1968.

Evelein, Johannes F., ed. *Exiles Traveling: Exploring Displacement, Crossing Boundaries in German Exile Arts and Writings 1933–1945*. Amsterdamer Beiträge zur Neueren Germanistik 68. Amsterdam: Rodopi, 2009.

Faber, Sebastiaan. "The Privilege of Pain: The Exile as Ethical Model in Max Aub, Francisco Ayala, and Edward Said." *Journal of the Interdisciplinary Crossroads* 3, no. 1, thematic issue "The Limits of Exile", edited by David Kettler and Zvi Ben-Dor (April 2006): 11–32.

Frank, Tibor. *Double Exile: Migrations of Jewish-Hungarian Professionals through Germany to the United States, 1919–1945*. Exile Studies. An Interdisciplinary Series, Volume 7. Oxford: Peter Lang, 2009.

Hacohen, Malachi Haim. "Dilemmas of Cosmopolitanism: Karl Popper, Jewish Identity, and 'Central European Culture.'" *The Journal of Modern History* 71, no. 1 (March 1999): 105–149.

Hacohen, Malachi Haim. "Kosmopoliten in einer ethnonationalen Zeit? Juden und Österreicher in der Ersten Republik" [Cosmopolitans in Ethnonational Times? Jews and Austrians in the First Republic]. In *Das Werden der Ersten Republik. ... der Rest ist Österreich*, edited by Helmut Konrad and Wolfgang Maderthaner, 2 vols., 281–316. Vienna: Gerold, 2008.

Hughes, Jon. *Facing Modernity: Fragmentation, Culture and Identity in Joseph Roth's Writing in the 1920s*. MHRA Texts & Dissertations vol. 67 and Bithell Series of Dissertations vol. 30. Leeds: Maney, 2006.

Judt, Tony. *The Memory Chalet*. London: William Heinemann, 2010.

Kaplan, Caren. *Questions of Travel: Postmodern Discourses of Displacement*. Durham: Duke University Press, 1996.

Kesten, Hermann (ed.). *Joseph Roth: Briefe 1911–1939*. Kiepenheuer & Witsch: Cologne, 1979.

Kuzmany, Börrie. *Brody: Eine galizische Grenzstadt im langen 19. Jahrhundert*. Vienna: Böhlau, 2011.

Lazaroms, Ilse Josepha. *The Grace of Misery: Joseph Roth and the Politics of Exile, 1919–1939*. Brill's Series in Jewish Studies 47. Leiden and Boston: Brill, 2013.

Lazaroms, Ilse Josepha. "Borderlands: Joseph Roth's Dystopian Imagination." *Simon Dubnow Institute Yearbook* 13 (2014): 215–236.

Penslar, Derek J. *Jews and the Military: A History*. Princeton and Oxford: Princeton University Press, 2013.

Snick, Els, ed. *Hotelmens: Reportages and Brieven – Joseph Roth*. Edited and translated by Els Snick. Illustrations by Peter van Hugten. Amsterdam: Bas Lubberhuizen, 2014.

Tonkin, Kati. *Joseph Roth's March into History: From the Early Novels to "Radetzkymarsch" and "Die Kapuzinergruft"*. Rochester and New York: Camden House Inc., 2008.

JEWS, COSMOPOLITANISM AND POLITICAL THOUGHT

Marxism, cosmopolitanism and 'the' Jews

Philip Spencer

ABSTRACT
Marxists have had a complex and contentious relationship to the question of both cosmopolitanism and antisemitism. The difficulties and problems they have encountered with each may, however, be related. They can be traced back to a repeated failure to take seriously Marx's initial critique of contemporary antisemites and his simultaneous adoption of a cosmopolitan approach to politics which set him apart from many of his peers. Rather than confronting antisemitism, many Marxists adopted the view that it contained some kind of rational kernel, whilst drifting towards an accommodation with forms of nationalism. Having ignored and largely failed to respond to the mortal threat that a radicalized antisemitism posed for Jews, the self-proclaimed Marxists ruling the Soviet Union then accused Jews of being both nationalists (of the wrong, Zionist sort) and cosmopolitans (now a term of abuse). There is, however, an alternative tradition that may be recovered, albeit on the margins of the Marxist movement, in the later work especially of Horkheimer and Adorno, and in some parallel way also of Hannah Arendt, that sees antisemitism from a cosmopolitan perspective as an inherently reactionary political force which (as it became genocidal) came to threaten both Jews and humanity at large.

Introduction

Marxists have long had a complex and contentious relationship to the question of both cosmopolitanism and antisemitism. The difficulties and problems they have encountered with each (and indeed created on occasion) may, however, be related.

With respect to cosmopolitanism, there has been over time a widespread (though not universal) failure to transcend the limitations of what at perhaps the deepest level, following Ulrich Beck and (more critically) Daniel Chernilo, we might now see as a kind of methodological nationalism, in which the nation-state is taken as the primary frame of reference.[1] Many Marxists (though not all) came to a growing accommodation to at least certain kinds of nationalism, and some ended up even explicitly rejecting cosmopolitanism itself as a set of overarching values and commitments.

With respect to antisemitism, there has been a widespread failure to take sufficiently seriously its increasingly destructive and reactionary character in the modern world. The threat posed to Jews by the Nazis in particular was not recognized by most Marxists as it was emerging. As that threat was realized in the Holocaust, there was only a weak and limited response from the organized Marxist movement. After the event, an ominous inversion took place, in what was seen by many to be the centre of that movement, which has ironically appeared to give a further and perverse twist to the history of antisemitism.

These are more than parallel developments. They have common roots which may be traced back to a widespread (though again not universal) failure to sustain and develop what was distinctive about Marx's original endeavours in the 1840s: his profound insights at a formative historical moment into the need for a politics that challenged the dominant ways in which the so-called 'national question' was coming to be framed (which occluded what is reactionary about nationalism as an ideology) and the need on the other to think much more deeply about the so-called 'Jewish Question' (a framing of the issue which similarly occluded what is reactionary about antisemitism).

This hiatus was to have extremely grave consequences both for Jews and for humanity as a whole to the degree to which Jews had become the cosmopolitan subject *par excellence*. Spread out across nation-states, they were to become the most (though not the only) vulnerable group as nationalism developed in the late nineteenth and twentieth centuries. Identified everywhere, to a greater or lesser extent, by nationalists as a problem for the imagined nation, Jews ended up losing what had only recently been granted (at best) - their rights as citizens, their right to have rights and, in the Holocaust, their human status, which was the distinctive focus of Marx's original arguments.

From a cosmopolitan perspective, the failure by Marxists to develop a coherent and sustained response to a radicalized antisemitism was particularly significant. The Marxist movement was, for over a century, potentially the main organized vehicle for a *radical* cosmopolitan politics, in a world order comprised of competing nation-states, each pursuing their own national interests, within the framework established at the Treaty of Westphalia in 1648 which proscribed states from intervening in the internal affairs of other states. In this context, the international solidarity which underpinned the creation of first the Second and then the Third Internationals, both largely dominated by Marxist ideas and movements, could have provided one of the few mechanisms for organising solidarity with the victims of the violence of modern states not only across borders (in the case of wars between states) but within them, when (in the case of genocide) they targeted minority groups for destruction.

A fundamental principle underpinning the creation of each of these organisations in the first place was a cosmopolitan one: of solidarity between members of an international working class. In its Marxist formulation, the proletariat was conceived of as a universal class, swelling in size to the point at which it would encompass all of humanity. Its cosmopolitanism was of what James Ingram has recently defined as a bottom-up and non-statist kind, even if this was modified to some extent when the Soviet Union came into existence.[2] At the most basic level which, as David Held argues[3], is where cosmopolitan solidarity begins, what the principle implied was that the International(s) would come to the aid of those most urgently in need, and prioritize rescue and refuge to those most acutely at risk, those who lacked any nation-state of their own to which they could flee – Jews certainly, and arguably also Roma and Sinti, although the Nazis perhaps exhibited slightly less destructive certainty in the latter case. Even those who could flee to other states were not guaranteed protection where they were granted (at best) a reluctant temporary refuge. Even here, as Derrida has recently reminded us, recalling Hannah Arendt's experience and observation, Jews were again acutely vulnerable to policing agencies which treated them at best with suspicion and at worst later collaborated eagerly with the Nazis in their renewed persecution.[4]

In such circumstances, only an organized non-state and radical cosmopolitan movement could have offered the unqualified aid that was so desperately needed. That aid would have had to be grounded in a more extensive notion of a right to hospitality than that advanced even by the most liberal cosmopolitans. As a radical form of cosmopolitanism, it would have to go beyond in particular, as Derrida has argued[5], Kant's explicit restriction to a fundamentally temporary right of visitation, in this case because those threatened by the Nazis could not go back to what could never again be 'home'. But Derrida's own reference point, the global city as the most relevant and viable site of cosmopolitan solidarity today, is in a way indicative itself of the legacy of the International(s)' failure, to the extent that the Marxist movement was never confined to cities alone.

None of this is to say that a different response would have been successful in saving anything like a majority of Jews from their fate. Clearly many other factors, far beyond the reach and responsibility of the Marxist movement, have to be taken into account in thinking about who could have come to the aid of Jews. But what is striking is how little reflection there has been on this issue from this perspective. Only a few thinkers working (at best) on the margins of the Marxist movement (notably Max Horkheimer and Theodor Adorno, and to some extent Hannah Arendt) have devoted significant effort, in the light of the catastrophe that had occurred, to retrieving some elements of the cosmopolitan way of responding to the antisemitism tradition that Marx himself inaugurated. However marginal and limited, these efforts may nevertheless, as I suggest in the concluding sections of this chapter, point to some continuing relevance for this tradition, as antisemitism continues to mutate and to threaten both Jews and humanity in the modern world.

Marx's early critique of nationalism

Marx's cosmopolitan critique of nationalism has of course to be placed, like his response to antisemitism, in its historical context. The 1840s might be characterized as both the high point and the turning point of liberal nationalism. In the decades that had followed the French Revolution, most progressive thinkers and movements believed, as the early French revolutionaries had done, that democracy and nationalism went hand in hand, that (as Sieyes had famously put it in 1789) the terms 'people' and 'nation' were 'synonymous'.

As far as the Jews were concerned, they had been included in the nation by French revolutionaries but only as individuals and only on certain conditions. As Clermont-Tonnerre famously put it in his speech advocating their emancipation, 'the Jews should be denied everything as a nation but granted everything as individuals', words which are ambiguous in both meaning and effect. From one liberal perspective, they could be interpreted to mean that Jews were required to abandon their traditional status as a 'nation within the nation'. Alternatively and more radically, however, they could mean that Jews should henceforth abandon any sense of collective identity at all and be subsumed within a homogenized nation.

This ambiguity was not accidental or purely contingent on that political context. Liberalism has not provided an unambiguously secure basis for confronting antisemitism, for a variety of reasons, which are largely beyond the scope of this paper, but which involve at the political level the manifold connections which developed throughout the nineteenth and twentieth centuries between liberalism and nationalism, and at the social level (insofar as this can be considered separately from the political) repeatedly expressed concerns about how even a liberal nation can be held together without a shared national culture, all too often not seen to include those who continued to think of themselves in some way or other as Jews.[6] At the dawn of modern liberalism in the Enlightenment, there was already a dominant view shared by many (though not all) thinkers that there was something inherently problematic about the maintenance in the modern world of a specifically Jewish identity. Just as many Enlightenment thinkers made all organized religion the object of criticism but treated Judaism with disproportionately more scorn and contempt, there lurked (beneath the new-found revolutionary toleration for Jews) an assumption on the part of both moderates and radicals that Jews would in return give up being Jewish altogether, because this particular identity was especially archaic and worthless.[7] As Pierre Birnbaum has shown in the case of the renowned emancipationist Abbé Gregoire, such assumptions were normally shared even by the most articulate and consistent advocates of Jewish emancipation in the new Republic.[8]

Marx criticized both assumptions: that the people and the nation were the same thing, and that Jews should be the object of particular suspicion. And he did so in the same period and on the same cosmopolitan lines, lines that have not been followed (though they could be) by most subsequent Marxists.

As Gilbert Achcar has recently argued, a cosmopolitan thread runs throughout Marx and Engels' work and it was particularly striking at the time he was developing his critique of Bruno Bauer, who came in for particular criticism specifically for his German chauvinism in *The German Ideology*.[9] Achcar argues that Marx's cosmopolitanism was distinct from prevailing conceptions which were, variously, philosophical, institutional, juridical or economic. It formed a core part of his historical materialist approach to history and politics which here, as elsewhere, involved a critique (rather than dismissal) of hitherto partial and one-sided conceptions.

A cosmopolitan perspective lay at the heart, in particular, of his conception of the proletariat as a universal class as 'the bearer', as Achcar puts it, 'of a global communist future', one which could not be fought for within the narrow and distorting confines of a nationalist frame of reference. On the one hand, Marx and Engels argued that 'working people have no country … the nationality of the worker is neither French, nor English, nor German, it is labour, free slavery, self-huckstering. His government is neither French, nor English, nor German, nor English, it is capital.'[10] At the same time, they claimed that 'the great mass of the proletarians are, by their nature, free from national prejudice and their whole disposition and movement is essentially *humanitarian, anti-nationalist*'.[11]

This may have been an overly optimistic assessment of the state of working-class consciousness at the moment in time but it formed only one part of a sophisticated and discriminating critique of nationalism as a form of politics, grounded as Erica Benner has argued, 'in a normative conception of the *human* community'.[12] This normative conception was fundamentally cosmopolitan, concerned not with what divided the international working class but with what was shared both materially and culturally. Above all, Marx's primary concern was to encourage solidarity across national boundaries, a solidarity which he believed was imperilled by the appeal of rival nationalisms.

This danger became particularly clear in the 1848 revolutions. Rather than uniting in a common struggle against the forces of reaction, German nationalists opted, as Langeswiehe has noted, 'to cooperate with counterrevolution to advance their interests against other nations'[13], rejecting out of hand the right of national self-determination, which they claimed for themselves, being applied to Danes, Poles, Italians or Czechs. Opposition to such divisive nationalism in 1848 came only from that internationalist part of the Left which was led by Marx himself.[14]

Within the organized Marxist movement, this critical stance was largely abandoned as various attempts were made to distinguish between different kinds of nationalism, some supposedly progressive, others reactionary. The most politically significant of these efforts was made by Lenin, who argued that there was a critical difference between the nationalism of the oppressor and the nationalism of the oppressed. Lenin's argument was largely instrumental in the first instance, put forward in the hope that Marxists might somehow be able to utilize nationalist resistance to Tsarist imperial rule. The task of developing what was initially a purely instrumental tactic into a more general position was, perhaps not insignificantly, entrusted to Joseph Stalin, the least theoretically equipped of all the Marxist revolutionaries, who contrived a set of rigid criteria, or 'mathematical formulae' as Enzo Traverso puts it[15], one of whose signal consequences was to repeat the old refrain that Jews in particular could not form a nation.

Not all Marxists, however, were prepared to abandon Marx's cosmopolitan standpoint, most notably Rosa Luxemburg, whose opposition to nationalism has often been far too casually dismissed as abstract and unrealistic. For her, like Marx, nationalism was essentially a category of bourgeois ideology; it was reactionary economically and politically; it divided workers across national boundaries by invoking the primacy of reified national identities over all other identities; where nationalists were successful in shaping the terms of national self-determination, it would only lead to new states oppressing the minorities in their midst.[16] Although antisemitism was not Luxemburg's own primary focus, this (as Anita Shelton has argued) was bound to have especially serious consequences for Jews, since they were a minority everywhere.[17]

The potential violence of nationalist ideology was realized in Luxemburg's lifetime on an extreme and unprecedented scale in the First World War, against which she called (albeit in vain) for the cosmopolitan solidarity of an international working-class movement. Only this, she believed, could save humanity from what she presciently defined as the threat of a general 'reversion to barbarism'.[18] Luxemburg's reference to barbarism was not purely rhetorical but drew explicitly on a suggestion made earlier by Engels that at some point the direction of history itself ('world history' is the term she used) might be at stake. If the proletariat did not rise to the challenge as an international class, a global war could bring about catastrophe for humanity itself.

If we extend Luxemburg's intuition to encompass both world wars[19], it could be argued that her cosmopolitan approach enabled her to have greater insight than many other Marxists at the time into the more profound consequences of the triumph of nationalism as the empires, which had dominated Europe for so long, fragmented. Where other Marxists followed Lenin into an uncritical support for the right of nations to self-determination, Luxemburg argued that this could all too easily be used to justify the claims of post-imperial nationalist elites who successfully achieved state power to oppress minorities within their own borders who were deemed to belong to other 'nations', or (in the case of the Jews) to no nation at all.[20]

Antisemitism and the 'Jewish Question'

Luxemburg was also rare, however, among Marxists of her generation in taking seriously Marx's understanding of the Jewish Question and in particular his critique of what we can now see as the proto-antisemitism of Bruno Bauer. Marx's response to Bauer appeared in the form of two seminal essays 'On the Jewish Question', published in 1843, in which he developed crucial elements of his own conception of human emancipation more generally. These essays, which were Marx's only sustained and focused writings on this issue, have been the subject of sustained debate for many years, between those who find in them (and in some of his later, more occasional remarks) damning evidence of antisemitism and those who seek to exculpate Marx from any such charge. Pierre Birnbaum has provided a substantial review of this debate, summarising the arguments on both sides. It may well be, as Birnbaum himself concludes, that Marx's essays and many of his subsequent comments are riddled with antisemitic expressions and tropes.[21] But there would have been nothing new or distinctive about any of this. What was new about Marx's critique of Bauer was that he challenged directly, and from a cosmopolitan perspective, the assumptions of the majority of even the most progressive Enlightenment thinkers that there was something uniquely problematic about Jews.

Where Bauer had argued, in what was by now a familiar vein, that Jews should only be given citizenship rights if they gave up being Jews, Marx strongly disagreed, insisting that it was fundamentally wrong to make such a demand, to single out Jews and Judaism and that Jews were as entitled to full rights in the political state as anyone else. The problem was not Jews or Judaism but the political state and a notion of human emancipation that was confined only to the political sphere. As Robert Fine has argued, this was a radical move on Marx's part.[22] It broke with what he has called 'the whole perspective of the Jewish question', one that saw the continued existence of Jews as a problem for an otherwise purportedly civil society or, in this context, purportedly unified nation. It could only be a 'Jewish Question' if the Jews were seen as the problem in the first place. Marx transformed the terms of this 'question'. If Jews did not have rights, then the problem was the society from which they were excluded. This is a cosmopolitan perspective because it assumes that all human beings have rights, by virtue of their common and equal human status, and that if there is a society which excludes them, there is a problem with that society, not with those who are denied rights. (This is not of course to say that Marx's own conception of rights is adequate, as he famously observed that 'not one of the so-called rights of man go beyond egoistic man'. But his argument does not imply that such rights are irrelevant but rather that they need to be further developed and extended universally and unconditionally, in this context to Jews).

As Lars Fischer has shown, Luxemburg was a signal exception in grounding her approach to antisemitism in Marx's critique of Bauer.[23] Most Marxists in the German Social Democratic Party, the largest and leading Marxist organisation in the Second International, were far more prone to adopt Bauer's construction of a 'Jewish Question', either out of ignorance or misunderstanding (wilful or otherwise). The general tendency was to be critical of Jews for not being willing to relinquish their collective identity in the struggle for general emancipation, and to treat 'philosemitism' as a bigger problem than antisemitism inasmuch as it denied a supposed Jewish harmfulness. As antisemitism became an increasingly significant political movement, albeit with ebbs and flows and mixed fortunes[24], one of the leaders of the SPD, August Bebel, called it 'the socialism of fools'. Bebel's adoption of this formulation[25] was obviously critical, but it could be taken to mean that antisemitism had some kind of rational kernel, that the hostility antisemites felt towards Jews was understandable but misdirected, and that antisemitism contained some kind of progressive energy that needed to be harnessed. To put it another way, even if it were the socialism of fools, it could be seen as some kind of socialism.

Marxism of course was not a monolith and glimpses of a more cosmopolitan approach can be found at the same time in the writings not only of Luxemburg but also of Trotsky, both of whom offered a more serious understanding of the destructive character of modern antisemitism. In the heat of the 1905 revolution, for example, Trotsky argued that so far from antisemites being won over to the socialist cause, as the 'rational kernel' approach would suggest, they played a pivotal role in the mobilisation of counter-revolutionary forces.[26]

A critical aspect of Marx's critique of Bauer, which unorthodox Marxists struggled to recover and develop, was his recognition that antisemitism had much less to do with what Jews were doing or not doing than with how 'the Jews' were imagined. Modern antisemites had come to see the world through a lens crafted by the 'Jewish Question': in a world of nation-states, they constructed 'the Jews' as an imaginary collectivity that was a problem for – and explained the problems of – what, following Benedict Anderson's pioneering work, we now understand as an also imagined nation.[27] The problem for Marxists was on the one hand that, in regressing to Bauer's perspective, they came to assume that there was a Jewish question for such a society which needed solving; and on the other that, in abandoning cosmopolitan presuppositions, they were left with no secure basis on which to respond to a form of antisemitism which went beyond (even if it started within) a national frame of reference. At a critical moment, these parallel developments within Marxism would make it increasingly difficult to mount an effective challenge to the idea that the 'Jewish Question' was one for each national society and for each nation-state to solve.

Failing to respond to Nazi antisemitism

These twin developments set severe limits in particular on how the organized Marxist movement was to respond to the radicalisation of antisemitism by the Nazis. For what is striking is how reluctant Marxists, whether they were Social Democrats or Communists, were to confront antisemitism as such, to make it any kind of priority. This was true both before the Nazis came to power and in the underground and resistance when they had done so.

Inside Germany, the Social Democrats, as Donald Niewyk has shown, did not appear to think that Nazi antisemitism was either deeply held or serious, and decided that it did not call for specific rebuttal, rarely taking direct action on this issue.[28] After the seizure of power, the underground was instructed not to prioritize the issue, on the grounds that it would make the work of the wider resistance more difficult, recognition at least implicitly that antisemitism was more popular than they originally estimated. Klaus Mann, son of the great novelist Thomas and one of the most vigorous left-wing opponents of the Nazis, though not himself a member of the Social Democratic Party, spoke for many on the non-Communist Left when he argued (as late as 1941) that 'antisemitism has already played too predominant a part in our propaganda … it is a dangerous mistake to overemphasize this one particular angle.'[29] No specific propaganda was ever produced to challenge Nazi arguments and, as Bankier argues, the Party's attitude appears to have been a compound of distrust, resentment and fear that it would be over-identified with the Jews.

If the Social Democrats had nevertheless made some effort to cultivate good relations with the Jewish community, the Communists had a rather more problematic record. In the various twists and turns of Communist politics, there were repeated episodes in which the Party itself flirted with antisemitic discourse. In 1923 for example the acknowledged leader of the Left in the Party at the time, Ruth Fischer, made an (in)famous speech in July 1923 to students urging them 'to crush the Jewish capitalists, and hang them from the lamp posts', although she then went on to urge them to hang other capitalists too.[30] In the early 1930s, the Party (in another effort to appeal directly to Nazi followers and supporters) produced leaflets depicting Hitler (of all people) in league with Jewish capitalists.[31] As with the Social Democrats, in the underground no efforts were made to confront antisemitism.[32] It was not until *Kristallnacht* that the Party's paper *Die Rote Fahne* finally gave the issue any prominence, but by the time of that state-sponsored violence, Jews had already been systematically removed from the German economy, polity and society.

German Marxists were of course not alone in failing to respond to the growing threat of Nazi antisemitism. The cosmopolitan resources in the writings of Marx and on the margins of the Marxist movement were not drawn upon almost anywhere on the organized Left when they were most needed, as the Nazi assault moved beyond the borders of the German nation-state to encompass Jews across Europe and beyond. The problem now facing Jews, however, had to be confronted from a cosmopolitan perspective, because the threat they faced from Nazi antisemitism was to their human status, to their membership of humanity itself. Nazi antisemitism had what Saul Friedlander has called a 'redemptive' character.[33] It articulated from the outset a picture of 'the Jews' as less than fully human and as a profound danger not just to Germany but to every nation, to Europe, to the Aryan race, and to humanity itself. Only through the elimination of 'the Jews' could Germany, or any nation, or Europe, or the Aryan race or even humanity itself be redeemed, be made whole and strong again. Nazi antisemitism was fundamentally a global project. It was nurtured inside one nation-state, drawing on existing traditions that held that Jews were not and could never be fully German[34] and developing new mechanisms which (re)bonded a nation from which Jews were now systematically excluded, not least through exemplary acts of violence.[35] That project was then broadened, in the process mobilising significant other nationalist forces especially in Eastern Europe in support of a genocidal project[36], which aimed to eliminate 'the Jews' from the world and excise them not just from every nation but from humanity itself.

All too often, resistance to this assault was circumscribed within a national frame of reference which could not make what was happening to Jews such a priority. In France, for example, where significant numbers of Jews had migrated before the war, fleeing antisemitism not just in Germany but from nationalist elites and movements further East, a distinction was first made between French and 'other', 'foreign' Jews to whom the French nation had no fundamental commitment. When the French state itself began its enthusiastic collaboration with the Nazis and began attacking French Jews too, much of the damage had been done because no priority had been given on the Left to solidarity with Jews and opposition to antisemitism as such. Even when French Jews were being deported to the camps, Communists in the Resistance refused to make antisemitism a major issue. No propaganda was produced which highlighted what was being done to the Jews in France or indeed elsewhere. The Communist section of the underground press (although of course it was not unique in this) effectively organized what Blatman and Poznanski have called a 'total silence ... even when an antisemitic propaganda campaign was launched and even when it directly targeted the resistance ... [T]hroughout the occupation, the resistance spared no effort to prove that its members had not signed up to the goal of defending the Jews.'[37]

None of this is to ignore the heroism of individual rescuers of individual Jews or the courageous actions of small groups, like the Baum group in Germany.[38] What Karen Monroe has called 'the hand of compassion' was offered by many remarkable individuals and some communities to Jews in extremely demanding conditions.[39] But it is difficult to discern any common political factor in what we know of such cases, which do not appear to have been confined in any significant way to individuals on the Left. If there is a politics which was shared, it may well have been at least implicitly cosmopolitan, and on occasion explicitly so, inasmuch as it involved a solidarity with Jews precisely because they were seen first and foremost as fellow human beings. But such a cosmopolitanism did not inform the strategic response of the organized Marxist movement anywhere at this time.

The Soviet response: from downplaying antisemitism to the simultaneous charge of 'Zionism' and 'cosmopolitanism'

The strategic response of most Marxists, organized as they largely were in Communist parties was not of course devised locally. It was designed and directed from the Soviet Union, a state whose interests and commitments by definition were supposed to transcend those of the nation-state. Here the refusal to take antisemitism seriously was to have particularly disastrous consequences in the short term and alarmingly perverse ones in the longer term.

As long as the Nazi-Soviet alliance held firm, the official policy of the state was to ignore what was being done to the Jews inside German-controlled territory. The border was sealed, although not that effectively, as some Jews did manage to flee East. When the attack on the Soviet Union began in 1941, after two years in which the Jews of German-occupied Poland had been subject to extreme violence, as Ben-Cion Pinchuk has shown, 'there was no plan that took into account the special dangers facing the Jewish population.'[40]

Reporting of what was happening to the Jews now inside Soviet territory was sporadic and inconsistent at best and there were repeated efforts to diminish the scale and intensity of the violence. The first report for example that 52,000 Jews had been murdered at Babi Yar was amended down to a figure of 1000.[41] How much of this was due to rising or resurgent antisemitism inside the Soviet Union in the 1930s has been much debated but what is clear is that there was no desire to prioritize what the Nazis were doing to the Jews.[42]

It was not for another year (a year and a half, that is, after the invasion of the Soviet Union, whose orders explicitly called for the mass killing of Jews) that the Soviet Union allowed itself to be associated with the statement published jointly by all the Allied governments and governments-in-exile on 'the Extermination of the Jewish Population of Europe by Nazi Officials'.[43] As even Altman and Ingerflow (who generally downplay Stalinist antisemitism in this context) have noted: 'Neither from the Soviet state nor from the Party was there a single appeal to underground organisations or the local population to help Soviet Jews.'[44]

The regime repeatedly insisted that the war had little or nothing to do with the Jews. In 1943 a Military Council leader, for example, confidently quoted Stalin as saying that 'some comrades of Jewish descent believe that this war is being fought to save the Jewish nation. These Jews are mistaken. We fight the Great Patriotic War for the salvation, the freedom and the independence of our homeland led by the Great Russian people.'[45] A year later, as the Red Army in its sweep west was discovering what remained of the extermination camps, the Soviet Extraordinary State Commission to Investigate German-Fascist Crimes was explicitly instructed to avoid stating that the victims of the massacres had been Jews.

It is true that a Jewish anti-Fascist committee had been set up by the Soviet regime in 1942 (alongside four other anti-Fascist committees) with the objective of mobilising support in the West for the Soviet war effort. As its name implies, however, it was not primarily about fighting antisemitism but Fascism, which is not the same thing (a confusion which has wrought some considerable havoc on efforts on the Left to think about and to respond to antisemitism). The JAC did nevertheless do what it could to publicize what the Nazis were doing, with many of its members (even long-standing Party members) seizing the opportunity to speak out directly about what the Nazis were doing to the Jews and often invoking in the process not only their own suppressed identity as Jews but a longer history and sometimes personal experience of antisemitism. One of the JAC's major projects, developed in partnership with the writer Ilya Ehrenburg (another who now felt he had to assert his hitherto suppressed Jewish identity) was a detailed record of Nazi violence published in early 1946 as *The Black Book: The Nazi Crime against the Jewish People*.

But the regime had been vigilant from the outset, spying with its usual paranoid suspicion on the members of the JAC (even though it had vetted and appointed them itself) and recording all actual or potential deviations from Party orthodoxy on the 'Jewish Question' for future use. Drafts of *The Black Book* had already aroused serious concerns, precisely for its emphasis on what had been done to Jews and was hastily withdrawn in late 1947 from publication, on the grounds that it contained 'grave political errors'. All copies were destroyed, along with the type set.[46] With the defeat of the Nazis, the committee had outlived its tactical utility, and noticeably long before the other anti-Fascist committees were closed down, the JAC was targeted. The first victim was its leading activist and spokesman the playwright Solomon Mikhoels, who was mysteriously murdered, on Stalin's personal orders, in fact, in January 1948. The committee was wound up and its leaders, some of them die-hard Stalinists, were arrested, tortured and charged and (almost all) shot.[47]

The two decisive terms of the charges laid against them appear at first sight as bizarrely contradictory. The leaders of the JAC (and then many others too) were charged with Jewish nationalism and Zionism on the one hand, and cosmopolitanism on the other. The apparent contradiction between the two charges was much less important, however, than what connected them: connotations of disloyalty, lack of patriotism, foreignness and, not least, worldwide Jewish conspiracy. Both charges flowed from accommodation to (in this instance, Russian) nationalism and both signified a further abandonment of Marx's cosmopolitan ways of thinking.

The charge of Jewish nationalism rested for its part on a selective nationalism which again claimed to distinguish between progressive and reactionary forms. Since the Jews could not constitute a nation according to Stalin's arbitrary criteria, then no progressive Jewish nationalism could exist. To think or speak otherwise was to threaten the cohesion and unity of the nations amongst whom Jews were dispersed and into which they were supposed to assimilate and disappear. The charge of Zionism demonstrated the supposed disloyalty of the Jews, not only clinging on to an identity they should have long foresworn when they were permitted to become members of the nation, but also implying a solidarity with other Jews which cut across the borders of the nation-state and superseded the primacy of the loyalty which nationalists demanded.

The charge of cosmopolitanism for its part was also premised on the primacy of national loyalty. The phrase 'rootless cosmopolitan Jew' was first cousin, as it were, to cognate terms like 'enemy of the people' or indeed 'enemy of the human species', which had emerged as tensions between democratic and nationalist logics began to come to the fore during the French Revolution.[48] During the Terror, the Jacobins had commonly laid the charge *hostis generis humani* against those they accused not only of counter-revolution, but also of betraying the French nation, whose interests were increasingly elided with those of humanity as a whole. A similar elision now occurred in the Soviet Union, where the particular (primarily Russian) national interests of the state were said to correspond with the interests of the world proletariat, and the interests of the world proletariat in turn to correspond with the interests of humanity in general.

Marx's sharp critique of the chauvinism lying behind Bauer's apparent universalism was now buried and indeed the very terms he used were inverted. As one loyal Stalinist put it: 'Cosmopolitanism is an ideology alien to the workers. Communism has nothing in common with cosmopolitanism.' Another described cosmopolitanism as 'a false, senseless, strange and incomprehensible phenomenon'. The cosmopolitan 'is a corrupt, unfeeling creature, totally unworthy of being called by the holy name of man'.[49]

Rethinking the question of antisemitism

These charges of course went beyond a further failure to think about antisemitism. They formed the basis of what was itself a distinctive contribution to the post-Holocaust repertoire of antisemitism (by no means confined to the Soviet Union), in which a new set of contradictory charges against Jews replaced the Nazi accusation that Jews were somehow responsible for both capitalism and Communism.

The question that arises here however is whether development like this was inevitable or if there was another potential path from Marx that could have been or needs to be developed. Those who think that Marx was himself an antisemite would, of course, have no hesitation in answering in the affirmative to the first hypothesis. Even many of those who are not convinced by this charge would argue that there is nothing in Marxism that provides the basis for an adequate response to the question of antisemitism. But they typically also assert that the reasons for this particular failure lie in a deeper failure – to understand the significance of nationalism and national identity, along with other non-class-based commitments and identities.[50]

The argument here has been different. It is that the adaptation of too many Marxists to nationalism, and the concession to the primacy of national identity, is itself an important reason for this failure. What I also want to suggest, in the concluding part of this article, that what is distinctive in Marx's own response to antisemitism and in his simultaneous response to nationalism, provides the basis for an alternative approach, which has been largely neglected. This alternative approach moreover was in fact taken up by some very important thinkers working on the margins of the Marxist tradition, or influenced by the cosmopolitan tradition within it, as they were forced to confront the Nazi radicalisation of antisemitism. It was this very radicalisation which forced them into a profound and essentially cosmopolitan rethinking of how antisemitism had developed and what was needed to respond to it.

I refer in particular here to the rethinking undertaken in the 1940s by the leading figures of the Frankfurt School, Max Horkheimer and Theodor Adorno, as news of the extermination of the Jews began to reach them. Even though their own work in every other respect was far more sophisticated and critical than anything produced at the time by other Marxists, especially those trapped within the dogmas of the Second and Third International, they had shared in the failure to take Nazi antisemitism seriously, and to give it any priority. Despite the fact that all the leading figures in the School were Jews themselves, they did not appear to think for a long time that this was of any relevance to their work as Marxists or that Marxism need concern itself in any significant way with antisemitism.[51] They were not of course alone in this. The universalist commitments which inspired many Jews to commit to the Social Democratic and (perhaps even more so) the Communist movements left little space for thinking about the dangers posed by antisemitism even or perhaps especially to themselves. There was a widespread tendency to think that they would be targeted primarily or exclusively as leftists not as Jews. (This was not true of course for members of the Bund or Marxist Zionists who did place a much greater priority on fighting antisemitism, although in both cases they too were to be disappointed to a greater or lesser extent by the weakness of a cosmopolitan response from their respective non-Jewish comrades).[52]

Horkheimer had produced one of the School's few works on the question only in 1938, five years after the Nazis had come to power, and two years after the Nuremberg laws had stripped Jews of their citizenship. In the course of what was in many respects a somewhat crude and reductionist analysis of the role of Jews in the economy, where they were assigned a central but now apparently doomed historical role as 'agents of circulation', Horkheimer claimed that Nazi antisemitism was only a temporary phenomenon, 'at most ... a safety valve for the younger members of the SA'.[53] This view was widely shared by his colleagues and, as late as 1942, Franz Neumann, who was the School's acknowledged expert on Nazism, insisted in *Behemoth* (his major work on the subject) that Nazi antisemitism was not important in its own right but only the means to another end, a 'spearhead of terror', which could be used or discarded to fit the needs of the day. At the very moment the extermination camps were becoming fully operative, Neumann insisted that 'the Nazis will never allow a complete extermination of the Jews'.[54]

To his considerable credit, Horkheimer then revised his own views and with Adorno rethought his entire approach to the question, an essential component of which was the adoption of a cosmopolitan perspective. It was not just that Horkheimer had come to realize, as he wrote to Marcuse, that 'the problem of antisemitism is much more complicated than I thought.'[55] It was that he now saw it as 'the focal point of injustice ... where the world shows its most horrible face'.[56] 'Whoever accuses the Jews today aims straight at humanity itself. The Jews have become the martyrs of civilisation ... To protect the Jews has come to be a symbol of everything mankind stands for. The Jews have been made what the Nazis always pretended they were – the focal point of world history.'[57]

Adorno emphatically agreed. 'Antisemitism is today really the central injustice, and our form of physiognomy must attend to the world where it shows its face at its most gruesome.'[58] They had now come to think that 'just as it is true that one can only understand antisemitism by examining society, it is becoming equally true that society itself can now only be understood through antisemitism.'[59]

They now devoted considerable attention to the history of antisemitism, first laying out a wide-ranging research agenda for tracing its genealogy going back to the first Crusades[60] and then going even deeper in their major work of this period, *Dialectic of Enlightenment*. The chapter on 'Elements of Antisemitism' formed not only the last section of the work but was, as Dana Villa has argued, the culmination of the overall argument.[61]

There is no space to go into this in any detail but what does bear emphasising here is the cosmopolitan vantage point that Adorno and Horkheimer adopted: that the history of antisemitism is intimately bound up with the history of humanity. What was projected on to the Jews, they argued, could tell us a great deal not about Jews but about tensions and contradictions inside society, about what could and could not be tolerated, about the nature and limits of civilisation, and ultimately how an unprecedented form of barbarism became possible. Going further than Luxemburg, they now saw barbarism not simply as relapse but something worse, something which changed the conditions of human existence and, in this context, the prospects for socialism at least for some time.

A crucial aspect of this argument has to do with difference and particularity, the very problem that lay at the heart of constructions of the so-called 'Jewish Question'. What Adorno and Horkheimer argued connected all the elements was an anxiety and intolerance of that particularity that could take different forms at different times, sometimes religious, sometimes economic, sometimes social, but which were most effectively channelled and institutionally 'embodied' in a nationalist framework.[62]

What they also insisted on was the need for any conception of society to allow for difference within an overall conception of humanity itself. From that perspective, the particular identity of Jews was not a threat or a problem for society (in the modern world, primarily the nation) but the opposite. It was not so much (or only) that they pointed to the contribution that Jews (and indeed Judaism) had made to the development of civilisation, or that every form of antisemitism was fundamentally destructive, but that they saw the particularity principle represented by Jews as a necessary and fundamentally cosmopolitan principle. The attack on Jews was, at root, an attack on diversity.

Back to and beyond Marx

This does not take us simply back to Marx but to his starting point. Marx does not develop to any significant extent a cosmopolitan sense of the diversity of humanity, though he was repeatedly critical of efforts to flatten out difference (notably in his Critique of the Gotha Programme), but he does reject any argument that singles out Jewish particularity as a problem. What Adorno and Horkheimer were doing was taking this rejection seriously and trying to think through its implications, both for the Jews and for humanity as a whole. They understood antisemitism in quite a rich and complex way as both an attack on a particular group *and* as an attack on humanity itself. A failure to respond to antisemitism was at the same time a failure to protect humanity, which would be irretrievably damaged by the annihilation of its Jewish element.

The damage was already very great of course. The Holocaust had destroyed a large percentage of Jews in the world, removed a Jewish presence from many nations who were now much more homogeneous than they had been before. It had proved possible to murder large numbers of people through the agency and apparatuses of a modern nation-state, with the willing collaboration of many fellow citizens and the passive compliance of many more. What had been scarcely imagined as a possibility even by the most vehement antisemites had now become a reality.

The Holocaust was a radical event in the history of both antisemitism and humanity which called for a radical response. Since Jews had not been protected within the nation-states across which they had been dispersed, new ways of thinking and new kinds of commitment were necessary which were in Horkheimer and Adorno's minds essentially cosmopolitan, because (like Marx) they were grounded in a normative commitment to the human community.

They were not alone, it has to be said, in coming to this conclusion at this critical time. Hannah Arendt, for all the differences she had with Horkheimer and (especially) Adorno, had been rethinking along similar lines. If she was not working within the Marxist tradition, she was arguably significantly influenced here by one Marxist in particular: Rosa Luxemburg.[63] Like Luxemburg, Arendt had identified a major problem with nationalism, in particular the way in which minorities who were dispersed across nation-states were placed in acute danger by a conception of rights which confined them only to those deemed to be loyal and worthy subjects of homogenising nation-states. Jews were especially vulnerable in this context, attacked as unreliable, as a source of corruption and (because they were supposedly purely self-interested) of division and decomposition.[64]

The solution proposed by Arendt on the one hand and Adorno and Horkheimer on the other was, as Seyla Benhabib has also suggested, fundamentally cosmopolitan[65], but it was also new. In having to think more deeply about antisemitism, they rethought our understanding of humanity, of the universal, as inherently diverse, as including particularity within it. This rethinking or development of cosmopolitanism was more than conceptual; it also carried with it a clear normative commitment to a solidarity across the boundaries of the nation-state with any group threatened with destruction in whole or in part. Or, to make it more concrete, with genocide, the crime after all that the radicalized antisemitism of the Nazis had visited upon the Jews, a crime which by its very nature required a cosmopolitan response.

Such a response was largely not forthcoming from one of the few sources from which it might have been mounted, the organized Marxist movement which by then had largely (though not completely) turned its back on the cosmopolitan principles originally espoused by Marx and on a (connected) understanding of antisemitism as a mortal threat *both* to Jews *and* to humanity itself. As that threat was realized in the Holocaust, there was some effort to retrieve and develop both these cosmopolitan principles and that understanding of antisemitism, albeit an effort that is by no means complete. To the extent to which antisemitism even after the Holocaust continues to pose a significant threat to Jews and to humanity itself, the history of how those principles and that understanding were both shaped and abandoned remains relevant. Even if the organized Marxist movement may no longer provide the kind of central focus it might once have done, there are still resources which can be quarried from that history for those who seek to develop a more adequate cosmopolitan response to such a threat.

Notes

1. Beck, "What Is Globalization;" Chernilo, "Social Theory's Methodological Nationalism."
2. Ingram, *Radical Cosmopolitics*. Ingram himself seems to think of this as only a recent development (which perhaps says something about how this tradition has disappeared from view).
3. Held, "Principles of Cosmopolitan Order," 12–13.

4. See the discussion in Derrida, *Cosmopolitanism and Forgiveness*, 15.
5. Ibid., 21.
6. For a thoughtful analysis of how these tensions expressed themselves in nineteenth-century Germany, see Stoetzler, *The State, the Nation and the Jews*. Stoetzler's argument is in many ways a systematic elaboration of insights first propounded by Adorno and Horkheimer, to whose cosmopolitan alternative we return in the concluding section of this article.
7. See in particular the recent study by David Nirenberg, *Anti-Judaism*.
8. Pierre Birnbaum, *Jewish Destinies*, chapter 1, "A Jacobin Regenerator: Abbé Grégoire," 11–30.
9. Achcar, *Marxism*.
10. From their critique of Friedrich List, the leading contemporary exponent of nationalism in economic theory (Marx and Engels 1976, 280). John Hall has tellingly described List as "the Marx of nationalism" (Hall 1998, 31).
11. Marx and Engels, *Communist Manifesto*, 6 (my emphasis).
12. Benner, *Really Existing Nationalisms*, 11 (my emphasis).
13. Langeswiehe, "Germany and the National Question."
14. On Marx's distinctive position at this time, see Hughes, *Nationalism and Society*.
15. Traverso, *Marxists and the Jewish Question*, 135.
16. Luxemburg, *The National Question*.
17. Shelton, "Rosa Luxemburg and the National Question."
18. Luxemburg, "The Junius Brochure," 269.
19. This extension is explored more fully in Spencer, "From Rosa Luxemburg."
20. For a good discussion on the homogenising policies of newly independent nation-states after the war, see Brubaker, *Nationalism Reframed*.
21. Birnbaum, *Geography of Hope*.
22. Fine, "Rereading Marx."
23. Fischer, *Socialist Response*.
24. See Pulzer, *Political Antisemitism*.
25. The formulation is often attributed to Bebel but it has been suggested that the term originated not with him but with an Austrian liberal, Ferdinand Kronawetter. See Jack Jacobs, *On Socialists and "the Jewish Question" after Marx*, chapter 2, "Eduard Bernstein: After All. A German Jew." Bebel was himself not entirely happy with the use of the term socialism in this context. In an interview conducted with Hermann Bahr in 1894, he expressed some reservations about this formulation, noting that if some workers encountered Jews as small capitalists, most Jews were themselves, especially in the East, workers or peasants, and that most Germans knew nothing about Jews at all. Hermann Bahr, "Der Antisemitismus- ein internationales interview" in Pias, *Hermann Bahr*. I am grateful to Olaf Kistenmacher for alerting me to this caveat.
26. Norman Geras has highlighted Trotsky's intuitions at this time and linked them to his later prediction in 1938 that, in the event of another war, the Nazis would attempt the annihilation of the Jews, a prediction made by no other political activists or thinker on the Left (or indeed anywhere else) at the time (Geras, *Contract*, 139, 159).
27. Anderson, *Imagined Communities*.
28. Niewyk, *Socialist, Anti-Semite and Jew*.
29. Cited by Bankier, "German Social Democrats and the Jewish Question," 521.
30. Quoted in Daycock, *KPD and NSDAP*. Fischer was not alone in using such language at this time. For further examples, including a speech by Herman Remmele, another prominent KPD figure, attacking Jewish cattle-dealers in Stuttgart in similar terms, see Conan Fischer, *German Communists*, 59–60.
31. On the overlap between Communist and Nazi propaganda on this issue, see Brown, *Weimar Radicals*.
32. The systematic silence of the Communist Party is discussed in some detail in Herf, "German Communism."
33. Friedländer, *The Years of Extermination*.
34. See in particular Schmidt, *The Continuities of German History*.

35. On the remaking of the nation, see Wildt, *Hitler's Volksgemeinschaft,* and on the violence Kühne, *Belonging and Genocide.*
36. On the ways in which the Nazis mobilized and legitimated unprecedented levels of antisemitic violence by other nationalists, see Kallis, *Genocide and Fascism.*
37. Blatman and Poznanski, "Jews and their Social Environment," 201.
38. The scale (and limits) of this resistance is analysed carefully in Cox, *Circles.*
39. Monroe, *The Hand of Compassion.*
40. Pinchuk, "Soviet Policy," 55.
41. Lustiger, *Stalin and the Jews,* 106.
42. The arguments have been carefully rehearsed by Harvey Asher, who concludes that Soviet policy was not so different to that of their Allies in some ways but that it was inflected both by what he calls a "culture of antisemitism" and by Soviet nationality policy in general ("The Soviet Union, the Holocaust and Auschwitz," 44). As Timothy Snyder has reminded us, this had had quite murderous consequences for some years, notably as a crucial factor in the Holodomor in Ukraine (Snyder, *Bloodlands*). As far as Jews were concerned, even if they were not the only victims of Stalin's paranoid suspicions of Ukrainians, Poles and many others, the number of Jews who had been killed because they were Jews by the regime by the end of the 1930s was actually far greater than those killed inside Nazi Germany by that moment in time.
43. Dan Plesch (*America, Hitler and the UN*) has recently brought the significance of this document back to our attention, arguing convincingly that it lay the foundation in many ways for the creation of the United Nations, and that the participation of all the Allies in publicising the document was a major step. But the Soviet Union did not lead from the front on this issue.
44. Quoted in Asher, "Soviet Union," 44.
45. Quoted in Lustiger, *Stalin,* 108.
46. Gitelman, "Politics and the Historiography of the Holocaust," 119.
47. On the appalling treatment of the members of the JAC, see Rubenstein and Naumov, *Stalin's Secret Pogrom.*
48. See the discussion of the different logics in Spencer and Wollman, *Nationalism,* 127–31.
49. Quoted in Pinkus and Frankel, *The Soviet Union and the Jews,* 152, 154.
50. This is Traverso's conclusion for example in *The Marxists and the Jews.*
51. Not all the members of the School of course were Jews, but all its leading members were, and according to Jack Jacobs, those few who were not could, at times, feel themselves somewhat excluded from the inner circle. Adorno's father was Jewish but his mother was not and he does not seem to have been brought up (unlike the others) with any sense of himself as Jewish. He was indeed for a time convinced that he could and should stay in Nazi Germany when all the others had fled. On the other hand, he turned out to be more alert to the dangers facing than the others and played a decisive role in helping Horkheimer reorient his entire approach and together to place antisemitism at the centre of their concerns. See Jacobs, *The Frankfurt School, Jewish Lives and Antisemitism,* especially 2–3, and 54–60.
52. The Polish Bund was part of the Socialist International, to which the German Social Democrats, whose difficulties we have briefly rehearsed, also belonged. The most significant Marxist Zionist group to consider in this context was probably Hashomer Hatzair, which sought (with growing difficulty) to combine Zionism with support for the Soviet Union, with mounting difficulty. On Hashomer Hatzair's efforts to deal with some of the contradictions here, see Kollat, "Marxist Zionism."
53. Horkheimer, "The Jews and Europe," 92.
54. Neumann, *Behemoth,* 125.
55. Horkheimer, *Gesammelte Schriften,* 17: 463–4.
56. Cited in Rabinbach, *The Cunning of Unreason,* 53.
57. Horkheimer, *A Life in Letters,* 223.
58. Quoted in Wiggershaus, *Frankfurt School,* 309.
59. Quoted in ibid., 690.
60. Horkheimer and Adorno, "A Research Project on Anti-Semitism."
61. Villa, "Arendt, Adorno and Auschwitz," 24.

62. Horkheimer and Adorno, *Dialectic of Enlightenment*, 176.
63. On the connection with Luxemburg in this respect in particular, see Spencer, *Luxemburg, Arendt*. Arendt's biographer, Elisabeth Young-Bruehl has also noted the importance of this connection in *Hannah Arendt: For Love of the World*, 399.
64. Some of the projections onto Jews which Arendt identified here match and indeed may be best understood by the categories Horkheimer and Adorno deployed in *Dialectic of Enlightenment*. These are discussed in very interesting ways by Carolyn Dean in her careful reflections on how difficult it was for intellectuals on the Left as much as the right to acknowledge the specificity of what had happened to the Jews. See her *Aversion and Erasure*, especially the concluding section.
65. Benhabib, "From 'The Dialectic of Enlightenment' to 'The Origins of Totalitarianism.'"

References

Achcar, Gilbert. *Marxism*. London: Saqi Books, 2013.
Anderson, Benedict. *Imagined Communities*. London: Verso, 1991.
Asher, Harvey. "The Soviet Union, the Holocaust and Auschwitz." In *The Holocaust in the East: Local Perpetrators and Soviet Responses*, edited by Michael David-Fox, Peter Holquist, and Alexander M. Martin, 29–50. Pittsburgh: University of Pittsburgh Press, 2014.
Bahr, Hermann. "Der Antisemitismus- ein internationales interview." In *Hermann Bahr: Kritische Schriften*, edited by Claus Pias, 3: 21–24. Accessed December 15, 2015. www.univie.ac.at/bahr/node/83302
Bankier, David. "German Social Democrats and the Jewish Question." In *Probing the Depths of German Anti-Semitism: German Society and the Persecution of the Jews 1933–1941*, edited by David Bankier, 511–532. Oxford: Berghahn, 2000.
Beck. Ulrich. *What Is Globalization?* Cambridge: Polity Press, 2000.
Benhabib, Seyla. "From 'The Dialectic of Enlightenment' to 'The Origins of Totalitarianism' and the Genocide Convention: Adorno and Horkheimer in the Company of Arendt and Lemkin." In *The Modernist Imagination: Intellectual History and Critical Theory*, edited by Warren Breckman, Peter E. Gordon, A. Dirk Moses, Samuel Moyn, and Elliot Neaman, 299–330. New York: Berghahn, 2008.
Benner, Erica. *Really Existing Nationalisms: a Post-Communist View from Marx and Engels*. Oxford: Oxford University Press, 1995.
Birnbaum, Pierre. *Jewish Destinies: Citizenship, State, and Community in Modern France*. New York: Hill and Wang, 2000.
Birnbaum, Pierre. *Geography of Hope: Exile, the Enlightenment, Disassimilation*. Stanford: Stanford University Press, 2008.
Blatman, Daniel, and Renée Poznanski. "Jews and their Social Environment: Perspectives from the Underground Press in Poland and France." In *Facing the Catastrophe: Jews and Non-Jews in Europe during World War Two*, edited by Beata Kosmala and Georgi Verbeeck, 159–228. Oxford: Berg, 2011.
Brown, Timothy. *Weimar Radicals: Nazis and Communists between Authenticity and Performance*. New York: Berghahn, 2009.
Brubaker, Rogers. *Nationalism Reframed: Nationalism and the National Question in the New Europe*. Cambridge: Cambridge University Press, 1996.
Chernilo, Daniel. "Social Theory's Methodological Nationalism: Myth and Reality." *European Journal of Social Theory* 9, no. 1 (2006): 5–22.

Cox, John. *Circles of Resistance: Jewish, Leftist, and Youth Dissidence in Nazi Germany.* Bern: Peter Lang, 2009.

Daycock, Davis W. *The KPD and the NSDAP: A Study of the Relationship between Political Extremes in Weimar Germany, 1923–1933.* PhD diss. London School of Economics, 1980.

Dean, Carolyn. *Aversion and Erasure: The Fate of the Victim after the Holocaust.* Ithaca, NY: Cornell University Press, 2010.

Derrida, Jacques. *Cosmopolitanism and Forgiveness.* London: Routledge, 2001.

Fine, Robert. "Rereading Marx on the 'Jewish Question.'" In *Antisemitism and the Constitution of Sociology*, edited by Marcel Stoetzler, 137–159. Lincoln: University of Nebraska Press, 2013.

Fischer, Conan. *The German Communists and the Rise of Nazism.* Basingstoke: Macmillan, 1990.

Fischer, Lars. *The Socialist Response to Antisemitism in Imperial Germany.* Cambridge: Cambridge University Press, 2007.

Friedländer, Saul. *The Years of Extermination: Nazi Germany and the Jews, 1939–1945.* London: Weidenfeld & Nicolson, 2007.

Geras, Norman. *The Contract of Mutual Indifference.* London: Verso, 1998.

Gitelman, Zvi. "Politics and the Historiography of the Holocaust in the Soviet Union." In *Bitter Legacy: Confronting the Holocaust in the USSR*, edited by Zvi Gitelman, 14–42. Bloomington: Indian University Press, 1997.

Hall, John. *The State of the Nation: Ernest Gellner and the Theory of Nationalism.* Cambridge: Cambridge University Press, 1998.

Held, David. "Principles of Cosmopolitan Order." In *The Political Philosophy of Cosmopolitanism*, edited by Gillian Brock and Harry Brighouse, 10–28. Cambridge: Cambridge University Press, 2005.

Herf, Jeffrey. "German Communism, the Discourse of 'anti-Fascist' Resistance and the Jewish Catastrophe." In *Resistance Against the Third Reich*, edited by Michael Geyer and John Boyer, 257–294. Chicago: Chicago University Press, 1994.

Horkheimer, Max. "The Jews and Europe." In *Critical Theory and Society*, edited by Stephen Eric Bronner and Douglas Kellner, 77–94. London: Routledge, 1989.

Horkheimer, Max. *Gesammelte Schriften*, vol. 17, *Briefwechsel 1941–48*. Edited by Gunzelin Schmid Noerr. Frankfurt am Main: Fischer, 1996.

Horkheimer, Max. *A Life in Letters- Selected Correspondence.* Translated and edited by Manfred R. Jacobson and Evelyn M. Jacobson. Lincoln and London: University of Nebraska Press, 2007.

Horkheimer, Max, and Theodor. W. Adorno. "Research Project on Anti-Semitism." *Studies in Philosophy and Social Science* 9, no. (1941): 124–143.

Horkheimer, Max, and Theodor. W. Adorno. *Dialectic of Enlightenment.* London: Allen Lane, 1973.

Hughes, Michael. *Nationalism and Society – Germany 1800–1945.* London: Edward Arnold, 1988.

Ingram, James D. *Radical Cosmopolitics – The Ethics and Practice of Democratic Universalism.* New York: Columbia University Press, 2013.

Jacobs, Jack. *On Socialists and the, Jewish Question after Marx.* New York: New York University Press, 1992.

Jacobs, Jack. *The Frankfurt School, Jewish Lives and Antisemitism.* Cambridge: Cambridge University Press, 2015.

Kallis, Aristotle. *Genocide and Fascism – The Eliminationist Drive in Fascist Europe.* London: Routledge, 2009.

Kollat, Israel. "Marxist Zionism." In *Varieties of Marxism*, edited by Shlomo Avineri, 227–270. The Hague: Martinus Nijhoff, 1977.

Kühne, Thomas. *Belonging and Genocide: Hitler's Community, 1918–1945.* New Haven: Yale University Press, 2010.

Langesweihe, Dieter. "Germany and the National Question." In *The State of Germany: The National Idea in the Making, Unmaking and Remaking*, edited by John Breuilly, 60–79. London: Longman, 1992.

Lustiger, Arno. *Stalin and the Jews: the Red Book – the Tragedy of the Jewish Anti- Fascist Committee and the Soviet Jews.* New York: Enigma, 2003.

Luxemburg, Rosa. "The Junius Pamphlet – the Crisis in German Social Democracy." In *Rosa Luxemburg Speaks*, edited by Mary-Alice Waters, 257–331. New York: Pathfinder, 1970.

Luxemburg, Rosa. *The National Question*. Edited by Horace B. Davis. New York: Monthly Review Press, 1976.

Marx, Karl, and Friedrich Engels. "Critique of List." In *Collected Works*, by Karl Marx and Friedrich Engels, vol. 4. London: Lawrence and Wishart, 1976.

Marx, Karl, and Friedrich Engels. "Manifesto of the Communist Party." In *Collected Works*, by Karl Marx and Friedrich Engels, vol. 6. London: Lawrence and Wishart, 1976.

Monroe, Karen. *The Hand of Compassion: Portraits of Moral Choice during the Holocaust*. Princeton: Princeton University Press, 2004.

Neumann, Franz. *Behemoth: the Structure and Practice of National Socialism*. London: V. Gollancz, 1942.

Niewyk, Donald. *Socialist, Anti-Semite and Jew – German Social Democracy Confronts the Problem of Anti-Semitism, 1918–1933*. Baton Rouge: Louisiana State University, 1971.

Nirenberg, David. *Anti-Judaism: the Western Tradition*. New York: W. W. Norton & Company, 2013.

Pias, Claus, ed. *Hermann Bahr: Kritische Schriften*, 3: 21–24. Accessed December 15, 2015. www.univie.ac.at/bahr/node/83302

Pinchuk, Ben-Cion. "Was There a Soviet Policy for Evacuating the Jews? The Case of the Annexed Territories." *Slavic Review* 39, no. 1 (1980): 44–55.

Pinkus, Benjamin, and Jonathan Frankel. *The Soviet Union and the Jews, 1948–67*. Cambridge: Cambridge University Press, 1984.

Plesch, Dan. *America, Hitler and the UN*. London: I.B. Tauris, 2011.

Pulzer, Peter. *The Rise of Political Anti-Semitism in Germany and Austria*. Harvard: Harvard University Press, 1988.

Rabinbach, Anson. "The Cunning of Unreason – Mimesis and the Construction of Antisemitism in Horkheimer and Adorno's *Dialectic of Enlightenment*." In *In the Shadow of Catastrophe – German Intellectuals between Apocalypse and Enlightenment*, edited by Anson Rabinbach, 166–198. Berkeley: University of California Press, 2001.

Rubenstein, Joshua, and Vladimir P. Naumov. *Stalin's Secret Pogrom: The Postwar inquisition of the Jewish Anti-Fascist Committee*. New Haven, CT: Yale University Press, 2001.

Schmidt, Helmut Walser. *The Continuities of German History: Nation, Religion, and Race Across the Long Nineteenth Century*. Cambridge: Cambridge University Press, 2008.

Shelton, Anita. "Rosa Luxemburg and the National Question." *East European Quarterly* 21, no. 3 (1987): 297–303.

Snyder, Timothy. *Bloodlands: Europe between Hitler and Stalin*. London: Bodley Head, 2010.

Spencer, Philip. "From Rosa Luxemburg to Hannah Arendt: Socialism, Barbarism and the Extermination Camps." *The European Legacy* 11, no. 5 (2006): 527–540.

Spencer, Philip, and Howard Wollman. "Good and Bad Nationalisms: a Critique of Dualism." *Journal of Political Ideologies* 3 (1998): 255–274.

Stoetzler, Marcel. *The State, the Nation and the Jews – Liberalism and the Antisemitism Dispute in Bismarck's Germany*. Lincoln: University of Nebraska Press, 2008.

Traverso, Enzo. *The Marxists and the Jewish Question*. New York: Humanities Press, 1994.

Wiggershaus, Rolf. *The Frankfurt School: its History, Theories, and Political Significance*. Cambridge: Polity Press, 1994.

Wildt, Michael. *Hitler's Volksgemeinschaft and the Dynamics of Racial Exclusion – Violence against Jews in Provincial Germany 1919–1939*. Oxford: Berghahn, 2012.

Villa, Dana. "Arendt, Adorno and Auschwitz – Genealogies of Total Domination." *New German Critique* 34, no. 1 (2007): 1–45.

Young-Bruehl, Elisabeth. *Hannah Arendt: For Love of the World*. New Haven: Yale University Press, 1982.

JEWS, COSMOPOLITANISM AND POLITICAL THOUGHT

New futures, new pasts: Horace M. Kallen and the contribution of Jewishness to the future

Jakob Egholm Feldt

ABSTRACT
Early in the twentieth century, American philosopher and educator Horace M. Kallen (1882–1974) constructed a cultural philosophy under the headline Cultural Pluralism. This philosophy was intended to have cosmopolitan effects in the sense that it had global ecumenical concerns for the social hope for all. Nevertheless, Kallen avoided the concept of cosmopolitanism because of the deep controversy over Jews and Jewishness entangled in the history of cosmopolitan thought since the Enlightenment. As an alternative, Kallen re-invented a new Jewish past to suit a future when Jewishness could be a model attitude for living in cosmopolis. This article shows how and why cosmopolitanism has been a problematic idea for Jewish thinkers such as Kallen, and it demonstrates how Kallen's early-twentieth-century ideas of Cultural Pluralism in many ways constitute a postcolonial cosmopolitanism *avant la lettre*.

Introduction

In this article I will discuss how American philosopher and educator Horace M. Kallen (1882–1974) constructed a new Jewish past to promote a pragmatist vision of the future that included what he saw as a social hope for all.[1] Kallen developed a philosophy of Cultural Pluralism that was explicitly concerned with the future living-together of different nations, but he distinguished his thought from cosmopolitanism due to its Hellene and Kantian history. I will investigate how Kallen's pluralist thought of the early twentieth century speaks to the contemporary plethora of cosmopolitanisms, and how Jewishness figured in his thought as a central resource for a future universe. My unfolding of Kallen's pluralism will emphasize history as the pool of experiences, or *Erfahrungsraum* in the words of Reinhart Koselleck, from which futures grow.[2] So even if it might seem as though cosmopolitan thought from Kant until today is about the future, cosmopolitan thought is equally about the past. It is also about which histories and which experiences appear conducive for the future of cosmopolitanism.[3]

Before analysing Kallen's pluralism, I will begin by outlining a few distinctions in cosmopolitan thought with particular relevance for my study. It is by no means an exhaustive review of the rich and growing body of cosmopolitan literature but it still reflects significant divisions between types of cosmopolitanism in today's debates. For my purposes here, it is particularly interesting how different types of cosmopolitanism enlist Jews and Jewishness for the cosmopolitan cause, or the opposite. This controversy over the potentials of Jewishness for future civility has ensued at least since the Enlightenment. As we will see, Kallen and other Jewish thinkers contributed significantly to what many today would call cosmopolitan thought but as cosmopolitan critics of cosmopolitanism. To Kallen and other Jewish thinkers, the particulars inside cosmopolitanism were 'Athens' and Christianity. When we seek to understand how and why cosmopolitanism has been a deeply problematic idea for Jews such as Kallen, on the one hand, and often outlined as a very Jewish idea on the other, it is necessary to go into some detail with these trajectories in cosmopolitan thought. In the recent blooming of cosmopolitan literature, this deep historical controversy of Jews and Jewishness *vis-à-vis* future global civility has largely been forgotten.[4]

Kantian cosmopolitanism, history and Jews

As remarked by Robert Fine, it seems like the cosmopolitan vision is more about the future than it is about the past.[5] The past appears less important to cosmopolitan thought than it appears to nationalism. Nationalists might talk a lot about the past and cosmopolitans about the present and the future, but since the Enlightenment and the beginning of modern cosmopolitanism, cosmopolitans have nevertheless been intensely occupied with history. When interpreting Kant's two seminal texts on cosmopolitanism ('Idea for a Universal History with a Cosmopolitan Perspective' [1784] and 'To Perpetual Peace. A Philosophical Sketch' [1795])[6], emphasis is often on how he envisioned that the global polis should be managed by international regulation, an international council and anchored by a principle of hospitality – and much less on what idea of history his visions rested on.[7] Kant could not see his cosmopolitan vision become true without a universal, progressive historical teleology. This means that Kantian cosmopolitanism is dependent on seeing the world as a unified time-space where it is possible to follow historically the evolution of the human spirit: the spirit of universal civility.[8] If we with Kant look at cosmopolitanism as the gradual progressive evolution of reason towards a universal, global common sense manifested in *a priori* givens such as 'natural law' and 'natural religion', then history's purpose is to rid us of historical burdens that are not compatible with universal civility.[9] Kant's cosmopolitanism is not a pluralist project. It is embroiled in a progressive, universal history by which men gradually develop their civilisational stages towards the end of history, which is a perpetual peace managed by a federation of free, republican states.[10] Accordingly, Kantian cosmopolitanism knows the end goal of human history (which is a global civil society); it knows the tools, and it knows the distinctions between the civilized and the non-civilized it knows those on the right path and those on the wrong. Kant did not think of his cosmopolitan vision as a pragmatic best-practice way to handle existing and coming conditions of life but as a definite plan of nature.[11]

To Kant, cosmopolitanism is a duty because it corresponds with nature's purpose for man to develop over the generations towards more advanced stages of civilisation. This purpose cannot be found in individual man, but in the species as a whole. Men are simply too short lived to envelop the grand purpose of the nature of humankind, but if a universal history is to be discernable, and indeed possible, at all, it must be organized along certain sets of propositions.[12] Among these propositions is that every creature's natural predispositions are destined to develop fully in accordance with their purpose. In Kant's words: 'An organ that is not meant to be used, or an arrangement that does not achieve its purpose, is a contradiction to the teleological theory of nature.'[13] If we do not accept this principle, we cannot understand history, says Kant. Then we are left with playing aimlessly and with a dismal reign of chance. When writing about Judaism, Kant was convinced that Judaism did not belong to the religion of reason. He did not believe that Judaism was such a useful organ in the world body included in the teleological theory of nature.[14] In Kant's view, Judaism was amoral and accordingly did not carry with it the potential of cosmopolitan duty. The amorality of Judaism derives from it being a polity more than a true religion. The Jews follow their god as a despot, as a set of statuary laws that leave no room for morality and freedom.[15]

Kant, Lessing, Dohm and other prominent Enlighteners advocated equal civil rights for Jews across Europe but what Miriam Leonard calls 'their Christian triumphalism' remained a problem for Jewish Enlighteners and reformers such as Moses Mendelssohn and later for both Moses Hess and Horace M. Kallen.[16] In a nutshell, the problem was that Jews and Jewishness were irrelevant for this historical and future vision. Individual Jews would have a place equal to other citizens but the qualities of Judaism and Jewishness were considered particular and historical, and thus fundamentally a pollution of the envisioned civility.[17] The history of the civil spirit went from Athens to Rome, from Rome to Christianity, and from Christianity to universality leaving Judaism as relics of history and Jews as living fossils. Though the cosmopolitanism of Kant and other Enlightenment reformers included equality for the Jews it also included a wished-for death of Judaism and Jewishness if perpetual peace were to be reached. The controversy for the Jewish enlighteners was not about laws, rights and the international management of hospitality, but about the scheme of historical progression that scandalized Jewishness in the civil sphere, in cosmopolis.[18]

Sociological cosmopolitanism and diversity

Jewishness lends itself more easily to cosmopolitan perspectives if we accept Yuri Slezkine's and others' 'Jewishness equals nomadism and mercurianism' line of thought.[19] Jews are displaced, homeless, diasporic, at home in the world, real Europeans, true global citizens, ethnic minorities, expatriates, in exile – to name the most used epithets of what signals both Jewishness and the cosmopolitan condition: a world in which most people live with mobility, difference, border-crossing risks, border-crossing ethnoscapes and mediascapes, global products and fashions.[20] In this way, Slezkine can make the cosmopolitan condition 'Jewish' in a way that is not much different from Breckenridge et al.'s 'minoritarian modernity'.[21] The cosmopolitan condition exists in the sociological perspective when the nation-state, the polity within borders in which you live, cannot secure your rights, prosperity and security without engaging in wars on the other side of the globe, without engaging in global environmental policies, or the global market economy. Under such conditions, cosmopolitanism is needed to make sense of this cacophony of mutually dependent associations and to secure the rights of individuals.[22]

In such perspectives cosmopolitanism cannot be defined as squarely as in the Kantian tradition. Cosmopolitanism is both structure and agency; something which can be studied, and should be studied, with a much more empirically sensitive attitude than through idealist notions of what cosmopolitanism *a priori* means.[23] Breckenridge et al. go as far as rejecting definitions: 'Cosmopolitanism may instead be a project whose conceptual content and pragmatic character are not only as yet unspecified but also must always escape positive and definitive specification, precisely because specifying cosmopolitanism positively and definitively is an uncosmopolitan thing to do.'[24] Instead, we should search for cosmopolitan archives globally and historically to learn about the practice of cosmopolitanism as it has been and as it is.[25] Studying global cosmopolitan archives includes the provincialisation of the European history of ideas. To assume that Kant's philosophy is relevant for cosmopolitan practice in Asia or Africa is simply Eurocentric.[26] In this perspective, the Jews or Jewishness has a model value to the world as other trans-national minorities, it seems, such as suggested by the Boyarins, who in 1993 claimed that the Jewish contribution to the world is 'diaspora' understood as the ability to maintain community and identity across time and territory without sovereignty and the suppressing of other peoples. Zionism is thus the real scandal in Jewish history.[27] In the Boyarins' perspective, the cosmopolitan world could learn from diasporic Jews that it is indeed possible to live in the world without a territory and without autochthony. Studying Jewish histories and cultures would then be lessons in and for the changing of the present and for the prospects of the future. It would be significant cosmopolitan archives to study.

The Jews and Jewishness is then a history, or histories, with potentials for the future, while the case is the opposite for philosophically oriented cosmopolitans of the Kantian orientation. In the perspective of the latter, the Jews are a minority who would benefit from being protected by hospitality, law and rights, while in the former perspective the Jews and Jewishness are a combination of a model and a prophecy to fit present and future conditions. For these reasons, many Jewish intellectuals have been wary of the concept of cosmopolitanism. Many have in concordance with recent postcolonial perspectives seen the Jews and other minorities as cosmopolitan victims of cosmopolitanism/universalism.[28] Already in 1783 in his work 'Jerusalem', Mendelssohn tried to unlock the dilemmas of a 'protected minority' by presenting an alternative universalism to counter the prevailing idea that Judaism was a historical burden for progress; Moses Hess called cosmopolitanism another word for 'a pure German soul' (1862), which, as we will see, was paraphrased by Horace M. Kallen in the 1910s, while many modern Zionists understand cosmopolitanism as an indirect threat to Israel and the Jewish right to national self-assertion.[29] In the following, we will see how a 'Jewish cosmopolitanism' unfolded in the work of American philosopher and educator Horace M. Kallen via a re-construction of the Jewish past. Read through Kallen's American pragmatism, 'the Jewish past' and 'the Jewish experience' offer the future of the world a different and better platform than Kantian idealism.

The changing past

> They are the people, the individuals who make and break the cultures they pass into and out of. They are the true subject matter of history when history is historical. Each is a span of time from birth to death, wherein his determined past works in his present to determine his undetermined future. His future is truly future in so far as it does not repeat his past and cannot be foretold from his past.[30]

Horace M. Kallen was in most ways a future-oriented thinker and educator. He was concerned with producing ideas and concepts for new and better ways of living that included increased freedom of creativity for the individual but always also included a social hope for all. As quoted above, 'future' meant newness and originality to Kallen in opposition to the repetition of pasts, that is, traditions. If we can foretell the future from the past, it is not really a future. Nevertheless, I will demonstrate how history in Kallen's thought worked as reservoir of experiences that could and should be rewoven for the sake of a better future. It is exactly in his efforts to invent a new Jewish history; in his efforts to invest new meaning in old vocabularies; in seeking to dissolve dichotomies between the particular and the universal that Kallen's work becomes an interesting cosmopolitan archive.

Kallen's legacy mainly revolves around his philosophy of Cultural Pluralism. There is a strong tendency in the reception of Cultural Pluralism that reads it as a reactionary position based on hereditary culture and grounded in racial categories that stands in opposition to a truly civil American culture. This reading is occupied with Kallen's use of categories such as 'race' and 'ethnic group' as the instruments of the symphony of civilisation more than the individual. Kallen's Cultural Pluralism is thus construed as a culturalist opposition to the melting pot that also neglected colour differences: a pluralism within whiteness.[31] In Noam Pianko's words, this tendency claims that Cultural Pluralism 'stands for the preservation of outmoded, primitive allegiances that are perceived as antithetical to cosmopolitan ideals'.[32] Pianko takes this as a grave misreading that fails to understand Kallen's context and takes its cues from a few quotes from Kallen's *The Nation* article 'Democracy and the Melting-Pot' from 1915.[33] Kallen's recent critics also overlook his attempts at investing a new pragmatist Jamesian meaning in old concepts such as history, culture and race. The avant-gardism that I here credit Kallen with comes to light when we look to other places than his trademark quotes and go into detail with his cultural thought and his constructions of Jewish history. In my reading, Kallen's life and work is an exemplary non-idealist cosmopolitan archive that shows how Jewishness could become a model for an international or transnational future.

In Kallen's thought, the *Erfahrungsraum*, histories and experiences, are the key resources for new associations, new connections, nexuses or links that can open up new or better futures for new and wider human unities that we desirefully can steer our imagination towards. History is thus a resource for making sense of the present for the purpose of actions towards the future. History is not true; it becomes true via its resourcefulness for our imagination. True ideas demonstrate their truth as a practical effect, as differences in action; accordingly readings of the past must prove themselves strong by their persuasive power, by their re-weaving of historical threads that give meaning to new experiences from which will follow that the world looks a little different and new horizons come within sight. Clearly, Kallen's ideas of history were solidly grounded in a Jamesian radical empiricism and a pragmatist attitude always emphasising 'the last things': the ways ideas are turned into differences of action. It is only when ideas are turned into action that we can know anything about the truth of an idea or its difference *vis-à-vis* other ideas. In Kallen's diagnosis, the modern world of mobility, industrial production and consumerism demanded new ways of associating with cultures and histories. Histories needed to be rewritten.

Turning Jewishness into a model

In his student days, Kallen discovered that the historical threads of 'Jewishness' could be rewoven in such a way that 'Jewishness' would turn out to be a productive attitude and resource for the future. According to his biographer Sarah Schmidt, Kallen was deeply dissatisfied with his father's religious understanding of Jewishness and considered that way of living a Jewish life parochial and narrow-minded.[34] The problem in particular was that this self-enclosed lifestyle did not encourage interaction, associating with society at large and with the general problems facing all Americans and even 'the world'. Like thousands of other new, young Americans, Kallen wanted to educate himself, integrate and free himself towards future horizons and as a consequence he was very sensitive to the barriers and injustices that immigrants were met with both by their old cultures and by the melting pot. Kallen's discovery of a to him relevant Jewishness was inspired by his encounter with and growing awareness of how naturally and self-evidently old-stock Americans appropriated particular values and particular pasts as true values of Americanism. As a student at Harvard, Kallen, and many other Jewish students, learnt how the self-evident organisation of culture is guided by prepositions that give directions and compasses to historical progression and cultural development in such a way that some associations are natural and logical while others need to 'melt' or clarify their unique contribution to natural order and historical logic.[35]

As Daniel Greene has shown, Cultural Pluralism became a philosophical and practical headline for Jewish student politics at universities across America. The Menorah Society and other organisations including Zionist organisations became nexuses for advancing cultural politics and variations of Jewishness that in many ways created what Kallen envisaged, namely unities through differences and meeting places among work, education, leisure, traditional cultures and religions in a marketplace of associations.[36] Organisations such as the Menorah Society moulded themselves after other university societies and actively sought the support of chancellors, professors and other distinguished personalities in order to receive a blueprint for the equality of the Jewish contribution to existing and eternal values of the university and society at large. Its leaders including Kallen were recruiting both Jews and non-Jews to the cause, which basically was to level true Jewish interests with true American interests thus dissolving conflicts between strong group loyalties, strong historicity and the common good. The survival of this project obviously included a strong re-evaluation of the kind of Jewishness that Kallen found his father to represent. Most existing varieties of Jewish life were not representative of the ethos and ethics Kallen and other Hebraists had in mind, which made it necessary to re-invent Jewishness.[37]

Discussions of the character of Jewishness and its contributions to civilisation have a long and complex history, but in the spirit of pluralism, Kallen wanted to find and promote its practical, living dimension as more than a set of religious and traditional lifestyles, and as more than a scholarly appreciation of Judaism's centrality for the modern understandings of monotheistic religion. Accordingly, he found it difficult to recognize the value of Wissenschaft des Judenthums (WdJ) despite its rebellion against Christological readings of Judaism and its struggle against the implicit and explicit antisemitism of the main currents of European theology.[38] The WdJ of Abraham Geiger and Reform Judaism led in Kallen's view not to the practical differences in life modes that would preserve the relevance of Jewishness for both Jews and the world because the WdJ and the reform ethos was intellectualistic and carried no binding to real life. In his conclusion, WdJ and Reform led to a Jewishness indistinguishable from the average Christian practice, and eventually modern Jewishness and modern Christianity would be the same no matter which idealist notions Jews or Christians could point to.[39]

Ultimately, Kallen rejected virtually all variations of Jewishness apart from Zionism. From today's perspective, this might seem somewhat peculiar, but it is important to bear in mind that Zionism did not spring from sources of *Völkish* nationalism. Most Zionist leaders were European, worldly intellectuals whose turn to Zionism had very little to do with a deep love for traditional Jewish life or with parochial European nationalisms. As Michael Stanislawski has shown, Zionism was in most ways an invention of Jewish cosmopolitans who at various paces drifted towards Zionism as the best possible answer for preserving their cosmopolitan outlook. Kallen himself was despite disagreements much more in tune with the Jewishness of Herzl, Nordau, Ahad Ha'am and Jabotinsky than with all other Judaisms since he was of the same kind: a trans-national intellectual emotionally much closer to Western or Russian art, literature, philosophy and politics than to the Jewish canon. Stanislawski's ironic remark about *Jugendstil* turning *Judenstil* in the case of Zionism could be said for Kallen's and Cultural Pluralism's turning modernity into Jewishness.[40] Kallen wrote in his introduction to his collection of articles, 'Judaism at Bay', that the kernel of Jewishness is its relation to modernity: 'Judaism is no longer identical with Jewishness and Jewishness is no longer identical with Judaism – I prefer to say, Hebraism – is a focus of modernity. It is the Jewish way of life become necessarily secular, humanist, scientific, conditioned on the industrial economy, without having ceased to be livingly Jewish.'[41]

Hebraism vs. Hellenism

Kallen's preference for the term Hebraism was anchored in a wish for creating an equal, even a superior, model of inspiration for the future than Hellenism and Christianity. Judaism was in his view a religious practice and philosophy while Jewishness and Hebraism more or less synonymously represented wider models of attitudes to life relevant for all people. In 1869 Matthew Arnold, in his influential *Culture and Anarchy*, opposed Hellenism and Judaism to each other as two distinct civilisational heritages that represented different cultural, historical and intellectual characters.[42] Not only did these -isms represent different cultural sign systems in a wider sense, they also constituted a particular way of thinking, imagining and practising life that manifested itself in the specific lives of Western Christians and Jews. Arnold claimed that more or less everything creative in the West had its source in Hellenism, while Judaism represented a strict and a moralist culture counter-balancing both Hellenism and Christianity.[43] Kallen used Arnold's depiction of the roles of the great Western civilisational forces as the offset to promote his rethinking of the particular contribution of Hebraism to the World. In the article 'Hebraism and Current Tendencies in Philosophy' from 1909, Kallen attacked 'Hellenism' via Arnold's definitions and declared that to be Hellenic meant to explain all variations of the world as mere aspects or appearances of static and structural forces, and to define all mutations with identity to something else.[44] Kallen's argument was that Hellenism represented an un-modern worldview where everything is given in advance and accordingly all experiences, observations and functionalities must represent something we already know when looking at it from the 'universal' perspective, from the perspective of structure and form. The deathblow to this way of thinking, according to Kallen, came with Darwin and *The Origin of Species*, which proved that

> to give species an origin is to abandon the notion of the eternity of forms and of the structural order of the universe. It is to espouse the flux, to allow for the reality of individuals as against classes, to allow for genuine freedom and chance in the world, to insist on the concrete instance rather than on the general law – in a word, to give an overwhelming scientific background to the Hebraic as against the Hellenic visions of the nature of reality.[45]

Kallen simply appropriated Darwin for a pluralist cultural Darwinism that removed the lid on the possible variations of the future universe. Spontaneous generation counted for human cultural variation as well as for animal species at the Galapagos. Newness entered the world as mutation, an event, a happening, as a practical, unplanned, solution to functional issues: how to survive, how to prosper. In the same way, survival of the fit could be enlisted for the pragmatist, pluralist cause by way of its fundamentally practical character. The fit were the individuals and the groups who managed to come up with solutions, mutate, relevantly *vis-à-vis* their environment. Thus, the pluralist variation of Darwinism did not emphasize strength as in masculine power, the dinosaur, but strength as adaptability, as the ability to function and prosper under continuously changing circumstances. And the Jews were the opposite of a dinosaur. They were the cultural group who were the most adaptable, the best at functioning and prospering under changing circumstances, and the best at mutating to function well in all environments, and accordingly true moderns.

From Hebraism to pluralism

To Kallen and his associates in the Menorah society and in Zionist circles, Hebraism was the inspirational source of central traits in Western civilisation – such as its sense of history, justice and science – to mention the most important of Hebraic influences.[46] Biblical narratives and law were, in the Hebraic perspective, seen as sources of historical trajectories stemming from a particular cultural genius that in the modern world is crucial for its very modern-ness.[47] While teaching at the University of Wisconsin, Kallen wrote a book entitled *The Book of Job as a Greek Tragedy* to demonstrate his turn of the role and place of Jewishness in modern cultural thought.[48] The book was widely discussed in progressive Jewish circles in America, and both criticized and applauded, for its bold attempt to rethink Jewishness' influence on modern Western culture.[49]

The concept of Hebraism promoted by Kallen and others did not in any way include an appraisal of traditional Jewish life as lived by poor immigrants from Eastern Europe or any sort of cultural conservatism that implied seclusion from other social groups or society at large. Rather, Hebraism was a summation of the progressive impulse in Jewishness, as Kallen saw it. Being Jewish was, in this line of thought, considered much more than a membership of a particular religious congregation. Jewishness implied being part of a great civilisational trajectory originating in the Biblical prophets who were both representatives and harbingers of the possibility of peaceful and constructive co-operation between nations.[50] The prophets' spirit of social justice, peace and inter-national co-operation simply ran through the history of the West. Being Jewish was indeed a particular identity, but this particular identity's attitude was Hebraism, which made a continuous, living contribution to the history of the West.

Loyal to Charles Sanders Peirce's pragmatic maxim, Kallen considered the life or death of cultures a matter of the practical bearings that these cultures are perceived to have in people's lives and in society at large.[51] If a culture is widely perceived 'dead' or a negative influence on society, it must no matter the degree of toleration professed by any society be considered as a space of improvement, a living museum, or a potential danger for the continued progress of society. For the Hebraists, the implications of this line of thought were to demonstrate the contributions of Hebraism to history in a perspective of continuation and difference from Hellenism and Christianity but no less significant and constructive for the prosperity and cultural richness of the World. Culture had a plurality of sources countering each other and contributing each with their own uniqueness to the common historical, cultural and social imagination. Needless to say, Hebraism was not by its proponents considered just any tree in the forest. In their view, Hebraism had invented and continuously developed defining aspects of modern Western civilisation such as 'science', 'the nation' and 'history'.[52]

In Kallen's ancient Hebrew world, Man did not have a grand scheme showing him the true order of the cosmos.[53] The realm of God, of the universe, was unknown to Man; the world chaotic, changing; both good and evil happened and order was in the hands of Man's self-reliance; his will to continue forward in the face of evil, disbelief, loss and chaos. Biblical Man was loyal to Life, the life of his people, and insisted in believing in goodness, justice and hopes for the future despite the evils he encountered on his path through life. Kallen thought this to be the core ethic of Hebraism. The Hebraic insistence on Life and carrying on no matter the hardships was captured by Job: *In the outcome, the Jews isolated man in the universe; 'I know that he will slay me,' says Job, 'I have no hope. Yet I will maintain my integrity before him.'*[54] If you struggle to carry on, this struggle may eventually deter your destruction but you do not know that it will. This was true realism to Kallen. In the Hebrew world, change was the leitmotif as opposed to structure, and no man was above another or free from sin. Dynamism, practicality and flexibility were essential qualities of Hebrew life, which made it functional and empirical, leading to clear ideas of the real quality of things.[55] The ancient Hebrews *existed* in the world and improvised their way forward, which made them much more than an inspiration for a pluralist present and future than a static Hellene cosmos. Kallen wrote of the idea of the universal that he associated with Athens and cosmopolis: 'What *exists* cannot be universal, in the Platonic sense of the word; and what is so universal cannot exist.'[56]

Hebraism was in Kallen's eyes pluralistic in its basic nature. The attitude to life of the Jews of the Hebrew Bible was not anchored in a clear and knowable structure but in a continuous flux. The ancient Hebrews lived in a plural universe in which other peoples and other gods existed. They fought for themselves against the wilderness and their enemies. They did not look at the world from a universalistic perspective but from a practical and particularistic one: how will we survive? How will we prosper? To Kallen, this Hebraist ethic was basically pragmatic. Man must experiment his way forward. This particularist but pragmatic and experimental attitude to life gave the world at least three of the central tenets of Western civilisation: science; the nation; and pluralism. These contributions represented community (the nation), pluralism (other groups and gods exist) and experimentation (science).[57]

Particular cultural-historical legitimacy in the present as well as a living relevance for the future simply derived from an idea of contribution in Kallen's work. Each social group in history made a contribution to the symphony of civilisation, some playing more important instruments and others playing louder. This contribution discourse is inherently paradoxical because it is so clearly an active constructivist project that erects its historical buildings and monuments on ruins and with a view to its own deconstruction.[58] Jews had a right to participate equally in the symphony despite their difference but in a sense this right had to be earned through education and proofs of contributions. It had to make itself true. That is why Kallen, a philosopher and secularist, had to invent Hebraist interpretations of the Hebrew Bible. He had to demonstrate that these texts were active and present as an ethical literature, which contribution was not historical in an antiquarian sense or the source of 'obedience' and 'narrow-mindedness' but a central tenet of our ideas of progress, freedom and human worldliness. They were essentially Jewish texts but their significance could be a model for all people living in the modern world of change, mobility and industrial production. They were cosmopolitan archives. Hebraism and Jewish history were living proof of change, adaptability, exchange and experimental openness towards the new.[59]

In Jewish journals in America such as *The Maccabean* and *The Menorah Journal* issues of how to promote Jewish causes were heatedly debated in the first decades of the twentieth century.[60] Hebraist-leaning positions such as that of Kallen but also Henry Hurwitz, Leon Simon, Norman Bentwich and other prominent intellectuals struggled with the dilemma between integration (acceptance), promotion (collective self-assertion) and what they saw as a basic right to be different. These three positions were not easily converged, each of them entailing an ontological problem for the other. Jewish self-assertion had to be true to authentic Jewishness. It had to demonstrate scientifically what Jewishness essentially is while at the same time erect a modern Jewish house adaptable to the present and future implicitly rejecting both Reform and Orthodoxy as constructive lifestyles. The Hebraists wanted to dissolve the dichotomy between the universal and the particular. To these American intellectuals, Jewish nationalism and a future Jewish state was an implication of Hebraism and indeed one of Hebraism's major contributions to the world universally, namely that people are naturally organized in families, groups and nations on the background of which they experience the world. This learning from the Jews and the Hebrew Bible is also a social ethic; it was by the Hebraists, but also by progressive intellectuals such as Randolph Bourne and John Dewey perceived as a potential for a trans-national solidarity between peoples.[61]

Cultural Pluralism

Kallen wanted to preserve and raise Jewishness into the future, but as an important aspect of securing and improving the social hope for all mankind. As a student at Harvard University, Kallen became closely involved with leading pragmatist thinkers such as William James and John Dewey. Pragmatism became Kallen's central matrix for understanding such seemingly diverse issues as Jewishness, education, international politics, social and cultural politics in America, Zionism and consumer politics, all of which he wrote extensively about. Out of these diverse interests, Kallen invented an elaborate cultural philosophy under the epithet Cultural Pluralism, heavily influenced by William James' pragmatist pluralism as an intended alternative to the popular melting-pot metaphor.

In 1915, Kallen wrote an article in *The Nation* entitled 'Democracy versus the Melting-Pot' in which he severely attacked Israel Zangwill's popular headline about the American Melting-Pot, where immigrants were melted into Americans, if they were adequately willing.[62] To Kallen, the concept of the melting pot was nothing short of a blind for majority predominance and discriminatory behaviour towards the millions of new Americans to which he belonged himself. The popularity of the melting-pot metaphor in the 1910s signalled to Kallen a deeply problematic attitude towards the newcomers grounded in a widespread perception that chronological time gave the right to forget that all Americans came from somewhere else. The few hundred years that separated old Americans from new Americans did not give old Americans the right to produce discrimination based on time. Many old-stock Americans misunderstood history in Kallen's view. Their production of histories was not conducive for present or future purposes. A recently invented sedentarism would simply betray the social hope for all that America represented.

In *The Nation*, Kallen gave the example of the Scandinavians coming to Minnesota to live more Norwegian lives than they did in Norway. His central argument was that people came to America to live as they wished in freedom and this wish most often led to Scandinavians living with Scandinavians, Jews with Jews, and Italians with Italians. Neighbourhoods and streets were not primarily divided into rich and poor but into national affiliations. Accordingly, the empirically observable American experience was not that people looked forward to being melted into Americans, but that they looked forward to re-constructing their lives most often in close cultural networks with their own kind. From this perspective followed that the melting pot was not really a democratic metaphor. The melting pot implied that the mould was already made; it included a heavy burden of *a priori* content defined by the former colonizers now autochthonous Americans. To the contrary, democracy, in Kallen's view, entailed a continuous reshaping of the mould via the empirical experience of peoples' practical lives. Implicitly, in Kallen's arguments we find a pluralist worldview where both groups and individuals navigate and utilize multiple temporalities and multiple ontologies in their continuous making sense of new experiences.

Of all the people coming to America, the Jews have showed themselves to be the most eager to adapt to new circumstances. 'They do not come to the United States from truly native lands, lands of their proper *natio* and culture. They come from lands of sojourn, where they have been for ages treated as foreigners, at most as semi-citizens, subject to disabilities and persecutions,' Kallen wrote of the Jews. He continued:

> Of all immigrants they have the oldest civilized tradition, they are longest accustomed to living under law, and are at the outset the most eager and the most successful in eliminating the external differences between themselves and their social environment. Even their religion is flexible and accommodating, as that of the Christian sectories is not, for change involves not change of doctrine, only in mode of life.[63]

The Jews were already on the move and not dependent on 'truly native lands' for their cohesion and group togetherness. This particular homeless trait of the Jews did not impede their home feeling, their sentimental bonds and their self-consciousness about being a particular group. The Jews are both perfectly amendable and perfectly parochially loyal, and, accordingly, in Kallen's words: 'In sum, the most eagerly American of the immigrant groups are also the most autonomous and self-conscious in spirit and culture.'[64] This example of the Jews served Kallen's core argument against the melting pot's proponents namely:

> Thus 'American Civilization' may come to mean the perfection of the cooperative harmonies of 'European Civilization', the waste, the squalor, and the distress of Europe being eliminated – a multiplicity in a unity, an orchestration of mankind. As in an orchestra, every type of instrument has its specific timbre and tonality, founded in its substance and form; as every type has its appropriate theme and melody in the whole symphony of civilization, so in society each ethnic group is the natural instrument, its spirit and culture are its theme and melody, and the harmony and dissonances and discords of them all make the symphony of civilization, with this difference; a musical symphony is written before it is played; in the symphony of civilization the playing is the writing, so that there is nothing fixed and inevitable about its progression and in music, so that within the limits set by nature they may vary at will, and the range and variety of the harmonies may become wider and richer and more beautiful.[65]

This lengthy quote serves to demonstrate how Kallen thought of the fundamental difference between the melting pot and Cultural Pluralism. Difference is natural and curbing the natural instruments will lead to pain and suffering as evidenced by the European tragedy. Instead of following already written scripts, the instruments must improvise, co-create, listen and experiment to find the harmonies, the futures, most open to the tone and timbre of all groups. Implicitly here, Cultural Pluralism reveals its significant differences from

Kantian or rights-oriented cosmopolitanisms in as much as rights-oriented, progressive, cosmopolitanisms are exactly already written scripts of human progression.

Cultural pluralism was to Kallen something radically empirical, something verifiable by experience, in opposition to idealist and *a priori* constructions of good or bad cultural organisation. Judgement over people's cultural associations should in Kallen's view not be made on the grounds of their group's language, gods or food habits, whether they were considered 'backward' or not, but on their willingness to liberate themselves and their group into the multitudes of associations of general society. With the Jews as a model, the medium of this liberation is strong group loyalties, obedience towards the law, self-consciousness and a strong wish for a better future. In fact, Kallen claimed that exactly these 'Jewish' qualities were 'the medium' to dissolute the conflict between particular and the universal. In the pluralist perspective, people are always members of various particular communities; people are always historical; everything that appears universal is particular if we look closely enough. What Kallen wished to demonstrate was that the most historical of all people, the Jews, were also the people who were the most eager to integrate, and who were the most adaptable to all sorts of circumstances. In a sense, adaptability, strong historicity and collective self-consciousness become functions of each other.[66]

A Jewish cosmopolitanism

In many ways, Cultural Pluralism resembles what Breckenridge et al. call 'minoritarian modernity' in its pragmatist rejection of idealist cosmopolitanism.[67] Kallen constructed Jewish archives that served as models for improvising the practical complexity of living together in a global world. His Job and his Hebraism was meant to outline a pluralist attitude and an alternative pragmatist variation of living together in and out of multiple associations of cultures and histories. Pragmatically, Kallen did not evaluate the Jewish archives he constructed in connection to their distance or proximity to the present or in relation to standard philology and Bible science. He read them like a pragmatist asking questions such as: how do they work, what do they do, what are their potentials? In this perspective, histories are always histories of effects, and the history of effects of Enlightenment cosmopolitanism towards the Jews was not a future to desirefully steer towards. As we have seen, the idea of cosmopolitanism in the Enlightenment tradition includes a deep controversy over Jews and Jewishness, which is invariably related to the idea of a unified historical progression and the development of global civility. Accordingly, global civility could not have a script to Kallen, and a singular history in one tempus must be rejected if Jews and other minorities truly had the right to be different. Despite its pragmatic character, Kallen's pluralism nevertheless included normative delimitations to what is the right pluralist attitude and what is not. As pointed out by Holton, the problem with the minoritarian modernity, what we could also call postcolonial cosmopolitanism, perspective is that nothing qualifies cosmopolitanism making it nothing or everything.[68] Holton argues that cosmopolitans need to have 'ecumenical concerns beyond the locality'.[69] In Kallen's pluralist thought, this equals the necessity of a social hope for all for attitudes to be truly pluralistic. In relation to today's plethora of cosmopolitan thought, Kallen's Cultural Pluralism would be a variation of cosmopolitanism that reminds us of the troubled historical effects of discourses of universalism, natural law and civility. In Jeffrey Alexander's words: 'Because of the vagaries of time, space, and function, civil capacities from the outset are primordialized, and the ability to perform adequately in civil society is understood as being restricted to those who possess the particular qualities of core groups.'[70] These restrictions to admission into the polis run as a red thread through modern Jewish history. Despite his blatant Eurocentrism and synonymous use of the West and civilisation as concepts often meaning the world, Kallen's thought nevertheless invokes many of the same themes as minoritarian modernity and postcolonial cosmopolitanism. *Avant la lettre*, Kallen's 'Jewish cosmopolitanism' insisted that true cosmopolitanism must be pragmatic, postcolonial, and experimental.

Kallen clearly saw his Cultural Pluralism as conditioned by the modern American world of migration, industrial production, urbanism, consumerism, democracy and science. America in many ways meant 'the modern world' while Europe and its nationalist struggles represented the world of yesterday. The social and cultural diagnoses of 'America' by pragmatist scholars such as Kallen, John Dewey and William James, but also public intellectuals like Randolph Bourne, correspond closely with what cosmopolitan theorists today take as reality. In David T. Hansen's words about John Dewey's cosmopolitanism, pragmatism is about the experimental space of learning in-between the self-that-was and the self-that-is; between the community-that-was, and the community-that-is; between the point of view-that-was, and the new point of view.[71] This repeats Kallen's words: 'the present is the past changing'. Kallen found the pragmatist attitude incarnated in Hebraism, while Hellenism represented an obsolete pre-Darwinian point of view. Jewishness grew *qua* new experiences into a model and a prophecy, but not just because the Jews were nomads. The Jews, not as Judaism but as Jewishness/Hebraism, promulgated and promoted the stream in human civilisation that will come into its own with modernity and even more so in the global future. Kallen's idiosyncratic Jewish cosmopolitanism sought the parochially loyal, the interested openness towards the world, and a cosmopolitan responsibility for the social hope for all in a blend where a new Jewish past was the medium, but the future was the goal.

Notes

1. Kallen, "Democracy Versus the Melting-Pot II," 217–18.
2. Koselleck, "'Erfahrungsraum' und 'Erwartungshorizont – zwei historische Kategorien," 349–75.
3. See as an example Pollock's essay on Sanskrit culture: Pollock, "Cosmopolitan and Vernacular in History," 15–53.
4. As also remarked by Miller and Ury: "Cosmopolitanism: the End of Jewishness?," 344.
5. Fine, *Cosmopolitanism*, 17–18.
6. I have used the collection of Kant's texts by Kleingeld et al., *Toward Perpetual Peace and other Writing on Politics, Peace, and History*.
7. Benhabib, *Another Cosmopolitanism*; Derrida, *On Cosmopolitanism and Forgiveness*; Fine, *Cosmopolitanism*; Miller and Ury, "Cosmopolitanism: the End of Jewishness."
8. Kant, "Idea for a Universal History with a Cosmopolitan Perspective," in Kleingeld, *Toward Perpetual Peace*, 8.
9. Leonard, *Socrates and the Jews*, 56.
10. Kleingeld, *Toward Perpetual Peace*, 78.
11. Kant, "Idea for a Universal History from a Cosmopolitan Perspective" in Kleingeld, *Toward Perpetual Peace*, 4.
12. Ibid.
13. Ibid., 4.
14. Munk, "Mendelssohn and Kant on Judaism," 217–18.
15. Ibid., 219.

16. Leonard, *Socrates and the Jews*, 53.
17. Alexander, *The Civil Sphere*, 463.
18. See also Goetschel, *Spinoza's Modernity*, and Mack, *German Idealism and the Jew*.
19. Slezkine, *The Jewish Century*.
20. See Beck, *Cosmopolitan Vision*, 1–14.
21. Breckenridge et al., *Cosmopolitanism*, 6.
22. See Beck, *Cosmopolitan Vision*, 78.
23. As advocated by Holton, *Cosmopolitanisms*, 1–25.
24. Breckenridge et al., *Cosmopolitanism*, 1.
25. Ibid., 10.
26. Ibid., 10. Obviously, the perspective in Breckenridge draws on well-established postcolonial and cultural-studies critiques of Western universalism.
27. Boyarin and Boyarin, "Diaspora: Generation and the Ground of Jewish Identity," 712, 723.
28. Mack, *German Idealism and the Jew*. See also Boyarin and Boyarin, "Diaspora: Generation and the Ground of Jewish Identity." In these perspectives, universalism is a camouflaged kind of racism.
29. Mendelssohn, *Jerusalem*; Hess, *Rome and Jerusalem*, 57. It is difficult to point to one specific place in Mendelssohn because *Jerusalem* is a long argument for an alternative universalism. But see for example his version of the plundering of the Temple on p. 114, which describes how universalists see the world with the eyes of barbarians.
30. Kallen, *Cultural Pluralism and the American Idea*, 54.
31. See Obenzinger, "Naturalizing Cultural Pluralism" and Sollors, *Beyond Ethnicity*.
32. Pianko, "The True Liberalism of Zionism," 300. Pianko further unfolds the positions in the reception of Cultural Pluralism.
33. Ibid., 300.
34. Schmidt, "Horace M. Kallen and the 'Americanization' of Zionism," 61.
35. Schmidt, *Horace M Kallen. Prophet of American Zionism*; Greene, *The Jewish Origins of Cultural Pluralism*, 14–35.
36. Greene, *The Jewish Origins of Cultural Pluralism*, 35–62.
37. Kallen, *Judaism at Bay*, 4.
38. See Gerdmar, *Roots of Theological Anti-Semitism* and Heschel, *Abraham Geiger and the Jewish Jesus*.
39. Kallen, "On the Import of 'Universal Judaism'" (1910); Kallen, "Judaism by Proxy" (1916). Both in *Judaism at Bay*.
40. Stanislawski, *Zionism and the Fin de Siècle*, 98.
41. Kallen, *Judaism at Bay*, 4–5.
42. Arnold, *Culture and Anarchy*.
43. Ibid., 147.
44. Kallen, *Judaism at Bay*, 10.
45. Ibid., p. 11.
46. Kallen, "Judaism and the Modern Point of View" (1911) in *Judaism at Bay*, 42–56; Konvitz, "H.M. Kallen and the Hebraic Idea," 215–26.
47. See also Slezkine, *The Jewish Century* who elaborates on this theme.
48. Kallen, *The Book of Job as a Greek Tragedy*.
49. Fried, "Creating Hebraism, Confronting Hellenism," 153.
50. Kallen, *The Book of Job as a Greek Tragedy*, 55.
51. Kallen, "Democracy versus the Melting Pot. A Study of American Nationality I, II."
52. Hebraists ranged from secularists such as Kallen, to religious reformers, scholars and Zionists such as Ahad Ha'am, who with different accents considered Judaism to be only an aspect of a wider cultural trajectory originating with the people who gave rise to the Hebrew Bible and the Prophets in particular. Kallen's varied expositions of Hebraism in articles and lectures led to heated debates in the Menorah Journal over the character of Hebraism, which points to the crucial nature of this debate *vis-à-vis* the place of Jews and Judaism in America early in the twentieth century see Fried, "Creating Hebraism, Confronting Hellenism," 146–74.

53. Kallen, *The Book of Job*, 10–11.
54. Ibid., 11.
55. See also Konvitz, "H.M. Kallen and his Hebraic Idea."
56. Kallen, "On the Import of 'Universal Judaism,'" in *Judaism at Bay*, 19.
57. Kallen, *The Book of Job*, 78.
58. See Rosman, *How Jewish is Jewish History* for an interesting discussion of historical contribution discourses.
59. Kallen, "Judaism and the Modern Point of View," in *Judaism at Bay*, 53–6.
60. Fried, "Creating Hebraism, Confronting Hellenism," 146–74.
61. Kronish, "John Dewey and Horace M. Kallen on Cultural Pluralism," 135–48.
62. Zangwill, *The Melting Pot. A Drama in Four Acts*.
63. Kallen, "Democracy versus the Melting-Pot II," 218.
64. Ibid., 218.
65. Ibid., 219.
66. Ibid., 218.
67. Breckenridge et al., *Cosmopolitanism*, 6.
68. Holton, *Cosmopolitanisms*, 17.
69. Ibid., 18.
70. Alexander, *The Civil Sphere*, 460.
71. Hansen, "Dewey and Cosmopolitanism," 128

ORCID

Jakob Egholm Feldt http://orcid.org/0000-0001-6418-8418

Bibliography

Alexander, Jeffrey. *The Civil Sphere*. Oxford: Oxford University Press, 2006.
Arnold, Matthew. *Culture and Anarchy. An Essay in Political and Social Criticism*. London: Smith, Elder and, 1869.
Beck, Ulrich. *Cosmopolitan Vision*. Cambridge: Polity Press, 2006.
Benhabib, Seyla. *Another Cosmopolitanism*. Oxford: Oxford University Press, 2006.
Boyarin, Daniel, and Jonathan Boyarin. "Diaspora: Generation and the Ground of Jewish Identity." *Critical Inquiry* 19, no. 4 (1993): 693–725.
Breckenridge, Carol, Sheldon Pollock, Homi K. Bhabha, and Dipesh Chakrabarty. *Cosmopolitanism*. London: Duke University Press, 2002.
Derrida, Jacques. *Cosmopolitanism and Forgiveness*. London: Routledge, 2001.
Fine, Robert. *Cosmopolitanism*. London: Routledge, 2007.
Fried, Lewis. "Creating Hebraism, Confronting Hellenism: The Menorah Journal and its Struggle for the Jewish Imagination." *American Jewish Archives Journal* 53, no. 1/2 (2001): 147–174.
Gerdmar, Anders. *Roots of Theological Anti-Semitism. German Biblical Interpretation and the Jews, from Herder and Semler to Kittel and Bultmann*. Leiden: Brill, 2009.

Goetschel, Willi. *Spinoza's Modernity. Mendelssohn, Lessing, and Heine*. Madison, WI: University of Wisconsin Press, 2004.

Greene, Daniel. *The Jewish Origins of Cultural Pluralism. The Menorah Association and American Diversity*. Bloomington: Indiana University Press, 2011.

Hansen, David T. "Dewey and Cosmopolitanism." *Education and Culture* 25, no. 2 (2009): 126–140.

Heschel, Susannah. *Abraham Geiger and the Jewish Jesus*. Chicago: University of Chicago Press, 1998.

Hess, Moses. *Rome and Jerusalem. A Study in Jewish Nationalism*. New York: Bloch Publishing Company, 1918 [1862].

Holton, Robert J. *Cosmopolitanisms. New Thinking and New Directions*. Basingstoke: Palgrave Macmillan, 2009.

Kant, Immanuel, and Pauline Kleingeld. *Toward Perpetual Peace and Other Writings on Politics, Peace, and History*. London: Yale University Press, 2006.

Kallen, Horace M. "Democracy versus the Melting-Pot I+II." *The Nation*, 18 and 25 February (1915), 190–194, 217–220.

Kallen, Horace M. *The Book of Job as a Greek Tragedy*. New York: Moffat, Yard and Company, 1918.

Kallen, Horace M. *Judaism at Bay. Essays toward the Adjustment of Judaism to Modernity*. New York: Bloch Publishing, 1932.

Kallen, Horace M. *Cultural Pluralism and the American Idea*. Philadelphia: University of Pennsylvania Press, 1956.

Konvitz, Milton. "H.M. Kallen and the Hebraic Idea." *Modern Judaism* 4, no. 2 (1984): 215–226.

Koselleck, Reinhart. "'Erfahrungsraum' und 'Erwartungshorizont – zwei historische Kategorien". *Vergangene Zukunft. Zur Semantic Geschichtlicher Zeiten* Franfurt/Main: Suhrkamp, 1989.

Kronish, Ronald. "John Dewey and Horace M. Kallen on Cultural Pluralism: Their Impact on Jewish Education." *Jewish Social Studies* 44, no. 2 (1982): 135–148.

Leonard, Miriam. *Socrates and the Jews. Hellenism and Hebraism from Moses Mendelssohn to Sigmund Freud*. Chicago: University of Chicago Press, 2012.

Mack, Michael. *German Idealism and the Jew. The Inner Anti-Semitism of Philosophy and German Jewish Responses*. Chicago: University of Chicago Press, 2003.

Mendelssohn, Moses. *Jerusalem. Or on Religious Power and Judaism*. Waltham: Brandeis University Press, 1983 [1783].

Miller, Michael, and Scott Ury. "Cosmopolitanism: the End of Jewishness?" *European Review of History: Revue européenne d'histoire* 17, no. 1 (2010): 337–359.

Munk, Reinier. "Mendelssohn and Kant on Judaism." *Jewish Studies Quarterly* 13 (2006): 215–222.

Obenzinger, Hilton. "Naturalizing Cultural Pluralism, Americanizing Zionism: the Settler Colonial Basis to Early-Twentieth Century Thought." *South Atlantic Quarterly* 107, no. 4 (2008): 651–669.

Pianko, Noam. "'The True Liberalism of Zionism': Horace Kallen, Jewish Nationalism, and the Limits of American Pluralism." *American Jewish History* 94, no. 4 (2008): 299–329.

Pollock, Sheldon. "Cosmopolitan and Vernacular in History." In *Cosmopolitanism*, edited by Carol Breckenridge, Sheldon Pollock, Homi K. Bhabha and Dipesh Chakrabarty. *Cosmopolitanism*. London: Duke University Press, 2002.

Rosman, Moshe. *How Jewish is Jewish History?*. Oxford: The Littman Library of Jewish Civilization, 2007.

Schmidt, Sarah. "Horace M. Kallen and the 'Americanization' of Zionism. In Memoriam." *American Jewish Archives*, April (1976).

Schmidt, Sarah. *Horace M. Kallen. Prophet of American Zionism*. New York: Carlson Publishing, 1995.

Selzkine, Yuri. *The Jewish Century*. Princeton: Princeton University Press, 2004.

Sollors, Werner. *Beyond Ethnicity: Consent and Descent in American Culture*. New York: Oxford University Press, 1986.

Stanislawski, Michael. *Zionism and the Fin de Siècle. Cosmopolitanism and Nationalism from Nordau to Jabotinsky*. Berkeley: University of California Press, 2001.

Zangwill, Israel. *The Melting Pot. A Drama in Four Acts*. New York: The American Jewish Book Company, 1921.

JEWS, COSMOPOLITANISM AND POLITICAL THOUGHT

Rootless cosmopolitans: German-Jewish writers confront the Stalinist and National Socialist atrocities

Cathy S. Gelbin

ABSTRACT
This article examines the impact of the Stalinist persecutions of Jews as 'rootless cosmopolitans' on the Jewish involvement with leftist ideas. In inter-war Germany and Austria, Jewish intellectuals played a disproportionate role in promoting both cosmopolitanist and leftist ideals. While belonging mostly to the bourgeois spectrum, many harboured close sympathies with the young Soviet Union, whose imperative of Communist internationalism seemed to chime closely with their own cosmopolitanist sentiments. This dream was shattered in the Stalinist purges of the 1930s and 1950s in particular, when Jews were persecuted as 'rootless cosmopolitans'. The author studies the novels by three German-speaking Jewish writers, Alice Rühle-Gerstel's *The Break*, Arthur Koestler's *Darkness at Noon* and Manès Sperber's *Like a Tear in the Ocean*, which were written in close proximity to the Stalinist crimes. She argues that these novels offer a unique insight into the seemingly impossible schism that leftist Jews faced in confronting the Stalinist crimes. In doing so, these novels enable us to trace the Jewish leftist predicament that both sustained the socialist–Communist project and ultimately called for its critical interrogation.

Between the 1920s and 1940s, Jews were drawn in disproportionate numbers to the idea of Communism, and thus became widely associated with revolutionary politics. At the same time, the brief period between the First World War and the Second World War saw a renewed cosmopolitanist engagement, particularly among those left-leaning Jewish intellectuals who sought to combine a renewed interest in their Jewish particularity – sparked by the twentieth-century Jewish renaissance – with an affirmation of their diasporic German, Austrian and European affiliations. In the course of the Communist project under the Soviet aegis, however, Jewish intellectuals increasingly found themselves as outsiders and, ultimately, presumed enemies.

As a result, Jewish writers who sympathized with the Communist Party found themselves among the earliest outspoken critics of the Stalinist crimes and began to address these in their writings from the late 1930s onwards. As this piece argues, their works enable us to trace the Jewish leftist predicament that sustained the socialist–Communist project on the one hand, and ultimately called for its critical interrogation on the other. And indeed, nowhere has the examination of the Stalinist crimes occurred in a more passionate and soul-searching manner than in writings by those German-speaking Jewish authors who were caught in the crossfire of the National Socialist and Stalinist regimes and their aftermath between the 1930s and the 1970s.

Communism, National Socialism and the Jews

Given the contested nature of comparisons between the Holocaust and other mass atrocities particularly in the context of Holocaust Studies, any comparative study of the National Socialist and Stalinist crimes requires careful framing. This is so especially since analogies between National Socialism and Stalinism have historically served to shore up Cold War divides and to allow the evasion of respective political and ethical responsibility for these events. This section of my article will, therefore, outline the historical and contemporary debates around the comparability of National Socialism and Stalinism, which both drew on and informed the fictional writings of the literary authors who form the centrepiece of this article.

During the period between both world wars, the partial affinities between cosmopolitanism and Communism seemed to be obvious, for the proponents of both ideas strove to transcend the rabid nationalism that had thrown Europe into the First World War disaster and fuelled the rising antisemitism and the National Socialists' ascent to power. For many Jews, both cosmopolitanist and leftist ideas thus held considerable attraction, and Communist internationalism in particular seemed to chime well with the cosmopolitanist sensibility. Both cosmopolitanist thought and the Communist fight for social justice offered left-leaning Jewish intellectuals a route to transcend the presumed stigma of Jewish particularity through affiliation with a universalist project. This was, of course, so because Communist internationalism was itself heir to the cosmopolitanist strand of philosophy in the German-speaking Enlightenment.[1] Under Stalin's rule, however, Soviet party Communism took an increasingly hostile stance towards cosmopolitanism and the Jews, and Communist internationalism was sidelined in favour of a new Soviet nationalism.

Yet until the second half of the 1920s, Jewish cosmopolitanist affinities with the Communist project were not merely imagined. Following the early revolutionary condemnation of antisemitism, Soviet propaganda of the 1920s officially forbade antisemitism as a 'reactionary relic of Tsarism'.[2] At the same time, Jewish particularism was seen to stand in opposition to the revolutionary idea of nationalism, according to which ethnic particularities were to be completely assimilated and integrated into the Soviet national project. In 1919, then, the Communist International, often also referred to as the Comintern or Third International, was founded in Moscow to safeguard proletarian internationalism and to promote the global Communist revolution. From the late 1920s onwards, the cosmopolitanist potential of this structure steadily declined as Communist internationalism was explicitly pressed into the service of unfailing support for the Soviet Union, and any aberration from its line deemed treason to the cause of Communism.

Communist internationalism was placed in explicit opposition to bourgeois nationalism, which was aligned with cosmopolitanism as the credo of the liberal bourgeois intellectual. During the 1930s, this campaign assumed increasingly antisemitic undertones as Leon Trotsky emerged as the figurehead of anti-Stalinist opposition. While even Stalin could not risk being openly antisemitic during this period of consolidation, his Great Purges all but destroyed a budding independent Jewish culture in the country.[3] But although antisemitism no doubt played an implicit role in conceiving and justifying these events, Jews were but one group among the millions of Stalin's Soviet victims between 1931 and 1939. These included an estimated six to nine million people who died of starvation in the process of the enforced collectivisation of agriculture between 1931 and 1933, as well as approximately three quarters of a million Soviet peasants, workers and ethnic-minority members killed in the course of Stalin's Popular Front politics between 1934 and 1939. Added to this were the numerous Communists of other nations, particularly German exiles from National Socialism, whom their own hard-line party comrades would secretly murder in the antifascist resistance struggle and behind the lines of the Spanish Civil War.[4]

As Stalin's byword shifted to antifascism to rally support for his leadership in the fight against Hitler and detract from his own mass killings, internationalism became an increasingly obsolete and suspect concept. During the first years of National Socialist rule, the Comintern had still served to keep German exiles in check and to betray to the party those who were deemed to have strayed from the Communist line. During the Great Purges, however, the Comintern's early leaders were killed together with large numbers of its staff, and Stalin finally disbanded the organisation in 1943.[5] The same year, Stalin began his concerted attacks on cosmopolitanism in order to stress Soviet patriotism against any indebtedness to foreign ideas. Stalin borrowed the term 'rootless cosmopolitanism' (*byezrodnui cosmopolit*) from the Russian critic Vissarion Belinsky, who had coined it during the early nineteenth century against the Westernisation of Russian culture, in particular to refer to those authors whose writing was influenced by German models. 'Rootless cosmopolitanism' soon stood synonymous for 'Jew' and the term was quickly integrated into Soviet antifascist ideology, the mirror image of the Nazis' conflation of Bolshevism with the Jews.

From 1946 onwards, then, when Andrei Zhdanov became director of Soviet cultural policy, Soviet rhetoric increasingly highlighted the goal of a pure Soviet culture freed from Western degeneration. This became apparent, for example, in a piece in the Soviet weekly *Literaturnya gazeta* in 1947, which denounced the claimed expressions of rootless cosmopolitanism as inimical to Soviet culture.[6] From 1949 onwards, then, a new series of openly antisemitic purges and executions began across the Soviet Union and its satellite countries, when Jews were charged explicitly with harbouring an international Zionist-cosmopolitanist conspiracy. During the 1930s, however, a number of Jewish writers had already felt a growing unease at Soviet politics and propaganda, which they believed to have antisemitic undercurrents. These concerns clashed with their continuing sympathies with the Communist project to liberate the world from social injustice, of which they saw antisemitism as one part.

Within the German Communist Party, which largely failed to express its solidarity with Hitler's Jewish victims and even excluded Jews from its resistance cells, deeming them a liability, the rifts were evidently clear.[7] In exile from National Socialist Germany, the situation of card-carrying Jewish intellectuals became increasingly untenable, given that they felt themselves to be in the crossfire of the National Socialists' persecutions and the Stalinist purges, both of which had deadly consequences. Too similar in sound were Hitler's references in his 1924 *Mein Kampf* to a 'poison injected by the international and cosmopolitan Jew[s]', who had formed a conspiracy to destroy the Aryan race,[8] to Stalin's 1950s charges that the Jews were 'rootless cosmopolitans' and had created an international Zionist conspiracy to destroy the Soviet Union and undermine its sphere of political influence in the post-war Eastern bloc.

Writing from her exile in the United States, the German-Jewish political scientist Hannah Arendt was the first to theorize in depth the possible points of comparison between Hitlerism and Stalinism in her *Origins of Totalitarianism* (1950).[9] Arendt's work arose from the post-1945 attempts to bring the National Socialist perpetrators to justice under the newly created label of 'crimes against humanity', and thus to instate what Seyla Benhabib has termed 'cosmopolitan norms of justice' inspired by Kant's call for a universal law in his *Perpetual Peace*.[10] In Cold War political rhetoric, the term totalitarianism then served to discredit the Eastern-bloc regimes against the supposedly cleansed democracies of the West, including West Germany.[11] Totalitarianism soon became a contested concept. Criticism came, for example, from Western intellectuals who were concerned about the legacy of the National Socialist past in Western Europe and in particular West Germany, where the term totalitarianism threatened to obliterate the barely acknowledged legacy of the National Socialist past. In *At the Mind's Limits*, the Austrian-Jewish writer and Auschwitz survivor Jean Améry thus debunked any analogies between Communism and National Socialism because, he argued, they were different in essence.[12] Citing a statement that the German writer Thomas Mann had given in exile, Améry concluded that 'no matter how terrible Communism may at times appear, it still symbolizes the idea of the man, whereas Hitler-Fascism was not an idea at all, but depravity' (31).

Although historians in the West have gradually abandoned the concept of totalitarianism, the last three decades have seen a growing body of comparative historiography on National Socialism and Stalinism. And yet, a nuanced discussion of the possible relationship between both systems and their politics of terror is yet to emerge. To date, such discussions display their roots in the Cold War rhetoric that sought to minimize the National Socialist atrocities through such analogies and thus absolve the Western allies of their varying histories of collaboration in the annihilation of European Jewry. In the 1980s, when such analogies emerged in the field of academic study, they were still met with wide outrage and considered an expression of fringe right-wing attitudes. Such was the response to two now infamous essays by Ernst Nolte, a professor of history at West Berlin's Free University.

In the first of these two pieces, 'Die negative Lebendigkeit des Dritten Reiches' ('The Negative Presence of the Third Reich', 1980), Nolte criticized the assumption that the 'violent crimes of the Third Reich are singular' (15). Instead, he drew a line of class-based terror from the French Revolution (and its right-wing responses) to Stalinist terror (and the National Socialist genocide as its response).[13] 'The events in Indo-China', Nolte concluded with regard to the recent discovery of Pol Pot's atrocities in Cambodia, 'should now have made apparent what precisely constitutes original and copy with regard to annihilation based on class, ethnicity, and group affiliation' (32). Nolte reiterated this claim in terming the National Socialist genocide against the Jews an 'Asiatic crime' in his follow-up article of 1986, 'Vergangenheit, die nicht vergehen will' ('The Past which Refuses to Pass'), which would spark off the landmark historians' debate in Germany.[14] In the course of this debate, Nolte's and others' subsequent attempts to legitimize academically comparisons between National Socialism and Stalinism became discredited. However, the opening of Soviet archives after 1989 brought new documentation to light, and such comparisons have since resurfaced under partially revised – and yet familiar – parameters.

In his foreword to the German historian Joachim Hoffmann's evocatively titled *Stalins Vernichtungskrieg* ('Stalin's War of Annihilation'), Manfred Kehrig, for example, conceded that the Second World War was 'a battle of life and death between two totalitarian systems, which used the same means and methods in order to achieve their political aims'.[15] Hoffmann's borrowings from Nolte are evident in his attempts to compare the 'mass murders' committed by the Stalinist regime 'due to motives of class struggle' to those of Hitler's regime due to motives of 'race struggle' (325). That Hoffmann really sought to redress the balance between the historical constellations of German Holocaust perpetrators versus their Jewish victims becomes apparent in his chapter on the Wehrmacht, which is subtitled 'The Anti-German War and Racial Propaganda of Hatred' and focuses extensively on the propagandistic war writings of the Soviet-Jewish writer Ilya Ehrenburg.

The narrow comparison between Hitler's and Stalin's regimes, and more specifically between Hitler's genocide against European Jewry and Stalin's atrocities against his own population, also stands at the centre of the Yale historian Timothy Snyder's 2011 study *Bloodlands*, which seeks to revise the term 'genocide' in favour of the generic 'mass killing'.[16] While Snyder's observations on the problematic political and discursive history of the term genocide are undoubtedly insightful, the blanket term of mass killings risks losing the discursive and political specificities of the National Socialist crimes, which found their justification in modern racial and broader genetic biology, and thus evince their historical basis in German and European antisemitic and colonialist mass violence. In particular, Snyder's rejection of the industrial notion of the Holocaust as overrated, given that as many of its victims were shot as were gassed, further limits his vision of the ideological, political and practical specificities of Hitler's and Stalin's killings.

This is, of course, not to say that the comparative study of atrocities is in and of itself illegitimate, but rather to point to their authors' inherently political agenda. By proposing the Holocaust as a function of modernity, the work of the Polish-British sociologist Zygmunt Bauman, in *Modernity and the Holocaust* for example, has often been misunderstood to suggest an arbitrariness of the Holocaust in relation to other mass atrocities, despite Bauman's explicit rejection of classing the Holocaust 'as another item (however prominent) in a wide class of that embraces many "similar" cases of conflict, or prejudice, or aggression'. What Bauman sought to undo instead was the focus on 'the *Germanness* of the crime' as 'an exercise in exonerating everyone else, and particularly *everything* else'.[17]

More recently, new studies such as Michael Rothberg's *Multidirectional Memories* have further demonstrated the necessity of a nuanced and contextual study of memories of the National Socialist atrocities and those committed in the European colonial territories.[18] Here, however, a nuanced examination of Stalin's crimes tends to fall by the wayside, such as when Rothberg critiques Hannah Arendt's linkage of 'disparate phenomena such as imperialism, Nazism, and Stalinism' (43) in her *Origins*. Such blanket rejections of any comparability of these phenomena disregards, for example, Russia's imperial policies in, and Orientalist conceptions of, Central Asia, which the Soviet Union inherited from its Tsarist predecessor and pursued under different parameters.[19] Furthermore, the overlapping experiences and memories of National Socialism and Stalinism form precisely part of Europe's multidirectional memories, which have been coming to the fore in German debates since unification.

Indeed, the close connections between the ways in which Stalinism and National Socialism implemented their systems of terror are evident given their overlapping temporality; their drive for total control of the state and organisation of its citizenry into politically streamlined mass organisations; as well as their mass atrocities and competing expansionist power struggles. The sidelining of Stalinism in these comparative studies around the Holocaust is thus itself born of the old Cold War divides, in which such comparisons carried the meanings of a Holocaust apologia. But nothing was further from the heart of those German-speaking Jewish writers who sympathized with the Communist cause and were caught in the crossfire between both regimes. Their writings offer a route of investigation into both systems that does not shirk the questions of political responsibility and personal agency on either side of the political divide.

Alice Rühle-Gerstel, *The Break*

Although Arthur Koestler's *Darkness at Noon*, first published in German in 1940, provided the famed template for this body of critical writing, it was preceded by Alice Rühle-Gerstel's novel *Der Umbruch oder Hanna und die Freiheit* ('The Break or Hanna and Freedom').[20] Today Rühle-Gerstel, who was born into a middle-class German-speaking Jewish family in Prague in 1894, is largely forgotten, even though her work has recently seen something of a revival on the German literary scene.[21] Between 1918 and 1932, Rühle-Gerstel lived in Munich and Dresden, where she authored several psychoanalytic, Marxist, feminist and sexological works. From 1932 to 1935, Rühle-Gerstel and her husband Otto lived in Prague, where Rühle-Gerstel's friendship and rumoured lesbian relationship with the Czech writer Milena Jesenská – Kafka's one-time lover and recipient of his *Letters to Milena* – brought her into contact with Czech opposition Communists and Trotskyists.[22] In 1936, Rühle-Gerstel followed her husband into Mexican exile, where she wrote *The Break* at the height of the Stalinist purges between 1937 and 1938. The novel, which critically examines the political cleansings among the German exile community in Czechoslovakia, would only be published posthumously in 1984. In Mexico, Rühle-Gerstel, who firmly saw herself as an internationalist and anti-Stalinist, struck up friendships with Diego Rivera, Frida Kahlo and Leon Trotsky, who was murdered there at Stalin's command in 1940. Deeply disillusioned personally and politically by her dual experience of National Socialism and Stalinism, Rühle-Gerstel committed suicide in 1943 by jumping from the window of her flat in Mexico City, just hours after her husband had passed away.

The Break weaves together the multiple political and personal dimensions which Rühle-Gerstel had addressed in her earlier essayistic oeuvre. These are also reflected in the novel's title, which in German stands for both rupture and the process of page make-up in newspaper print. The lead protagonist Hanna's realisation in the newspaper office where she finds employment in Prague that 'Make-up occurs every day' (260) reflects the huge political and personal ruptures of the time, which here variously signify the National Socialists' rise to power; Hanna's emigration from Berlin to Prague; her gradual alienation from the Communist-led exile movement; and her liberation from both bourgeois and the Communist Party's conceptions of female subjectivity and sexuality. Rühle-Gerstel's dissent from hard-line party politics thus lies precisely in her holistic conception of the Marxist personality type, which retains the important features of individuality – marked as 'bourgeois' in official party propaganda – even under the conditions of class struggle and the fight against Fascism.

In Rühle-Gerstel, as later in Koestler, Jewishness remains an implicit or subdued feature in the narrative. This reflects the high degree of assimilation which often marked the background of those Jewish authors who later joined the Communist movement. For these authors, the revolutionary relegation of Jewishness as a 'secondary problem' that would be resolved through class struggle thus did not pose an inherent problem to their already secularized self-conception. But this did not necessarily mean that they rejected their Jewishness. Rather, many Jewish Communists saw their political engagement as the necessary consequence of the lethal history of European antisemitism since the Middle Ages. Given the extraordinary contribution of German-speaking Jews, including Karl Marx, Ferdinand Lassalle and Rosa Luxemburg, to the socialist and Communist movements, Jewish Communists could see themselves as part of a specifically Jewish legacy within the political fight for social justice. Their secular Jewish awareness rendered these writers sensitive to the early signs of the antisemitism in Stalinist politics, which also lay dormant in the 1930s propaganda against bourgeois intellectuals and internationalists.

Jewish themes and associations in their writings serve as a site of disturbance of, and resistance against, the grip of Stalinism. While Rühle-Gerstel's *The Break*, for example, makes only passing reference to Jews, who are mentioned alongside other émigrés and among the politicized, the lead protagonist Hanna Aschbach – ostensibly the daughter of a Czech mother and a German father – bears implicit Jewish connotations through her name, as well as through her brother's occupation as a banker. Having grown up bilingually, Hanna's predicament of non-belonging, which results from having grown up in between national affiliations, echoes the deterritorialized state of Jewish identity in the diaspora. Hanna's sense that because '[h]er father was German, her mother was Czech, she belonged neither here nor there' (34) thus invokes Gregor Samsa's fantastical wanderings across all the planes of his room in Kafka's *Metamorphosis*, which have been read to symbolize the shifting ethnic, national and cultural locations of acculturated Jews in early twentieth-century Prague.[23] For Hanna, this predicament of non-belonging fuels her work for the party, for 'we are internationalists, words such as strange lands, home country, abroad mean nothing to us, for there are comrades everywhere' (66).

Hanna's internationalism, however, renders her a singular figure in the text, and her constant perception by other protagonists as an outsider reflects the ostracized status of the Jew as perpetual outsider, which Hannah Arendt would describe so memorably in *The Jew as Pariah* (1944) just a few years later.[24] Such moments of alienation are numerous in the text, for example when the staff at the German refugee hostel treat Hanna with suspicion due to her 'face, which seemed so foreign to the workers' (63), as well as her educated middle-class origins. Hanna is then interrogated by one of their leaders, who accuses her of having stolen the till from her local resistance group back in Berlin. This is only the beginning of Hanna's decline, which ends when the party itself betrays her to the police for having engaged in political work, thus invalidating her refugee status and causing her extradition from Czechoslovakia.

In the novel, the process of political disillusionment is focalized through Hanna. Upon her arrival in Prague, Hanna still idolized the Soviet Union that she had experienced during a visit in 1931, with its spirit of awakening due to its new agricultural programme and five-year plan, and the Russians' fervent love for their country. Now, however, 'the second five-year plan had come around, the masses continued to starve heroically' (120), while the most efficient workers were beginning to enjoy a better lifestyle. Wasn't this, Hanna ruminates, akin to the 'worst type of capitalist slave-driving for the piece rate'? (120) By suggesting that the mass starvation of millions of Soviets during the early 1930s was not simply a necessary stage in the construction of the new Soviet society, but the product of wilful negligence at best and cynical calculation at worst, Rühle-Gerstel injects the official Communist narrative of Soviet moral and social superiority with severe doubt.

Final doubt is shed on the Soviet project when, further on in the novel, comparisons with the National Socialist persecutions become ever more explicit. Hanna thus feels the Czech party's attempts to bring its members into line with new Soviet directives 'to be awfully similar to Hitler's persecutions into the third and fourth generations' (168), and the Communist daily to 'write almost as nationalistically as a fascist paper' (348). An inkling of the violent nature of the purges shines through the ellipses in the unfinished sentence when Hanna peruses the newspaper's reports 'of vast party purges and its threats of an iron broom that … set in such small print so as to be hard to read' (348). The party ultimately stands for 'right wing' (402) politics.

Hanna's alienation from Stalinist party Communism runs parallel to her move towards two alternative male figures, Leon Trotsky and Anatol Svoboda, both of whom the novel ultimately treats with hesitation, albeit in different ways. Although Trotsky does not make an appearance in the novel himself, the text sees several of Hanna's friends turn to Trotskyism as a rallying point against hard-line Stalinist party Communism. But Rühle-Gerstel does not let Hanna herself replace Stalin with the new political father figure of Trotsky. Instead, we see Hanna make her way to Spain, where the Popular Front is as yet a leftist movement in flux and offers itself more readily to Rühle-Gerstel's vision of a more fluid Marxist internationalist, gender and sexual politics beyond party structures. But the novel's ending, which leaves Hanna alone in the geographic no-man's land between Bohemia and Austria, suggests that this is a utopian vision that cannot be realized under the contemporaneous political conditions.

The other, more tangible alternative in the novel is offered by the figure of Anatol Svoboda, editor of the Czech newspaper, which incidentally bears his last name, where Hanna has been placed by the Prague party chapter. Svoboda means 'freedom' in Czech, and both Anatol and his paper represent the positively configured bourgeois attributes of 'libertarianism, patriotism, and cosmopolitanism as its leitmotifs' (72). Of course, the party had quickly denounced the new publication, but the novel conveys the considerable allure of its values through Hanna's infatuation with the much younger Anatol. For a while, Hanna and Anatol emerge as nearly like-minded protagonists. The son of a Hungarian mother and a Czech father, Anatol, like Hanna, implicitly displays the physical and intellectual attributes of the Jew. Upon their first encounter, Hanna thus perceives Anatol with his 'glowing […] dark eyes' (98), 'olive-yellow' (136) complexion, and 'strange, non-European' (ibid.) appearance as 'nervous, nervous, a nervous aesthete …' (98). After all, the claims of the Jews' hybrid racial origins, together with their alleged special proclivity for neurasthenia and lacking cultural essence, lay central to the mythology of modern racial antisemitism.[25]

With her husband Karl, a Communist resister and sex educator, interned in a National Socialist jail in Germany, Hanna feels herself to be temporarily single and thus free to embark on a relationship with Svoboda, in which she finds herself fully orgasmic for the first time in her life. The conditions of exile and political illegality allow Hanna to temporarily suspend the constraints of both bourgeois and Communist conceptions of heterosexual relationships, and her liaison with Svoboda ultimately catalyses her growing dissidence from the

Communist Party. This portrayal seems to reiterate, and apply to Stalinism, the German-Jewish Marxist psychoanalyst Wilhelm Reich's construction of the sexually repressed personality as the essential predicament of the authoritarian regimes that Fascism epitomized. Conversely, then, according to Reich's *The Mass Psychology of Fascism* (1933), 'the objective loosening of the reactionary shackles placed on sexuality' would effectively disable the politically repressive regime.[26]

This process also seems at work in Rühle-Gerstel's *The Break*, where the liberation of Hanna's libido develops alongside her dissident status in the party. Tellingly, the consolidation of Stalinist party politics materializes towards the novel's end in the announcement of a new and more restrictive sexual politics. The party's previous approach had been governed by pragmatism, whereby sexuality was only a secondary issue, given the primacy of political struggle. In the past, both Hanna and Karl had defended this view. But in her encounter with Anatol, Hanna realizes that the party's view of sex as a 'hygienic measure' (165) to safeguard the primacy of political struggle has left her sexually unfulfilled even in her relationship with her beloved Karl. Yet the ending of the novel reinstates the importance of political struggle over the sexual and the wider personal, albeit under reconfigured parameters, as Hanna leaves behind both Karl and Anatol for an uncertain journey to join the Spanish Interbrigades. In doing so, Hanna symbolically rejects both the party Communism of her adult life and the bourgeois cosmopolitanism of her upbringing, which both men represent respectively, and instead embraces a truly internationalist stance.

Hanna's departure from all male-defined co-ordinates of her previous life suggests the nomadic rootlessness of the modern woman, which oddly recalls Weininger's notion of women and Jews as signifiers of rootless modernity.[27] Unlike Weininger, however, Rühle-Gerstel does not present this rootlessness as an essentialized paradigm of the woman and the Jew. Instead, she suggests Hanna's nomadism as the only viable stance to disrupt the ideologies of modernity – National Socialism and party Communism, as well as bourgeois liberalism and its cosmopolitan configuration – that have led society into a literal dead end.

Arthur Koestler, *Darkness at Noon*

When Arthur Koestler wrote his seminal novel *Darkness at Noon* (1940), he obviously did so with far more extensive knowledge of the Great Purges than Rühle-Gerstel had available in 1937–8.[28] The son of a Hungarian-Jewish father and an Austrian-Jewish mother, Koestler was born in Budapest in 1905. He joined the Zionist movement while a student in Vienna, becoming head of the Association of Zionist Student Leagues and forming the Activists' League, an organisation sympathetic to Wladimir Jabotinsky's Zionist right wing. This led to his rejection by the socialist Kibbutzim after his emigration to Palestine in 1926, which would provide a first point of dissonance with the socialist movement. In 1931, while living in Berlin, Koestler nonetheless joined the Communist Party. In 1933, he went into exile in Paris, just after having visited the Soviet Union. He left the Communist Party in 1938 and, after a four-month internment in the notorious Le Vernet camp, found refuge in Britain in 1940. He died in London in 1983.

Darkness at Noon provided the first concerted attempt to address the Great Purges. The novel conveys the profound disillusionment and shock that Koestler felt during his 1933 visit to the Soviet Union, during which he encountered what would become his novel's central theme. This was Stalinism's betrayal of its own subjects, which he had encountered during his Soviet visit and which he now located in the foundations of Stalinist ideology and politics. Set in a Soviet jail, the novel explores the Stalinist purges of first-guard revolutionaries between 1936 and 1938 through the eyes of the accused former Comintern representative Nicolas Salmanovitch Rubashov. Through Rubashov, Koestler places the Jew at the centre of the Stalinist narrative and its critical examination, as well as pre-empting the post-1945 Stalinist persecution of Jews among the Communist guard. Similarly to Rühle-Gerstel's Hanna, however, Rubashov's Jewishness remains only implicit, a narrative strategy reflecting the subordinate role of Jewishness within both assimilationist and Communist identity politics.[29] Rubashov's Jewish origins are suggested through his middle name, Salmanovitch, which indicates that his father bore the Hebrew first name Salomon (Shlomo). In this context, Rubashov's intellectual pretences, his internationalist convictions, and extensive travels abroad, which link him to the image of the Jew as a nomad, add further meaning. While installed as a functionary, Rubashov's 'long difficult to understand' (KD, 15) speeches at conferences, which suggest his abstract intellectualism – a mode of thinking that antisemitic discourse ascribed to the Jews – had praised the Comintern and the world revolution. Now, the party deems him a 'Querulous intellectual' (KD, 29) and thus suspect.

As was the case with so many, Rubashov's faithful service, first to the revolution, then to the Communist state, predestines him for, rather then protects him from, the purges. Once a dedicated Communist, Rubashov has delivered others presumed to be political deviants to the deadly purges. These, however, have left him increasingly disillusioned until his turn has come. The same is true for another convict in the jail. This is the former chairman of the Comintern, a thinly veiled reference to the real-life figure of Grigory Zinoviev, also a Jew and former leader of the Comintern, who was executed in the purges in 1936. Zinoviev's case illustrates the complex relationship between Communist perpetrators and their victims, for he himself had provided the ideological justification for the Stalinist mass murder when he declared at a 1918 meeting of Bolsheviks that 'we must carry along with us 90 out of the 100 million of Soviet Russia's inhabitants. As for the rest, we have nothing to say to them. They must be annihilated.'[30] But by 1936, as Stalin was establishing his new Soviet nationalism, a close involvement in the Comintern meant a death sentence, no matter how faithful a functionary had been to the early revolutionary cause. As Rubashov's interrogator Gletkin states:

> The policy of the International had to be subordinated to our national policy. Whoever did not understand this necessity had to be destroyed. Whole sets of our best functionaries in Europe had to be physically liquidated. We did not recoil from crushing our own organizations abroad when the interests of the Bastion required it. (KD, 226)

As Koestler shows, the particular horror of the Stalinist persecutions lay in the victims' extensive collaboration and identification with their persecutors because the previous generation of victims had been the hangmen in the past. In his earlier role as a Comintern functionary, Rubashov himself had travelled on a mission abroad to purge Communist resisters in National Socialist Germany because they had customized the party's leaflets to speak more effectively to the masses. This was deemed an aberration from the party line, even if it occurred in the service of its cause. Most importantly, however, Stalinism also achieved its lethal effect by compelling its victims to behave according to their own belief system. Rubashov thus conceives his relationship with his interrogator, Ivanov, as that of twins 'nourished by the umbilical cord of a common conviction. [...] They had the same moral standard, the same philosophy, they thought in the same terms. Their positions might just as well have been the other way round' (KD, 110). Out of sheer party discipline, the victims performed the part of the traitor because that was what their leaders required of them.

Unlike Rühle-Gerstel's *The Break*, which outlines, through its female figure Hanna, an internal position of dissent from Stalinism within the Communist idea, any internal resistance has become eroded in Koestler's novel. Stalinism has consumed the Communist idea in its entirety, and having previously been the hangmen, the victims have lost any position of moral authority over their perpetrators. This is, of course, yet another moment where the psychological mechanisms at work in Stalin's and Hitler's atrocities seem to overlap. In his final book *The Drowned and the Saved* (1986), Primo Levi, too, observed an 'identification or imitation, or exchange of roles between oppressor and victim' in his study of the Jewish special squads at Auschwitz, who were forced to aid the SS in processing the dead bodies produced in the gas chambers.[31] Therein, however, also lie the essential differences in the ideological conception of the Soviet and the German atrocities. For in the National Socialist camps, the seeming convergence between masters and slaves never suspended the hierarchy of power that marked the biologized difference between the masters and their slaves, whereby all Jews were designated to die, whether they had been accessories to the murder or not. Such essentialized differences did not exist between Stalin's henchmen and their victims, and Stalin could thus ideologically contaminate his victims in a way that National Socialism, which viewed its Jewish victims as subhuman outsiders and therefore did not require them to identify with its cause, did not demand.

This is, of course, not to say that Stalin's crimes equalled or outweighed Hitler's, but rather to pinpoint the finer nuances by which both ideologies enveloped and utilized their victims in different ways. In *Darkness at Noon*, however, National Socialism and Stalinism still look deceptively similar on the surface. This emerges most clearly in the novel's final scene, when Rubashov, having made a false confession, is convicted and led down the steps of a basement to his execution. In his dying moments, he dreams of his arrest, wondering whether it is the portrait of Stalin or Hitler which is looking down on him:

> He with the ironic smile or he with the glassy gaze? A shapeless figure bent over him, he smelt the fresh leather of the revolver belt; but what insignia did the figure wear on the sleeves and shoulder straps of its uniform – and in whose name did it raise the dark pistol barrel? (KD, 254)

Such analogies, however, do not serve to absolve individual responsibility by pointing one's finger at another, presumably similar, evil. If anything, such comparisons serve as a last call to awaken the human and leftist conscience in particular, in order to disrupt everyday complacency towards such atrocities. Koestler's later writing suggests that these analogies between National Socialism and Stalinism result from the timing of *Darkness at Noon*, which was written several years before the National Socialists' Final Solution unfolded. Before the erection of the death camps, it was possible to read Stalin and Hitler as evil twins who both utilized seemingly similar mechanisms to manipulate the masses and ensnare their political victims. The knowledge of the death camps changed that. When the bare outlines of that news emerged, albeit riddled with inaccuracies in detail due to the sparse information available, there is no question for Koestler about the unique nature of that crime. As he wrote in his essay 'On Disbelieving Atrocities' (1944) on the annihilation of European Jewry: 'It is the greatest mass-killing in recorded history; and it goes on daily, hourly, as regularly as the ticking of your watch.'[32]

Manès Sperber, *Like a Tear in the Ocean*

In making the Holocaust the universal paradigm of the human loss resulting from modern mass violence, Manès Sperber's *Like a Tear in the Ocean* similarly suggests the uniqueness of the National Socialist genocide, while simultaneously probing into its intersections with Stalinism.[33] Sperber's trilogy on the Communist struggle in times of war, written in German but first published in French between 1948 and 1952, delivers extensive descriptions of Stalinist atrocities as well as referring to the National Socialists' destruction of European Jewry, albeit by refraining from a representation of the gas-chamber killings themselves. Sperber was born into an Orthodox Jewish family, in eastern Galicia in 1905, where he received a traditional Jewish upbringing. Like Koestler, Sperber joined the Communist Party while living in Berlin, and he left the party while living in exile in Paris. In 1942, by then in Swiss exile, Sperber began writing the first book of his trilogy, which he completed in 1948. Having returned to Paris, he wrote the second and third volumes of the trilogy between 1948 and 1951.

The case of Willi Münzenberg and his associates is echoed throughout the first two volumes of Sperber's trilogy. In 1918, Münzenburg, a non-Jew from a working-class family, had co-founded the German Communist Party. Münzenberg was a leading Comintern member, and he remained a loyal Stalinist until the beginning of the Great Purges in 1936. But when Münzenberg refused to purge the KPD, his own life became endangered. Within two years, the vast majority of Münzenberg's associates had been expelled or killed by the NKVD, and in 1940 Münzenberg himself was found strangled in a forest in south-eastern France. His killers are widely believed to have been Stalin's agents. The historic figure of Münzenberg is echoed in Sperber's protagonist Herbert Soennecke, once a popular leader of the working class and a friend of Rosa Luxemburg, who is brought to trial in Moscow, accused of being a Trotskyite and shot. By the end of the novel, most of Soennecke's associates, just like Münzenberger's, have been killed by the GPU or delivered into the National Socialists' hands. 'Nowhere else in the world have so many Communists been killed as in Russia' (1:,332), Sperber has one of them, a man called Albert Gräfe, say. The party delivers Gräfe to the Gestapo, but he survives National Socialist torture, jail and camp internment, believing it was Soennecke who betrayed him. Meanwhile, his lover Erna, led by the party to believe it was her fault, commits suicide. Later on, in Swiss exile, Gräfe survives a violent attack by party agents, who then betray him to the Swiss police as a double agent of the Gestapo and GPU. In the end, he is murdered by Fascist Croatians while in flight through Yugoslavia.

Betrayal of his most faithful comrades lay at the heart of Stalin's power politics. Sperber reveals the anatomy of this system's total moral evisceration of its subjects in the section dealing with the farcical investigation and murder of Soennecke and two of his comrades in Moscow. As the interrogator, a 'clever and obviously experienced' man (1: 349) explains to Soennecke, the true reason for his conviction is found in his being 'an old revolutionary, and therefore, *ipso facto*, an opponent of the present regime' (all emphasis in the original, ibid.). But unless Soennecke falsely confesses to having planned Stalin's assassination, all parties and their organs, as well as intellectual sympathizers globally, will be instructed to denounce him as a National Socialist agent and counter-revolutionary the next day. This process is necessary, the interrogator states, to cleanse the party's reputation from the many grave mistakes it has committed: 'Afterwards the water's dirty, but the Party's clean. Under what epithet a man dies is utterly unimportant' (1: 351).

As Sperber's account of the interrogation suggests, the merged identities of hangmen and victims safeguards the smooth running of this system. For up until this point, and despite nagging doubt, Soennecke has delivered his own comrades to their incarceration and death. Therefore, the interrogator argues, Soennecke's refusal to die himself according to this logic bears no scrutiny. Conversely, the hangman's compliance was ensured by giving him a previous taste of the Gulag, 'and there's no place in the world where dying's easier' (1: 350). But Soennecke dies steadfast, despite threats to target his children.

As Sperber suggests, Stalinist ideology depended on a supreme degree to its internalisation by the individual, to the extent of total self-sacrifice and self-effacement for the clean reputation of the party. As Hannah Arendt argued in her *Origins*, the demand for 'total, unrestricted, unconditional, and unalterable loyalty of the individual member' (323) formed the hallmark of totalitarian movements.[34] This is the 'atomized individual' (338) of modern society, whose lacking social ties form the essential precondition for its total surrender to the party or movement. Arising from the great upheavals of the Bolshevik Revolution, Arendt argued, the early Soviet Union thus became a laboratory for the workings of totalitarian power. Soviet propaganda specialized in coercing the 'isolated mass man' (353) into fabricated self-confessions of guilt, which were essentially predicated on this individual's great dependency on the party or movement for its sense of personal truth and belonging.

In *Like a Tear*, the leading protagonist Doino Faber, who like Sperber hailed from the provinces of Tsarist Russia and abandoned his traditional Jewish upbringing for Communism, represents Arendt's atomized modern individual per se. As a child, Faber had been taught to wait for the Messiah, who would do away with the Tsar's executions of innocent people. Having grown older, he rejected such a passive stance and instead chose, in the words of his friend Stetten, a different kind of 'Messiah, only now he calls him "world revolution" or perhaps a "classless society"' (1: 146). This atomized state becomes even further pronounced under the intersecting conditions of political illegality, exile and the Stalinist persecutions. The text's unpredictable shifts into a multitude of characters and perspectives, whose identities often emerge only after several pages of narration, reflect the isolated condition of Sperber's protagonists, who are struggling for moral integrity and, ultimately, sheer physical survival. In this situation, leaving the party, or being marked a traitor by it, is tantamount to death:

> Perhaps it is the anguish of solitude and of being deprived of all future. What is usually called sadness contains within itself the consolations of self-pity. But this particular anguish destroys that pity: it petrifies your heart and immobilizes time itself. (2: 70)

The novel lets Faber's Jewishness emerge as a humanising feature that will enable him to take on the role of witness and break through his emotional ossification. Before their execution, both Soennecke and his associate Vasso had outlined the survivor's role in identifying individual responsibility for the Stalinist atrocities and preserving the memory of the crimes, without either rejecting Communism on the one hand, or succumbing to the logic of his murderers on the other. The trilogy's prologue, which relates a modern version of the biblical story of the burning bush, reflects the centrality of Jewish paradigms for Sperber's vision of the dashed hopes of Communism. The fires of the burning bush, from which the hidden Hebrew god speaks to Moses in the Torah, has led humans to live in its light, until one day the branches and even the roots of the bush are consumed to ash. But the new masters kill everyone who expresses their sense of betrayal that the miracle has failed. Hope, the novel suggests, only lies in the steadfast rejection of power and in the embracing of the victims' stance in its stead, as the only resistance that does not repeat injustice. At the end of the novel, Faber thus reaffirms his earlier realisation 'that power corrupts, and that, therefore, the man who has it inevitably misuses it' (1: 145), by rejecting political action. This development runs parallel to his renewed interest in Jewish tradition, if only as an intellectual blueprint. Faber's ultimate recovered memory of the Jewish legend of the Lamed Vov, the 36 just men who are said to exist in every generation, and whose merits ensure the continued existence of the world, thus maintains the imperative of justice, albeit in a reconfigured way.

Faber's embrace of a non-violent stance runs parallel to the story of the Jews of Wolyna, whom his counterpart Edi, a secular Viennese Jew and social democrat, encounters in Poland on the eve of the Germans occupation of their town. Faced with their imminent annihilation, the rabbi and his son refuse to follow Edi's call for armed resistance. 'Try, just once, to describe a battle', the rabbi's son tells Edi, 'and you will find that all those actions taken together are smaller and more shapeless than a tear in the sea' (3: 190). The centrality of this statement for the novel, which is reiterated in its title, is apparent. These teachings, then, chime with the convictions of Faber's Viennese friend and professor of history, von Stetten, who represents 'the corpse of Austria' (1: 228) with its destroyed liberal legacy. Through this construction, Sperber aligns the Jews with the lost cosmopolitanist cause of the inter-war period, which has died a violent death in the National Socialist and Stalinist persecutions.

Conclusion

Sperber wrote the last two volumes of his trilogy against the backdrop of renewed Stalinist purges, in which the persecution of internationalists assumed a clearly antisemitic tone. The 1930s purges had occurred on the back of the Stalin-Trotsky split. When in 1948 Yugoslavia embarked on a more liberal version of Communism under Josip Broz Tito, a new series of purges began across the Soviet satellite countries. The antisemitic tone of the new purges culminated in the infamous Prague show trial in November 1952, when Rudolf Slánský, Secretary General of the Czech Communist Party, and 13 other high-ranking members of the Czech Communist establishment were charged with high treason, and Zionist conspiracy, murder, espionage, Titoism. Eleven of the 14 defendants were Jews. Slánský and 10 others were hanged, the remaining three sentenced to life. While the National Socialist and Stalinist persecutions of the Jews by no means ended the Jewish engagement with cosmopolitanism, the concept of the 'Jewish cosmopolitan' would, from now on, be ever more contested.

As I have argued in this piece, exiled leftist Jewish intellectuals and writers led the way in the critical examination of the Stalinist and National Socialist crimes. The literary authors discussed in this article – Alice Rühle-Gerstel, Arthur Koestler and Manès Sperber – stand as exemplars for this body of writing. Given the close historical proximity of Stalin's crimes to Hitler's, it seems almost inevitable that these writers would draw analogies between the atrocities of both systems, if perhaps mainly to draw attention to the Stalinist persecutions that were happening in their midst. Indeed, these intellectuals' experiences of political and racial persecution by the National Socialists significantly brought into focus their budding critique of Stalin's regime. This was particularly so because Hitler's rise to power, their flight into exile, and the beginning of Stalin's Great Purges not only closely coincided but were also intricately linked. The soul-searching writings of these authors with their quest for personal responsibility offer an important vantage point from which to consider the obvious similarities and differences between Hitler's and Stalin's crimes. They open up perspectives that resist the relativisation of either atrocity, a strategy that had always, from the start, served to permit the avoidance of political and individual responsibility on either side of the political divide.

Notes

1. See Philip Spencer, who reads Marx's critique of Bruno Bauer as an expression of Kantian cosmopolitanism because of Marx's insistence that Jews and Judaism should have the same political rights as all other individuals (in this volume). See also Fine, "Rereading Marx on the 'Jewish Question.'"
2. Quoted in Grüner, *Patrioten und Kosmopoliten*, 42 (my translation).
3. See Claussen, "Versuch über den Antizionismus," 15.
4. For these figures, see Grüner (note 2), 136 and 147, as well as Snyder, *Bloodlands*, 67.
5. For these figures, see Courtois et al., *The Black Book of Communism*, 298–301.
6. Leder, *My Life in Stalinist Russia*, 288.
7. See Kwiet and Eschwege, *Selbstbehauptung und Widerstand*, 113f.
8. Hitler, *Mein Kampf*, 459.
9. Arendt, *The Origins of Totalitarianism*.
10. Benhabib, *Another Cosmopolitanism*, 15ff.
11. See Fine, *Political Investigations: Hegel, Marx, Arendt*, 107.
12. Améry, *At the Mind's Limits*.
13. Nolte, "Zwischen Geschichtslegende und Revisionismus? Das Dritte Reich im Blickwinkel des Jahres 1980."
14. Nolte, "Vergangenheit, die nicht vergehen will," 45 (my translation)
15. Kehrig, "Zum Geleit," 11 (my translation).
16. Snyder, *Bloodlands*.
17. Bauman, *Modernity and the Holocaust*, 2 and xii (all emphasis in the original).
18. Rothberg, *Multidirectional Memory*.
19. See Tolz, *Russia's Own Orient*.
20. Rühle-Gerstel, *Der Umbruch oder Hanna und die Freiheit* (all translations mine).
21. This biographical sketch follows Anna Marková's afterword, "Alice Rühle-Gerstel, eine deutsch-jüdische Intellektuelle aus Prag," in Rühle-Gerstel, *Der Umbruch* (note 20), 417–41.
22. Kafka, *Letters to Milena*.
23. Robertson, *Kafka: Judaism, Politics, and Literature*.
24. Arendt, *The Jew as Pariah*.
25. See Gilman, *Difference and Pathology*.
26. Reich, *The Mass Psychology of Fascism*, 224.
27. Weininger, *Sex & Character*.
28. Koestler, *Darkness at Noon*.
29. This subdued importance of Jewishness also marked Koestler's attitudes. See Cesarani, *Arthur Koestler*, 398.
30. Pipes, *The Russian Revolution*, 820.
31. Levi, *The Drowned and the Saved*, 48.
32. Koestler, "On Disbelieving Atrocities," 90.
33. Sperber, *Like A Tear in the Ocean*.
34. See Arendt, *Origins*.

Funding

This work was supported by the Arts and Humanities Research Council [grant number AH/K003771/1].

Bibliography

Améry, Jean. *At the Mind's Limits: Contemplations by a Survivor on Auschwitz and its Realities*. Translated by Sidney Rosenfeld and Stella P. Rosenfeld. Bloomington: Indiana University Press, 1980.
Arendt, Hannah. *The Jew as Pariah: Jewish Identity and Politics in the Modern Age*. New York: Grove Press, 1978.
Arendt, Hannah. *The Origins of Totalitarianism*. Orlando: Harcourt, 1985.
Bauman, Zygmunt. *Modernity and the Holocaust*. Ithaca, NY: Cornell University Press, 1996.
Benhabib, Seyla. *Another Cosmopolitanism*. Oxford: Oxford University Press, 2008.
Carew Hunt, Robert Nigel. *A Guide to Communist Jargon*. London: Geoffrey Bles, 1957.
Cesarani, David. *Arthur Koestler*. New York: Free Press, 1998.
Claussen, Detlev. "Versuch über den Antizionismus." In Léon Poliakov, *Vom Antizionismus zum Antisemitismus*. Translated by Franziska Sick, Elfriede Müller, and Michael T. Koltan, 7–20. Freiburg: Ça ira, 2013.
Courtois, Stéphane, et al., eds. *The Black Book of Communism: Crimes, Terror, Repression*. Translated by Jonathan Murphy and Mark Kramer. Cambridge, MA: Harvard University Press, 1999.
Fine, Robert. *Political Investigations: Hegel, Marx, Arendt*. London: Routledge, 2001.
Fine, Robert. "Rereading Marx on the 'Jewish Question': Marx as a Critic of Antisemitism?" In *Antisemitism and the Constitution of Sociology*, edited by Marcel Stoetzler. Lincoln, NE: University of Nebraska Press, 2014.
Gilman, Sander L. *Difference and Pathology: Stereotypes of Sexuality, Race, and Madness*. Ithaca: Cornell University Press, 1985.
Grüner, Frank. *Patrioten und Kosmopoliten: Juden im Sowjetstaat 1941–1953*. Cologne: Böhlau, 2008.
Hitler, Adolf. *Mein Kampf*. Translated by Ralph Manheim. Boston: Houghton Mifflin, 1943.
Hoffmann, Joachim. *Stalins Vernichtungskrieg 1941–1945: Planung, Ausführung und Dokumentation*. Munich: Herbig, 2000.
Kafka, Franz. *Letters to Milena*. Translated by Philip Boehm. New York: Schocken Books, 1990.
Kehrig, Manfred. "Zum Geleit." In Joachim Hoffmann, *Stalins Vernichtungskrieg 1941–1945: Planung, Ausführung und Dokumentation*. Munich: Herbig, 2000.
Koestler, Arthur. "On Disbelieving Atrocities." In *The Yogi and the Commissar, and other Essays*, 81–93. London: Hutchinson, 1965.
Koestler, Arthur. *Darkness at Noon*. Translated by Daphne Hardy. London: Hutchinson, 1973.
Kwiet, Konrad, and Helmut Eschwege. *Selbstbehauptung und Widerstand: Deutsche Juden im Kampf um Existenz und Menschenwürde, 1933–1945*. Hamburg: Christians, 1984.
Leder, Mary M. *My Life in Stalinist Russia*. Bloomington, IN: Indiana University Press, 2001.
Levi, Primo. *The Drowned and the Saved*. New York: Vintage International, 1989.

Nolte, Ernst. "Vergangenheit, die nicht vergehen will. Eine Rede, die geschrieben, aber nicht gehalten werden konnte." In *Historikerstreit: Die Dokumentation der Kontroverse um die Einzigartigkeit der nationalsozialistischen Judenvernichtung*, ed. n.n., 39–47. Munich: Piper, 1987.

Nolte, Ernest. "Zwischen Geschichtslegende und Revisionismus? Das Dritte Reich im Blickwinkel des Jahres 1980." In *Historikerstreit: Die Dokumentation der Kontroverse um die Einzigartigkeit des nationalsozialistischen Judenvernichtung*, edited by n.n., 13–35. Munich: Piper, 1987.

Pipes, Richard. *The Russian Revolution, 1899–1919*. London: Fontana Press, 1990.

Reich, Wilhelm. *The Mass Psychology of Fascism*. Translated by Vincent R. Carfagno. London: Penguin Books, 1970.

Robertson, Ritchie. *Kafka: Judaism, Politics, and Literature*. Oxford: Oxford University Press, 1985.

Rothberg, Michael. *Multidirectional Memory: Remembering the Holocaust in the Age of Decolonization*. Stanford, CA: Stanford University Press, 2009.

Rühle-Gerstel, Alice. *Der Umbruch oder Hanna und die Freiheit*. Berlin: Aviva, 2007.

Snyder, Timothy. *Bloodlands: Europe Between Hitler and Stalin*. London: Bodley Head, 2011.

Sperber, Manès. *Like A Tear in the Ocean*. Translated by Constantine Fitzgibbon. 3 vols. New York: Holmes and Meier, 1988.

Tolz, Vera. *Russia's Own Orient: The Politics of Identity and Oriental Studies in the Late Imperial and Early Soviet Periods*. Oxford: Oxford University Press, 2011.

Weininger, Otto. *Sex & Character*. London: Heinemann, 1906.

JEWS AND THE NEW COSMOPOLITANISM

Inviting essential outsiders in: imagining a cosmopolitan nation

Claire Sutherland

ABSTRACT
The article uses the archetype of a cosmopolitan, diasporic Jewish community to reassess the 'imagined community' of the nation. It takes as its starting point the notion of 'Essential Outsiders' mooted by Anthony Reid and Daniel Chirot in their so-titled, comparative study of Jewish and Chinese entrepreneurs in Europe and South-East Asia respectively. Drawing on Benedict Anderson's methodological writings, the article discusses the possibility and desirability of such cross-cultural and continental comparisons. It uses work by Pheng Cheah, Heonik Kwon and Angharad Closs Stephens to examine the relationship between cosmopolitanism and nationalism, questioning whether this is indeed as antagonistic as it might first appear. Building on this analysis, the article explores alternatives to the bounded 'imagined community', of which 'Essential Outsiders' form a constituent part. The article considers new ways of thinking the nation using the guiding metaphor of ghosts and haunting. It asks: can the idea of Jews as 'Essential Outsiders' prompt the development of new models of national belonging for the twenty-first century?

This article uses the archetype of a cosmopolitan, diasporic Jewish community to reassess the 'imagined community' of the nation.[1] It takes as its starting point the notion of 'Essential Outsiders' mooted by Anthony Reid and Daniel Chirot in their so-titled, comparative study of Jewish and Chinese entrepreneurs in Europe and Southeast Asia, respectively.[2] Drawing on Benedict Anderson's methodological writings, the article discusses the possibility and desirability of such cross-cultural and continental comparisons. It uses work by Pheng Cheah, Heonik Kwon and Angharad Closs Stephens to examine the relationship between cosmopolitanism and nationalism, questioning whether this is indeed as antagonistic as it might first appear. Building on this analysis, the article explores alternatives to the bounded 'imagined community', of which 'Essential Outsiders' form a constituent part. The article considers new ways of thinking the nation using the guiding metaphor of ghosts and haunting, and asks, can the idea of Jews as 'Essential Outsiders' prompt the development of new models of national belonging for the twenty-first century?

Daniel Chirot's introduction to *Essential Outsiders* and Pheng Cheah's account of *Spectral Nationality* take the wars and ethnic violence of the late twentieth century as a starting point for analyses of cosmopolitan and national belonging, respectively. As Cheah puts it, '[n]ationalism has almost become the exemplary figure for death' thereby prefiguring his analytical use of spectrality in the Derridean sense of mutually constitutive meanings and 'hauntings'.[3] On a less abstract level, the anthropologist Heonik Kwon explores how ghosts are an inextricable part of national commemoration, using Vietnam as a case study. Like Cheah, he points out that '[m]ass war death is an integral part of modern national memory'[4] and shows how official nation-building discourse in Vietnam has co-opted remembrance of war dead for its own legitimating purpose in the face of pre-existing rituals that once comfortably combined the local and international, or cosmopolitan. The official commemoration of war 'heroes', coupled with the systematic forgetting of those who fought for and fell on the losing side in the Vietnam War, contrasts sharply with very different practices at the local level. These, in turn, recall traditions of hospitality in European cities before the age of nationalism, as discussed by Derrida.[5] Rather like the 'city time' evoked by Angharad Closs Stephens and discussed later in this article, Kwon shows how the local and cosmopolitan are brought together in commemorative rituals, thereby bypassing the national to create a 'cosmopolitan vernacular'.[6] This is achieved by dividing the spirit world not into local and foreigner or victor and traitor, as in the national construct, but rather into ancestors and their categorical opposite, ghosts. The following section looks at how the concept of the nation and nation-building, understood as state-led nationalism, could be reinscribed with more cosmopolitan understandings of belonging by focusing on the problematic figure of the cosmopolitan Jew.

Cosmopolitanism and nationalism

Jews were one of the 'vanguard minorities', among the first to experience the negative impact of nationalist ideology in Europe.[7] From the late nineteenth century onwards, Zionism offered the Jewish diaspora its own nationalist focus, but Jews were still expected to 'fit' the dominant ethnocultural narrative in their nation-state of residence. To this extent, their predicament was comparable to that of many migrants in today's nation-states, where 'the congruence of political unit and culture will continue to apply'.[8] In nineteenth- and twentieth-century Europe, anti-Semitic tropes assumed Jewish unity and solidarity as a corollary to that of the nation, when in fact Zionist, Communist, entrepreneurial, liberal and Orthodox Jews often had little in common other than their unenviable status as 'Essential Outsiders'.[9] Such a status is only meaningful in relation to nationalism's need for an 'Other' ascriptive identity, the self-defining opposite that is necessary to construct the nation. As the archetypal 'Essential Outsider', the figure of the cosmopolitan Jew throws nationalism's inherent 'Othering' into stark relief: 'All that was needed to set off some such hostility in the age of nationalism was the existence of distinctive minority communities'.[10] In this sense, the Jewish connection with cosmopolitanism is indeed a palimpsest, an ancient story continually reinscribed with new struggles and protagonists. To quote Jakob Egholm Feldt in this issue : 'Jews are displaced, homeless, diasporic, at home in the world, real Europeans, true global citizens, ethnic minorities, ex-patriates, in exile, to name the most used epithets of what signals both Jewishness and the cosmopolitan condition.' However, the protean nature of the Jewish cosmopolitan condition – an epithet also often applied to nationalism – may provide a key to transcending heteronormative definitions of national belonging.

Antisemitic associations of cosmopolitanism with rootlessness and disloyalty portrayed it as the polar opposite of nationalism, but this simplistic dichotomy assumes an understanding of the nation as a bounded entity moving through linear time that has itself been subjected to sustained critique.[11] The ambivalent figure of the cosmopolitan Jew is thus a fitting starting point from which to consider cosmopolitanism in the context of contemporary nation-building and belonging. How does the Jewish experience resonate with that of other 'Outsiders' to the nation-state? How can we invent 'imagined communities' that do not construct a binary between the nation and the cosmopolitan? Is it possible to break down that border and bring the cosmopolitan into the national fold? In other words, can we imagine new forms of cosmopolitan unity that take place through the nation-state, rather than transcending it?[12]

Imagining the nation is all about constructing the borders of national belonging and is thus inherently exclusionary. A closed, racial definition of the nation tends towards policies intolerant of immigration and intermarriage. Taken to extremes, this can lead to chauvinism, so-called 'ethnic cleansing' and Fascism. A more open definition of the nation, however, lowers the barriers to national belonging for non-natives and is thus compatible with multicultural or even cosmopolitan approaches to nation-building. In the national context, we can say that 'the concept of cosmopolitanism is more individualistic and flexible, less inclined to reify cultures as fixed repertoires of behavior and catalogues of heritage'.[13] Nevertheless, the concept of the nation necessarily entails a group of insiders and outsiders, namely those who are included within the 'imagined community' and those who are not. Migrants and minorities most often find themselves at the margins of the nation-building process, which is why they are key to rethinking nationality. Migrants and minorities are the 'Other' that serves to constitute the nation; it is often easier to delimit the nation in terms of what it is not than to make sense of its *de facto* diversity, a diversity that resonates with Jakob Egholm Feldt's above-cited definition of Jewishness and the cosmopolitan condition. To that extent, then, nationalism cannot do without its 'Essential Outsiders', whether they be Jewish or other migrant minorities.

The definition of cosmopolitanism as 'moral obligations to foreigners that are equal to our obligations to our compatriots' simply reproduces the national referent as a way of distinguishing self from other.[14] A more satisfactory definition escapes this dichotomy whilst emphasising that cosmopolitanism takes many forms: 'Cosmopolitanism is a set of projects toward planetary conviviality'.[15] As a way of thinking about 'outside' influences on society and culture, cosmopolitanism can open up the national paradigm to become a more negotiated, evolving and diverse space[16] Gerard Delanty, for example, points out that the national has 'always been embroiled with immanent cosmopolitan orientations' and Mary Kaldor suggests that 'nationalisms could be harnessed to a cosmopolitan politics'.[17] David Held's cosmopolitanism, in turn, 'is concerned [with] political order in a world where political communities and states matter, but not only and exclusively'.[18] Held's model posits concurrent citizenship at state, regional and global levels. As such, cosmopolitanism could conceivably contribute to nation-building by disrupting unitary narratives of nationhood and belonging. European citizenship provides one example of how this can look in practice.

Pheng Cheah argues that the nation was not originally conceived as a closed, atavistic community, but rather as a rational community that had much in common with the universalism of cosmopolitanism.[19] As Craig Calhoun put it: 'Nationalism was also (at least often) an attempt to reconcile liberty and ethical universalism with felt community.'[20] Cheah explores the origins of nationalism in German Idealism and Romanticism, arguing that 'myths of the organic community' depicting nationalism as atavistic and oppressive have misinterpreted its foundational aim as a means of actualising freedom.[21] In this, Cheah contends, nationalism is no different from cosmopolitanism and forms part of 'a continuing series of territorialized and deterritorialized models for realizing freedom'.[22] Eminent German philosophers like Herder, Schiller, Humboldt and Fichte combined a cosmopolitan outlook with a belief that the nation was the most appropriate vehicle for realising universal ideals. As such, the frequent opposition of nationalism and cosmopolitanism is unhelpful:

> [It] fails to recognize that nationalism is also a universalism because both it and cosmopolitanism are based on the same normative concept of culture [...] understood not as ideological indoctrination, but as a cultivational process where universal ideals are incarnated in the daily practices of a collective's individual members.[23]

Of course, the idea of an organic community went on to be hijacked by the same *Blut und Boden* ideology that peddled antisemitic tropes of the rootless, cosmopolitan Jew. Drawing on the work of Jacques Derrida, who also recognized the nation's potential to encapsulate universal ideals, Cheah uses a haunting metaphor to describe this development: 'Any process of actualization is inevitably haunted and can go awry'.[24] It remains to be seen whether this actualisation process also needs to create – and denigrate – the figure of an 'Essential Outsider'.

Cheah uses Derrida's concept of spectrality to suggest that the nation is constantly overshadowed by the state and its official national culture. This prevents postcolonial nations in particular from realising moral freedom through political community, in the way that Fichte and Hegel first envisaged. People may have temporarily 'reappropriated the state during decolonization', but this liberation has not lasted due to the deadening force of state-sponsored capital and nation-building.[25] Derrida's 'hauntology' portrays this as an inevitable and limiting feature of the nation as a means of actualising freedom, thereby conjuring a spectre that is necessary and unavoidable but also negative. Cheah himself, however, is less dismissive than Derrida of nationalism's potential yet to realize freedom in the face of global capital and other attendant aspects of globalisation. In other words, Cheah still believes in the potential of the nation (as opposed to the nation-state) as a means of realising universal ideals. Building on this theoretical insight, which Cheah illustrates with reference to the South-East Asian financial crisis of the late 1990s, we turn to some of the methodological considerations that flow from comparing nations.

As a South-East Asianist, Benedict Anderson's hugely influential *Imagined Communities* built on his knowledge of the region. Similarly, his subsequent work entitled *The Spectre of Comparisons: Nationalism, Southeast Asia and the World* rejected the Eurocentric bias inherent in much of the nationalism-studies literature. Instead, it adopted South-East Asia as a 'ground of comparison', understood as 'both the empirical or objective basis from which comparison begins as well as the interest or principle of reason that motivates each particular activity of comparison'.[26] Anderson used the image of looking through an inverted telescope to illustrate how the colonial period and his own European background both coloured his perception of South-East Asia and its 'imagined', constructed contours. The spectrality of the European legacy, its haunting of South-East Asian understandings of sovereignty and nation-building, is also taken up in Partha Chatterjee's critique of Anderson's work. In Chatterjee's view, so-called Third World nationalism is not subject to the same logic of seriality and classification that Anderson posits as nationalism's universal grammar.[27] Specifically,

Chatterjee questions Anderson's notion of nationalism as bound up in 'homogenous, empty time', understood as people's ability to imagine the 'steady, anonymous, simultaneous activity' of their compatriots and members of other nations beyond their own.[28] Contrary to Anderson's argument that nationalism superseded Christianity and religious community, Chatterjee argues that different registers of belief and cultural commonality continue to exist side by side. This analysis resonates with the work of Heonik Kwon, who contrasts individuals' spiritual *Vergangenheitsbewaeltigung* (or coming to terms with the past) through the worship of ghosts and defunct relatives, with the state's very different framing of officially recognized heroes and martyrs.[29] Through its combination of the political and the spiritual, then, the postcolonial experience in South-East Asia is an intriguing lens through which to view nationalism. Ironically, Kwon's account of ghosts offers a glimpse of an alternative cosmology that escapes Derrida's 'hauntology'. It steps outside the heteronormative framework implied by Benedict Anderson's 'imagined communities', namely bounded national communities existing side by side in 'homogenous, empty time'. Instead, we can envisage a more fluid imaginary that is reminiscent of Jakob Egholm Feldt's earlier-cited evocation of Jewishness and the cosmopolitan condition but, following Cheah, one that does not leave behind the concept of the nation entirely.

Comparing nations through Anderson's inverted telescope introduces a new frame of reference to the Eurocentric norm, thereby encouraging reflection on the nation from a different perspective. Anderson gives as an extreme example the shock of hearing President Sukarno of Indonesia describe Adolf Hitler as a great nationalist leader.[30] Such an approach does not entail a simple one-to-one comparison between Europe and South-East Asia. Rather, it presupposes that South-East Asia today is haunted or shaped by its European colonial legacy, of the kind that Asian intellectuals educated in the colonising metropolis brought back to their homelands. Yet many other influences also persist, such as the precolonial past, which 'lives on as a ghost that returns from outside time'.[31] Similarly, the ghosts of ancestor and spirit worship can haunt and ultimately subvert everyday nation-building practices. As Chatterjee suggested, these offer glimpses into alternative cosmologies and ontologies that challenge Benedict Anderson's own understanding of homogenous empty time and begin to question nationalism's 'Othering' of 'Essential Outsiders'. As we have seen, the inherent fluidity of cosmopolitan Jewish identity resists and transcends this archetypal 'Othering', pointing towards unbounded ways of thinking the nation.

Nationalism's tendency to construct the community in terms of what it is not makes comparison an inherent, core component of nationalism. Anderson's grounds of comparison provide an analytical framework oriented towards 'how nations are imagined rather than what they imagine themselves as', that can be applied to how cosmopolitanism might conceivably be integrated with nationalism.[32] Further, the South-East Asian perspective suggests that studies of nationalism should consider enduring spiritual and cultural dimensions alongside its political and ideological facets. Following Chatterjee, this article (re)introduces parallel and often conflicting notions of space and time to the analysis of nationalism, of the kind that Anderson suggests were superseded by modern nationalism. At the same time, it learns from Cheah and Anderson's theoretical approach to nationalism as universal and inherently comparable. In practice, this means taking up Chatterjee's critique of synchronicity to explore parallel and intertwined spiritual and cultural practices in Vietnam, as brilliantly illuminated through Heonik Kwon's scholarship.

Anderson and Cheah's use of the haunting metaphor complements Kwon's analysis of ghostly presences on the margins of Vietnam's official nation-building. The spatial and ideological divisions of the Vietnam War, which have shaped official commemorations of war dead, are not followed or respected in the spiritual realm, opening up the possibility of a very different form of nation-building. In sum, the present approach seeks to reconcile Cheah and Anderson's position that nationalism can have universal ambitions with Chatterjee's critique of universalism as a Eurocentric concept not applicable to postcolonial countries. In other words, it combines the abstract homogeneity of a world organized into nation-states with the extreme heterogeneity of nation-building within these states, starting with hierarchies of ethnicity and belonging and the delimitation of insider and outsider. Rather than being used in contrast to national belonging, the figure of the cosmopolitan Jew has been used to critique and to step outside exclusionary nationalist discourse, in an attempt to recover nationalism's originary universalism. The next section explores this idea in practice.

Ghosts and ancestors

Heonik Kwon approaches the political – specifically the enduring trauma caused by Cold War conflicts – from an anthropological perspective.[33] A key theme of his body of work is the way in which ritual practice, including the veneration of ancestors and ghosts in contemporary Vietnam and Korea, serves to transcend the ideological division of the Cold War and begin to lay its legacy to rest. In both country cases, Kwon has explored the gradual rehabilitation of war dead from the losing side and the consequent reconciliation that is made possible within and between estranged families and communities. His analyses also have a wider significance for considering the relationship between cosmopolitanism and nationalism that has not been taken up before now. In Vietnam, the resurgence of spiritual practice since the beginning of economic liberalisation (*doi moi*) in the mid-1980s has opened up new spaces for imagining the nation to include the anti-Communist diaspora, in a national narrative based on the shared practice of ancestor worship.[34] In South Korea, the democratic transition of the 1990s was characterized by public debates about coming to terms with massacres committed in the lead-up to the Korean War.[35] In both cases, a rapprochement between descendants of the victims on each side has been made possible through ritual performances that transcend entrenched divisions and offer a glimmer of hope for a more inclusive form of national belonging.

The spiritual realm of the Vietnamese village that Kwon describes is not retrenched behind a bamboo hedge but ranges across ideological and national borders, encompassing the wandering souls of an Algerian conscript, French soldiers, American GIs and a South Korean marine among others.[36] These ghosts are believed to be 'wandering souls' because they have died a violent or untimely death and have no homes, or ancestral altars, to go to. It is also important to note that when communal houses were destroyed in the Indochinese Wars, the guardian and ancestral spirits housed therein were believed to join the ranks of wandering souls until a new home could be built for them. That is, displaced ancestors were worshipped indiscriminately (but temporarily) alongside ghosts, because the fundamental distinction between the two turned on whether they had a place of rest. Regardless of kinship with villagers, then, displaced ancestors became ghosts once more. This suggests that having a home is even more crucial than descent in anchoring an ancestor securely in his or her rightful social space, an insight that resonates with the love of homeland and the spectre of statelessness that pervades the dichotomous discourse of nation and cosmopolitanism. This insight is crucial because it testifies to a cosmology built on residence and repose – or security – rather than one fundamentally structured around kinship, or ethnic myths of descent.

In Vietnam, offerings are made to ghosts not only because they are roaming spirits to be placated, but also in recognition of their restless, liminal plight. This gesture of solidarity and hospitality 'bespeaks a reciprocal relationship of sympathy between the displaced spirits of the dead and the living person in exile'.[37] It highlights a possible parallel between the spirit realm and the 'real world' of displacement, migration and diaspora that Derrida grappled with in his essay *On Cosmopolitanism*. In other words, could a similar act of hospitality be extended to the 'unknown and unrelated'.[38] A hierarchy of belonging between ancestors and strangers exists in the Vietnamese spirit world, just as the national imaginary distinguishes those who belong to the national 'family' from those who do not. What might be learnt from this belief system for the wider temporal world (though the two are already intimately bound together in the Vietnamese case), is how to manage the border between foreigner and kin and how to extend hospitality across this division. The figure of the cosmopolitan Jew, by resisting neat, homogenous categorisation, already began to break down the negatively charged dichotomy between national belonging and 'Essential Outsider'. Kwon's analysis of the Vietnamese spirit world goes a little further in showing a cautious welcoming of the other; the practice of worshipping ghosts accepts 'their rights to exist in the village world', even if their 'social standing' is not as high as that of ancestors.[39] So many million Jews were heinously denied their right to exist, but one legacy of the cosmopolitan Jewish archetype, as expressed by Jakob Engholm Feldt, is to point away from homogenisation towards fluidity and inclusiveness.

Elsewhere, Kwon has shown how local acts of remembrance for the dead can be considered a threat to the ruling regime and its interpretation of history, thereby highlighting the personal as political and even potentially treasonous. For example, Korean families who had exhumed and reburied relatives summarily shot as suspected Communist sympathizers in the first weeks of the Korean War were pursued by the subsequent anti-Communist regime: 'human remains became the object of radical conflicts between the postwar state authority and the bereaved families'.[40] In the Vietnamese case, Communist victory in 1975 brought official condemnation of practices like ancestor worship, deemed 'superstitious'. Relaxation of this rule came with the economic liberalisation of the 1980s, which saw a resurgence in ancestor worship and its corollary of spirit worship. The fact that the Vietnamese state has unbottled these genies undoubtedly has implications for its future nation-building, which has hitherto focused on a classic, linear narrative of national *longue durée* and dogged resistance to foreign invasion.[41] More generally, however, 'the unbound marginality of unassimilated death' hints at a possible model for considering cosmopolitan forms of belonging to a community, in which 'wandering souls' are not cast out but comforted regardless of nationality, ideology, age or gender.[42]

Kwon argues that the invention of national unity entailed 'the invention of disunity between the local and the cosmopolitan'.[43] This has obscured the fact that 'home is not necessarily a place where cosmopolitanism is in exile'.[44] Kwon's work on Vietnamese spirit worship illustrates one way of conceptualising and treating 'locals' and 'strangers' that is different from the current nation-state norm of 'insider' and 'outsider'. It is difficult to transpose the model Kwon describes to the contemporary, 'haunted' world of nation-states.

National communities like the United Kingdom do not currently present themselves as 'sites of consolation' – far less hospitality – to migrants, displaced people and refugees. UK government policies surrounding immigration, fuelled and fanned by the prominence of the UK Independence Party (UKIP), seek to limit and reduce the number of 'wandering souls' reaching British shores. Immanuel Kant's definition of hospitality as the absence of hostility towards foreigners is not reflected in immigration debates, despite the efforts of some media outlets and business groups to emphasize the benefits they bring to the UK economy. Instead, the focus in both the UK and the European Union (EU) is on limiting and controlling migrant numbers, and the EU's approach to securing its external borders echoes Anderson's classic definition of the nation in terms of bounded seriality.

To Kant, 'hospitality signifies the claim of a stranger entering foreign territory to be treated by its owner without hostility [...] so long as he conducts himself peaceably, he must not be treated as an enemy'.[45] Kant clearly restricts his right of hospitality to visitation, rather than residence: 'It is not a right to be treated as a guest to which the stranger can lay claim – a special friendly compact on his behalf would be required to make him for a given time an actual inmate'.[46] This unconditional right to hospitality is thus precarious and short-lived, probably better-suited to a wealthy, cosmopolitan jet-setter than to the 'working class cosmopolitan'.[47] Critiques of high-flying cosmopolitans point to the ease with which they can cross borders, usually thanks to a passport from a leading industrial nation-state.[48] It is much harder to be this kind of cosmopolitan on a Vietnamese passport than, say, a British or American one.[49] Such cosmopolitans can afford to look down on nationalism and patriotism when they are secure in the enjoyment of privilege, but few enjoy this luxury. As Cheah reminds us, however, cosmopolitanism and nationalism are based on the same universal principles, and there is analytical potential in looking beyond the oft-repeated opposition between the concepts to find common ground. Analyses of Vietnamese spirit worship offer an unexpected means to this end.

Just as official Vietnamese nation-building has decreed those to be remembered and those to be forgotten in the aftermath of its civil war, so nationalism's binaries of insider and outsider decide who is to be abandoned at the margins and who is to be brought into the fold. Kwon draws attention to parallels with the Greek tragedy of Antigone by Sophocles.[50] Antigone buries both her brothers, one who died a heroic, patriot's death and the other abandoned as a traitor outside the city walls. This incurs the wrath of King Creon and Antigone's own death. Creon placed political loyalty above Antigone's right to mourn and remember, in the same way as the Vietnamese nation-state manipulates national commemoration to the exclusion of a great many victims judged ideologically unsound. Vietnamese spirit and ancestor worship works against this, just as Antigone defied Creon. Likewise, as the figure of the cosmopolitan Jew reminds us, it is possible to defy the national dichotomies of insider and 'Essential Outsider', just as Derrida sought to do in his call for cities of refuge and a new cosmopolitics. Recognising ancestral rights is not antithetical to showing hospitality, and to this extent cosmopolitanism 'does not contradict the morality of community solidarity'.[51] According to this reading, strangers are no longer 'essential outsiders' but integrated into a political space. They have a right, albeit not an equal right, 'to dwell in the place'.

> [Such] actions point to a particular vision of society – a society in which both natives and strangers have the right to dwell in the place. For the dead, this means that strangers to the political community of the nation can join the local ritual community of kinship as ancestors.

Those who are not entitled to join this ritual unity can still benefit from the sites of consolation prepared in the exterior of the communal unity.[52]

The final section offers some thoughts on how this 'right to dwell in the place' might be transposed to the world of the living.

Home and homeland

Rather like looking through Benedict Anderson's methodological metaphor of an inverted telescope, Heonik Kwon's work on the ritual commemoration of Vietnam's ghosts of war offers a completely different frame of reference to Anderson's own conception of the national 'imagined community' in terms of bounded seriality. Angharad Closs Stephens, for her part, explicitly rejects cosmopolitan critiques that tend to 'travel together' with the nation in a binary way and offers the 'melée' of the city as an alternative to nationalist discourse.[53] Closs Stephens' analysis attempts to go beyond the nation rather than risk reinforcing its conceptual framework. Unlike Cheah, she believes the nation is irretrievably haunted. In other words, she also recognizes that cosmopolitanism is tied to nationalism, but cautions that it reproduces the conceptual armoury of the nation at the same time as trying to undermine it. Instead, she looks to the city as a model of unbounded, potentially inclusive conceptions of community that orient citizenship debates away from their nationalist foundation.

Closs Stephens asks 'what might politics look like when we don't approach "it" as something that takes place within a bounded developmental community?'[54] Such a radical reading of contemporary citizenship delinks it completely from the bounded, sovereign state and gestures towards the multifaceted figure of the cosmopolitan Jew as described by Jakob Engholm Feldt. Here, the nation-state disappears as a unitary actor of any sort, and gives way to an understanding of politics as a relational web that is 'contingent and dynamic'.[55] Rather than 'take as an entry point the sovereign state as a political entity', this approach 'suggest(s) that citizenship is constituted through a range of concrete political struggles'.[56] The focus on encounters, coexistence, exchange and conflict as constitutive of citizenship seeks to capture some of citizens' multiple identities. Even if one accepts the persistence of the nation-state, this approach is helpful in transcending the nation/cosmopolitan dichotomy to allow for greater cosmopolitanism within nation-building narratives. For example, Closs Stephens proposes the notion of 'city time [...] that refuses a sense of completion'.[57] This contrasts with Anderson's adoption of Walter Benjamin's 'homogenous empty time', so central to his conceptualisation of the nation as an 'imagined community'.

Closs Stephens points to 'the absurdity, as well as the violence, of aligning territory with identity'.[58] To illustrate this, she looks to the 'affective community' created by loss, specifically the nationalist responses to the '7/7' bombings in London and '9/11' in the United States. This nationalist imaginary is shown to be exclusive in its creation of a community of mourning. For example, she highlights then UK Prime Minister Tony Blair's use of the national 'we' in the wake of the London bombings to evoke solidarity with, but not inclusion of, law-abiding Muslims. Similarly, the Vietnamese Communist Party's 'forgetting' of those who died for the Republic of Vietnam (a.k.a. South Vietnam) in its post-war nation-building narrative deserves the critique that 'the continuing and complex experience of loss [...] is not something that can be easily located or atoned for through nationalism and retaliation'.[59] Kwon's work shows just how complex the 'experience of loss' can be, and also offers hope that the 'Essential Outsider', as embodied in the figure of the cosmopolitan Jew, the law-abiding Muslims in Closs Stephens' example, or the wandering soul in Vietnamese spirit cosmology, can be imagined as something else than the constitutive 'Other'. That is, they can be offered more than Kantian hospitality or solidarity, namely the 'right to dwell in the place'.

Not content to critique how the nation is imagined spatially, Closs Stephens also questions the community as some sort of inherited whole, passed down intact from generation to generation. As Michael Herzfeld has noted: 'The absurdity of the human condition surely comes to a head with official claims to everlasting nationhood'.[60] Instead, Closs Stephens presents community as a 'messy' confluence of 'citizens, non-citizens, insiders, outsiders, aliens and strangers'.[61] Her analysis of Daniel Libeskind's deconstructed design for his wing of Berlin's Jewish Museum and Peter Eisenman's Berlin memorial to the murdered Jews of Europe develops this argument. Eisenman's memorial has no obvious entrance and exit: it is not a labyrinth. The educational exhibition that attempts to explain and situate the Holocaust is relegated underground. Libeskind's design is similarly disorienting. Its uneven planes and dead-ends do not lead the visitor along a marked path: 'It implies a thinking of community without a point of origin or transcendence that the community can mourn or aspire towards'.[62] By extension, this kind of community is not clearly delineated in space and time, making it difficult to identify who belongs to that community and who is excluded. Such a community dissolves the insider/outsider dichotomy through radical unfixity.[63]

As Closs Stephens points out: 'A closed system that seeks to rationalize citizens into homogenous units is necessarily haunted by other, more open ways of imagining political community'.[64] Following Derrida but unlike Cheah, Closs Stephens rejects the nation, because she does not see it as a means of achieving those 'more open ways of imagining'. She rightly points to how official commemoration of the dead is also a means of maintaining the nation. But, just as official Vietnamese mourning of its national heroes is haunted by a different way of remembering the spiritual realm, so the 'imagined community' of bounded seriality is haunted, following Cheah, by a potentially more productive national metaphor that permits 'more open ways of imagining'. Closs Stephens' choice of examples to illustrate her conception of 'messy' community is telling, and brings us back to the archetype of the cosmopolitan Jew as symbolising so much more than the nation's 'Essential Outsider'.

Ilan Baron has shown how the need to imagine community in more open ways than Benedict Anderson's theory permits is an on-going, pressing concern for the Jewish diaspora's evolving relationship with Israel. Unlike Zionism, that is expressly connected with territory as 'homeland', the diasporic Jewish experience offers 'a pluralistic view of political identity and political spaces that does not wed the idea of the nation to that of the state'.[65] This recalls Closs Stephens' comment above as to 'the violence, of aligning territory with identity'. As Lazaroms shows in this issue, Joseph Roth's life is one illustration of the 'narrowing of the European Jewish lifeworlds' that made it impossible to realize any sort of deterritorialized Jewish nationalism, and squeezed Jewish identity out of the racially or ethnically defined straitjacket of the nation-state. Roth contested those national borders, but at a price.

Lazaroms uses the notion of home as the dividing line between nationalism and cosmopolitanism. Roth's cosmopolitanism claimed the right to travel and feel at home wherever he wished. This is a conceit which, then as now, goes hand in hand with possessing the correct papers and the financial means to criss-cross the borders delimiting sovereign states, but approximates to 'the right to dwell in the place'. As previously noted, so-called 'working class cosmopolitans' have less wherewithal to do so than moneyed professionals with a *passepartout* passport. To be homeless in the age of nations is always precarious, and most often considered pernicious by those wedded to the nation-state system (see Gilman in this issue). As Roth's life shows, displacement is not easy, and lived cosmopolitanism is by no means always a celebratory state. In Roth's case, however, his ability to feel at home seems to have been limited to continental Europe, thereby replacing his natal home with a European home and apparently making him unable to go into exile in the United States or the United Kingdom. There is a tension 'between real and metaphorical displacement' (Lazaroms, this issue), and Roth's peripatetic lifestyle did not extend to travelling worldwide or abandoning national distinctions completely. Nevertheless, his experience as a cosmopolitan Jew allows us to get to grips with the complex consequences of resisting life as an 'Essential Outsider' and bravely stepping outside the exclusionary logic and homogenising dichotomies underpinning the nation-state system.

The premise that people belong in a specific national place is a function of the nation-state system, into which those who cannot or will not be 'put back in their place' do not fit: 'The political organization of identities into nation-states, and the forced migration of those nations' Others are outcomes of struggles over national identity and a feature of population management through refugee regimes and accompanying immigration, naturalization, and citizenship policies.[66] The artists Rachel Garfield analyses in this issue set out to imagine how home might look outside of the nation-state structure or beyond a single place, thereby problematising the idea of home as a secure haven. Brun and Fàbos offer the tripartite conceptualisation of 'home – Home – HOME' to denote, respectively, the daily acts of homemaking, feelings of belonging expressed through heritage and values, and the global political and historical context in which ideas of home are framed and understood. In analysing the impact of prolonged displacement on refugees and others, Brun and Fàbos note how analyses of '"the national order of things" have included the narrative of home as elsewhere, refugees as out of place, and the close association and inseparable bond between home and homeland'.[67] In an attempt to dissociate home from a single, fixed national place that is in opposition to movement and migration, the authors point out that different places can provide the components of home, Home and HOME, such as economic security and a sense of belonging. Economic migrants may accommodate themselves to this situation better than forced migrants, however, who may well struggle to maintain multiple links due to their legal status.

Refugees and migrants are marginal to the state and thus threaten its control of the national construct, hence the proliferation of policing, registration and detention in border zones. Just as Brun and Fàbos emphasize that home is not static nor necessarily in a single place, so the artistic media of collage and photomontage convey the fluidity of diasporic identity, to the extent that 'the Jew has no originating location' (see Garfield in this issue). Garfield recognizes the 'discomfort of *not* belonging', but also that rejecting the national referent can be an 'unsettling' form of resistance to the nation-state construct. Once again, the Jewish diaspora experience offers insights into how we might imagine a home without homeland. The cosmopolitan Jew as defined above by Jakob Engholm Feldt embodies resistance to essentialising 'Othering' and opens up the possibility of critiquing the nation-state construct – as Cheah and Closs Stephens have done – or stepping outside it to illuminate alternative cosmologies and ontologies, as in the work of Kwon.

Today, the existence of Israel has a tendency to 'overshadow' (Cristaudo in this issue) the diaspora experience, resulting in some members of the Jewish diaspora's uneasy relationship with the country (see also Taberner in this issue). Whilst recognising that the nation-state system was bound to make Israel central to Jewish identity, Baron notes that:

> Israel is neither the be-all and end-all of Jewish identity nor the culmination of Jewish history, as if Jews have nothing else to offer and there is no Jewish life in the Diaspora. This argument is belittling of Jewish Diaspora communities, marginalizing them and ignoring how they are important centers of Jewish life in their own right.[68]

The experience of the Jewish diaspora, bracketing Zionism, can be read as a lesson in cosmopolitanism that contrasts with Kantian cosmopolitanism in that it is deterritorialized (see Engholm Feldt in this issue). That is, it does not engage with the language of minority, homeland and hospitality, all of which refer to 'imaginations of place'.[69] As Xun Zhou (this issue) states with reference to Hong Kong's Jewish community today: 'Their deep roots are their shared Jewish identity no matter where they are from originally.' This resonates with the concept of home as analysed above, in that origins and native place fall away to make way for a more complex and multifaceted sense of belonging. In contrast to this deterritorialized identity, Horace Kallen highlighted the hegemony of the nationalist narrative of *longue durée* and its haunting of an ostensibly egalitarian metaphor like the US melting pot (Engholm Feldt in this issue). Today, the 'dominant *ethnie*', as exemplified by the archetypal White Anglo-Saxon Protestant and what Cristaudo (this issue) calls 'Enlightened/Puritan "value triggers"' in the United States, still sets the standard for national belonging and gives the lie to a supposedly future-oriented 'imagined community' premised on something like the American dream.[70] Instead, we see the emergence of so-called 'paranational communities' (Seyhan cited in Taberner, this issue) of migrant or ethnic minority residents in nation-states who lack citizenship and/or nationality, in the strict sense of belonging to the nation as an 'imagined community'. The German phrases *Migrationshintergrund* and *Ausländische Mitbürger* are indicative of this disconnect.

Migrants and minorities are categories deriving their meaning from the existence of nation-states, which set out to integrate, if not assimilate them according to official nation-building discourse. A cosmopolitan reading of the nation would resist this. In order to avoid cosmopolitanism becoming a hegemonic project of its own, however (a kind of nationalism writ large), it is necessary to pay attention to colonial difference and cosmopolitan projects – pluralized as cosmopolitanisms – emerging from elsewhere than the global north.[71] The preceding discussion of South-East Asian grounded comparison and Vietnamese spirit worship has gone some way towards addressing this imperative. As Walter Mignolo puts it: 'Inclusion doesn't seem to be the solution to cosmopolitanism any longer, insofar as it presupposes that the agency that establishes the inclusion is itself beyond inclusion'.[72] In effect, Mignolo is arguing for the same cultural pluralism as Horace Kallen was, only from an explicitly postcolonial perspective that highlights on-going power inequalities and rejects a supposedly universal project with Eurocentric foundations, such as Ancient Greece or the Enlightenment. Instead, Mignolo recasts cosmopolitanisms as a multiperspectival critical dialogue. In so doing, he shifts the focus away from the dichotomy between the particular and an arguably Eurocentric universal, with its tendency 'to universalize "Western" values in order to pathologize the values of others' (Fine in this issue, see also Taberner in this issue). According to this reading and in the spirit of a special issue highlighting Jewish contributions to the cosmopolitan project, so-called 'Essential Outsiders' – whether migrants, minorities or the archetypal Jewish cosmopolitan – should be recast as active participants or agents of cosmopolitanisms, rather than passive recipients waiting to be included in an imagined national community.

Conclusion

Anderson's 'imagined community' deftly sums up an enduring and frequently exclusionary phenomenon. Philip Spencer (this issue) reminds us of Rosa Luxembourg's early critique of nationalism: 'Where nationalists were successful in shaping the terms of national self-determination, it would only lead to new states oppressing the minorities in their midst.' As the Jewish diaspora experience clearly shows, national self-determination is frequently selective, and emancipation is not necessarily extended beyond the dominant *ethnie*. The contributions to this special issue show how Jews were not imagined as part of the national community. But, following Cheah, this failure of imagination need not mean that nationalism itself is inherently pernicious and should be jettisoned both in theory and practice. The same charges levelled against Jews, such as a perceived lack of patriotism or loyalty to the nation-state, continue to underlie all the integrationist and assimilationist measures imposed on would-be citizens, including citizenship tests and oaths of loyalty to queen and country. Nevertheless, the concept of the nation does hold analytical potential for 'more open ways of imagining' that could incorporate a productive relationship with cosmopolitanism and provide the basis for a voluntaristic model of belonging that builds on 'the right to dwell in the place'. Key to this is distinguishing citizenship as a legal concept from the accretions of nationality – understood in its strict sense of belonging to the nation – in order to disentangle the hierarchies of legal and ethnic belonging that frequently characterize nation-states today.

The depth and richness of theory, comparison and interdisciplinarity in Benedict Anderson's body of work offers endless inspiration across a wide range of disciplines. It has also given rise to a substantial body of literature critiquing the concept of 'imagined community' and its attendant characteristics of 'homogenous empty time' and the logic of seriality. Taking the Jewish diaspora as the archetypal 'Essential Outsiders' that are the nation's constitutive 'Other', Anderson's notion of the inverted telescope has been used here to consider the 'imagined community' from a South-East Asian perspective. Having after establishing the relationship between nationalism and cosmopolitanism, Heonik Kwon's work on Vietnamese spirit worship laid the groundwork for evoking another form of cosmopolitan community. The 'right to dwell in the place' is a concept that can be extended to any individual, regardless of origin. For example, the American G.I. has a place inside the Vietnamese cosmology of spirit worship. By contrast, he remains an 'Essential Outsider' (along with adherents of the defunct southern Republic of Vietnam) in official Vietnamese nation-building.

The notion of exile, like that of diaspora, is connected to a point of origin and a myth or desire of return that distinguishes it from the cosmopolitan construct of the global traveller. As such, exile and diaspora are bound up in the logic of a world organized into nation-states, understood as places of belonging or 'homelands'. However, this article has put forward a notion of home that is not linked to the 'violence' of aligning territory with identity or the 'absurdity' of claiming national *longue durée*. 'The nation-state model does not provide much room for a deterritorialized Diaspora nationalism' because it assumes that every individual has a citizenship or myth of origin, that their identity and belonging must be defined in terms of where they or their family have come from, and that exile is something to be endured until return is possible.[73] Cosmopolitanism frees individuals of these ties that bind and allows for a more multifaceted understanding of home, but it is not a global panacea divorced from the nation-state system, as Lazaroms notes in this issue.

It would be inappropriate to dismiss the on-going importance of state citizenship when the hope of security it can move millions of migrants and refugees to make huge personal sacrifices. However, an analysis founded on 'the right to dwell in the place' begins to address the shadowy side of citizenship regimes that make it possible to deport foreign nationals, to offer differential access to citizenship based on descent and country of origin, and to erect ethnically derived barriers to naturalisation, such as citizenship tests.

This article has sought to retain the concept of the nation – one that is not haunted by the nation-state – as a potentially productive component of cosmopolitanisms that are actively shaped by all those outwith the dominant discourses of belonging, such as those defined as migrants and minorities in relation to the nation-state. It has explored notions of deterritorialized home that are not derived from a national homeland and that decouple 'the right to dwell in the place' from state-enforced markers of integration into the 'imagined community' of the nation. As an alternative, 'the right to dwell in the place' gestures towards a legal standing different to that derived from a state-sanctioned 'homeland', one akin to 'anational citizenship' and based on domicile as a legal concept well-established in international private law and an avenue for further research.[74]

Notes

1. Anderson, *Imagined Communities*.
2. Daniel Chirot and Anthony Reid, eds. *Essential Outsiders: Chinese and Jews in the modern transformation of Southeast Asia and Central Europe*.
3. Cheah, *Spectral Nationality*, 1.
4. Kwon, "The Ghosts of War," 22.
5. Derrida, *On Cosmopolitanism and Forgiveness*.
6. Taylor, cited in Kwon, "Ghosts of War," 24.
7. Reid, "Entrepreneurial Minorities," 39 and 51.
8. Reid, "Entrepreneurial Minorities," 59.
9. Chirot, "Conflicting Identities," 13.
10. Chirot, "Conflicting Identities," 15.
11. This understanding of nationalism, developed by Benedict Anderson in *Imagined Communities* has been critiqued by, among others, Kelly in "Time and the Global," Chatterjee in "The Nation in Heterogeneous Time" and Closs Stephens in *The Persistence of Nationalism*.
12. Sutherland, "German Politics and Society."
13. Cheesman, *Novels of Turkish-German Settlement*, 44.
14. Brock and Brighouse, *The Political Philosophy of Cosmopolitanism*, v.
15. Mignolo, "The Many Faces of Cosmo-Polis," 721.
16. See Sutherland, "German Politics and Society;" Pace Closs Stephens, *The Persistence of Nationalism*.
17. Delanty, *The Cosmopolitan Imagination*, 17 and Kaldor, "Nationalism and Globalisation," 176.
18. Held, "Principles of Cosmopolitan Order," 10.
19. Cheah, *Spectral Nationality*.
20. Calhoun, "Cosmopolitanism and Nationalism," 444.
21. Cheah, *Spectral Nationality*, 17.
22. Cheah, *Spectral Nationality*, 6.
23. Cheah, *Spectral Nationality*, 8.

24. Cheah, *Spectral Nationality*, 8.
25. Cheah, *Spectral Nationality*, 384.
26. Cheah and Culler, *Grounds of Comparison*, 2.
27. Chatterjee, "The Nation in Heterogeneous Time."
28. Anderson, *Imagined Communities*, 26.
29. Kwon, "Ghosts of War in Vietnam."
30. Anderson, *The Spectre of Comparisons*, 1.
31. Cheah and Culler, *Grounds of Comparison*, 15.
32. Cheah and Culler, *Grounds of Comparison*, 5.
33. Kwon, *After the Massacre*, "The Ghosts of the American War in Vietnam;" "Healing the Wounds of War;" *The Other Cold War*.
34. Sutherland, "Nation-Building in China and Vietnam" and "Vietnamese Diasporic Citizenship."
35. Kwon, "Healing the Wounds of War."
36. Kwon, "The Ghosts of War," 34.
37. Kwon, "The Ghosts of War," 28.
38. Kwon, "The Ghosts of War," 28.
39. Kwon, "The Ghosts of War," 29.
40. Kwon, "The Korean War Mass Graves," no page.
41. Sutherland, *Soldered States*.
42. Kwon, "The Ghosts of War," 35.
43. Kwon, "The Ghosts of War," 24.
44. Harvey, *Cosmopolitanism and the Geographies of Freedom*, 169.
45. Kant, cited in Derrida, *On Cosmopolitanism and Forgiveness*, 21.
46. Kant, cited in Derrida, *On Cosmopolitanism and Forgiveness*, 21.
47. Werbner, "Global Pathways. Working Class Cosmopolitans."
48. Mandel, *Cosmopolitan Anxieties*, 50.
49. Ong, *Flexible Citizenship*.
50. Kwon, "The Ghosts of War."
51. Kwon, "The Ghosts of War," 41.
52. Kwon, "The Ghosts of the American War," no page.
53. Closs Stephens, *The Persistence of Nationalism*.
54. Closs Stephens, "Citizenship Without Community," 32.
55. Closs Stephens and Squire, "Politics Through a Web," 553.
56. Closs Stephens and Squire, "Politics Through a Web," 553, 555.
57. Closs Stephens, "Citizenship Without Community," 36.
58. Closs Stephens, *The Persistence of Nationalism*, 83.
59. Closs Stephens, *The Persistence of Nationalism*, 84
60. Herzfeld, *Cultural Intimacy*, 4.
61. Closs Stephens, "Citizenship without Community," 38.
62. Closs Stephens, "Citizenship without Community," 40.
63. Laclau and Mouffe, *Hegemony and Socialist Strategy*.
64. Closs Stephens, "Citizenship without Community," 40.
65. Baron, *Obligation in Exile*, 9.
66. Brun and Fábos, "Making Homes in Limbo," 10.
67. Brun and Fábos, "Making Homes in Limbo," 7.
68. Baron, *Obligation in Exile*, 22.
69. Pollock et al., "Cosmopolitanisms," 579.
70. The phrase "dominant ethnie" is from A.D. Smith, *Nations and Nationalisms*.
71. Pollock et al., "Cosmopolitanisms."
72. Mignolo, "The Many Faces of the Cosmo-Polis," 736.
73. Baron, *Obligation in Exile*, 23.
74. Kostakopoulou, *The Future Governance of Citizenship*.

Bibliography

Anderson, Benedict. *Imagined Communities*. London: Verso, 1991.
Anderson, Benedict. *The Spectre of Comparisons: Nationalism, Southeast Asia and the World*. London: Verso, 1998.
Baron, Ilan. *Obligation in Exile*. Edinburgh: Edinburgh University Press, 2014.
Brock, Harry, and Gillian Brighouse (eds.). *The Political Philosophy of Cosmopolitanism*. Cambridge: Cambridge University Press, 2005.
Brun, Cathrine, and Anita Fábos. "Making Homes in Limbo: A Conceptual Framework." *Refuge* 31 (2015): 5–17.
Calhoun, Craig. "Cosmopolitanism and Nationalism." *Nations and Nationalism* 14 (2008): 427–448.
Chatterjee, Partha. "The Nation in Heterogeneous Time." *Futures* 37 (2005): 925–942.
Cheah, Pheng. *Spectral Nationality*. New York: Columbia University Press, 2003.
Cheah, Pheng, and Jonathan Culler (eds.). *Grounds of Comparison*. London and New York: Routledge, 2003.
Cheesman, Tom. *Novels of Turkish-German Settlement: Cosmopolite Fictions*. Rochester: Camden House, 2007.
Chirot, Daniel. "Conflicting Identities and the Dangers of Communalism." In *Essential Outsiders: Chinese and Jews in the Modern Transformation of Southeast Asia and Central Europe*, edited by Daniel Chirot and Anthony Reid. Washington: University of Washington Press, 1997: 3–32.
Closs Stephens, Angharad. "Citizenship Without Community: Time, Design and the City". *Citizenship Studies* 14 (2010): 31–46.
Closs Stephens, Angharad. *The Persistence of Nationalism: from Imagined Communities to Urban Encounters*. London and New York: Routledge, 2013.
Closs Stephens, Angharad, and Vicki Squire. "Politics through a Web: Citizenship and Community Unbound". *Environment and Planning D: Society and Space* 30 (2012): 551–567.
Delanty, Gerard. *The Cosmopolitan Imagination*. Cambridge: Cambridge University Press, 2009.
Derrida, Jacques. *On Cosmopolitanism and Forgiveness*. London and New York: Routledge, 2005.
Harvey, David. *Cosmopolitanism and the Geographies of Freedom*. New York: Columbia University Press, 2009.
Held, David. "Principles of Cosmopolitan Order." In *The Political Philosophy of Cosmopolitanism*, edited by Harry Brock and Gillian Brighouse. Cambridge: Cambridge University Press, 2005: 10–27.
Herzfeld, M. *Cultural Intimacy*. 3rd ed. Abingdon and New York: Routledge, 2016.
Kaldor, Mary. "Nationalism and Globalisation." *Nations and Nationalism* 10 (2004): 161–177.
Kelly, John. "Time and the Global: Against the Homogeneous, Empty Communities in Contemporary Social Theory." *Development and Change* 29 (1998): 839–871.
Kostakopoulou, Dora. *The Future Governance of Citizenship*. Cambridge: Cambridge University Press, 2008.
Kwon, Heonik. *After the Massacre: Commemoration and Consolation in Ha My and My Lai*. Berkeley: University of California Press, 2006.
Kwon, Heonik. "The Ghosts of the American War in Vietnam." *The Asia-Pacific Journal* 23 (2008): Online.
Kwon, Heonik. *Ghosts of War in Vietnam*. Cambridge: Cambridge University Press, 2008.
Kwon, Heonik. "The Korean War Mass Graves." *The Asia-Pacific Journal* 23 (2008): Online.
Kwon, Heonik. "The Ghosts of War and the Spirit of Cosmopolitanism." *History of Religions* 48 (2008): 22–42.

Kwon, Heonik. "Healing the Wounds of War: New Ancestral Shrines in Korea." *The Asia-Pacific Journal* 24 (2009): Online.

Kwon, Heonik. *The Other Cold War*. New York and Chichester: Columbia University Press, 2010.

Laclau, Ernesto, and Chantal Mouffe. *Hegemony and Socialist Strategy*. London: Verso, 1985.

Mandel, Ruth. *Cosmopolitan Anxieties: Turkish Challenges to Citizenship and Belonging in Germany*. Durham: Duke University Press, 2008.

Mignolo, Walter. "The Many Faces of Cosmo-Polis: Border Thinking and Critical Cosmopolitanism." *Public Culture* 12 (2000): 721–748.

Ong, Aihwa. *Flexible Citizenship*. Durham: Duke University Press, 1999.

Pollock, Sheldon, Homi Bhabha, Carol Breckenridge, and Dipesh Chakrabarty. "Cosmopolitanisms." *Public Culture* 12 (2000): 577–589.

Reid, Anthony. "Entrepreneurial Minorities, Nationalism and the State." In *Essential Outsiders: Chinese and Jews in the Modern Transformation of Southeast Asia and Central Europe*, edited by Daniel Chirot and Anthony Reid. Washington: University of Washington Press, 1997: 33–71.

Smith, Anthony D. *Nations and Nationalism in a Global Era*. Cambridge: Polity and Blackwell, 1995.

Sutherland, Claire. *Soldered States: Nation-Building in Germany and Vietnam*. Manchester, NH: Manchester University Press, 2010.

Sutherland, Claire. "German Politics and Society from a Cosmopolitan Perspective." *German Politics and Society* 29 (2011): 1–19.

Sutherland, Claire. "Nation-Building in China and Vietnam." *East Asia: An International Quarterly* 29 (2012): 1–13.

Sutherland, Claire. "Vietnamese Diasporic Citizenship." In *Handbook of Global Citizenship Studies*, edited by Engin Isin and Peter Nyers. London and New York: Routledge, 2014: 522–531.

Werbner, Pnina. "Global Pathways. Working Class Cosmopolitans and the Creation of Transnational Ethnic Worlds." *Social Anthropology* 7 (1999): 17–35.

'Cosmopolitan from above': a Jewish experience in Hong Kong

Xun Zhou

ABSTRACT
The case of Hong Kong provides a substantial re-examination of what it means to be a cosmopolitan from above, both historically in terms of real colonial presence and power – that of the British Empire at the height of its pink-flushed world domination – and as a 'model minority' under such circumstances as well as in the postcolonial world of modern Hong Kong. The history of the Jews in Hong Kong illustrates the pitfalls in assuming the view of 'cosmopolitan of the above' is uniform or indeed 'from above'. The confusion of the cosmopolitan with the utopian goals of transhistorical views of mobility with the lived practice of Jews in British and now Chinese Hong Kong is a powerful corrective of this view. Focusing on Hong Kong, this former British Colony and now a Special Administrative Region (SAR) of the People's Republic of China, situated simultaneously at the centre and at the periphery of debates about the cosmopolitan, this article adds a new dimension to the parallel discussions of Jewish cosmopolitanism in Europe and North America.

Postcolonial theory deals with cosmopolitanism in a somewhat contradictory manner. As the Filipino-American literary theorist E. San Juan Jr. notes:

> Based on the orthodox tenets laid out by Edward Said, Homi Bhabha, and Gayatri Spivak – the 'founding fathers' of this discursive territory, postcolonial theory seeks to explain the ambivalent and hybrid nature of subjects, their thinking and behaviour, in the former colonies of the Western imperial powers, mainly the British Commonwealth societies. It seeks to prove that the colonial enterprise was not just a one-way affair of oppression and exploitation, but a reciprocal or mutual co- or inter-determination of both metropolitan master and 'third world' subaltern. Whatever the subtle differences among mainstream postcolonial critics, they all agree that colonialism, for all its terror and barbarism, presents a rhetorical and philosophical anomaly: the postcolonial subject as identical and different from the history textbook's portrayal of the submissive and silent victim of imperial conquest.[1]

Stuart Hall qualifies this by noting that such approaches to the cosmopolitan are often rooted in discrepancies between what he calls the 'cosmopolitan of the above', that of 'global entrepreneurs following the pathways of corporate power', and the 'cosmopolitan from below', those who have been uprooted from their native lands due to extenuating circumstances and often against their wills.[2] The case of Hong Kong provides a substantial examination of what it means to be a cosmopolitan from above, both historically in terms of real colonial presence and power – that of the British Empire at the height of its pink-flushed world domination – and as a 'model minority' under such circumstances as well as in the postcolonial world of modern Hong Kong. The history of the Jews in Hong Kong illustrates the pitfalls in assuming the view 'from above' is uniform or indeed 'from above'. The confusion of the cosmopolitan with the utopian goals of trans-historical views of mobility with the lived practice of Jews in British and now Chinese Hong Kong is a powerful corrective of this view.

Today there are between 6000 and 10,000 Jews living in this densely populated cosmopolitan city and place of transit. While the beautiful Edwardian free-baroque-style Ohel Leah Synagogue is hailed as one of Asia's oldest synagogues, Hong Kong is now arguably the centre of Jewish life in Asia. The Hong Kong Jewish Community Centre (popularly known as the JCC), located in a tall, modern luxury apartment tower in central Hong Kong, is its focal point. In this article, I will examine how in different historical periods, from under British rule for the most of the nineteenth and twentieth centuries to the years following Hong Kong's handover to the Communist China in 1997, the various Jewish groups in Hong Kong have adopted and re-adopted 'cosmopolitanism' as their identity while remaining Jewish. It is a cosmopolitanism of economic mobility and graduated visibility, that of the model minority in a world in which being Jewish has been at best tolerated and at worst a stigma. Focusing on Hong Kong, this former British Colony and now a Special Administrative Region (SAR) of the People's Republic of China, situated simultaneously at the centre and at the periphery of debates about the cosmopolitan, this article will add a new dimension to the parallel discussions of Jewish cosmopolitanism in Europe and North America.

A short history

Today Hong Kong's Jewish community consists of members from all over the world: India, South Africa, the United States, Canada, Britain, Germany, Israel, Iraq and many other lands. Some of them have been in Hong Kong since its founding in the second half of the nineteenth century, and they, alongside the Chinese population in Hong Kong, as well as the Indians, the Muslims, the Parsees and the British, have helped to transform this small *outpost*, or diseased jungle, as some called it, on the eastern periphery of the British Empire into a cosmopolitan global city and the financial centre of Asia.

The first group of Jews arrived in Hong Kong in 1842, after the First Anglo-Chinese War – better known as the First Opium War. Most of them came via what were then British Bombay and Calcutta. A number of them had already been trading in nearby Canton for a number of years. The history of modern China is, as pointed out by John King Fairbank, the doyen of Chinese studies, inextricably entwined with that of the opium trade.[3] As its prime brokers, the first groups of Jewish traders in Hong Kong were part of the making of that history. After settling down in Hong Kong, as well as in Shanghai from the 1860s onwards, these Jews, although they had acquired the British nationality, were however not assimilated to become either British or Chinese. As global entrepreneurs of the nineteenth century, they adopted cosmopolitanism as their 'new' identity. In this sense they serve as fascinating examples of cosmopolitanism from below and not simply assimilated Jews.

Prior to the First Opium War in 1839, the Sephardic textile merchant David Sassoon (1792–1864), originally from Baghdad, had already been selling opium to the Chinese for a number of years. During the First Opium War, with the support of the British Army, he sent his second son, Elias David Sassoon, to Hong Kong to cash in on the opium trade. In the aftermath of the War, the Treaty of Nanking in 1842 forced the Qing China to open five ports to foreign trade. Three years later, in 1845, the Sassoons opened a branch of their commercial operations in Shanghai, one of the five treaty ports. As the anti-opium campaign intensified in China and international pressure to stop the opium trade increased, the business became highly contested but even more lucrative. When the Manchu government imposed a ban on opium, the Sassoons and other traders, many of them Jewish, seized the opportunity and began to control its price. By 1870 David Sassoon, Son & Co. was indisputably the largest opium importer in China.[4] The firm dominated more than one third of the total Indian opium trade to China.[5] With the money their forefathers had made on opium, the younger generation of the Sassoons, as well as other Jewish merchants such as the Kadoories and Silas Hardoon, were able to widen their business interests into shipping, banking and land speculation in Hong Kong as well as in Shanghai.

Silas (Saleh) Aaron Hardoon was the most controversial figure in Baghdadi Jewish circles in the Far East. Born in Baghdad, he moved as a child with his impoverished family to British Bombay, where Hardoon senior established close business ties with the Sassoon family. As an adult, Silas first took employment at David Sassoon, Sons & Co. in Hong Kong and Shanghai. Eventually he became partner and manager of E.D. Sassoon & Co.'s Shanghai branch – an enterprise of Elias David Sassoon. In the late nineteenth and early twentieth centuries, Shanghai grew to become Asia's most important cosmopolitan commercial hub. Hardoon took full advantage of this. With the influx of Chinese refugees from surrounding countryside and towns into Shanghai as the result of the Taiping Rebellion in the 1860s, the city grew exponentially. Land became ever more valuable. Opium and land speculation made Hardoon at one point the richest man in the Far East. He became known as the 'Rothschild of the East'. In Shanghai, Hardoon married a Euro-Asian woman who was also an ardent follower of Buddhism. Hardoon also became closely associated with various Chinese social groups in Shanghai. His home, the Aili Garden, was a Chinese-style garden designed by the famous Buddhist revolutionary monk and Chinese patriot Huang Zongyang. Through Huang, Hardoon became acquainted with the founder of the Chinese republic, Sun Yat-sen, and hosted a number of Chinese revolutionary meetings at the Aili Garden. However, throughout his life in Shanghai, Hardoon avoided becoming assimilated to the Chinese way of life or the life of colonialists. While he embraced cosmopolitanism as his identity and his involvement with Jewish circles in Asia were minimal, he remained Jewish. Together with his wife, the couple adopted a number of Jewish children as well as White Russian children who had fled to China after the Bolshevik Revolution, and brought them up as Jews. The most colourful and controversial episode came after Hardoon's death. His 'Jewish' funeral was conducted by a Jewish rabbi, but during it Buddhist monks and Taoist priests cited *sutra* and performed Taoist rituals. One day later at the memorial service, some Chinese funeral specialists performed elaborate mortuary rites in Confucian style, resembling those carried out during Chinese funerals.[6]

In its earliest days, most members of the Hong Kong Jewish circle were Sephardic merchants. As the number of Jews increased gradually over the years, a formal Jewish life began to establish itself. In 1855 a Jewish cemetery was laid out behind the Chinese village of Wong Nei Chong (in today's Happy Valley), and two years later the first Jew was buried there, at the same time as the Crown Lease was granted. By the 1860s, as the opium trade prospered, more Jews moved to Hong Kong as employees or partners of David Sassoon, Sons & Co. and its rival firm, E. D. Sassoon & Co. As the Jewish population grew, it also became necessary to have regular places of worship for the ever-expanding Jewish community. From 1867 the community began to lease premises on Hollywood Road in central Hong Kong Island. This was the earliest synagogue in Hong Kong. Fourteen years later it was relocated to the north side of Staunton Street, not far from its former location.

As the Jewish community grew in size, tensions within the community also grew. According to Carl T. Smith, at the end of nineteenth century, 'class as well as religious division had become a feature of the community'.[7] In the 1880s and 1890s pogroms brought an influx of Jewish refugees from Russia and the Balkans. Unlike their Sephardic counterparts, these Ashkenazi Jews from Europe were mostly poor. They found employment in badly paid jobs as barmen, innkeepers, cleaners and so on. A number of women resorted to prostitution. There were also regular police reports showing that some Ashkenazim were involved in street brawls, assaults and in using indecent language, a particularly British colonial crime. These incidents caused great embarrassment to the well-established and fairly wealthy Sephardic community. These newcomers were of a different social, cultural, linguistic, religious and economic background. They did not find it easy to adjust to the Sephardic tradition of Hong Kong Jewish life, and were not willing to be identified with the Sephardim. Some of these so-called 'German' Jews hired a hall and formed a temporary congregation of their own. The Ashkenazi congregation mostly met on Jewish holidays such as New Year and Yom Kippur. According to Emmanuel Raphael Belilios, another successful Jewish opium trader from Calcutta and then a senior member of the Jewish community, when the Ashkenazim could not form a *minyan* (the 10 male Jews necessary for communal prayer) amongst themselves, they did join with the Sephardim.

Belilios is a prime example of the complexity of speaking about a homogenous Jewish sense of identity as colonial subjects in Hong Kong. At the beginning of my article, I introduced Stuart Hall's distinction a 'cosmopolitan of the above', that of 'global entrepreneurs following the pathways of corporate power', and a 'cosmopolitan from below'. The question of how individuals such as Belilios, as well as Hardoon in Shanghai as mentioned earlier, integrated themselves into a Jewish community, defined as homogenous in a colonial British setting, shows how the cosmopolitan can become an alternative identity in such conflicted contexts. Venetian by origin, Belilios did not always see eye to eye with other Sephardim who had originally come from the Arab lands and for whom Arabic was their *lingua franca*. (Until 1925 Arabic remained the main language spoken by the majority of Sephardim in Hong Kong, and these Sephardic merchants were sometimes referred to at the time as 'merchants from Arab lands'). To ease the tension, Belilios devoted his time and energy to strengthening his social and political position in British Hong Kong. It is worth mentioning that, being a British subject, Belilios, as well as many other Sephardim in Hong Kong, desperately wanted to be identified with the British elites but remain Jewish in a cosmopolitan sense.

To begin with he played the Jewish card by making attempts to establish ties with the British Prime Minister, Benjamin Disraeli. This resulted in his building the Beaconsfield Arcade in central Hong Kong named in Disraeli's honour. In 1879 Belilios gave £1000 to the British Governor of Hong Kong to erect a statue of Disraeli there, but his offer was rejected by Disraeli himself. After that Belilios devoted his time and wealth to philanthropy. Through his engagement in philanthropy, he became a cosmopolitan. He used the money to set up a medical-scholarship fund named after Belilios and also helped to establish the

Alice Memorial Hospital.[8] The hospital served as one of the major teaching hospitals for students of the Hong Kong College of Medicine for Chinese, the earlier incarnation of the Faculty of Medicine of the University of Hong Kong, today one of the most prestigious medical schools in the world. Sun Yat-sen, the 'father of Chinese nation', was one of the first graduates of the college.

Subsequently Belilios donated more money to the Hong Kong colonial government to build the Central School for Girls to give 'an ordinary middle-class English education to the daughters of Chinese, English, and Indian residents of China'. The school was later renamed Belilios Public School in his honour, and is still standing today. Belilios was also famous for his philanthropic work to promote the welfare and education of Chinese girls who were driven to crime and prostitution by poverty, and he set up a fund to build a probation home for girls. In 1893 he was made a Companion of St Michael and St George for his significant contribution to Hong Kong society, and became the first Hong Kong resident to receive this honour.[9] Between 1881 and 1900 Belilios also served on the Hong Kong Legislative Council.

As Belilios became more involved with the British ruling class in Hong Kong through his philanthropic work, he moved further away from the Sephardic community. One major conflict he had with other Sephardim was over the building of the new synagogue. Belilios wanted the new synagogue to welcome their Ashkenazi brothers from Europe, but the location he had chosen was not acceptable to other members of the Jewish community. Belilios had bought a plot of land on the prestigious Kennedy Road, and he proposed to sell a portion to the synagogue trustees to build the new synagogue. But Jacob Elias Sassoon in Bombay refused to go along with it. In the meantime other members of the Jewish community in Hong Kong also opposed Belilios' proposal, arguing that the Kennedy Road location was inappropriate, as the shabby appearance of the poor Jews from Europe would disgrace the community in this wealthy British neighbourhood.[10] As a result, Belilios resigned as one of the managers of the fund for the new synagogue. In Hong Kong today, Belilios is remembered as a philanthropist and cosmopolitan, not as a Jew.

Meanwhile, the Kardoories emerged as the leading figures in the Jewish community. Like Belilios, the Kadoories were also famous for their philanthropic work amongst the non-Jewish population of Hong Kong, and left lasting legacies. In the 1910s the Kadoories opened a school for the Chinese and another for the Hindus, as well as Helena May, a home for English working girls in Hong Kong. In addition, the Kadoories were amongst some of the most prominent families in Hong Kong's economic and civic culture. Even today their names are enshrined in the names of streets, buildings and institutions across the territory. The Peninsula Hotel, one of Hong Kong's most famous landmarks, is but one example. As the founders of China and Light, the Kadoories were also responsible for illuminating the streets of Hong Kong and supplying electricity for 80% of the territory's population.

Married in England to an English Sephardi, Elly Kadoorie was deeply attracted to Victorian English life. With the intention of introducing the concept of the English club to Hong Kong Jewish society, he turned the Hong Kong Jewish Recreational Club into a Victorian club fit for Hong Kong colonial life. In 1920 Israel Cohen, a British Jew and Communist travelling through Hong Kong, remarked that the Jewish Recreational Club was 'the finest Jewish institution' and was equipped with something of the comfort characteristic of a social or political club in the West End of London. There was a large and tastefully furnished room with a grand piano ... a reading room ... a billiard-room that was seldom neglected, and a bar presided over by a white-jacketed Chinese mixer who could dispense you any cocktail that you chose.'[11] Besides a billiard room, the club also brought tennis, bowling and croquet – all Victorian games – to the Hong Kong Jewish community. Here we have all the external markers of colonial cosmopolitanism now translated into a Jewish setting.[12]

Under Lawrence Kadoorie's leadership, a major innovation was introduced to Ohel Leah Synagogue. At the New Year services in 1938, a certain number of prayers were read out in English as well as in Hebrew, despite opposition from some members of the synagogue. Ohel Leah was, of course, a Sephardic synagogue. The movement of Hong Kong Jewry into the world of British Jewry is very interesting. By the nineteenth century the original Sephardic community in London, still very much present in congregations such as the seventeenth-century Bevis Marks Synagogue, had been eclipsed by German and Eastern European Ashkenazi Jewry. In Hong Kong, the presence of 'Baghdadi' Jews meant that the movement towards 'reform' in the *minhag* in London was relatively late coming to Ohel Leah.

Yet with all its accomplishments and some of its prominent members' efforts to become Anglicized, the Hong Kong Jews were never wholly accepted by the British elites in Hong Kong. Not being 'British enough' in a way helped them to maintain their Jewish identity in this self-consciously cosmopolitan British colony – cosmopolitan in that it lived off being a transit point for trade and relied on the movement of peoples as well as the movement of goods. While they were major players in the economic as well as the political life of the city, the 'Baghdadi' Jews remained too 'Oriental' for the late nineteenth- and early twentieth-century British. They were cosmopolitan from below in Stuart Hall's sense. But this marginalisation was not limited to Jews from beyond the Empire. Matthew Nathan, one of Hong Kong's high achievers as well as the only Jewish governor (1903–7) is an example. Nathan, who initiated Hong Kong's urban planning and the city's infrastructure, was instrumental in Hong Kong's future development. During his tenure, the construction of the Kowloon–Canton Railway, Hong Kong's first and most important railway, and the only one built during the entire British rule, began. And Nathan Road, Kowloon's major and most famous road, also known as Hong Kong's Golden Mile, was named after him to honour his monumental achievements and his contribution to Hong Kong. His superior at the Colonial Office, Sir Reginald Antrobus, praised him as a 'first rate official'.[13] Despite his achievements, however, being a bachelor and Jewish, as well as lacking university education and bureaucratic experience, Nathan remained an outsider. He was loathed by the British ruling class in Hong Kong and was not a welcome figure at their regular Victorian tea parties and charity balls. One of his presumed faults was that as the governor he was the nominal head of St John's Cathedral, but being a professing Jew, he did not attend the Church of England Sunday services. It was a real relief to him when he was spared laying the foundation stone of an Anglican cathedral in Hong Kong, but this event further diminished his popularity amongst Hong Kong British society.[14] Nathan also became a constant target for gossip because he was a bachelor in an age that had grown more and more anxious about homosexuality after the Oscar Wilde trials in the 1890s. During this time he took an active part in Hong Kong Jewish life and helped the community to secure the lease to extend the Jewish cemetery. Although being Jewish contributed to his downfall in Hong Kong, in a way it strengthened his Jewish identity. After Hong Kong, he did toy briefly with the Anglican faith, but in the end he rejected it. During his assignments in South Africa and Ireland, Nathan made an effort to attend the Anglican Church regularly, but remained absent from all Easter services. By 1858 the extensive debate following Lionel de Rothschild's election to the House of Commons in 1847 had eventually led the House to change the oath to permit observant Jews to serve in that body. By the end of the century Jewish civil emancipation was not in question, but the social acceptance of Jews in conservative arenas such as Whitehall (the Foreign Service) meant that they could not 'flaunt' their Jewishness. Being present as part of the community at Easter services was considered to be a quasi-official obligation. Throughout the rest of his life, Nathan remained a professing Jew.[15]

Jewish life in twentieth-century Hong Kong

Hong Kong's Jewish community, like other colonial, peripheral but substantial communities, such as the Chinese, the Muslims and others in Hong Kong, has inevitably been influenced by its political and historical environment. The Sino-Japanese War of the 1930s and 1940s cast a shadow on the life of Hong Kong, and it impacted on Hong Kong Jewish life. In some ways, one could argue that the war brought the Hong Kong Jewish community closer to their fellow Jews from other parts of the world, including those refugees from Europe and Jewish charitable organisations in the United States.

On Christmas Day 1941 the Japanese Army marched into Hong Kong and occupied this thriving British Colony. Civilian nationals of those countries that were at war with Japan were kept in POW camps. As many Hong Kong Jews had acquired British nationality, they did not escape this treatment. After occupying Hong Kong, the Japanese authority implemented a policy aimed at restoring 'Asia values' in Hong Kong and returning the city to the East Asians. In the process of the Japanese eradication of 'the poisonous remains of British cultural leftovers'[16], the Victorian-style Jewish Recreational Club, which frequently provided entertainment for the British forces that were fighting the Japanese, was badly damaged. With the intention of providing entertainment for those 'soldiers with Jewish persuasion', Lawrence Kadoorie instigated the formation of the Jewish Ladies' Committee. In the meantime, on the issue of helping the Jewish refugees, the Hong Kong Jewish community stood together with a common goal.

The Jewish refugees escaping the war in Europe began to pass through Hong Kong as early as 1938, after China had entered the war with Japan and Shanghai was under Japanese occupation. The long-established Jewish Benevolent Society was the first to assume responsibility for taking care of them. As the Jewish community leader, Lawrence Kadoorie appealed to Hong Kong Jews to unite and help these refugees: 'Today more than ever is it the duty of every Jew to realize his responsibilities.'[17]

As soon as the war ended in 1945, life and social structure in Hong Kong returned more or less to normal, and many of those who had escaped during the conflict returned. By 1947 the population in Hong Kong had grown to 1,750,000. Refugees crowded into Hong Kong, and many of them were Jewish refugees from Europe who had found refuge in China and were now waiting for their passage to Palestine, North America or Australia. Many of them, however, lacked the necessary paperwork to stop in Hong Kong, which had returned to British rule. The American Jewish Joint Distribution Committee (JDC) was then sponsoring and co-ordinating the transportation of these refugees. During the war years, they had already worked closely with Horace Kadoorie to provide relief work for the Jewish refugees in Shanghai. They co-ordinated with Lawrence Kadoorie, Horace's brother, in Hong Kong, using the Kardoories' British connections to try to obtain the proper authorisation for the refugees to stay in Hong Kong while in transit. The Kadoories regularly visited the Hong Kong Immigration Department to ensure those Jewish refugees due to arrive had ready the visas necessary for resettlement to the then British Palestine, North America, Europe and Australia. As Hong Kong was already crammed with displaced persons as well as the repatriated British, there was a concern that the influx of Jewish refugees would compete for the city's limited resources. This meant even transit visas were difficult to obtain. The Kadoories wrote thousands of letters to governments, NGOs and individuals to guarantee successful repatriation. The Kadoories, as the guarantors of the Jewish refugees, housed them in the grand Peninsula Hotel as they waited for the next ship. This was the Kadoories' effort to assure the colonial government that these Jews would not be a burden to Hong Kong, and to avoid antisemitism. Some years earlier, in fear of increased antisemitism, Lawrence Kadoorie had warned the community that '[i]n trying to help those of our people who have lost their all, we must remember that to take work from others in order to fulfill this object will cause that very anti-Semitism that we must try at all costs to avoid.'[18]

In addition to the Kadoories, the Hong Kong Jewish community, while still readjusting to post-war life after returning from Japanese war camps, worked closely alongside the National Jewish Welfare Board in helping their fellow Jews in transit. Just as Primo Levi, the Italian Sephardi, embraced Yiddish as the language of the Jews after his concentration-camp experience[19], one could argue that after a half century of conflicting interests, the Second World War brought the Sephardic and the Ashkenazi Jewish groups in Hong Kong together. Their common effort during and after the war marked the beginning of their on-going collaboration. Many individuals from the existing Jewish community offered their hospitality and friendship to their refugee brothers. A makeshift synagogue was set up at the Peninsula Hotel, and the Hong Kong Jewish Women's Association, a larger reincarnation of the earlier Jewish Ladies Committee, was formed to help distribute goods to the refugees.

As more and more refugees departed Hong Kong, the Hong Kong Jewish community began to devote its energy to rebuilding Jewish life in the British colony. In 1949 the Kadoorie family once again made a generous financial contribution to the reconstruction of a new Jewish Recreational Club. Besides those older Sephardic members, a growing number of Ashkenazi Jews began to take an active role in the club and in Hong Kong Jewish life as whole.

But the community's post-war effort to rebuild their Jewish life was soon interrupted. In 1966 and 1967, when China was experiencing the upheaval of the Cultural Revolution, Hong Kong was also in chaos. Anti-British riots were a regular feature. Extreme leftists, many of them Communist supporters and closely linked to the People's Republic of China (PRC), were bombing cars, killing people and engaging in all kinds of destructive activities. These riots also caused tremendous financial damage to Hong Kong. According to estimates, the damage caused by the 1966 riot alone was HK$20 million. These events affected Hong Kong's Jewish community as well as individuals within the community. Some four months after Michael Kadoorie was appointed to the Board of China Light & Power Co., Ltd. (CLP), another leftist riot took place that was intended to immobilize Hong Kong's industry in order to deprive the Hong Kong government of its sources of revenue and eventually get rid of British rule.[20] About 70% of the employees at CLP went on strike. Joining with many other prominent businessmen, the Kadoories stood firmly on the side of the British. A few years later, Lawrence Kadoorie was knighted by the Queen for his contribution to the British Empire.[21]

Whilst the leaders of the Hong Kong Jewish community such as the Kadoories were preoccupied with the political events taking place at the time, Hong Kong's communal Jewish life was very much neglected. David Buxbaum, a Jewish student living in Singapore, visited Hong Kong during this period. He noted that the Hong Kong Jews were 'a community without much Jewishness. Having come from Singapore, we were surprised at the lack of school, a shochet, a kosher mikva, a rabbi, or a regular minyan service.' And according to him, even the much-lauded Jewish Relief Council was poorly maintained.[22]

As the 1970s dawned, things began to pick up in Hong Kong, and individuals grew wealthier. Members of the Jewish community felt a need to bring Jewish culture and religion back to Hong Kong Jewish life. Providing Jewish children with a Jewish education became a pressing topic for the Hong Kong Jewish community. Prior to the Second World War, the community used to send their children to Jewish schools in Mainland China. As the majority of Jews had left China after the war and with the Communist seizure of power in 1949, all Jewish schools in China had ceased to exist. In 1969 a Hebrew school opened its doors to promote Jewish education in Hong Kong. Under the leadership of Judy Diestel, an active member of the Jewish community who had lived in Shanghai during the Second World War, school attendance grew, and the school quickly became a focal point of the community. Here, Sephardic and Ashkenazi children and their parents met. The latter worked together to support the school in many of its activities. As Diestel put it:, 'The community evolved around the school, sharing in its spirit, its events and, in the mutual need for a Jewish environment.'[23]

Towards the end of the 1970s Hong Kong, by then the world's third largest financial centre became more cosmopolitan. This cosmopolitanism also marked the ever-growing Hong Kong Jewish community. Prior to 1997 the Ohel Leah congregation changed from a primarily Sephardic congregation to one consisting of some 200 families who came from the United States, Israel, the Netherlands and 14 other countries. This demographic change was partly due to the gradual opening of the PRC, the aim of which was to engage economically with the rest of the world. Hong Kong, being so close, became a regular and popular stopping point for those wishing to do business with or in China. Jewish businesses, especially many Israeli companies, used Hong Kong as a launch pad into the Mainland market. In addition to bankers and businessmen, there were also a number of journalists and students. Some were long-term residents, and many more were on temporary assignments. This was markedly different from members of the older Sephardic community, most of whom were permanent residents of Hong Kong. These 'new' Jews added new dimensions and challenges to the existing Hong Kong Jewish life.

Faced with these changes, the Jewish community in Hong Kong, being at the economic crossroads of the New Asia, adopted this new cosmopolitanism as their 'new' identity as opposed to the old cosmopolitanism of the British Empire. Services at Ohel Leah Synagogue, for example, began to follow the Ashkenazi form as the Baghdadi Jews gave way in their numbers to Jews from Western Europe and North America. A student from an Orthodox Ashkenazi *yeshiva* was appointed the rabbi of the synagogue in 1986, and a couple of years later he went on to open the first Chabad house in Hong Kong. The Chabad (Lubavitcher) movement is by definition not only rooted in specific Orthodox practices, but also cosmopolitan in that it caters to Jews of any and all definitions, with, of course, the understood notion of proselytising them. Around the same time, the United Jewish Congregation was formed to cater to the needs of the Reform-Liberal group. Being relatively small in size yet very diverse, the Hong Kong Jewish community has developed some unique arrangements: Ohel Leah and the Jewish Community Centre are maintained by an Orthodox trust, which also sponsors the United Jewish Congregation – the only example in the world of a Reform congregation being funded by an Orthodox one.

The religious restrictions imposed by the Communist government on the mainland presented further opportunities for the Hong Kong Jewish community, especially as the 1984 Draft Agreement between Britain and China over Hong Kong's handover guaranteed Hong Kong the freedom of 'religious belief'. For a while, the Jewish Community Centre and Ohel Leah Synagogue provided material and educational support for Jewish communities on the mainland. For instance, until very recently, Jewish communities in China went to Hong Kong for Passover supplies, and as a result Hong Kong acquired the role as the centre of Jewish life in Asia.

Being Jewish in post-1997 Hong Kong

In 1997 the British handed over Hong Kong to the Communist government in China, and Hong Kong became a Special Administrative Region. This event profoundly affected Hong Kong society and, in turn, impacted on the Jews of Hong Kong. Prior to the handover residents, including Jews, wondered to what degree the Communist Party would want to control Hong Kong, as the 1984 Draft Agreement between Britain and China had made no specific provisions for how Hong Kong's social and economic systems would be preserved, or how the transition to Chinese rule would be made. At the time only 3% of Hong Kong residents were ethnically non-Chinese, and the Jews were among this small minority. There were then only about 2500 Jewish residents in Hong Kong. A few of the older generation who came to Hong Kong in 1949 after the Communists took over China, were troubled by the uncertain future. Some worried that what had happened in Shanghai in 1949 could happen in Hong Kong. While many of the younger generations of Jews had foreign passports, quite a few elderly members of the Jewish community did not. Being cosmopolitans became a factor they worried about: 'I have never felt isolated or rootless as a Jew in Hong Kong', lamented one older member of the Jewish community. In a time of uncertainty, the need to be Jewish grew stronger: 'For years there has been a vital Jewish community here and elsewhere in Asia, and I pray there will always be.'[24] Being Jewish was seen as belonging to a multicultural Hong Kong mix but with a strong religiously rooted component. The echo of the anxiety of Diaspora Jewry about a Jewish community always on the edge of attack and dissolution is paralleled by the cosmopolitan notion of a Jewry always present, no matter what the context.

Ironically, while wealthy and middle-class ethnic Chinese flooded into Canada and Australia to purchase properties at very high prices in the hope of gaining a foreign citizenship, those expatriates with foreign passports, including many Jewish residents, stayed in Hong Kong to wait and see what would happen. The Diestels were among them. Having moved to Hong Kong from Shanghai after the Second World War, they were by then the leaders of the Jewish community. Living in the same luxury apartment block as Hong Kong's new chief executive, Tung Chee-hwa, the Diestels were full of optimism, which was shared by a number of well-to-do Hong Kong Jews. They embraced the religion of Hong Kong: money. Five years prior to the handover, the trustees of the Hong Kong Jewish community leased half of its property on Robinson Road in the Mid-Levels district, originally owned by the Sassoon brothers, to Hong Kong's biggest property developer. This deal made the Hong Kong Jewish community one of the wealthiest Jewish communities per capita in the world. This wealth was seen by many as a guarantee of the community's future. In addition, the 'Eisenberg connection' added another layer of warranty for the community. Shoul Eisenberg, another Second World War Jewish refugee from Europe who lived briefly in Shanghai, was one of the most influential China brokers for world trade since the 1950s. He was also instrumental in re-establishing diplomatic and trading relations between China and Israel in 1992. At the time of the handover, his protégé Avishay Hamburger was in charge of the local Israel Chamber of Commerce in Hong Kong. By the mid-1990s, Israel had become China's second biggest trading partner, and the Israel Chamber of Commerce in Hong Kong played a pivotal role in promoting trade with Israel. With Eisenberg behind them, many members of the Jewish community were certain that Beijing would be unlikely to do anything drastic to harm the ever-thriving China-Jewish ties.

By the year 2000 the Communist government had done very little to change Hong Kong except to turn it into an even greater money-making machine. As the wealth of Hong Kong SAR grew, many Hong Kong Chinese who had fled before 1997 returned home. Joining them were thousands of expatriates from other ethnic backgrounds, including Jews. Although the SARS virus crisis in 2003 initially hit this expansion of Hong Kong, it quickly recovered, and there followed an even greater sense of optimism. As a result, its economy grew at a remarkable rate. The optimistic notion that nothing could beat Hong Kong persisted during the 2008 worldwide economic recession, and many more Jewish businessmen, bankers and young entrepreneurs seeking opportunities and employment moved to this Asian financial centre as Asia came to represent the future at this gloomy time.

In 2010 Hong Kong's Jewish population grew to 5000, literally doubling since 1997. Though it remains small compared to those in Europe and North America, this Jewish community is remarkably active and diverse. There are Jews 'from everywhere, even from countries where I didn't know there were Jews, like Zaire'[25], Asher Oser, Ohel Leah's newly appointed rabbi, remarked. This new trend is matched by five congregations: in addition to Ohel Leah Synagogue, there is now a United Jewish Congregation on Hong Kong Island; three Chabad Houses covering all of Hong Kong; and two Sephardic Orthodox congregations covering Kowloon and Hong Kong Island. Yet cosmopolitanism did not disappear completely. While Jews from different backgrounds and regions have a choice of congregations, they are also brought together by the Jewish Community Centre, a Jewish day school and a Jewish newspaper and magazine.

In 1995 the new Jewish Community Centre (JCC) replaced the former Jewish Recreational Club. Replacing the former Victorian games, the JCC is equipped with modern amenities including a luxury swimming pool. In addition to providing recreational facilities for the Hong Kong Jewish community, the centre also houses a mikvah, a dairy restaurant, a meat restaurant and, more recently, a kosher shopping centre catering to observant Jews. The kosher products served or sold are all imported. Those from the United States and Canada bear printed *hasgachot*, while products from Australia and England are listed in *kashrut* guides. Besides the JCC, there are now a number of kosher restaurants throughout Hong Kong, and one can now even find kosher products in Hong Kong's major supermarket. So keeping kosher is no longer a problem in Hong Kong. At the same time kosher food is becoming an integral part of non-Chinese international 'healthy' cuisine, which can be enjoyed by anyone, not just Jews.

For many years, one major concern for many Jewish families was their children's education: specifically, finding ways to give their children a Jewish education but at the same time maintain a highly competitive international standard. Carmel School's Elsa High School, Hong Kong's first Jewish high school, became the answer as it bridges these two different requirements. Its curriculum combines the best elements of religious and secular education with a firm foundation in an internationally recognized syllabus. While Jewish students love the Jewish experience they get at Elsa High, students from other religious or secular backgrounds enrol in the school because it offers a high-standard British education and extends their awareness and understanding of various economic, political, historical and geographical perspectives.[26] Elsa High offers a Jewish perspective to non-Jewish students in Hong Kong, while Hong Kong Jewish residents also benefit from the cosmopolitan experience of living there. The South Africa-born Judy Green is the chairwoman of the Hong Kong Jewish Historical Society. She recalls in a discussion with the author that during her many visits to the Hong Kong Jewish cemetery, situated right behind a Buddhist monastery: 'You can hear the nuns chanting. It's very peaceful.'

While Green finds Buddhist chanting peaceful, Hong Kong's international community enjoys Asia's one and only Jewish film festival. The Hong Kong Jewish Film Festival was first launched in 2001 by the Canadian businessman Howard Elias and his friend as a small screening party. Over the years, it has grown to become one of highest-rated film festivals in Hong Kong. In an interview with CNN, Elias claimed the festival to be 'non-partisan':

> Even if someone is not active in the Jewish community, they come to the festival, which is great. There's no religion to it, except the fact that we're kosher. It's just a big party. We're the only Jewish film festival in Asia – there's nothing else between Jerusalem and Sydney. We've had people come from Shanghai and Beijing, and the Israeli ambassador to Myanmar came a couple years ago.[27]

In addition, the festival is also reported to have become a very Hong Kong affair rather than solely a Jewish one. In 2009 according to Elias, about a third of its audience was local Chinese, and they 'absolutely loved the festival'.[28]

But the question is: is there room for Jewishness in this cosmopolitan city? For Rabbi Asher Oser, the current rabbi of Ohel Leah Synagogue, being Jewish in secular and cosmopolitan Hong Kong is what Jewish life is about. 'What Judaism does is it tries to make sense of those contradictions,' he says. Rabbi Oser predicts that there will eventually be an 'Asianization of Judaism', but he does not quite know what that would entail. Like many other members of the Hong Kong Jewish community, Rabbi Oser was born in Australia, educated in Canada, and most recently served as the rabbi for a congregation in Providence, Rhode Island. 'There are few Jews here, and it's a transient place, yet there are deep roots,' he said in an interview.[29] Being rooted in this transient place sums up not only Hong Kong Jewish life but also life in Hong Kong in general. For the Hong Kong Jewish community, their deep roots are their shared Jewish identity no matter where they are from originally. The postcolonial world of contemporary Hong Kong allows the notion of a cosmopolitanism from above, to use Stuart Hall's label, more specifically the cosmopolitanism of the Jewish merchant and the banker, to trump the national identity of Jews as Israelis, Americans or British. Oser's romantic vision of an 'Asianization of Judaism' evokes precisely this cosmopolitan levelling effect but from above, not from below. What the reality will bring with the now radicalized diminution of the promised guarantees of freedom, including freedom of religious assembly, with Hong Kong now being part of the PRC, is at present unclear. This is not solely a Jewish concern. The fear for the future is currently being experienced by the majority population living in Hong Kong. But the new cosmopolitanism of Hong Kong's Jewish life may decay into a tourist attraction, like the present evocation of an earlier Jewish life in Shanghai or Kaifeng. In this respect, the Jewish experience in Hong Kong will become a monument rather than a lived experience.

Notes

1. San Juan Jr., "The Limits of Postcolonial Criticism."
2. Stuart Hall in conversation with Pnina Werbner, "Cosmopolitanism, Globalisation and Diaspora."
3. See Dikötter, Zhou, and Laamann, *Narcotic Culture*, 234.
4. "Commercial Reports from Her Majesty's Consuls in China: 1879," British Parliamentary Papers (Trade Reports) [C.2718] China. No. 3 (1880), 215.
5. "Further Memorials Respecting the China Treaty Revision Convention," British Parliamentary Papers [C.80] China. No. 6 (1870), 21.
6. Betta, "Silas Aaron Hardoon (1815–1931)."
7. Smith, *A Sense of History*, 400.
8. Eitel, *Europe in China*, 563–4.
9. *Times*, 1893, quoted in Choa, *The Life and Times of Sir Kai Ho Kai*, 58.
10. Smith, *A Sense of History*, 400–1.
11. "The Journal of a Jewish Traveller," *Bulletin Igud Yotzei Sin* 57, no. 402 (August–September 2010): 88–9.
12. Cf. Wilson and Swan, *Glenferrie Hill Recreation Club*.
13. Colonial Office Papers, Public Record Office, London 446/50. Minutes by Sir Reginald Antrobus, 28 January 1906.
14. Haydon, *Sir Matthew Nathan*.
15. Chasin, *Citizens of Empire*, 47.
16. "Cultural Activities in the New Hong Kong: A Special Article from the Hong Kong Broadcasting Office," *New East Asia* (September 1942), 107–8.
17. "Lawrence Kadoorie's Speech at the Jewish Recreational Club," February 1939. From the Hong Kong Heritage Project archive.
18. Ibid.
19. Gilman, "To Quote Primo Levi," 293–316.
20. Cheung, *Hong Kong's Watershed*, 63.
21. "Obituary: Lord Kadoorie," *Independent*, 26 August 1993.
22. David Buxbaum, quoted in "A Brief Sojourn in Asia and the Flourishing of Jewish Life," 20.
23. Maynard in association with Ngan, "A History of the Jewish Community in Hong Kong," 25.
24. Tarnapol, "Pondering the Future under Chinese Rule," 35.
25. Christopher DeWolf, "Keeping Kosher," *China Daily*, 8 December 2010. http://www.chinadaily.com.cn/hkedition/2010-12/08/content_11666891.htm (Accessed 21 February 2014).
26. DeWolf, "Keeping Kosher."
27. DeWolf, "Interview: Howard Elias."
28. DeWolf, "Interview: Howard Elias."
29. Christopher DeWolf, "Keeping Kosher," China Daily, 8 December 2010. http://www.chinadaily.com.cn/hkedition/2010-12/08/content_11666891.htm (Accessed 21 February 2014).

Disclosure statement

No potential conflict of interest was reported by the author.

References

Archival sources

"Commercial Reports from Her Majesty's Consuls in China: 1879." British Parliamentary Papers (Trade reports) [C.2718] China. No. 3 (1880), 215.

"Further Memorials respecting the China Treaty Revision Convention." British Parliamentary Papers, 1870 [C.80] China. No. 6 (1870), 21.

Colonial Office Papers, Public Record Office, London 446/50, minutes by Sir Reginald Antrobus, 28 January 1906.

Printed sources

"A Brief Sojourn in Asia and the Flourishing of Jewish Life." *Jewish Asia Times* 5, no. 1 (April 2010), 20.

Betta, Chiara. *Silas Aaron Hardoon (1815–1931): Marginality and Adaptation in Shanghai*. PhD diss.: University of London, 1997.

Chasin, Stephanie. *Citizens of Empire: Jews in the Service of the British Empire, 1906–1940*. Los Angeles, CA: University of California Press, 2008.

Cheung, Gary Ka-wai. *Hong Kong's Watershed: the 1967 Riots*, Hong Kong: Hong Kong University Press, 2009.

Choa, G. H. *The Life and Times of Sir Kai Ho Kai: A Prominent Figure in Nineteenth Hong Kong*. Hong Kong: Chinese University Press, 2000.

"Cultural Activities in the New Hong Kong, a Special Article from the Hong Kong Broadcasting Office." *The New East Asia*, September (1942), 107–108.

DeWolf, Christopher. "Interview: Howard Elias, Founder of Asia's only Jewish Film Festival." CNN.com. 12 November 2009. Accessed 12 February 2014. http://travel.cnn.com/hong-kong/play/interview-howard-elias-founder-asias-only-jewish-film-festival-963969

DeWolf, Christopher. "Keeping Kosher." *China Daily*, 8 December 2010. Accessed 21 February 2014. http://www.chinadaily.com.cn/hkedition/2010-12/08/content_11666891.htm.

Dikötter, Frank, Zhou Xun, and Lars Laamann. *Narcotic Culture: A History of Drugs in China*. Chicago: University of Chicago Press and Hurst & Co, 2004.

Eitel, E. J. *Europe in China*. Hong Kong: Kelly and Walsh, 1895.

Hall, Stuart in conversation with Pnina Werbner. "Cosmopolitanism, Globalisation and Diaspora." In *Anthropology and the New Cosmopolitanism: Rooted, Feminist and Vernacular Perspective*, edited by P. Werbner, 345–360. ASA Monographs 45. Oxford: Berg, 2008.

Haydon, Anthony. *Sir Matthew Nathan: British Colonial Governor and Civil Servant*. Brisbane: University of Queensland Press, 1976.

Gilman, Sander L. "To Quote Primo Levi: If You Don't Speak Yiddish, You're not a Jew." In *Inscribing the Other*, 293–316. Lincoln, NE: University of Nebraska Press, 1991.

"The Journal of a Jewish Traveller." *Bulletin Igud Yotzei Sin*, LVII, no. 402 (2010), 88–89.

"Lawrence Kadoorie's Speech at Jewish Recreational Club." February 1939. From Hong Kong Heritage Project archive.

Maynard, Debra, in association with George Ngan. "A History of the Jewish Community in Hong Kong." In *A Vision Fulfilled*. Hong Kong: The Jewish Community Centre, 1995.

"Obituary: Lord Kadoorie." *Independent*, 26 August 1993.

San Juan Jr., E. 2005. "The Limits of Postcolonial Criticism: The Discourse of Edward Said." *Solidarity*. http://www.solidarity-us.org/current/node/1781

Smith, Carl T. *A Sense of History*. Hong Kong: Hong Kong Education Publishing, 1996.

Tarnapol, Paula. "Pondering the Future Under Chinese Rule." *The Jewish Monthly* (March 1986), 35.

Wilson, Pamela F., and John M. Swan. *Glenferrie Hill Recreation Club: A Memoir 1907 2001*. Swan: J. M, 2008.

JEWS AND THE NEW COSMOPOLITANISM

The possibilities and pitfalls of a Jewish cosmopolitanism: reading Natan Sznaider through Russian-Jewish writer Olga Grjasnowa's German-language novel *Der Russe ist einer, der Birken liebt* (All Russians Love Birch Trees)

Stuart Taberner

ABSTRACT
In his *Jewish Memory and the Cosmopolitan Order* (2011), Natan Sznaider shows how Jewish thinkers both before and after the Holocaust have advanced universalist ideas out of their particularist Jewish identities, connecting the Jewish experience to contemporary cosmopolitan concerns such as Human Rights, genocide prevention and international justice. Sznaider focuses on Hannah Arendt and illustrates how this post-Holocaust Jewish thinker both defended her rootedness in her Jewish identity and drew universalising conclusions from it. This article explores Sznaider's notion of a 'Jewish cosmopolitanism' in tandem with a close reading of Russian-Jewish writer Olga Grjasnowa's 2012 German-language novel *Der Russe ist einer, der Birken liebt* (All Russians Love Birch Trees). The empathy Grjasnowa's protagonist feels for the plight of Palestinians reveals her commitment to a universalist ideal of Human Rights even as she remains rooted in her Jewish identity: her activism draws on the transmission of the trauma of the Holocaust down through the different generations of her family. At the same time, Grjasnowa's novel also suggests some of the limitations – and indeed problems – of Sznaider's conceptualisation of a Jewish cosmopolitanism.

A Jewish cosmopolitanism?

In *Jewish Memory and the Cosmopolitan Order* (2011), Israeli sociologist Natan Sznaider shows how Jewish thinkers before and after the Holocaust have advanced universalist ideas out of their particularist Jewish identities, connecting the Jewish experience to contemporary cosmopolitan concerns such as Human Rights, genocide prevention and international justice. In the opening section of this article, we examine Sznaider's elaboration of a historically grounded and implicitly diasporic 'Jewish cosmopolitanism' as a response to what he sees as the increasing Jewish ethno-nationalism of the state of Israel. Next, we turn to Russian-Jewish writer Olga Grjasnowa's *Der Russe ist einer, der Birken liebt* (All Russians Love Birch Trees, 2012). Like Sznaider's *Jewish Memory*, Grjasnowa's German-language novel posits a Jewish cosmopolitanism that insists upon the 'Jewishness' of the Holocaust *and* its universal significance, but this work of fiction also probes the limitations of a cosmopolitanism that aims to channel Jewish trauma into a principled solidarity with others. Finally, we ask whether Sznaider's 'Jewish cosmopolitanism' can avoid the pitfalls of undifferentiated sentimentality and self-indulgence (or self-consolation), or avoid a potentially fraught stylisation of Jews as 'exemplary'.

In late 2014, Prime Minister Binyamin Netanyahu provoked international consternation, and not insignificant domestic concern, when he forwarded to the Knesset a bill to introduce a definition of Israel as the 'national state of the Jewish people' into the constitution. For Netanyahu's critics, including two of his coalition partners, the proposed legislation contradicted the ideal prominently featured in Israel's Declaration of Independence of 1948, namely the new state's duty to 'ensure complete equality of social and political rights to all its inhabitants'. It appeared that Netanyahu was determined to set aside Israel's foundational rhetorical commitment to cosmopolitan principles – which had in any case always clashed with the everyday reality of discrimination against its Arab citizens – in favour of an uncompromising assertion of Jewish ethno-nationalism. For German-Jewish commentator Micha Brumlik, Netanyahu's reframing of Israel's purpose could only end in catastrophe, not only for Israeli Arabs and Palestinians seeking to realise *their* national aspirations, but also for Jews. It would incite the biggest crisis since the Holocaust, as Jews in the diaspora – committed to their Jewishness as an expression of universalist values – would reject Israeli chauvinism as no better than any other expression of aggressive particularism.[1]

Brumlik, of course, is not the only thinker to have observed the tension between universalism and particularism in Jewish existence, especially in the diaspora, and to argue that Jewishness loses its prophetic significance when it sacrifices the former for the sake of the latter. Promoting a Jewish Enlightenment (Haskalah) in the late eighteenth century, Moses Mendelssohn emphasised Judaism's universalist *ethical* underpinning, shared with the other Abrahamic faiths – reason, tolerance, love – as an indispensable counterpart to the Jewish people's special covenant with God, forged through revelation. Indeed, Jewish enlighteners (*maskilim*) emphasised the humanistic aspects of Judaism while depicting Jews in the diaspora as mediators between the particular and the universal.[2] In more recent times, American scholar and public intellectual Alan Wolfe, in his provocatively titled (and hotly debated) book *At Home in Exile: Why Diaspora is Good for the Jews* (2014), has argued that 'in a world in which nation-states are primarily concerned with protecting their own, however, the diaspora remains the place where a universalistic Judaism will survive best'.[3] (Here, Wolfe's *At Home in Exile* to some extent recalls Juri Slezkine's 2004 *The Jewish Century*, which prefers a cosmopolitan nomadism for Jews to the normalising tendencies of the nation-state Israel). Jews in the diaspora, Wolfe suggests, are not only charged with preserving the universalist impulse intrinsic to Judaism, at risk of being of extinguished in Israel as it 'turns to the right' (*HE*, 7). It seems that they are also – in the wake of 9/11 and the clamorous claims of 'national security' – charged with preserving universalism itself.

Wolfe's allusion to the signal assertiveness of nation-states in the present day – focused on their citizens' physical protection, often to the detriment of their liberties, and on the targeted (and not so targeted) elimination of perceived threats – reminds us why the debate on universalism and particularism has become so vital, and not only for Jews in Israel and in the diaspora. People across the world are today faced today with the bewildering simultaneity of: (1) globalisation, that is, the massively intensified flow of people, products and ideas across frontiers resulting from the post-Cold War liberalisation of trade and the communications revolution; (2) the emergence of what German sociologist Ulrich Beck terms the 'world risk society', or the reality that ethnic conflict, civil war, refugee crises, mass migration, terrorism, climate change and other symptoms of global instability pay no heed to borders; and (3) the renewed emphasis on the agency of the nation-state and on (national, ethnic, religious) identity within this new global fluidity. Being both more dependent on one another and yet also hyperaware of the differences that exist (or are created) between us – privileged or marginalised; citizen or non-citizen; Christian, Muslim or Jew – we are conscious, however dimly, that the question of how we can live *together* defines our age.

For scholars working across philosophy, political science, sociology and cultural studies, this question has prompted a reinvigorated engagement with cosmopolitanism, whether in its Classical formulation (Diogenes the Cynic, the Stoics), its Enlightenment elaboration by (mainly German) eighteenth-century thinkers such as Kant, Lessing and Herder, or in relation to (say) contemporary Human Rights discourse and international law (Benhabib), supranational federations (Habermas, Beck, Held), or a 'vernacular' or 'discrepant' postcolonial cosmopolitanism (Bhabha, Clifford, 'Travelling Cultures'). At its core, this academic concern with cosmopolitanism responds to a historically contingent but no less urgent real-life need to find ways to deal equitably – that is, ethically – with others in a world characterised by increased proximity and increased conflict while sustaining what we feel defines *us*. Most explicitly attempting to resolve the apparent conflict between the (moral, political and ethical) imperatives of universalism and the (emotional, identificatory and motivational) appeals of particularism – especially in the aftermath of 9/11 and the war on terror – Martha Nussbaum and Kwame Anthony Appiah have proposed a 'rooted cosmopolitanism' in which allegiance to people closest to us (or to a nation) underpins our responsibility towards global 'others'.

A concern with the tension between universalism and particularlism is – today – thus not only a matter for diaspora Jews seeking to reconcile their identity as a 'nation' with their lived reality as a globally dispersed minority. Yet the fact that 'the Jew' has for centuries been constructed as a trope for precisely this tension – and for cosmopolitanism, defined positively (mobile, multilingual, worldly) or negatively (placeless, unpatriotic, modern) – means, as Cathy Gelbin and Sander Gilman argue, that even as Jews have 'largely vanished from the debate about cosmopolitanism [they] remain the palimpsest of academic discourse'.[4] Benhabib often refers to her Sephardic Jewish heritage in Turkey[5], and allusions to the scapegoating of 'rootless cosmopolitan' Jews abound in Beck's work (e.g. *Cosmopolitan Vision* [2006] and *Cosmopolitan Europe* [2007]), whereas for Bhabha Jewishness even appears to embody a kind of essential(ist) cosmopolitanism: 'a form of historical and racial *in-betweenness*'.[6]

Israeli sociologist Natan Sznaider goes a step further. Sznaider, who was born in Germany to Polish Holocaust survivors and moved to Israel aged 20, presents 'the Jewish condition' not simply as a trope for the tension between universalism and particularism – now the defining feature of the global present – but (potentially, at least) as an *exemplary* cosmopolitan resolution of this tension. In *Jewish Memory and the Cosmopolitan Order* (2011), a compelling case is made for the legitimacy (and value) of particularity – a distinctively Jewish voice – *within* the universalist aspirations of cosmopolitanism. Above all, however, Sznaider's suggestion that Jews can continue to assert, and indeed insist on, their specificity even as they circulate as citizens of the world is even more ambitious than the rooted cosmopolitanism championed by Nussbaum and Appiah. In *Jewish Memory and the Cosmopolitan Order*, Jews move from being a mere referent (or even commonplace) within debates on cosmopolitanism – an archetypal case study – to a source of inspiration. 'Jewish cosmopolitanism', Sznaider argues, may (come to) be seen as a 'global civilising force': 'It does not wait passively for redemption but provides a politics of redemption.'[7]

Sznaider echoes Wolfe in arguing that 'today Jewish cosmopolitanism is in danger of disappearing' as it is 'swallowed up by an increasingly aggressive Jewish ethnic nationalism' (*JM*, 147), and he too sees this as a potentially catastrophic cause of estrangement between Israel and Jews in the diaspora. But for Sznaider, the revival of Jewish cosmopolitanism is not only something to be wished for, a universalism to counter the retreat within the borders of the nation. It also implies something akin to a messianic imperative to save the world.

Jewish cosmopolitanism and cosmopolitan memory

But what is Jewish cosmopolitanism, and what makes it so special? For Sznaider, the answer to this question derives from his re-reading of Hannah Arendt.[8] Indeed, *Jewish Memory and the Cosmopolitan Order* both pays homage to this influential German-Jewish philosopher who fled the Nazis for the United States and asserts her continued, indeed deepened, significance for contemporary global politics. 'The choice of Arendt', Sznaider insists, 'is not arbitrary. Perhaps more than that of any other thinker of the twentieth century, the urgency of her writing on totalitarianism, critical judgment, and evil remains relevant today' (*JM*, 2). Certainly, it is no coincidence that sociologists, political theorists and philosophers have (re)turned to Arendt to help them think through anew the banality of violence and indiscriminate killing, the relationship between political thought and political action – how sentiment becomes deed, and what inspires democratic in preference to destructive acts – and how we might cultivate a proper '*amor mundi*' (love of the world, which was Arendt's initial choice of title for her 1958 book *The Human Condition*). Benhabib, for example, refers often to Arendt in her 2004 Berkeley Tanner lectures, released as *Another Cosmopolitanism*, and in 2010 she published the volume *Politics in Dark Times: Encounters with Hannah Arendt*, with contributions by distinguished thinkers on Arendt's work on freedom, equality and responsibility, the nation-state, the failure of politics, and evil.

Sznaider's specific interest, however, is in Arendt's thinking about Jewishness, and in her elaboration of the relationship between Jewishness and worldliness. To this extent, we can surmise that Sznaider's ambition is to fill with *particular* content Arendt's universalising musings on 'world-building', for instance in *The Human Condition*, in which she famously declares that the world is 'a human artefact, the fabrication of human hands, as well as affairs which go on among those who inhabit the man-made world together', continuing:

> To live together in the world means essentially that a world of things is between those who have it in common, as a table is located between those who sit around it; the world, like every in-between, relates and separates men at the same time.[9]

Arendt describes here how a world is created in common in the spaces *between* men (and women) as they bring to its construction particular experiences that intersect with but also diverge from others' – particularism *and* universalism, or a rooted cosmopolitanism, therefore. Sznaider's concern is with Arendt's elaboration of which specifically *Jewish* experiences might add something to this world-building. 'It is my intention', he expands, 'to show how she constantly navigated between universalism and particularism through her understanding of political judgment, the revolutionary tradition, federal republicanism, and other issues she examined through the prism of the Jewish fate' (*JM*, 3–4).

In *Jewish Memory and the Cosmopolitan Order*, Sznaider shows that Arendt – typically considered a 'secular thinker whose relationship to Jewish thought was one of critical distance' (*JM*, 3) – was profoundly committed to translating 'some rather unpolitical [Jewish] thinking into political action' (*JM*, 22). In chapters on Arendt's relationship with, transmission of, and essays on Kafka, Walter Benjamin, Gershom Scholem, Moritz Goldstein, Simon Dubnow and Salo Baron, Sznaider reveals how Arendt sought to universalise from (without denying the specificity of) these *Jewish* writers and intellectuals to intervene in broader contemporary debates on totalitarianism, liberty, and human rights. At the same time, Sznaider's own intellectual loyalty, which he honours through his detailed re-evaluation of Arendt's indebtedness to the same individual, is most likely ultimately owed to Benjamin. Certainly, the title *Jewish Memory and the Cosmopolitan Order* hints at this allegiance. Benjamin – far more readily than Arendt – is associated with particular Jewish (messianic) traditions of memory-work related to disruption and dispersal, *tikkun olam* ('repairing the world', deriving from medieval Jewish mysticism), and hoped-for redemption, and the book's unexpected twist will be to align Arendt, the resolutely political thinker, with this metaphysical thinking. More obviously, the introduction begins with a quotation from a letter Benjamin once wrote to his Zionist friend Ludwig Strauss that effectively sums up Sznaider's postulation of the indispensability of a Jewish cosmopolitanism: 'It would be bad for Europe if the cultural energies of the Jews were to leave it' (*JM*, 1).

Arendt is recast as a Benjaminian figure. The urgency to repair history drives her dedication to a universalist ideal of Human Rights yet – in Sznaider's reading – this cosmopolitan commitment does not conflict with Jewish particularism, but is infused by it. History does not preclude cosmopolitanism – the particular historical experience of this or that group need not disrupt universalism or be dissolved within it – for it is possible to grasp that which is generalisable while also insisting on what is specific. Arendt, Sznaider claims, exemplifies 'the cosmopolitan potential' of the *Jewish* experience, 'which straddles the interstices of universal identifications and particular attachments' (*JM*, 5).

Here it is important to emphasise that for Sznaider (and, he argues, for Arendt) 'history' and 'experience' are not general terms denoting some generalised state in which Jews have lived 'in the past' – exile, dispersion and diaspora. Rather, he is talking about *events*, and, of course, for the most part about one event (or assemblage of events) in particular, namely the Holocaust. This distinction is vital, since it connotes just how radical Sznaider believes Arendt to have been. In *At Home in Exile*, Alan Wolfe rightly prognoses that 'particularism's appeal in the wake of both the Holocaust and the birth of Israel [...] was all but inevitable' (*HE*, 72), and he ends with an impassioned plea to focus less on this *event* and more on the existential condition of Jewish existence through two millennia, namely exile: 'But the events of the 1930s and the 1940s are not the only events constituting Jewish memory [...] By bringing back to life the universalist ideals developed during their long residency in exile, a new generation of Jews can offer the best hope for a revival of a Jewish future' (*HE*, 215). For Sznaider, on the other hand, Arendt's insistence on the Holocaust as a specifically Jewish experience *and* an injunction to think in universalist terms not only precludes its appropriation as the foundation stone of Israeli ethno-nationalism. It also suggests that the Holocaust is in fact the only sustainable basis for a truly *situated* Jewish cosmopolitanism – a Jewish cosmopolitanism that is locatable in time and space rather than one that can seem ahistorically diffuse. (As, indeed, it does in Wolfe's formulation). In brief, Sznaider asks us to take seriously – and to place the appropriate emphases within – Arendt's oft-cited criticism of the Jerusalem court in *Eichmann in Jerusalem* (1963) that it failed to recognise that the Nazi genocide was a 'crime against Humanity, perpetrated upon the body of the Jewish people, and that only the choice of victims, not the nature of the crime, could be derived from the long history of Jew-hatred and anti-Semitism' (cited in *JM*, 119).

Sznaider's reading of Hannah Arendt in *Jewish Memory and the Cosmopolitan Order* is primarily intended to reclaim the Holocaust from the particularist claims of Israeli nationalism. Yet it most likely also responds to criticism levelled (perhaps unfairly) against Sznaider's earlier book, written with Daniel Levy, *The Holocaust and Memory in The Global Age* (2006; originally in German, 2001), namely that his (and Levy's) prognosis of a 'cosmopolitan memory' of the Holocaust de-emphasises its Jewishness in favour of its universal significance. In fact, this may be the purpose of Sznaider's replaying, in *Jewish Memory*, of Arendt's exchanges with Hans Magnus Enzensberger in the mid-1960s, when she contradicted his attempt to read her *Eichmann in Jerusalem* as demonstrating that the Holocaust was *only* about the destructiveness of capitalist modernity. For Sznaider, Arendt's retort to Enzensberger exemplifies that Jewish memory is not at odds with cosmopolitan memory. It is an instantiation of cosmopolitan memory that transmits Jews' particular implication in events of world-historical dimension and universal significance.

Cosmopolitan memory, as described by Sznaider and Levy in *The Holocaust and Memory in The Global Age*, emerges from the 'historical link between memories of the Holocaust and the emergence of a moral consensus about human rights'.[10] It encompasses the by-now global acknowledgment of the enormity of the Holocaust and its role in mobilising confrontations with other atrocities. Cosmopolitan memory is akin to what Michael Rothberg calls multi-directional memory – the circulation of Holocaust motifs through other traumatic pasts (and presents) – but the claim made for it is larger, namely that it connects injustice everywhere not just to the Holocaust as a crime perpetrated, as Arendt says, upon the body of the Jews, but also to its universal significance as the basis of contemporary ethics. In the post 9/11 era, Sznaider and Levy argue in their next book – bearing the programmatic title *Human Rights and Memory* – 'memories of past abuses [...] drive human rights remedies and have further raised the cost of committing such abuses'.[11] The Holocaust, it is implied, is in this context always the 'originary memory'. Jewish memory – and Jewish cosmopolitanism – is not only a *particular* form of cosmopolitan memory, therefore. It is also a *privileged* form, insofar as it transmits the Holocaust as the foundational moment of contemporary Human Rights discourse and – to reiterate Sznaider's claim in *Jewish Memory* – insofar as it 'does not wait passively for redemption but provides a politics of redemption' (*JM*, 142).

However, it should be apparent from the present analysis that Jewish cosmopolitanism – rooted in the existential experience of exile, dispersion and diaspora, but also concretely in the historical singularity of the Holocaust – is not simply a Jewish bequest to humankind *in universum*. As repeatedly suggested above, it also defines a pluralistic Jewish identity to counter the 'Jewish ethnic nationalism' that Sznaider (with others) sees as increasingly dominant in today's Israel (*JM*, 147). But more than this – and going beyond longstanding debates on an Israeli centre versus a diasporic periphery[12] – we might now also wonder whether the *exceptional* quality of the Jewish experience within the contemporary re-framing of cosmopolitanism as a call-to-action emerging from *memory* implies the exceptionalism of Jewish identity itself. What does it mean for a modern Jewish identity to have this representative, even exemplary, status? And we might wonder whether this Jewish exceptionalism – suggesting Jewish mediation between the particular and the universal, but also recalling a long history of negative as well as positive conceptualisations of 'Jewish chosenness' – might be a less unproblematic solution to the cosmopolitan challenge of our age than, in Sznaider's compelling prose, it might at first appear.

In the closing chapter of *Jewish Memory*, Sznaider gives a brief account of the twentieth-century graphic artist Bruno Schulz (born 1892 in the Drohobych, at the time part of the Austro-Hungarian Empire, later Poland, occupied first by the Soviets then the Nazis, and after 1990 belonging to Ukraine). His purpose is to show something of the Jewish pluralism that he has described. Schulz wrote in Polish, was fluent in German, and knew some Yiddish and Hebrew (*JM*, 142–3). But it is also to relate how Schulz's work has been (mis)appropriated, by different individuals and entities, always as *either* particular *or* universal but never both. Schulz, Sznaider recounts, was forced to paint the walls of the home of the SS officer Felix Landau with scenes from German fairy tales – in 2001, the mural was discovered by a German documentary filmmaker, Benjamin Geisler, but then shortly afterwards removed to Israel, to Yad Vashem. For Sznaider, Yad Vashem's emphasis on the Jewish particularity of Schulz's life and fate (he was murdered because he was Jewish), is as misguided as Geisler's desire to universalise (or de-ethnicise) the Holocaust victim as 'simply Bruno Schulz' (Geisler in interview with Celestine Bohler; cited in *JM*, 145) within what – in his book *Shattered Spaces* and in a essay in this special edition – Michael Meng terms 'redemptive cosmopolitanism'. (Speaking specifically about modern-day Germany, Jack Zipes notes, the 'contemporary German fascination for things Jewish' and Karen Remmler an 'imagined cosmopolitanism that would return Germany to a sense of 'normalcy').[13] The interplay of particularism *and* universalism, Sznaider concludes, is the only perspective from which a 'realistic cosmopolitanism' can be developed. This is the lesson to be learnt not only from Arendt, but also even from more manifestly 'Jewish' twentieth-century figures such as Scholem, Feuchtwanger, Baron, Schulz and Kafka (*JM*, 146).

In what follows, we examine a more recent imaginative work, Olga Grjasnowa's 2012 novel *Der Russe ist einer, der Birken liebt* (All Russians Love Birch Trees), in order to further test Sznaider's hypothesis, as it were. On the one hand, Grjasnowa embodies the re-emergence – in Germany of all places – of significant centres of Jewish life in Europe, with the cultural and linguistic plurality that that implied before the Holocaust. This increasingly high-profile young writer, born in 1984, is one of about 200,000 'Kontingent-Juden' (so-named in German bureaucratese: quota Jews) who were permitted from the early 1990s to emigrate from the former Soviet Union until restrictions were imposed in 2005.[14] She speaks Russian and some Azeri (she grew up as part of the Russian minority in Azerbaijan) and chooses to write in German. On the other hand, even as it both exemplifies this transnational perspective and largely reproduces Sznaider's ideal of a Jewish cosmopolitanism rooted in the particular memory of the Holocaust, *Der Russe* (most likely intentionally) may also reveal the continued difficulty of translating this ideal into a way of living.

Der Russe ist einer, der Birken liebt

Writing in 2002, Leslie Morris and Karen Remmler name Katja Behrens, Maxim Biller, Esther Dischereit and Barbara Honigmann as 'only four of a growing number of second-generation and, more recently, third-generation writers for whom the memory of the Shoah plays a major role in the self-understanding as Jewish writers living in Germany'.[15] A little more than a decade later, this timely avowal of a renaissance of German-language fiction by self-identified Jewish authors following the end of the Cold War and German unification is in need of some updating. First, the number of authors with a Jewish background has continued to increase, as a result of the influx of Jews from the former Soviet Union but also of Jewish immigration – often a second or third relocation – from elsewhere in Eastern Europe, the United States and even Israel. (Second-generation writer Doron Rabinovici had already moved as a child from Israel to Austria in 1964, as did Rafael Seligman to Germany in 1957). Vladimir Vertlib, for example, is a multiple migrant of Russian-Jewish background. Born in Leningrad in 1966, Vertlib's family moved first to Israel, then to Austria, Italy and Austria again, then Italy (again), the Netherlands, and Israel once more, the United States and – acquiring citizenship – back to Austria. His novels *Abschiebung* (Deportation, 1995) and *Zwischenstationen* (Interim Stations, 1999) are largely based on his family's travels.[16] Similarly, Irene Dische, the daughter of Jewish refugees 'returned' to Germany from her parents' adopted country, the United States, and now publishes in both English and German.

Second, the marked (and to-be-expected) concern of first- and second-generation writers with the Holocaust, and with the incongruity of Jewish *life* in Germany after the Shoah, has attenuated somewhat in the work of the third generation. On the one hand, this has to do with the passing of time. But it may also have to do with the fact that, especially for younger Jewish writers from the former Soviet Union, the Holocaust seems less salient than more recent persecution. As Y. Michal Bodemann and Olena Bagno explain: 'While other Jews in Germany experience the Second World War as the great trauma, this is not necessarily so for the Russian Jews; for them, present-day Russian anti-Semitism and earlier the Gulag, have often been the greater traumatic experience.'[17] To the extent that Jews in the Soviet Union were largely spared from the Holocaust, authors of Russian-Jewish extraction may tend to focus more on Soviet persecution and prejudice, or – in ways which remain taboo for other Jewish writers in German – even to draw parallels between the Nazi and Soviet dictatorships. (Vertlib's *Das besondere Gedächtnis der Rosa Masur* / The Extraordinary Memory of Rosa Masur, from 2001, recounts Stalin's anti-Jewish purges *and* Germans' current exoticisation of the Jewish immigrants whose ancestors they once victimised).[18] Third, and related to this more indirect relationship to the Holocaust, writers of this new generation now set their own histories in the context of other minorities' experiences of dislocation and marginalisation, especially in the present day. The Russian-Jewish immigrant Wladimir Kaminer, for example, is famous for his mocking of Germans' stereotyping of their *ausländische Mitbürger* (foreign co-citizens) – also implied in Grjasnowa's parodic title 'All Russians Love Birch Trees' – whereas Julya Rabinowich's *Die Erdfresserin* (The Woman Who Eats Dirt, 2012) thematises the trafficking of women across borders and the persecution of undocumented migrants.[19]

Third-generation writers, particularly from the former Soviet Union, are thus above all concerned with the often harsh reality of immigration to Germany. Lena Gorelik's *Meine weißen Nächte* (My White Nights, 2004) and Alina Bronsky's *Scherbenpark* (2008; *Broken Glass Park*, 2010), for instance, relate the difficulties that both Jewish *and* non-Jewish migrants encounter in gaining employment, decent housing and social acceptance.[20] To this extent, these novels reflect both the specific 'stagnating integration process' of Russian-Jewish immigrants to Germany, as Schoeps and Glöckner describe it[21], and the wider emergence of what Azade Seyhan defines as 'paranational communities', that is, groups 'that exist within national borders or alongside the citizens of the host country but remain culturally or linguistically distanced from them and, in some instances, are estranged from both the home and the host culture'.[22] In the work of Kaminer, Rabinowich, Gorelik and Bronsky, as in Grjasnowa and fellow Russian-Jewish writers Vladimir Vertlib and Katja Petrowskaja, protagonists with Russian(-Jewish) backgrounds interact almost always only with other recent migrants, or with second- or third-generation Turkish-Germans, intensifying the 'vague linkage between "things Jewish" and things "Turkish"' that Leslie Adelson identified in 2000.[23] (Maxim Biller's 2003 *Esra* makes this linkage explicit[24], as does the 1998 novel *Gefährliche Verwandschaft* / Dangerous Relation by Turkish-German writer Zafer Senocak).[25] To this extent at least, Russian-Jewish writers in German – *and* Turkish-German writers – engage with multiculturalism as a given social reality in today's Federal Republic of Germany.

Yet 'Jewishness' is nevertheless still more than just another ethnic marker. In works by Jewish *and* non-Jewish writers, Jewishness suggests both the deterritorialising effect of contemporary transnationalism – 'the ideal of fixed territories of culture', Regina Römhild argues, is 'a fiction, and mobility becomes the common ground for the proliferation of diasporic life-worlds, cultures and identities'[26] – and the redemptive potential of cosmopolitan memory. The Holocaust, or textual palimpsests of the Holocaust[27], intervenes into such narratives to urge empathetic identification with (other) historical trauma as well as the disruptions of the present.[28] In Turkish-German Feridun Zaimoglu's *Hinterland* (2009), the unexpected (even uncanny) appearance of Orthodox Jews at the railway station in Bratislava encapsulates both the forced migrations of the Soviet, Ottoman *and* Nazi empires thematised throughout the novel and the dis- and relocations of globalisation today: 'Dutzende von orthodoxen Juden drängelten sich auf dem Bahnsteig, woher kamen sie, wohin gingen sie, wollten sie alle etwa in den Zug steigen?'[29] (Dozens of Orthodox Jews were pushing on the platform, where did they all come from, where were they going, did they really all want to get into the train?) At the same time, the fact that these Jews are willingly boarding a train – rather than being forced onto one – may offer hope that historical trauma can be overcome, and that mobility might cause a cosmopolitan subversion of borders.

In Grjasnowa's *Der Russe*, it appears that this subversion of the nation has already taken place. Mascha, the novel's Russian-Jewish protagonist, associates almost exclusively with other migrants. The sole significant exception is her German boyfriend Elias, whose 'hohe Wangenknochen, blaugraue Augen und dunkle Wimpern' (high cheekbones, blue-grey eyes and dark eyelashes) mark *him* out as the 'exotic other' – for Mascha's mother, in a striking inversion of age-old stereotypes of Jews, his strange beauty and innate ability to please others, embody his 'Hochstaplerzüge' (imposter's characteristics), for which, however, she cannot help but love him.[30] And even Elias is from the former German Democratic Republic, a place 'to the east' that is perceived by Mascha and her migrant friends as backward and provincial (and racist). To this extent, Elias too might be considered a migrant within the post-unification Federal Republic. His efforts to research and understand Mascha's pre-migration history in Azerbaijan in the months before his untimely death (*DR*, 150) – he dies in hospital some time after he breaks his femur – may be motivated by a desire to become part of this transnational solidarity, just as her melancholic fixation on him after he has gone may suggest her desire to include him, posthumously at least, and to recognise him not just as a 'German' but as a fellow exile with his own story. Before Elias's death, in fact, their relationship was tense, in part on account of their different positioning in relation to current debates on people with a 'Migrationshintergrund' (migration background) and Germany's evolution into a society that is not so much multicultural as *'postmigrantisch'* (postmigrant; *DR*, 12).

Germany exists only as a deterritorialised space in which the displaced and the dispossessed reassemble and share memories of trauma. Mascha's ex-boyfriend Sami (for whom she longs throughout the novel, even as she mourns Elias too) was born in Beirut during the civil war; Cem is Turkish-German and a homosexual; and the Kurdish refugee Sibel is scarred across her body from the beatings inflicted by her father and older brother. Sibel was Mascha's first lesbian affair, and, here again, Mascha is prone to melancholic fixation. In each case, a traumatic past predicts Mascha's empathetic identification, even over-identification, with her fellow migrants, and also with Elias. Her visits following Elias's death to his family home in East Germany are most likely a belated acknowledgment of the dislocation he suffered in fleeing both the beatings he had received from his alcoholic father and, more generally, the constraints of his East German background (*DR*, 90).

Mascha's own traumatic memory is delayed, even displaced, however. And it is not the foundational Jewish memory that, following Sznaider, we might expect to motivate the empathetic investment that she demonstrates through her readiness to prompt her fellow migrants to recount the abuses they have suffered. The past that Mascha struggles to speak of – she cannot tell Elias, even when he asks directly – is not the Holocaust. It is the violent clashes between ethnic Armenians and Azeris in Azerbaijan in 1992, and specifically – the reader is to surmise – the brutal expulsion of Armenians in retaliation for the Khojaly massacre of 25–26 February, when 161 Azerbaijani civilians were killed in the Armenian-majority Azerbaijani enclave of Nagorno-Karabakh. Throughout the novel, Mascha is haunted by the image of the body of a young woman in a light-blue underskirt lying before her 'mit verdrehten Beinen und blutenden Unterleib' (legs twisted, with bleeding abdomen; *DR*, 107).

Yet Mascha's horrific experiences in Baku in 1992 *do* ultimately relate to the Holocaust. Just as Sami, Cem, Sibel and Elias prompt Mascha's delayed confrontation with her own horrific experiences in Baku in 1992 – enabling their cosmopolitan solidarity – so does Mascha's account as a Jewish witness to a pogrom inflicted on her Armenian neighbours, prompt her (re-)telling of her grandmother's narrow escape from the Germans. In the novel's closing pages, Mascha finally arrives at the 'original trauma' of the Holocaust:

> Weißt du, in meiner Kindheit gab es einen geprackten Koffer zu Hause, für den Fall der Fälle. In unserem Fall war es die ehemalige Aktentasche meines Großvaters, und darin waren frische Unterhosen, Familienfotos, Silberlöffel und Goldkronen, das Kapital, das sie unter dem kommunistischen Regime akkumulieren konnten. Die Armenier waren schon lange aus der Stadt fortgejagt worden, und nicht wenige von ihnen wurden exekutiert. Meine Oma, die die Shoah ... (*DR*, 276)
>
> (You know, in my childhood there was a packed suitcase at home, just in case. In our house, it was my grandfather's old briefcase, with fresh underwear, family photos, silver spoons and gold crowns, that capital that they were able to accumulate under the communist regime. The Armenians had long been chased out of the city, and not a few were executed. My grandma, the Shoah ...)

Mascha's grandmother had given refuge to fleeing Armenians (*DR*, 282), for which she was denounced by neighbours, most likely forcing the family's migration. What *she* takes from the Holocaust, therefore, is not a particularist narrative of Jewish victimisation but rather a universalist obligation to offer sanctuary. Here, Grjasnowa's novel points beyond the mere depiction of multiculturalism as a contemporary social reality, or even as an inherently limited ideal of mutual respect between communities living alongside or even separately from one another, and gestures toward *cosmopolitanism*. In contrast to Kant's famous but somewhat limited definition of hospitality as the essence of 'cosmopolitan right' in *Perpetual Peace* (1795) – 'the right of a foreigner not to be treated with hostility because he has arrived on the land of another'[31] – , moreover, we glimpse a modern understanding of cosmopolitanism as universal human rights. This cosmopolitan ideal extends beyond the absence of molestation to proactive protection and, as important, to empathetic identification with traumatised others based on a universalised mobilisation of Jewish memory.

Reading back through the novel from the perspective of its conclusion, we surmise that Mascha's Jewish memory – distilled from her grandmother's knowledge of the Holocaust, as it were – motivates her investment in the traumatic experiences of others. Above all, her fluid (bi-)sexuality connotes not only the undermining of the heteronormative nation. In this, she joins many other 'unsettling' transnational protagonists in contemporary German-language literature, who, in their turn, frequently often 'typed' as Jewish, to the extent that Jews have long been characterised as sexually *and* 'nationally' deviant.[32] Her alternating attraction for both men and women also additionally intimates her strikingly embodied desire to *know* the other, even as she herself finds it difficult to tell of her experiences in Azerbaijan. (The traumatic memories of others 'screen' her memories of Azerbaijan, just as these memories screen her grandmother's memories of the Holocaust). Indeed, more or less the only character with whom she 'just' has sex, without any subsequent desire for emotional intimacy, is the Israeli Ori, who is trauma-free and a staunch defender of his country's defence of its national(ist) aspirations. Mascha's sustained sexual intimacy with his sister Tal – easily accepted by Ori, who seems to recognise that he does not have a 'story' to engage Mascha – may have to do with the fact that Tal felt compelled to abandon her daughter following the breakdown of her relationship, and with Tal's 'scandalous' activism on behalf of Palestinian victims of the Israeli response to the second Intifada.

Parts three and four of the novel are set in Israel and the West Bank. On completion of her advanced qualification in interpreting, Mascha sleeps with her comically named German professor Windmühle (windmill) – as in 'tilting at windmills', most likely a satirical allusion here to Germans' vainglorious bluster about 'making amends' – and secures his endorsement for a post with a German aid organisation in Tel Aviv charged with monitoring 'the situation in Israel'. 'Diese Organisation hatte sich wie Dutzende andere perfekt in den Konflikt integriert' (This organisation, like dozens of others, had integrated itself seamlessly into the conflict), she comments sardonically, adding that if the fighting were to cease they would no longer be able to boast to potential sexual partners that they lived in a war zone (*DR*, 183). She flies to Israel, has her laptop blown up by bored security personnel at the airport, moves into an apartment with sea views, makes contact with relatives, including her cousin Hannah who is disappointed that she doesn't look sufficiently Jewish (*DR*, 167), and takes advantage of the lack of real work at the office to mourn Elias, crave Sami and pursue Tal.

In Israel, Mascha is forced to confront head-on the question that she had hitherto managed to evade in the transnational, cosmopolitan togetherness she enjoyed in Berlin, namely what her Jewishness means to her. The fact that she speaks Arabic – initially learnt from Sami, then consolidated during her studies – but not Hebrew, is a repeated source of bafflement, and even affront, for her Israeli companions. And she instinctively rejects the Israeli nationalism embodied not only by Ori, but also by her relatives, the various officials she encounters, and Russian-Jewish settlers in the occupied territories. This does not mean that she entirely repudiates Israel. Watching CNN reporting on Israeli's incursions into the West Bank with Cem in Germany, she had felt the need to counter what she saw as the media's lachrymose presentation of the Palestinian fate (*DV*, 59) – before she travels to Israel, it seems that were some limits to her universalising empathy. But, lacking any sincere understanding of, or even interest in Jewish ritual, she needs to forge a secular Jewish identity that does not depend on a departicularised diasporic solidarity with other migrants – in Germany, she is more Russian than Jewish – or an inflamed Israeli nationalism.

Jewish memory of the Holocaust, and more broadly identification with the suffering of others, may enable just such an identity. In Germany, Mascha objects to a fellow student's gauche philosemitism: 'Ich habe einen deutschen Pass. Ich bin nicht Israel' (I have a German passport. I am not Israel; *DR*, 6); in Israel, she insists on her German citizenship, to the great irritation of her cousin Hannah (*DR*, 166), and she speaks German with Sam, a potential lover, and allows him to take her for a Russian immigrant (*DR*, 178), just as she had always emphasised her Russian rather than Jewish origins in Germany too. In the fourth and final part of the novel, however, Mascha crosses into the West Bank, where for the first time, and notwithstanding the obvious risk, she embraces an unambivalent identity. 'Ich bin jüdisch' (I am Jewish; *DR*, 274), she declares to Ismael, the Palestinian man who offers her refugee after she escapes Tal, Tal's new love interest, and the ineffective Israeli peace delegation for which she was to interpret (none of the Israelis speaks Arabic). With Ismael – the former Hamas supporter, who now sees the error of his earlier intolerance and religious fundamentalism (*DR*, 273-4) – she finally seems able to speak of herself, and of her own trauma. She lives in Germany, and she is Russian by nationality, but she was born in Azerbaijan, where she endured both antisemitism and civil war (*DR*, 265–74). And above all she is a Jew – secular, profoundly conscious of her history, *and* cosmopolitan.

The cosmopolitan understanding Mascha achieves with Ismael – the name given to Abraham's first son in Jewish, Christian and Muslim scripture, though each tradition has different interpretations of his role and significance – may even be more genuine than the solidarity she experienced with fellow migrants in Germany. Mascha and Ismael do not have sex, even though this is an obvious possibility in his room overnight, and nor does their sharing of trauma imply a blurring of the self-evident differences between their histories and current situations. In other words, *their* cosmopolitan exchange is based not on physical intimacy or on the dissolution of their particularist identities within an undifferentiated universalism, but on the recognition of difference – the scars inflicted on his arm by an Israeli bullet; for her: 'Meine Oma, die Shoah ...' (*DR*, 276) – and even of the ultimate unknowability of the Other. The brief relationship forged by Mascha and Ismael, therefore, is characterised by the unsentimental recognition of our detachment identified by Arendt as the condition for authentic engagement with the other – 'the world, like every in-between, relates and *separates* men at the same time'[33] – and, as important, for political action: 'Because compassion abolishes the distance, the worldly space between men where political matters, the whole realm of human affairs, are located, it remains, politically speaking, irrelevant and without consequences.'[34] Accompanying Ismael, Mascha is welcomed at a Palestinian wedding, in spite of the discomfort some guests feel at her presence. In a dream-like state, she narrates, at length, the horrors of the civil war in Azerbaijan – her recollection of tanks shelling buildings invokes the suffering that the Palestinians at the wedding with her have endured, and will endure. At the very end of the novel, the reader grasps that Jewish memory – the

Holocaust – is not just the keystone of a secular Jewish identity. It also entails an injunction to think globally, and to *act* in defence of universal human rights.

Thus far, Grjasnowa's *Der Russe* appears to endorse, and even embody, the possibility of a Jewish cosmopolitanism in which the Jewish particularity of the Holocaust is seen to possess a universal, even redemptive significance. However, one of the benefits that readers gain from literature – in addition to aesthetic pleasure – emerges out of the way fiction may nuance the 'ideal types' that populate generalising works of philosophical enquiry such as Sznaider's *Jewish Memory*. Grjasnowa's Mascha inhabits *Der Russe* not only as an exemplar of Sznaider's cosmopolitan Jewish memory, therefore, but also as the embodiment of the inconsistencies and self-absorption of real human beings. And it is in its focus on the difficulties that individuals encounter in translating principle into practice that Grjasnowa's novel helps us to conceptualise some of the limitations – and indeed problems – of Sznaider's conceptualisation of a Jewish cosmopolitanism.

At Israel's principal Holocaust memorial centre Yad Vashem, Mascha seems almost to be paraphrasing Sznaider when she insists on the universalist meaning of the Holocaust and rejects the ethno-nationalism of Jewish settlers in the West Bank:

> 'Wir dürfen nichts vergessen', sagte Tante # 13.
> 'Natürlich nicht', sagte ich. 'Allerdings reicht das alleine nicht'.
> 'Wie meinst du das?', fragte Hannah.
> 'Selbst die fanatischsten Siedler gedenken des Holocaust', sagte ich. (*DR*, 193)
>
> ('We must forget nothing', said aunt number 13.
> 'Of course not', I said, 'Though that's not enough'
> 'What do you mean?', asked Hannah.
> 'Even the most fanatical settlers commemorate the Holocaust', I said).

Elsewhere, however, we wonder whether Mascha's cosmopolitan solidarity truly reflects her principled openness to others or simply a more egotistical longing for consolation. In the West Bank, swastikas drawn by Hamas fighters trigger not so much a rational engagement with the need to create alliances *across* traumatised communities as jumbled memories of the Caspian Sea, her mother and Elias: 'Zurück zu meiner Mutter, ich wollte, dass sie mich beschützt. Ich wollte zurück zu Elischa, mich an sein Hemd klammern und seinen Geruch einatmen, sein Gesicht wieder klar vor mir sehen' (Back to my mother, I wanted her to protect me. I wanted to get back to Elias, to cling to his shirt and breathe in his smell, see his face before me again) (*DR*, 280).

The refusal of sentimentality that characterises Arendt's (and Sznaider's) cosmopolitanism – the essential unknowability of the other must be acknowledged if the temptation to colonise is to be resisted – is, in practice, difficult if not impossible to sustain. The attitude of respectful detachment towards one another that Mascha and Ismael manage to achieve together will scarcely be tested over time. It is clear from the outset that her sojourn with him will be brief, and as soon as she can she phones Sami, her Beirut-born ex-lover, and enjoins him to leave behind his girlfriend in Germany and extract her from Palestine. At the end of the novel, Mascha opts to return to the emotionally satisfying, but undifferentiated, empathetic solidarity that she had appeared determined to exceed during her time in Israel. It seems unlikely that she will continue, once back in Germany, to channel traumatic memory into political engagement.

Even if sentimentality can be avoided, there is still a danger that 'the Jew' once more becomes little more than a cipher. Sznaider's emphasis on the specifically Jewish experience of the Holocaust styles Jewish memory, as previously noted, as both central to cosmopolitan memory and, more broadly, as *representative*. But in what sense representative? If Jewish memory *embodies* the suffering of all humankind, then the Holocaust's title as the most egregious example of the cruelty people throughout the ages have inflicted upon one another creates a manner of detachment that is different in kind from the distance that Arendt sees as the essential basis of equality between the multitude of others who 'have the world in common'. Jews stand apart, fetishised as descendants of the Holocaust or resented for their aloofness – *their* difference from *us* is not the same as our difference from other 'others'. Or, if Jewish memory *speaks for* others who have been traumatised, must detachment mutate into disassociation, as the Jewish experience is deployed in the service of others? On her return to Germany, Mascha will no doubt endure the painful philosemitism of her fellow student Daniel, and continue to have to repress her Jewish (rather than Russian) past even amongst her fellow migrants.

If Jewish memory no longer motivates any practical, political cosmopolitan commitment, therefore, the risk may be that it becomes merely an instrument for the ritualistic expression of what Gillian Rose ("Beginning of the Day") calls 'Holocaust piety', or a vessel for the containment of a whole world of traumas, or both at the same time. In any event, Jewish memory appears 'flattened', to the extent that the particularity of the Holocaust acquires a citational quality, in Derrida's sense of a communicative act that, through its constant iteration, is intended to testify to truth but in fact signals the ever present possibility of inauthenticity. Jewish identity is not only once again reduced to the Holocaust. It is also defined, and delimited, either as a conduit for empathy and affect or as a container for universal suffering rather than as substantial in and of itself.

In the final analysis, it is difficult to surmise what kind of political engagement Sznaider envisages in *Jewish Memory and The Cosmopolitan Order* beyond his admiration for Arendt's lofty insistence on the particularity of the Jewish experience within the universality of Human Rights, and on the indispensability of cosmopolitan exchange based on the acknowledgment of difference. How is a cosmopolitan Jewish memory, and identity, to be actively articulated, beyond the sort of well-meaning rhetoric formulated by the Israeli activists that Mascha accompanies into the West Bank? Does Sznaider expect 'regular' Jewish individuals – outside the circle of intellectuals that feature in *Jewish Memory* – to confront injustice more *concretely*, locally and globally, and perhaps especially in relation to Israel? But why not expect this of all people? Why expect more of Jews, and therefore perhaps less of others? It might seem to be an odd consequence of the Holocaust that Jews should be expected to internalise its lessons more fully than others. Indeed, the most striking, and positive, aspect of Grjasnowa's depiction of Mascha is that she is as flawed – as human – as all the novel's other characters. The author's suggestion seems to be that there can be no requirement for the Jew to be 'better' than those she or he lives amongst.

Conclusion

Sznaider's *Jewish Memory and The Cosmopolitan Order* presents a timely and challenge to think again about Jewish identity, and to expound a positive 'Jewish cosmopolitanism' to set against the prejudice that, historically, has accompanied that designation. However, insofar as *Der Russe* exemplifies through its form and content precisely the movement back and forth between particularity and universalism that Sznaider praises in Arendt – and the Polish-speaking Jewish graphic artist Bruno Schulz – Grjasnowa's novel may offer something more concrete, and potentially more radical. The most 'cosmopolitan' aspect of *Der Russe ist einer, der Birken liebt*, in truth, is not its elaboration of Holocaust memory as the basis of human rights practice and solidarity across borders. Rather, it is its own inherent transnationality that is key, and not only the fact that it was written in the German language by an author of Russian-Jewish background but also, just as, if not more, important, the way it connects German, Middle Eastern and Eastern European pasts and presents. This in itself already undermines the parochialism of the nation, and indeed national narratives. We might debate, with Leslie Morris, whether this represents a 'translation of Jewishness into […] an imagined transnational community',[35] or we might set Grjasnowa's novel within the broader 'transnationalisation' of German-language (and other) writing in recent years, including fiction by Jewish, other 'minority', but also 'majority' authors.[36] In any event, the increasing traversability of national borders and national cultures that we are witnessing in the contemporary era – along with a pervasive ethnocentric backlash – has reignited the debate on cosmopolitanism and seems to require *all* of us, Jews and non-Jews, to look beyond our ethnic and national limit(ation)s. It might be inspiring to think, however, that we would wish to become citizens of the world *without* reference to the Holocaust – because global citizenship is seen as a desirable goal in itself – and without requiring Jews to be, once again, somehow *exemplary*.

Grjasnowa's next novel after *Der Russe*, titled *Die juristische Unschärfe einer Ehe* (*The Judicial Uncertainty of A Marriage*, 2014), certainly has no requirement for an exemplary Jew. Jonoun, the novel's American-Jewish migrant to Germany, is blithely unaware of the trauma her girlfriend Leyla has suffered at the hands of the repressive authorities in her home country Azerbaijan, and of the distress she causes Leyla's (homosexual) husband Altay. And she appears to have no connection whatsoever to the Holocaust. Without the possibility of a redemptive cosmopolitanism rooted in memory – whether Jewish or any other – however, the issue now is that the only cosmopolitanism that seems able to assert itself against the nation-state as an instrument of global consumer capitalism (Germany, along with other Western countries) or of repression (Azerbaijan and other countries in the region, even after the Arab Spring) is the elite cosmopolitanism of the super-wealthy as they jet around the globe in search of either tax-friendly or legally dubious regimes. Sznaider's Jewish cosmopolitanism may be utopian – or even problematic – but it is surely to be preferred to the depressing reality of the only form of cosmopolitanism that, thus far, actually seems to have succeeded in establishing itself as truly global.

Notes

1. Brumlik, "Wem gehört der Staat Israel?"
2. See Miller and Ury, "Cosmopolitanism: The End of Jewishness?," 345.
3. Wolfe, *At Home in Exile*, 7. Hereafter *HE* in brackets following quotations in the main body of the text.
4. Cathy Gelbin, from the preamble to the conference call for "Cosmopolitanism and the Jews", which Gelbin co-organised with Sander Gilman on 11–12 May 2014 at the Leo Baeck Institute London, Queen Mary University. Details online at: http://www.leobaeck.co.uk/archives/4188 (Accessed January 9, 2015).

5. See Benhabib's, "Interview with Harry Keisler."
6. Bhabha, "Unpacking My Library Again," 14.
7. Sznaider, *Jewish Memory*, 142. Hereafter *JM* in brackets following quotations in the main body of the text. The allusion to waiting passively for redemption, of course, recalls the debate between those (especially Orthodox and Ultra-Orthodox) Jews who insist that the Messiah's coming cannot be forced and those who believe that political action in the here and now is permitted as a means of provoking redemption.
8. Sznaider anticipates, and indeed summarises in advance, his discussion of Arendt in *Jewish Memory and the Cosmopolitan Order* in his 2007 article "Hannah Arendt's Jewish Cosmopolitanism: Between The Universal and The Particular."
9. Arendt, *The Human Condition*, 52.
10. Levy and Sznaider, *Human Rights*, 20.
11. Levy and Sznaider, *Human Rights*, 151.
12. Sznaider in fact is one of a number of scholars who have attempted to re-evaluate the long-standing division between Jewish life in the diaspora and Jewish life in Israel. See, for example, Sander Gilman and Milton Shain, *Jewries at the Frontier*.
13. Remmler, "Encounters Across The Void," 21.
14. See Popper, "Germany Is Moving To End Mass Immigration of Jews From Russia."
15. Morris and Remmler, "Introduction," 1.
16. See Lorenz, "Vladimir Vertlib, a Global Intellectual."
17. Bodemann and Bagno, "In The Ethnic Twilight: The Paths of Russian Jews in Germany," 163.
18. See my "Performing Jewishness in The New Germany."
19. See Mayr, "Europe's Invisible Ghettos."
20. See Biendarra, "Cultural Dichotomies and Lived Transnationalism."
21. Schoeps and Glöckner, "Fifteen Years of Russian-Jewish Immigration to Germany," 144.
22. Seyhan, *Writing Outside The Nation*, 10.
23. See Adelson, "Touching Tales of Turks, Germans, and Jews."
24. See my "Germans, Jews and Turks in Maxim Biller's Novel *Esra*."
25. See Garloff, "Interreligious Love in Contemporary German Film and Literature."
26. Römhild, "Global Heimat Germany."
27. "The palimpsest" has become a key term in memory studies. See, for example, Huyssen, *Present Pasts* and Silverman, *Palimpsestic Memory*.
28. Margaret Littler ("Cultural Memory") has written more generally of the way connections between German, Eastern and Central European, and Turkish histories in contemporary texts creates relationships of "affect", such that "moments of intensity have deterritorialising force, and intimacy takes on new and unfamiliar forms" (193). Brigid Haines ("Writing") also notes the increasing trend towards depicting the transnational entanglement of German history and German identity, especially in the work of German-language writers with Eastern and Central European backgrounds.
29. Zaimoglu, *Hinterland*, 359.
30. Grjasnowa, *Der Russe ist einer*, 10. Hereafter *DR* in brackets following quotations in the main body of the text.
31. Kant, *Towards Perpetual Peace*, 329.
32. See Gilman, *The Jew's Body*. In her next novel, *Die juristische Unschärfe einer Ehe*, from 2014, Grjasnowa interestingly problematises the way Western nations' increasingly liberal attitude towards homosexuality is now frequently deployed to mark Islam as regressive and incompatible with "our" values. This is what Jabir Puar in *Terrorist Assemblages* refers to as "homonormativity" post-9/11.
33. Arendt, *The Human Condition*, 52. My emphasis. There has been much discussion in the scholarly literature of Arendt's insistence on the irrelevance of compassion.
34. Arendt, *On Revolution*, 86–7.
35. Leslie Morris "How Jewish Is It?," 112.
36. See my "Transnationalism in Contemporary German-Language Fiction." My book project *German-Language Literature and Transnationalism* will be published in 2017.

Funding

This work was supported by the Arts and Humanities Research Council, UK [grant number AH/K000853/1].

ORCID

Stuart Taberner http://orcid.org/0000-0002-3913-9363

Bibliography

Adelson, Leslie. "Touching Tales of Turks, Germans, and Jews: Cultural Alterity, Historical Narrative, and Literary Riddles for The 1990s." *New German Critique* 80 (2000): 93–124.
Arendt, Hannah. *The Human Condition*. London: The University of Chicago Press, 1958.
Arendt, Hannah. *On Revolution*. Harmondsworth: Penguin, 1990 [1963].
Benhabib, Seyla. *Another Cosmopolitanism*. New York: Oxford University Press, 2006.
Benhabib, Seyla. *Politics in Dark Times: Encounters with Hannah Arendt*. Cambridge: Cambridge University Press, 2010.
Benhabib, Seyla. "Interview with Harry Keisler." Conversations with History Series at the Institute of International Studies, UC Berkeley. Accessed January 25, 2015. http://globetrotter.berkeley.edu/people4/Benhabib/benhabib-con1.html
Bhabha, Homi. "Unpacking My Library Again." *The Journal of the Midwest Modern Language Association* 28, no. 1 (1995): 5–18.
Biendarra, Anke. "Cultural Dichotomies and Lived Transnationalism in Recent Russian-German Narratives." *Transnationalism in Contemporary German-Language Literature*, edited by Elisabeth Herrmann, Carrie Smith-Prei, and Stuart Taberner, 209–227. Rochester, MN: Camden House, 2015.
Bodemann, Y. Michal, and Olena Bagno. "In The Ethnic Twilight: The Paths of Russian Jews in Germany." In *The New German Jewry and The European Context*, edited by Y. Michal Bodemann, 158–176. New York: Palgrave, 2008.
Brumlik, Micha. "Wem gehört der Staat Israel?" Taz, 07.12.2014. Accessed January 25, 2015. www.taz.de/Debatte-Nationalismus-in-Israel/!150785
Clifford, James. "Traveling Cultures." In *Cultural Studies*, edited by Lawrence Grossberg, Cary Nelson, and Paula A. Treichler, 96–116. London: Routledge, 1992.

Garloff, Katja. "Interreligious love in Contemporary German Film and Literature." *Judaism, Christianity, and Islam: Collaboration and Conflict in The Age of Diaspora*, edited by Sander Gilman, 153–164. Hong Kong: Hong Kong University Press, 2014.

Gilman, Sander. *The Jew's Body*. New York and London: Routledge, 1991.

Gilman, Sander, and Milton Shain, eds. *Jewries at the Frontier, Accommodation*. Identity and Conflict. Urbana: University of Illinois Press, 1999.

Grjasnowa, Olga. *Der Russe ist einer, der Birken liebt*. Munich: Hanser, 2012.

Haines, Brigid. "Writing from Eastern and Central Europe." In *Contemporary German Fiction*, edited by Stuart Taberner, 214–227. Cambridge: Cambridge University Press, 2007.

Huyssen, Andreas. *Present Pasts: Urban Palimpsests and the Politics of Memory*. Stanford: Stanford University Press, 2003.

Kant, Immanuel. *Towards Perpetual Peace*. Translated by Mary Gregor. In Kant, *Practical Philosophy*, 311–352. Cambridge: Cambridge University Press, 1996.

Levy, Daniel, and Natan Sznaider. *The Holocaust and Memory in a Global Age*. Philadelphia, PA: Temple University Press, 2006.

Levy, Daniel, and Natan Sznaider. *Human Rights and Memory*. Philadelphia, PA: Pennsylvania State University Press, 2010.

Littler, Margaret. "Cultural Memory and Identity Formation in The Berlin Republic." In *Contemporary German Fiction*, edited by Stuart Taberner, 177–195. Cambridge: Cambridge University Press, 2007.

Lorenz, Dagmar. "Vladimir Vertlib, a Global Intellectual: Exile, Migration, and Individualism in The Narratives of a Russian Jewish Author in Austria." In *Beyond Vienna: Contemporary Literature From The Austrian Provinces*, edited by Todd C Hanlin, 230–262. Riverside: Ariadne Press, 2008.

Mayr, Maria. "Europe's Invisible Ghettos: Transnationalism and Neoliberal Capitalism in Julya Rabinowich's *Die Erdfresserin*." In *Transnationalism in Contemporary German-Language Literature*, edited by Elisabeth Herrmann, Carrie Smith-Prei and Stuart Taberner, 144–161. Rochester, MN: Camden House, 2015.

Meng, Michael. *Shattered Spaces. Encountering Jewish Ruins in Postwar Germany and Poland*. Cambridge, MA: Harvard University Press, 2011.

Miller, Michael, and Scott Ury. "Cosmopolitanism: The End of Jewishness?" *European Review of History: Revue européenne d'histoire* 17, no. 3 (2010): 337–359.

Morris, Leslie. "How Jewish Is It? W.G. Sebald and the Question of Contemporary German-Jewish Writing." In *The New German Jewry and the European Context. The Return of the European Diaspora*, edited by Y. Michal Bodemann, 111–128. New York: Palgrave Macmillan, 2008.

Morris, Leslie, and Karen Remmler. "Introduction." In *Contemporary Jewish Writing in Germany: An Anthology*, edited by L. Morris and K. Remmler, 1–32. Lincoln: University of Nebraska Press, 2002.

Popper, Nathaniel. "Germany Is Moving To End Mass Immigration of Jews From Russia." *The Jewish Daily Forward*, 24.12.2004. Accessed January 25, 2015. http://forward.com/articles/4029/germany-is-moving-to-end-mass-immigration-of-jews

Puar, Jabir. *Terrorist Assemblages: Homonationalism in Queer Times*. Durham, NC: Duke University Press, 2007.

Remmler, Karen. "Encounters Across The Void." In *Unlikely History. The Changing German-Jewish Symbiosis*, edited by Leslie Morris and Jack Zipes, 3–29. New York: Palgrave, 2002.

Römhild, Regina. "Global Heimat Germany. Migration and the Transnationalization of the Nation-State." *Transit* 1, no. 1 (2005). Accessed January 25, 2015. http://escholarship.org/uc/item/57z2470p

Rose, Gillian. "Beginning of The Day: Fascism and Representation." In *Modernity, Culture and "The Jew"*, edited by Bryan Cheyette and Laura Marcus, 242–256. Cambridge: Polity Press, 1998.

Rothberg, Michael. *Multidirectional Memory: Remembering the Holocaust in the Age of Decolonization*. Stanford: Stanford University Press, 2009.

Schoeps, Julius H., and Olaf Glöckner. "Fifteen Years of Russian-Jewish Immigration to Germany: Successes and Setbacks." In *The New German Jewry and The European Context*, edited by Y Michal Bodemann, 144–157. New York: Palgrave, 2008.

Seyhan, Azade. *Writing Outside The Nation*. Princeton, NJ: Princeton University Press, 2001.

Silverman, Max. *Palimpsestic Memory: The Holocaust and Colonialism in French and Francophone Fiction and Film*. New York and Oxford: Berghahn Books, 2013.

Slezkine, Yuri. *The Jewish Century*. Princeton, NJ: Princeton University Press, 2004.
Sznaider, Natan. "Hannah Arendt's Jewish Cosmopolitanism: Between the Universal and the Particular." *European Journal of Social Theory* 10, no. 1 (2007): 112–122.
Sznaider, Natan. *Jewish Memory and The Cosmopolitan Order*. Cambridge: Polity Press, 2011.
Taberner, Stuart. "Germans, Jews and Turks in Maxim Biller's Novel *Esra*." *The German Quarterly* 79, no. 2 (2006): 234–248.
Taberner, Stuart. "Vladimir Vertlib's *Das besondere Gedächtnis der Rosa Masur* [Performing Jewishness in The New Germany]." In *Emerging German-Language Novelists of the Twenty-First Century*, edited by Stuart Taberner and Lyn Marven, 32–45. Rochester, MN: Camden House, 2011.
Taberner, Stuart. "Transnationalism in Contemporary German-Language Fiction." *Seminar* 47, no. 5 (2011): 624–645.
Wolfe, Alan. *At Home in Exile: Why Diaspora Is Good for the Jews*. Boston, MA: Beacon Press, 2014.
Zaimoglu, Feridun. *Hinterland*. Cologne: Kiepenheuer & Witsch, 2009.
Zipes, Jack. "The Contemporary German Fascination for Things Jewish: Toward a Jewish Minority Culture". In *Reemerging Jewish Culture in Germany. Life and Literature since 1989*, edited by Sander Gilman and Karen Remmler, 15–46. New York and London: New York University Press, 1994.

Cosmopolitan Europeans? Jewish public intellectuals in Germany and Austria and the idea of 'Europe'

Anita Bunyan

ABSTRACT
The recent Eurozone crisis and the outbreak of political and populist Euroscepticism pose an unprecedented challenge to advocates of the post-war 'Idea of Europe'. In the United Kingdom and France, some of the most eloquent and impassioned defences of 'Europe' have been penned by Jewish intellectuals. The historian Walter Laqueur, the philosopher Bernard-Henri Levy and journalists such as David Aaronovich, for example, have all rallied to the cause of 'Europe'. This article will focus on the responses of Robert Menasse and Henryk Broder, two Jewish intellectuals from Austria and Germany, who have recently published powerful reflections on the European idea. Menasse's polemic of 2012, *Der Europäische Landbote* (The European Courier), defends the idea of Europe as a 'Friedensprojekt', or 'peace project', and the European Union as an institutional antidote to the destructive power of nationalism and the self-interest of the nation-state. Broder's bestselling book of 2013, *Die letzten Tage Europas: Wie wir eine gute Idee versenken* (The Last Days of Europe: How we are Scuppering a Good Idea), embraces 'European values' but launches a critique of a European Union which stifles pluralism and critical debate. This paper analyses how Menasse and Broder define the idea of 'Europe' and argues that, despite their differences, in form and content, the work of Menasse and Broder draws on a common tradition of enlightened cosmopolitanism as well as informs the renewed academic debate in the humanities and social sciences about the place of 'cosmopolitanism' in our global world.

The recent Eurozone crisis and the outbreak of political and populist Euroscepticism pose an unprecedented challenge to advocates of the post-war 'Idea of Europe'. In the United Kingdom and France, some of the most eloquent and impassioned defences of 'Europe' have been penned by Jewish intellectuals. The historians Walter Laqueur and Diana Pinto, the philosopher Bernard-Henri Lévy and the journalist David Aaronovich, for example, have all rallied to the cause of 'Europe'.[1] This article will focus on the responses of two Jewish intellectuals, Robert Menasse and Henryk Broder, from Austria and Germany respectively, who have recently published powerful reflections on the European idea. Menasse's polemic of 2012, *Der Europäische Landbote* (The European Courier), defends the idea of Europe as a 'peace project', and the European Union as an institutional antidote to the destructive power of nationalism and the self-interest of the nation-state.[2] Broder's bestselling book of 2013, *Die letzten Tage Europas; Wie wir eine gute Idee versenken* (The Last Days of Europe: How we are Scuppering a Good Idea), embraces 'European' values, but launches a scathing critique of a European Union which stifles pluralism and critical debate.[3]

Despite these differences, however, Menasse and Broder's arguments about the state of Europe today draw on a common tradition of enlightened cosmopolitanism and inform the renewed academic debate in the humanities and social sciences about the place of 'cosmopolitanism' in our global world.[4] Cosmopolitanism is a contested concept.[5] Contemporary thinkers disagree on whether it is a convenient mask for the hegemonic aspirations of powerful states or a visionary ideal with great potential for the appreciation and management of difference in a global and mobile world.[6] Broder and Menasse's personal experiences of migration, emigration and remigration infuse their work with a cosmopolitan quality. Broder, who describes himself, tongue-in-cheek, as 'a German expat of Polish-Jewish immigrant background', moved to Germany from Poland in 1958 at the age of 12.[7] The son of Holocaust survivors, he became an outspoken essayist whose witty and incisive polemics challenge the complacent orthodoxies of political, social and cultural discourse in contemporary Germany.[8] Menasse, who describes his identity as 'Viennese', was born and grew up in Vienna but lived for almost seven years in Brazil where he worked as a lecturer and critic.[9] The son of a Jewish *Kindertransport* child who returned to his home city of Vienna after the war, Menasse is a novelist, critic and one of Austria's most prominent and probing public intellectuals.[10]

The cosmopolitan perspective these Jewish intellectuals bring to bear on the question of Europe informs their reflections on some of the key questions that concern contemporary theorists of cosmopolitanism. How is an appreciation of difference to be reconciled with a consensus about shared sets of social and political norms?[11] Is cosmopolitanism synonymous with 'rootlessness' or can it be reconciled with experiences of rootedness and belonging?[12] What is the relationship between cosmopolitanism and the concept of post-nationalism?[13] Who controls the cosmopolitan narrative – the political and intellectual elites or ordinary citizens?[14] How does the concept of cosmopolitanism relate to the experience and visions of migrants in a global and mobile world?[15] And finally, is the 'Idea of Europe' a cosmopolitan vision and reality or a concept cynically exploited by egoistic nation-states or an increasingly totalitarian Brussels bureaucracy?

Menasse and Broder felt compelled by a sense of impending European catastrophe to pen their reflections on the European idea. Broder captured the political atmosphere in Europe in typically vivid fashion when he likened the situation of Europeans to that of a motorist careering down a mountain with defective brakes.[16] In a similar vein, Menasse solemnly pronounced Europe to be 'on the eve of destruction'. Europe had reached a decisive crossroads in its history, but it was as yet unclear 'whether the system of nation states or the system designed to transcend the nation state would be destroyed'.[17]

On the surface, the responses of Menasse and Broder to the European crisis could not be more different. Indeed, although he does not mention him by name, Broder's polemic could be read as a direct riposte to that of Menasse. For Menasse, 'Europe' is, above all, a cultural-political project, designed to maintain peace by undermining nationalism. Rooted in the experience of war and genocide, the idea of Europe is embraced by Menasse as a post-national 'peace project'.[18] The idea was 'not just to reconcile the hostile nations, but completely to transcend the nation and secure real and lasting peace by making national economies interdependent.' The strength of this particular 'cultural-political project' was that it was constructed on a firm economic basis as the inhabitants of Europe found it logical to co-operate economically. Now that austerity has replaced prosperity, Menasse argues, the European idea has to be more actively promoted than ever before: a 'more pro-active, self-confident and better-funded cultural politics' is required.[19]

Broder, by contrast, is repelled by the idea of Europe as a cultural-political laboratory where Europeans are transformed into guinea pigs or objects of a large-scale experimental attempt to create a European identity.[20] For Broder, European identity is an essentialist phenomenon, a geographical reality: 'Stating "I am a European" is as fatuous as saying "I take a shower every day." It's embarrassing when a commonplace is elevated to the status of something exceptional.'[21] European identity does not need to be artificially constructed and Broder dismisses the earnest efforts of 'Professional Europeans' to do so:

> I do not want to be an honorary European or required to feel European. Especially not by people who have turned their European identity into a full-time occupation. Europe, says the French philosopher Bernard-Henri Lévy, is 'not a place, but an Idea'. That sounds good at first, but it's a hollow phrase that can be interpreted to suit anyone's taste.[22]

In contrast to Menasse, Broder's situation as a Jewish European makes him highly sceptical of the peace rhetoric deployed by European functionaries such as Martin Schulz, President of the European Parliament, and he likens it pointedly to what he sees as the empty rhetoric of 'the oft-quoted German-Jewish symbiosis, which never existed'.[23] He attributes Europe's peaceful post-war existence quite emphatically to the United States and not the EU: 'The community of prosperity and peace to which Schulz refers owes its peace and prosperity to the intervention of foreign powers, the Marshall Plan and to the fact that for half a century the Americans laid a protective hand over Western Europe.'[24] Europe's peace-keeping record, by contrast, is, in Broder's view, abysmal, and 'engaged Europeans' who advance this argument are wilfully blind to the fact that 'Europe today is not even capable of solving regional conflicts such as those in Northern Ireland or the Basque country, not to mention the civil war in Yugoslavia which was watched, for a long time, by a helpless and clueless Europe.'[25]

At worst, Broder argues, the rhetoric of peace and Holocaust memory is manipulated by Eurocrats such as Martin Schulz in the interests of a bloated European bureaucracy: 'An effort such as this, in which there is an absurd relationship between input and output, needs legitimacy. No wonder it always has to be a matter of Auschwitz, war and peace, and the future of humanity.'[26] As a Jewish intellectual, Broder is particularly sensitive to the fact that this dubious discourse can be deployed to support the project of deeper political integration in Europe:

> Europe or Auschwitz. [...] To summon up the 'demons of the past' to testify to the need for a united Europe in the present, is not just irresponsible, it is also dangerous because it raises questions about who will call the shots in a unified or united Europe. The children of yesterday's poachers are now playing gamekeeper.[27]

Menasse and Broder also differ in their interpretation of the relationship between the EU and the concept of the nation. Menasse sees the EU as a post-national bulwark against nationalism and the self-interested power of the nation-state. Broder, in contrast, contends that the EU is itself a 'meta-nationalist' and increasingly totalitarian phenomenon. Both positions are undoubtedly informed by their experience as Jewish Europeans. Menasse presents the national idea as an anachronism and exposes contemporary definitions of 'Austrian' and 'German' national identity to ridicule. In a seemingly light-hearted conversation with a German colleague in Brussels, he tests linguistic, cultural and constitutional definitions of 'German' national identity and finds them wanting:

> What is typically German and bestows you with a national identity?
> I don't know. All sorts of things. For example ... she threw her hands up in the air and
> said in exasperation:
> There are lots of things. Little things perhaps, but they're important! German bread,
> for example![28]

In the end, Menasse observes archly, a superior type of bread is all that distinguishes Germans from their fellow Europeans. As multiple definitions of 'Germanness' fall by the wayside, Menasse's German colleague resorts to culinary definitions to buttress her sense of national identity. The Austrians are no more convincing on the subject. They cannot invoke the concept of Austria as a 'cultural nation' (Kulturnation) because it erodes the vital distinction between Austrian and German national identity. The civic notion of the 'political nation' (Staatsnation), by contrast, is, according to Menasse, not exclusive enough for many Austrians: '"Political nation" then? God forbid! We had only just got rid of the Jews, and if we now declared ourselves to be a political nation in the sense defined by the French revolutionaries, once again anyone could come along ...'[29] As a result, Austrians resort to aesthetic definitions of the nation, citing its beautiful landscape as a source of identification. However, Menasse's Jewish experience drives him to reveal the dark side of these flawed but powerful forms of national identification in his ironic but heartfelt comments on the Austrian state's mindless and cynical post-war embrace of nationalism which, among other things, required Jewish Austrians forced to emigrate during the Third Reich to produce 'character references' before being allowed to return to the land of their birth: 'I was born in Austria, the country that decided to learn from history, after all the devastation and criminal acts produced half a century before by nationalism and national conflicts – and itself become a nation.'[30] For Menasse, the post-national EU is an antidote to an Austrian national discourse which downplays its genocidal past.

Ultimately, national identity is, in Menasse's view, 'a shabby ideology that frequently leads to war and crimes against humanity'.[31] He denounces nationalism as the ideology that led to the Holocaust:

> The ideology of the self-determined, self-confident, self-glorifying nation, the
> dynamic of nationalism, the 'eternal enmity' between nations, the attempt to defend,
> if necessary with violence, 'national interests' against other nations, have cost
> countless millions of human lives, brought endless suffering to the living and, in its
> most uninhibited form, culminated in that atrocious crime against humanity,
> symbolizes today by 'Auschwitz'.[32]

Even in the more peaceful circumstances of post-war Europe, Menasse argues that anachronistic forms of national identity lead to irrational political decision-making on the part of nation-states. He notes, for example, that the costs of German unification consumed 4% of West German GDP and puts forward the intriguing suggestion that it would have been cheaper and less humiliating for the GDR to have joined the EU instead of West Germany: 'The costs of German reunification are not too high for German national consciousness, and anyway are necessary – but the costs of European unification seem astronomical.'[33] The widely touted concept of the 'national interest' is, he argues, a deception perpetrated by the state on the citizens of the nation: 'The only interests that are defended are those of the nation's political and economic, or indeed financial, elites.'[34] In Menasse's view, the nation-state represents the selfish interests of a political and economic elite in pursuit of neo-liberal policies.[35]

Menasse celebrates the fact that the EU was designed by the post-war elites to maintain peace by overcoming nationalism and the nation-state. However, he bemoans the limited ability of the EU to develop truly supra-national solutions to the challenges Europe faces. This is due to a fundamental structural problem. For Menasse, the supra-national intentions of the system are disfigured by the 'birthmarks of the old nationalism'.[36] The supra-national power of the European commission has been progressively weakened by national governments pursuing national interests in the European Council and these systemic problems have produced the Eurozone crisis:

> The system that has produced this crisis is precisely the institutional edifice that is specific to the European Union: a poorly balanced relationship between supra-national institutions (Commission, Parliament) and an institution where national interests, national circumstances and national fictions et cetera are defended (the Council).[37]

The worst offenders in this respect are the Germans. In Menasse's view, the Germans are not driven by a truly cosmopolitan vision but instead by a desire to defend their national interest: 'It is German politicians who, with unwavering consistency, have turned a European institution, the Council, into a council for the defence of the national interest, in particular their own.'[38] Menasse argues that Angela Merkel's generation fails to appreciate that the European idea is grounded in the crimes of German nationalism: 'Unlike the generation of Helmut Kohl, she has not been shaped by the shocking devastation and crimes for which German nationalism was to blame. [...] Can her socialisation offer any historical goal other than the achievement and reaffirmation of a united, democratic Germany?'[39] The Eurozone crisis is therefore for Menasse a political rather than economic phenomenon, caused by the self-interest of nation-states and the failure of the supra-national European institutions to curb their power.[40] As a consequence, he would strengthen the powers of the European Commission, which he finds to be an open and transparent post-national institution: 'In the European Commission and the European Parliament, two truly supra-national institutions were created with the aim of driving forward post-national developments.'[41]

Menasse sees the EU as the post-national solution to an economic crisis caused by the political and economic self-interest of the nation-state. Broder, on the other hand, regards the EU as the problem. Far from being post-national, 'Europe', he argues, is becoming a monstrous meta-nation which threatens the liberty and prosperity of Europeans.[42] He is therefore highly critical of those who see the EU as an antidote to nationalism. The economic crisis of the Eurozone has, he argues, ruined lives and threatens social cohesion on the continent. This high social cost should at the very least cause 'engaged Europeans' to revise the mantra that 'the EU is the ideal framework for the peaceful coexistence of nations and a guarantee against nationalism, hatred and centrifugal tendencies. [...] The way the EU functions at present is not bringing nations together, but driving them apart.'[43] He rejects the idea that the supra-national institutions of the EU can prevent nationalist 'adventures' or the rise of antisemitism. Developments in Hungary, for example, of which Broder, as a Jew, is no doubt especially aware, have starkly revealed the impotence of the supra-national union in this respect:

> The EU may be in a position to prescribe to the Czechs which kind of sandwich spread they can describe as 'Maslo', but it is not in a position to prevent fascist and anti-Semitic parties from taking part in the Hungarian elections. All it can do is watch the situation in Hungary 'with concern'.[44]

Like Menasse, Broder has little time for the concept of national sovereignty: 'As far as I'm concerned, "national sovereignty" is not an object that I would defend with my life. I couldn't care less whether I am stopped by a German or a French police officer, or whether I am fleeced by a German, Dutch or European tax office.'[45] The problem, however, is that the European elites are not post-nationalists, but deluded meta-nationalists determined to impose costly political visions on the peoples of Europe:

> Cultural community, Life Model ... 'Renationalisation' is taking place at a European level, for borders cannot stop the march of either stupidity or nationalism. [...] For that reason, all the talk about the fact that a strong Europe is the best antidote to 'renationalisation' is ... nothing but idle talk. The opposite is the case. As we have seen, commitment to Europe is a cheap opportunity to behave as a Meta-nationalist, without falling under suspicion of actually being one.[46]

Menasse and Broder's conflicting interpretations of the EU are reflected in their antithetical attitudes to the controversial figure of the EU bureaucrat. Menasse moved to Brussels to carry out research for his book and, contrary to his own expectations, found himself developing a deep admiration for the bureaucrats of Brussels. Unlike the self-interested political elites of Europe's nation-states, the European bureaucrat of *Der europäische Landbote* is a truly enlightened and cosmopolitan visionary who embodies the 'European' values that Menasse seeks to promote. The bureaucrats are, he concludes, 'real Europeans: polyglots, highly qualified, enlightened, rooted in their cultures of origin, but liberated from the irrationalism of a so-called national identity'.[47] Less corrupt or nepotistic and more meritocratic than their national counterparts, the bureaucracy of the European Union is also the cheapest in Europe, costing a mere 0.06% of European GDP.[48] The EU, he notes, employs fewer bureaucrats than the city of Vienna but, unlike nation-states or municipalities, is regularly castigated for its 'regulation-mania' and unelected 'Moloch of bureaucrats'.[49] Menasse insists, however, that European bureaucrats are progressive, rational and dedicated to defending the European common interest. They are, in many ways, heirs to the enlightened tradition of the Josephine bureaucracy of the Austro-Hungarian Empire for which Menasse, the Austrian, appears to have more than a sneaking regard.[50] Unlike the 'provincial' actors of Europe's nation-states, the transnational bureaucrats of the European Union can develop long-term strategic solutions to questions of European social policy, taxes, asylum and migration: 'The much-maligned EU bureaucracy demonstrates how an organization can develop rational solutions when it is liberated from short-term thinking.'[51]

The European bureaucrat of Broder's experience is no enlightened cosmopolitan visionary, but instead the mindless functionary of an increasingly totalitarian system. If Menasse's view of the European bureaucrat is shaped by his Austrian situation, Broder's appears to be shaped by his experience of the German and Polish Communist experiments and by his personal experience of disenchantment with the Left wing of the German political spectrum. The EU is 'a modern Frankenstein story' with 'a rampant bureaucracy' and Broder fears that 'yet another optimistic vision for humanity is in the process of acquiring totalitarian features'.[52] The EU in its current form is 'a product of the omnipotent fantasies of impotent bureaucrats [...] The Brussels EU-aristocracy lives and works on its own planet, far away from the rest of the world.'[53] In reality, the EU is 'a gigantic delusion', a political project financed by a bastard economy working in the interests of banks, not people.[54] Broder's EU bureaucrat is self-aggrandising, yet professionally incompetent.[55] He castigates the pointless industriousness with which the functionaries of the Union try to impose uniformity on the lives of Europeans: 'Most eurocrats know that they are taking part in a programme of occupational therapy. [...] They're aware that they are engaged in completely nonsensical activity.'[56] They cost too much, but are clearly underemployed: 'Could it be that the bureaucracy is not fully occupied? That it's constantly in search of something that hasn't yet been regulated, like a housewife who also hoovers under the carpet?'[57] And despite the costs, Europe's staggering youth unemployment rates reveal that 'the relationship between effort and achievement is pathetic'.[58]

The same malaise is evident in the pointless activity of the European Parliament which Broder likens to the Supreme Soviet of the USSR: 'The EU-"Parliament" is the only representative body in the so-called "free world" that does not have the right to initiate legislation.'[59] Indeed, on a visit to Strasbourg, he is amused, yet not surprised, to find former East German Communist Lothar Bisky transformed seamlessly into a late-career MEP: 'So, a stalwart of the GDR, who had been washed away with the sewage of a real-life socialist system in decline, was playing Euro-politics.'[60] As Bisky admits to Broder: 'I needed to effect a dignified departure.'[61] Broder mocks the impotence of what he sees as this toothless and irrelevant Parliament: 'A parliament that is so powerless can only bustle about to compensate for its lack of relevance.' Indeed, a visit to the Parliament in Strasbourg enables him to contrast the absurd amount of time expended on trivialities such as 'how high the minimum amounts of anethole and thujone need to be before a drink can be described as absinthe' to the cursory treatment of consequential matters such as foreign policy:

> And between a round of absinthe and a virtual visit to a betting office, the Members of Parliament held discussions with the EU's High Representative for foreign affairs, Catherine Ashton, about the situation in Egypt, North Korea, Ukraine, Syria and Mali – all before elevenses.[62]

Indeed, unlike Menasse, Broder is deeply troubled by the myopia of the Union's institutions and its dangerous neglect of foreign-political and military realities. Instead: 'Grown-ups play politics, like children playing shop or Monopoly. The only difference is that in Brussels you play with real money.'[63]

Menasse sees the national elites as the greatest threat to European peace and cohesion. Broder regards the Union's elites as the problem. Unsurprisingly therefore, their views about further political integration diverge considerably. Menasse urges Europe's politicians to think creatively and to develop a vision of deeper political integration: 'In the first place it would be desirable to have political integration, at least of the Eurozone countries.'[64] Broder, however, is sceptical of visions. A United Europe, he argues, would be a journey into the unknown 'in which even the guys on the bridge of the ship have no idea where they're heading and how much it will cost'.[65] He admits that 'in the course of writing, I had growing doubts about whether "Europe" – in the sense of "The United States of Europe" – had ever been a good idea.' He has come to the conclusion that, like other totalitarian projects, "Europe" is now little more than 'a project of the elites, the jet-setters and air-miles collectors, the connoisseurs and treasure-hunters'.[66] It is a product of incompetent megalomania and he rejects the creation of a European super-state as an antidote to nationalism.[67]

However, for all their dramatic differences of opinion about the merits of the EU, shaped undoubtedly by their Jewish, but also their respective Austrian and German situations,

Menasse and Broder's reflections on Europe and defence of 'European values' are anchored in a common tradition of enlightenment and cosmopolitanism.[68] Menasse, for example, places the future of Europe in the hands of its enlightened citizens. Drawing on the ideas of Habermas and Negt, he outlines his vision of a post-national European democracy of free and rational citizens.[69] Menasse dismisses the nation-state and the concept of the 'national interest' as anachronisms from the nineteenth century and calls instead for a new, more democratic, constitution for a Europe of the regions:

> As a prerequisite for a democratic Europe, a democratic offensive must call for the abolition of the Council, the bestowal of full parliamentary powers on the European parliament and the election of representatives on a regional rather than on a national basis. Is that not what we were promised? A post-national, subsidiary Europe of the Regions?[70]

Citizens would elect a new kind of European Parliament which would complement the work of the enlightened European bureaucrat and create a rational framework to tackle the challenges of 'a continent without nations'.[71] Parliament and a Commission elected by parliamentarians would control finance, taxation and economic policy, as well as take responsibility for legal and social frameworks. Regional affairs would be controlled by the regional parliaments of the new European Federal Republic.[72]

On closer inspection, however, and very much in keeping with the tradition of European Enlightenment thought, Menasse's vision of a post-national democracy of free and enlightened European citizens is, albeit understandably, elitist and overly-idealistic.[73] He praises the European visionaries who, traumatized by war and genocide, drove forward the creation of the European community against the will of popular opinion in France and Germany.[74] He visibly struggles to suppress his contempt for 'the masses' who display no interest whatsoever in the question of post-national democracy.[75] For Menasse, the great advantage of a European over a national bureaucracy is precisely the fact that it is an independent and 'enlightened bureaucracy' that is not in thrall to the vagaries of popular opinion and 'to the backwardness of large sections of the population to be found in EU-member states, to their prejudices and subservient desire for authoritarian leaders'.[76] Indeed, despite his support for a European Parliament with meaningful powers, he expresses reservations about the modern democratic process and a degree of nostalgia for the age of governance by enlightened bureaucracy: 'The educated citizen is a prerequisite for democracy. If the educated are outvoted by baiting crowds whipped up by the mass media, then democracy becomes homicidal.'[77] It is an elitist position, arising, no doubt, from his Jewish-Austrian family's experience of persecution in Vienna in the 1930s. Menasse's vision of a United Europe based on peace, shared values and post-national forms of negotiation is also highly idealistic. He defines it in explicit opposition to the model of the United States of America which, he argues, represents the 'old European' values of conquest, immigration and nation-building.[78] Key issues such as control of security, defence and foreign policy are simply ignored by Menasse, as if they had no place in the post-national European order.[79]

Broder's vision for Europe is also indebted to an Enlightenment tradition of critical thinking and rational debate. 'The real European', he declares, is 'a critical European'. 'Professional Europeans', by contrast, stifle pluralism and critical debate and deny Europe's citizens the opportunity to think and make choices about the future of Europe for themselves: 'And the nomenklatura fear nothing more than an honest discussion about what they have done with the "European Idea".'[80] The critical vigilance of the individual citizen is the only antidote to what Broder regards as the deeply troubling totalitarian character of the EU. Ruled by a profoundly undemocratic Commission, the EU subordinates the interests of its citizens to that of an unproductive virtual economy:

> Whereas in the real economy people make tables out of trees, boiled beef out of cattle and fruit brandy out of apricots, in the world of finance people make money out of money. [...] Sales and profits are generated in a closed system. [...] Virtual business is done with virtual money.[81]

The cycle of deception and self-deception is, he suggests, similar to that practised by totalitarian regimes such as the GDR.[82] Indeed, Broder likens the suppression of internal dissent and the promotion of the European idea through expensive marketing campaigns such as 'I want Europe' to totalitarian propaganda methods: 'There were also campaigns of this sort in the socialist era [...] A system that celebrates itself in this fashion is already on the way out.'[83] Always inclined to thought-provoking provocation, Broder describes the award of the Nobel Peace prize to the EU in 2012 as an 'Agitprop event', designed to deflect criticism of the Union.[84] In this respect, he argues, the European Union increasingly resembles the Soviet Union:

> In principle you could criticise everything, only you couldn't call the system itself into question. For it guaranteed peace. That was the ultimate argument that justified everything: occupational and travel bans, press censorship, denunciations, sham elections and the privileges enjoyed by the ruling class. The sacrifices demanded of ordinary people would contribute to securing peace. [...] A little bit of unemployment, paternalism, expropriation, uniformity and, soon, inflation are not pleasant, but hardly too high a price to pay for the preservation of peace.[85]

A system that can only tolerate 'constructive' criticism gravely endangers the principle of intellectual freedom, and Broder reserves some of his most scathing criticism for Martin Schulz's 'authoritarian, almost totalitarian way of speaking. Criticism? Yes, please! But only if it's constructive. And what constitutes constructive criticism will be determined this time not by the Central Committee of the Communist Party of the Soviet Union but by the President of the European Parliament.'[86] Quoting David Cameron's declaration of 2013 that '[t]he greatest threat to the EU is not those who call for change but those who denounce new ideas as heresy', Broder notes that '"EU-critics" and "EU-sceptics" are treated like heretics.'[87] But '[c]riticism and scepticism are the weapons of the citizen. Only a subject would allow himself to be bossed around without contradiction.'[88] Broder castigates Schulz for deploying a discourse, with a long tradition in German political culture, which scapegoats critics of Europe and blames them for Europe's problems in his book *The Giant in Chains*[89]:

> What does that remind us of? Exactly! Of the 'grumblers, querulants and quibblers (Nörgler, Querulanten und Kritikaster)', who denigrated good ideas for the hell of it. Of the Stab-in-the-back legend which was used to explain German defeat in the First World War. Of the 'rootless comrades (die heimatlosen Gesellen)', who are loyal to nothing but themselves. Of the 'corrosive elements (zersetzenden Elemente)', which threatened the wellbeing of the nation in the Third Reich, of the 'subversive elements' and 'hostile and negative forces (feindlich-negativen Kräfte)' that prevented the flourishing of socialism in the GDR. Of the 'class enemy' that was responsible for everything that went wrong in the Soviet Union. Of the 'attack dogs, predators and philistines (Pinscher, Uhus und Banausen)' who were causing mischief in Ludwig Erhard's time, of the 'rats and bluebottles (Ratten und Schmeißfliegen)' who pursued Franz Josef Strauß everywhere, of the 'locusts (Heuschrecken)', as Franz Müntefering described investors 'who spare no thought for the people whose

jobs they destroy'. Seen in this context, Schulz's 'Blame game' perpetuates an old tradition.[90]

Indeed, at the heart of Broder's reflections on Europe lies a coruscating critique of the politics of 'paternalism', a tradition that he finds deeply embedded in German political culture. He rejects the vision of a united Europe as a project of German elites who want to impose their own form of reparations or 'Wiedergutmachung' for past misdemeanours on the rest of Europe.

> The great vision of the 'United States of Europe' is a project of elites who support and promote each other, of politicians who want to go down in history, and – at the same time – German do-gooders who see 'Europe' as an antidote to the poison of nationalism. A good-will gesture that should ensure that we Germans are loved in all those places where the German army and the SS left behind scorched earth. A sort of reparations for Europe. [...] No wonder that we Germans are accused of wanting to save the world, or in this instance Europe, whether people like it or not. [...] Whoever really wants to preserve peace in Europe should beat an orderly retreat, and the sooner the better.[91]

The discourse of atonement is deceptive, however. For the German 'Euro-nationalists', Broder argues, European unity is a substitute for German national greatness: 'Germans with withdrawal symptoms dream about a "United Europe" – as a substitute for the dream of national greatness. The fact that in a unified Europe it's the Germans who generally call the shots, makes the dream even more beautiful.'[92] At worst, Broder accuses Germans of hypocritical and cynical exploitation of the Holocaust in defence of this 'meta-nationalist' project:

> Former Chancellor Schmidt completely ... excelled himself when he declared that the Germans bore more responsibility than other nations for Europe 'because we murdered six million Jewish fellow citizens in an industrial fashion.' Not that he would have said that the Germans bore more responsibility than other nations for Israel's security, not that he would have suggested that Germany should argue in the European Council for the recognition of Hezbollah as a terrorist organization, not that he would have said anything remotely relevant – he proclaimed six million dead Jews to be German fellow citizens to highlight Germany's special responsibility for Europe.[93]

Broder, the Jewish 'fellow citizen', by contrast, urges critical scrutiny of a German 'Euro-Patriotism' which he denounces as 'the politics of paternalism and homogenization'.[94] He calls for vigilance in, for example, the sphere of economic policy, noting the contrast between the economist Hans-Werner Sinn's description of European economics as a 'Ponzi-Game' and Wolfgang Schäuble's insistence that everything is under control.[95] He calls, in conclusion, for a democratic public debate and then referendum about the future of Europe. 'It's time to put an end to the diktats that decree there is no alternative, and to the politics of emergency decrees from above.'[96]

Both Menasse and Broder try to reconcile their democratic visions for Europe with the cosmopolitan values of the German Enlightenment.[97] Menasse celebrates the post-national, cosmopolitan atmosphere he finds in Brussels.[98] The city embodies 'the concrete, living and lively vision of a post-national Europe [...] ultimately a relaxed but orderly chaos of identities!'[99] Multilingualism is the norm in Brussels where 'the monolingual individual is the stranger'.[100] But Menasse's Europeans are no rootless cosmopolitans.[101] Mindful, no doubt, of the pejorative use of the term to describe Europe's Jews, Menasse stresses the idea that

Europe's cosmopolitan identity is rooted in regional diversity: 'Europe is in reality a Europe of the regions. It ought to be the purpose of European politics to give political expression to this reality.'[102] The cosmopolitan bureaucrats he admires are rooted not in their respective nations, but in the regional *Heimat*.[103] Polyglots they may be, but they are 'rooted in their culture of origin':[104]

> In reality though, people are rooted in their regions and moulded by the life of their region. Anyway, what is 'national identity' compared to local patriotism (Heimatgefühl)? To have a 'Heimat' is a human right, a national identity is not. The 'Heimat' is where smells and intonation strike a particular chord, the one place in life where one is not a visitor, where linguistic peculiarities and odd traditions engender, if not necessarily approval, nevertheless a certain sense of belonging. 'Heimat' is the one place where things that are diffuse and unclear become tangible and sharp, where the bread has a particular taste, where emotions are heightened, and anger at the small-mindedness as great as the love one has for the particular cast of mind. Regional identity is the root of European identity.[105]

On a personal level, Menasse thus reconciles his Viennese and European identities and constructs a post-national sense of belonging that reconciles particular and more universal identities. It is an idea that has much in common with Appiah's concept of 'the cosmopolitan patriot' who 'can entertain the possibility of a world in which everyone is a rooted cosmopolitan, attached to a home of one's own, with its cultural particularities, but taking pleasure from the presence of other, different places that are home to other, different people'.[106] Menasse's cosmopolitan vision for Europe also echoes that of Ulrich Beck who criticizes Enlightenment universalism for neglecting particularity.[107]

Broder's Brussels is not the embodiment of European cosmopolitanism, but its enemy. He celebrates the fact that Europe's diversity has not been destroyed by the levellers of Brussels: '"My" Europe is still there: the Rynek in Cracow, the Bloemgracht in Amsterdam, the Naschmarkt in Vienna.'[108] He opposes Brussels' attempts to impose a 'one-size-fits-all' model of economic management across Europe, but by describing the Eurozone as an attempt to impose a 'Northern' mentality on 'Southern' Europe and comparing it to a merger between Formula One and the Red Bull Soapbox Race, he perpetuates stereotypes of national 'character'.[109] His cosmopolitan celebration of European diversity is, however, more attuned to the contemporary realities of mobility and migration than Menasse's rather static definition of *Heimat*, or homeland, allows:[110] 'Migration is, and has always been, movement away from poverty. From the moment human beings first straightened themselves up on the African Steppe, they have been in search of a better life …'[111] Broder's acceptance of migration as a universal reality implicitly challenges conventional concepts of *Heimat* which define it as a place of origin. In Europe today, it must be possible for migrants to construct a new *Heimat* which can coexist with the one from which they have come. That the enlightened values of the new European *Heimat* must be honoured is, however, non-negotiable for Broder.[112]

Menasse and Broder's post-national and cosmopolitan reflections on Europe can be criticized on several levels. Menasse's vision has an elitist, Eurocentric and idealistic quality, while Broder's often teeters on the edge of hyperbole and a bleak cynicism. Despite this, their situation as Jewish public intellectuals sharpens their insights into the potential dangers of nationalist, populist, quasi-totalitarian and paternalistic discourses. It undoubtedly shapes Menasse's vision of the rooted, as opposed to rootless, cosmopolitan. Broder's German perspective and, most likely, his estrangement from the German Left reinforce this deep antipathy towards totalitarian tendencies while Menasse's Austrian situation bolsters his critique of the self-interested provincialism of the European nation-states and celebration of the enlightened, transnational bureaucrat. Moreover, it is no coincidence that both Menasse and Broder situate their writings quite explicitly in a German-speaking intellectual tradition of political critique and enlightenment.[113] While Menasse takes inspiration from Georg Büchner's efforts to raise the popular political consciousness of the nineteenth-century German peasantry in his tract *Der hessische Landbote* (The Hessian Courier), Broder alludes to Karl Kraus's great satirical critique of authoritarian and nationalist discourse, *Die letzten Tage der Menschheit* (The Last Days of Mankind). As in Kraus's dramatic montage about Europe during the First World War, Broder notes grimly that in his stocktaking of Europe almost a century later: 'The worst quotes are not fictional.'[114] Like those of their intellectual predecessors, Menasse and Broder's contribution to the contemporary debate about the political future of the European continent is invaluable for keeping alive, at a critical juncture, a deep-rooted spirit of critical enquiry and fearless debate, with thought-provoking implications for contemporary debates about the relationship between cosmopolitanism and the idea of 'Europe'.[115] This is particularly vital where, at the time of writing in 2016, the debates about Britain's relationship with the European Union have once again exposed the naked self-interest of Europe's nation-states.

Notes

1. Laqueur, *The Last Days of Europe* and *After the Fall*; Pinto, "I'm a European Jew – and No, I'm not Leaving;" Lévy, *Left in Dark Times*; Aaronovitch, "Europe Isn't Just About the Economy, Stupid." On Jews and the political culture of post-war Europe, see Beller, "Ist Europa gut für die Juden?"
2. Menasse, *Der europäische Landbote*. Translated into English by author. Since 2013 Menasse has also published articles and given speeches in defence of a United Europe. See Menasse, "FAQ Europa." He is also a member of the "Reflection Group" of the transnational "New Pact for Europe" project.
3. Broder, *Die letzten Tage Europas*. Translated into English by author. See also his satirical television documentary *Entweder Broder: Die Europa Safari*.
4. On the "new cosmopolitanism" see Fine, *Cosmopolitanism*, 2–6.
5. On Cosmopolitanism as a contested concept today, see Neilson, "On the New Cosmopolitanism," 111; Fine, *Cosmopolitanism*, 18.
6. As examples of opposing interpretations of cosmopolitanism, see Brennan, *At Home in the World*, who presents it as a tool of US-centred transnationalism, and Cheah and Robbins, *Cosmopolitics*; Beck, *Cosmopolitan Vision*; and Appiah, "Cosmopolitan Patriots" who emphasize its political and social potential and viability.

7. Broder, *Die letzten Tage*, 21.
8. Sander Gilman credits Broder with reviving the rich genre of the German-Jewish *feuilleton* or newspaper essay. See Gilman and Friedberg, *A Jew in the New Germany: Henryk Broder*, xi. See also Markwort, "Hurra, wir gratulieren!"
9. Menasse, *Der europäische Landbote*, 85.
10. Reiter, *Contemporary Jewish Writing*, 97, 84–9, 102–10; Beilein, *86 und die Folgen*.
11. On the difference between "cosmopolitanism" and "multiculturalism" see Beck and Grande, *Cosmopolitan Europe*, 14.
12. On the association between cosmopolitanism and rootlessness see Neilson, "On the New Cosmopolitanism," 111 and Appiah, "Cosmopolitan Patriots," 618.
13. Appiah, "Cosmopolitan Patriots," 624, and Beck and Grande, *Cosmopolitan Europe*, 16.
14. Fine, *Cosmopolitanism*, 40.
15. Ibid., x.
16. Broder, *Die letzten Tage*, 222.
17. Menasse, *Der europäische Landbote*, 108.
18. Ibid., 82.
19. Ibid., 82.
20. Broder, *Die letzten Tage*, 194.
21. Ibid., 11.
22. Ibid., 21.
23. Ibid., 114.
24. Ibid., 115.
25. Ibid., 85.
26. Ibid., 50.
27. Ibid., 48–9.
28. Menasse, *Der europäische Landbote*, 87.
29. Ibid., 66.
30. Ibid., 65–6.
31. Ibid., 64.
32. Ibid., 8.
33. Ibid., 22.
34. Ibid., 59.
35. "Der neoliberale Einfluss kommt über die nationalstaatlichen Interessen herein." Menasse, *Der Europäische Landbote*, 57.
36. Ibid., 84. See also Ulrich Beck's description of the EU as a "deformed cosmopolitanism" arising out of the egoism of member states. Beck and Grande, *Cosmopolitan Europe*, 20.
37. Menasse, *Der europäische Landbote*, 51, 82.
38. Ibid., 31.
39. Ibid., 47–8.
40. Ibid., 91, 93.
41. Ibid., 21, 49.
42. Broder, *Die letzten Tage*, 166.
43. Ibid., 87–8.
44. Ibid., 166.
45. Ibid., 165.
46. Ibid., 161, 166.
47. Menasse, *Der europäische Landbote*, 23.
48. Ibid., 24.
49. Ibid., 15, 17, 22.
50. Ibid, 20–3.
51. Ibid., 71–2.
52. Broder draws here on Enzensberger, *Sanftes Monster Brüssel*. Broder, *Die letzten Tage*, 79, 14.
53. Broder, *Die letzten Tage*, 89.
54. Ibid., 9.

55. Ibid., 42, 65.
56. Ibid., 106.
57. Ibid., 171.
58. Ibid., 215.
59. Ibid., 44.
60. Ibid., 107.
61. Ibid., 109.
62. Ibid., 184.
63. Ibid., 185.
64. Menasse, *Der europäische Landbote,* 90.
65. Broder, *Die letzten Tage,* 186.
66. Ibid., 192.
67. Ibid., 218, 220.
68. On Menasse's desire to identify with proto-Enlightenment figures such as Rabbi Manasseh and Spinoza, see Reiter, "Die Geschichte der Marranan." On Broder's defence of Enlightenment values, see Broder, "Toleranz hilft nur den Rücksichtslosen."
69. Menasse, *Der europäische Landbote*, 15, 95. Habermas, "Why Europe needs a Constitution," 17; Negt, *Gesellschaftsentwurf Europa.*
70. Menasse, *Der europäische Landbote,* 84.
71. Ibid., 102.
72. Ibid., 88. See also Menasse and Guerot, "For a European Republic."
73. Outram, *Enlightenment.* See also Beck's critique of the Enlightenment's hegemonic "humanistic universalism" which posed a threat to pluralism. Beck, *Cosmopolitan Vision,* 49. See also Fine's critique of Habermas' new cosmopolitanism and the emphasis Fine places on "the role of political judgement on the part of ordinary citizens." Fine, *Cosmopolitanism,* 40.
74. Menasse, *Der europäische Landbote,* 11–12.
75. Ibid., 95.
76. Ibid., 26–7.
77. Ibid., 42.
78. Ibid., 99–101.
79. Ibid., 88.
80. Broder, *Die letzten Tage,* 10.
81. Ibid., 27–9.
82. Ibid., 141.
83. Ibid., 81–2.
84. Ibid., 113.
85. Ibid., 116–7.
86. Ibid., 123.
87. Ibid., 122, 117.
88. Ibid., 10.
89. Schulz, *Der gefesselte Riese.*
90. Broder, *Die letzten Tage,* 163–4.
91. Ibid., 125–6.
92. Ibid., 167.
93. Ibid., 175.
94. Ibid., 208.
95. Ibid., 197.
96. Ibid., 222.
97. Fine, *Cosmopolitanism,* 4; Reiss, *Kant: Political Writings*; Bohman and Lutz-Bachmann, *Perpetual Peace.*
98. Cosmopolitanism and post-nationalism are not necessarily synonymous. Menasse goes further than many advocates of cosmopolitanism (who, for example, highlight the merits of postcolonial nationalism) in forcefully willing the demise of the nation-state. See Appiah's attempt to reconcile cosmopolitanism and concepts of the nation in "Cosmopolitan Patriots," 624.

99. See Appiah's distinction between cosmopolitanism which "celebrates the fact that there are different local human ways of being", as long, crucially, as these differences "meet certain general ethical constraints" and "humanism" which he finds "consistent with the desire for global hegemony." Appiah, "Cosmopolitan Patriots," 621.
100. Menasse, *Der europäische Landbote*, 29.
101. On the pejorative connotations of the association between Jews and Cosmopolitanism, see Miller and Ury, "Cosmopolitanism: the End of Jewishness?," 347.
102. Menasse, *Der europäische Landbote*, 67. On representations of Jews as the personification of rootless cosmopolitanism, see Koffman, "Figures of the Cosmopolitan."
103. Cf. Beck's notion of "cosmopolitan nationalism" in Beck, *Cosmopolitan Vision*, 49.
104. Menasse, *Der europäische Landbote*, 23.
105. Ibid., 88. Menasse defines nationalism as the "politischer Missbrauch von Heimatliebe" in Menasse, "FAQ Europa," 12.
106. Appiah, "Cosmopolitan Patriots," 618.
107. Beck, *Cosmopolitan Vision*, 49. Cf. Fine, who is critical of the conservatism of cosmopolitans who attach "cosmopolitanism to an already strong and confident sense of belonging (whether it is Ghanaian village society, or post-war German constitutional democracy, or the European way of life, or indeed American democracy)". Fine, *Cosmopolitanism*, x, 38.
108. Broder, *Die letzten Tage*, 193.
109. Ibid., 120–1.
110. Menasse regards the nation, not the region, as a "Fiktion," but underestimates the extent to which regions and *Heimat* also contain fictional elements. Menasse, "FAQ Europa," 16. On the concept of "Heimat," see Blickle, *Critical Theory*. On more mobile concepts of "belonging" see Adelson, "Against Between."
111. Broder, *Die letzten Tage*, 93.
112. See Broder, *Hurra, wir kapitulieren!* where he satirizes the willingness of Europe's political and intellectual elites to appease militant Islamists who challenge European values.
113. Elsewhere Menasse situates himself in a tradition of intellectual dreamers such as Novalis and Zweig whose utopian thoughts about Europe have obeyed "einer nachhaltigen Vernunft": Menasse, "FAQ Europa," 7. See also Martin Meyer's praise of Menasse's ability to think against the grain of convention in his Laudatio to Menasse on his receipt of the Max-Frisch-Preis in 2014. http//www.nzz.ch/feuilleton/utopie-als-freiheit-als-kritik-1.18300308.
114. Broder, *Die letzten Tage*, 191.
115. See also Menasse's public interventions and calls for creative discussion in, for example, Menasse and Guerot, "For a European Republic."

Bibliography

Aaronovitch, David. "Europe Isn't Just About the Economy, Stupid." *The Times* 21 (May 2015).
Adelson, Leslie A. "Against Between." *New German Critique* 80 (2000): 93–124.
Appiah, Kwame Anthony. "Cosmopolitan Patriots." *Critical Inquiry* 23, no. 3 (1997): 617–639.
Beck, Ulrich. *Cosmopolitan Vision*. Cambridge: Polity, 2006.
Beck, Ulrich, and Edgar Grande. *Cosmopolitan Europe*. Cambridge: Polity, 2006.
Beilein, Matthias. *86 und die Folgen. Robert Schindel, Robert Menasse und Doron Rabinovici im literarischen Feld Österreichs*. Berlin: Erich Schmidt, 2008.
Beller, Steven. "Ist Europa gut für die Juden?" *Jüdisches Echo* 58 (2009): 11–23.
Blickle, Peter. *Critical Theory of the German Idea of Homeland*. Rochester: Camden House, 2002.
Bohman, James, and Matthias Lutz-Bachmann (eds.). *Perpetual Peace: Essays on Kant's Cosmopolitan Ideal*. London: MIT Press, 1997.
Brennan, Timothy. *At Home in the World: Cosmopolitanism Now*. Cambridge, MA: Harvard University Press, 1997.
Broder, Henryk M. *Hurra, wir kapitulieren! Von der Lust am Einknicken*. Munich: Pantheon, 2007.
Broder, Henryk M. "Toleranz hilft nur den Rücksichtslosen. Dankesrede für den Ludwig-Börne-Preis." *Spiegel Online*, 25 June 2007. http://www.spiegel.de/kultur/gesellschaft/henryk-m-broder-toleranz-hilft-nur-den-ruecksichtslosen-a-490497.html.

Broder, Henryk M. *Entweder Broder: Die Europa Safari*, DVD. Directed by Joachim Schroeder, Claudio Schmid, and Tobias Streck. Munich: Indigo, 2010.

Broder, Henryk M. *Die letzten Tage Europas. Wie wir eine gute Idee versenken*. Munich: Albrecht Knaus Verlag, 2013.

Cheah, Pheng, and Bruce Robbins (eds.). *Cosmopolitics: Thinking and Feeling beyond the Nation*. Minneapolis, MN: University of Minnesota Press, 1998.

Enzensberger, Hans Magnus. *Sanftes Monster Brüssel oder die Entmündigung Europas*. Berlin: Suhrkamp, 2011.

Fine, Robert. *Cosmopolitanism*. London: Routledge, 2007.

Gilman. Sander L., and Lilian M. Friedberg, eds. *A Jew in the New Germany: Henryk Broder*. Urbana: University of Illinois Press, 2004.

Habermas, Jürgen. "Why Europe needs a Constitution." *New Left Review* 11 (2001): 5–26.

Koffman, Eleonore. "Figures of the Cosmopolitan: Privileged Nationals and National Outsiders." In *Cosmopolitanism and Europe*, edited by Chris Rumford, 239–256. Liverpool: Liverpool University Press, 2007.

Laqueur, Walter. *The Last Days of Europe: Epitaph for an Old Continent*. New York, NY: Thomas Dunne, 2007.

Laqueur, Walter. *After the Fall: the End of the European Dream and the Decline of a Continent*. New York, NY: Thomas Dunne, 2012.

Lévy, Bernard-Henri. *Left in Dark Times: a Stand against the New Barbarism*. New York, NY: Random House, 2008.

Markwort, Helmut."Hurra, wir gratulieren! Laudatio für Henryk Broder." http://www.achgut.com/dadgdx/index.php/dadgd/print/002165

Menasse, Robert. *Der Europäische Landbote*. Die Wut der Bürger und der Friede Europas. Vienna: Paul Zsolnay Verlag, 2012.

Menasse, Robert. "FAQ Europa." *Europa-Bottom-Up. Arbeitspapiere zur europäischen Zivilgesellschaft 1*. Berlin: Maecenata Stiftung, 2013, 525.

Menasse, Robert, and Ulrike Guerot. "For a European Republic." http://www.socialeurope.eu/2013/04/for-a-european-republic/.

Meyer, Martin. "Laudatio auf Robert Menasse. Utopie als Freiheit als Kritik. " http://www.nzz.ch/feuilleton/utopie-als-freiheit-als-kritik-1.18300308.

Miller, Michael L., and Scott Ury. "Cosmopolitanism: the End of Jewishness?" *European Review of History: Revue européenne d'histoire* 17, no. 3 (2010): 337–359.

Negt, Oskar. *Gesellschaftsentwurf Europa*. Plädoyer für ein gerechtes Gemeinwesen. Göttingen: Steidl, 2012.

Neilson, Brett. "On the New Cosmopolitanism." *Communal/Plural: Journal of Transnational and Cross-Cultural Studies* 7, no. 1 (1999): 111–124.

Outram, Dorinda. *The Enlightenment*. Cambridge: Cambridge University Press, 2013.

Pinto, Diana. "I'm a European Jew - and No, I'm not Leaving." *New Republic* 26 (March 2015).

Reiss, Hans (ed.). *Kant: Political Writings*. Cambridge: Cambridge University Press, 1991.

Reiter, Andrea. "Die Geschichte der Marranan, ein Paradigma jüdischer Identität in Österreich nach der Shoah? Robert Menasses Die Vertreibung aus der Hölle." *Aschkenas* 20, no. 1 (2011): 167–186.

Reiter, Andrea. *Contemporary Jewish Writing*. Austria after Waldheim. New York: Routledge, 2013.

Schulz, Martin. *Der gefesselte Riese*. Europas letzte Chance. Berlin: Rowohlt, 2013.

JEWS AND THE NEW COSMOPOLITANISM

Drifting towards Cosmopolis

Ruth Novaczek

ABSTRACT
This is an artist's text where an experimental filmmaker explores cosmopolitanism in her own work and that of others. Talking about eclectic cosmopolitan theory, this article maps the role of the wanderer in literature and film. Investigating the cross-pollination of image, sound and text in experimental filmmaking, the writer charts her own position as a mediator of cultural elements in a globalised world, and the implications of feminist subjectivity. The article charts the making of the author's cosmopolitan films made between the late 1980s and 2015, as well as the development of a practice that reflects a transnational consciousness. The text embeds a discussion of diaspora, and of appropriation and citation as the inevitable result of accelerated media profusion. Jewish identity is explored through text, and a dialogue with the world, refracted through subjective bricolage. A contextual introduction to the author's films, this text explores diaspora, nomadism and Jewish and feminist consciousness in a globalised world. The film draws on eclectic sources to describe an identity in flux and a rhizomatic rather than rootless relation to diaspora. The text references Henry James, Rosi Braidotti, Jacques Derrida, Chris Kraus and others to sketch a transnational vision of twenty-first-century cosmopolitanism and *ecriture feminine*.

'He's what's called a cosmopolite' says Isabel Archer in Henry James' *Portrait of a Lady*'. 'That means he's a little of everything and not much of any.'[1] So goes the conversation among Isabel Archer, Henrietta Stackpole and Ralph Touchett on the virtues of travel, so common in Henry James' novels. Of course James is talking about the moneyed and idle rich, but their quest is nonetheless a restless search for home, a nineteenth-century American rootlessness. A little of everything is not such a bad proposition, but making something out of not much might be a strategy towards twenty-first century cosmopolitanism. James' protagonists, compelled to move for reasons of health, leisure or mere curiosity paint a portrait of the *fin de siècle* where travel had become a part of life for the wealthy. The 1890s saw railways, motor cars, aeroplanes and the moving image become viable transports for some. For Henrietta, newly arrived in England from the United States, Ralph's vague sense of belonging nowhere in particular is simply the mark of a leisured dilettante, drifting aimlessly. My own work echoes this rootlessness; my films are made in different locations, cut together, their seams visible, to form the backdrop for the narrative in which I place my

Figure 1. Frame grab from *Sense* (2005).

wandering protagonists. Cutting from New York to Paris, Tel Aviv to Spain, the imaginary landscapes of my fragmented Jewish origins are represented by a world without borders.

When I was living in Brooklyn, the local cab service offered limos to the airport, and I shot a lot of footage of the road to Newark or JFK from the car: the liminal edges of the city. I was hopping back and forth between London and New York, editing in both places. Many twenty-first-century artists, who are often based in two or more cities, are driven by restlessness and wanderlust. My own uprootings and wanderings began in my teens in the twentieth century on 'family' holidays[2] which made me question the idea of a fixed sense of home. I was raised to assimilate outside the walls of our flat in London, and to hide my Jewishness at school. I endured intermittent antisemitism from schoolmates. And I wasn't interested in going to the synagogue every week with my single, divorced mother, sitting upstairs in the women's gallery. The lighting of candles in our gloomy apartment on a Friday night was sad and joyless. My part-Sephardi mother crept around like a mouse. I learnt French with enthusiasm, whereas Hebrew was a chore; I learnt to write but the linguistics weren't taught, so I couldn't grasp the context. But nonetheless that language and its letters were on the periphery of my thinking: not only was G-d invisible, but didn't speak English! Being Jewish was never explained clearly: 'It's both a culture and a religion in one' my mother told me. I felt a sense of threat, menace and perplexity I couldn't properly understand; I wanted a new future, not fear and shadows; I wanted a real life in the world. Helene Cixous writes of the 'exinclusions' associated with the letter "J", the 'stigmata' of 'passovers, transfers, expulsions … doors slammed in your face'.[3] At private school, where I was one of three Jews, I had often been referred to as 'foreign' so I decided I was, just like my refugee father. Jewish cosmopolitanism is rooted in the vicissitudes of the forced flight of previous generations rather than Diogenes' utopian claim to citizenship of the world. To be foreign is to reclaim the potential of the temporary, and to realise the limitations of universal and neutral notions of identity. Stalin's *bezhrodnyi kosmpolit*, rootless cosmopolitans, represented the pro-Western intellectuals who served as a euphemism for Jews: a suspected anti-patriotic fifth column. Where globalisation and the Internet offer a virtual cosmopolitanism, questions of sharing rather than a renewed colonialism prevail, but the virtual traveller is not embodied. The first moment in stepping off a plane, the feel of the air, the smell of a place offers new familiarities, new places and experiences, a broader hospitality. Cixous' exilic voice must nonetheless wrestle with the letter 'J', as a citizen and as the subject of her subjectivity with which she writes herself. The films I'll discuss here involve a filmmaking process that asks how Jewish and other subjectivities might find a transversal and transmedial cosmopolis, where crossing paths, and the traces they leave, shore up a phenomenological mood borne of experience, not dependent on the fixity of place. My own trajectory on this route began when I moved to Italy in my teens to escape London and my life there. I had broken up with my boyfriend and discovered I was adopted. My senses were shattered; I needed to leave the scene of my traumas. I hoped that living in a new language would at least change the view, and it did. That experience established what I now understand as an inevitable cosmopolitanism that springs up in response to the realisation that 'home' can be unstable. And home can be anywhere you embrace the language.

'The human condition itself has become cosmopolitan,' writes Ulrich Beck, and this, he says, requires 'a reconfiguration of our modes of perception'.[4] Artist and educator Gregg Bordowitz challenges the role of perception in the twenty-first century, claiming: 'Some theories attempt to nullify the distinction between a viewing subject and the object of its perception ... Other theories attempt to remove the ground entirely from the field of perception by situating all encounters in a constantly shifting cosmos – like a pool of water swirling in a rainstorm altered drop by drop.'[5] Certainly technology has enabled and been enabled by, a corporate colonialism masquerading as globalism that attempts cognitive mapping to multiply consumption, regardless of the (human) cost. A twenty-first century cosmopolitan is compelled to re-vision herself as an agent of post-colonialism, a fighter against commodification, working from the margins to outsmart the accelerated backlash of power and its minions. Artists tend to enact this resistance by playing with language. On one level my film work critiques the British national identity in which I feel myself trapped by ignoring it altogether. By cross-cutting locations and conversations between cultures, I embed a dimension that evades the frame that entraps me. Cross-pollination, the product of cosmopolitanism, is an energy that any traveller brings to the web that cultures inevitably weave. Crusaders, pilgrims, Vikings, Visigoths, and the Arab, Roman, Persian and Ottoman imperial armies travelled across vast distances and mixed with the populations they ruled. This web is already dense, already rhizomatic in its momentum and shape, forming vernaculars at the borders, or erasing them. Without imperial motive the Bedouin, Berber, Inuit and Maori people roamed according to seasons and traditions. While the cosmopolitan has always existed as the mobile aspect of humanity, today we're indeed asked to reflect on the reconfiguration of our modes of perception. Jews wandering in the wake of empires, or fleeing persecutions were not wanderers or tourists. Neither were African slaves, forced from their homes in any sense the leisured travellers James portrays. The idea that the cosmopolitan is rootless is the slander of old curses[6]. As so many refugees and exiles have made plain, no one leaves home unless force is involved.

The protagonists in my films are cosmopolitan because they're ambiguous, and in *Cheap Philosophy*, I assume a range of disguises, accents and wigs. Both place and being are kaleidoscopic, unbound to national or temporal identity. The characters in *Cheap Philosophy*, and *Rootless Cosmopolitans,* exist in an almost timeless era: the 1950s, the nineteenth century or the 1960s – they're hard to place. Just as location is vague and transgressive in my work, so is identity. Both place and protagonist surf, float, cut and drift in my films, and finally the ending closes the circle, and makes sense of the disparate elements.

Figure 2. Ruth Novaczek in *Cheap Philosophy* (1994).

Today cosmopolitanism might reinscribe the transience or impermanence of origins, and the intellectual mobility of individuals or groups. Jews, among others, have carried ideas and objects across the globe. For Amoz Oz and Fania Oz-Salzberger, 'Jewish continuity, even Jewish uniqueness, depends not on central places, monuments, personalities, or rituals, but rather on written words and an ongoing conversation between generations.' They write of a textual inheritance at the heart of Jewish diasporism: 'Ours is not a bloodline but a text-line.'[7] What then does my generation carry across borders? My grandmother, according to my father, smuggled literature across the non-borders of what was the Austro-Hungarian Empire; she was obviously a woman of the book. So am I. In fact, literature leads me into my films, a development from my pre-film days when I let books guide me with no particular destination, they led me somewhere. As an artist this is at the heart of research: a cultural cosmopolitanism that embraces music, literature, art and cinema from everywhere, which is increasingly easy to access. Conscious of my father's family having moved from one place to another, I adopted 'nomadism' as the basis of my practice, surfing and browsing, wandering through time and place. Walter Benjamin's collage of notes and observations, the *Arcades Project* browses and surfs Parisian culture as a *flaneur* and *bricoleur*.

Begun in 1927, Benjamin's notes, essays and fragments interrogate literary, philosophical and architectural subjects through the device of the Paris arcades, as a documentation of daily life that also surfs the intellectual map of the time. Akin to a collective dream, the texts draw on a vast range of sources, to weave a midrashic cartography. These wanderings through the conceptual arcades of the early twentieth century, published in 1982, anticipate the cut-up, the sprawling historiographies of the future.[8] The forerunner of the department store, the arcades symbolised Paris as the cosmopolitan capital of the nineteenth century; the department store symbolises a cultural browsing that Benjamin anticipates, a loose wandering, and also a gathering together of disparate things. This fragmented narrative, broad and varied, abandoned in 1940 when Benjamin was forced to flee Paris, illustrates a linking and thinking I have applied to the narrative construction of my own films. 'The montage form – with its philosophic play of distances, transitions and intersections, its perpetually shifting contexts and ironic juxtapositions – had become a favorite device in Benjamin's later investigations.'[9]

When the *Arcades Project* was published in German in 1982, I had discovered art, music and film; my father's Super-8 camera became mine and I bought a few rolls of Ektachrome and tried it out. Eventually montage became the means to transpose filmic ideas, images and sounds into a formal practice. At art school identity debates and questions of subjectivity were emerging in work by Black and feminist artists. I was perplexed by a Jewish identity built on the Holocaust, and symbolised by Anne Frank.[10] My graduation film *Tea Leaf* (1986) utilised the raw, direct tone of post-punk to narrativise my own subjectivity and identity in a confessional story which cut and overlaid layers of images and sounds to recount a story of complex identity positions and subjective detail. The voiceover for the film had emerged as I cut together images, and spontaneously remembered experiences I'd repressed. I recorded these fragments on a cassette recorder in the edit room. In retrospect I regret the raw outpouring of trauma, yet the process taught me that film has a magic whereby the submerged story can reveal itself through the juxtaposition of images. It opened a Pandora's Box which, according to the writer Kamila Shamsie, is not just an outpouring of evil, but also of hope. 'Hope's crimes' she writes, 'can only be successful if they are an inside job' in the midst of sorrow.[11] The repressed anger and humiliation in *Tea Leaf* (1983) revealed an inner subjective optimism.

By the late 1980s I wanted to address Jewishness better, to find a contemporary approach to identity. I made *Rootless Cosmopolitans* (1989) at a time when I was looking for a more abstract practice yet I wanted to make a specifically Jewish film. It opens with the declaration 'let's face it, it isn't exactly trendy to be Jewish' and tells the story of the lovers Estelle and Lily. It riffs on Jean-Luc Godard's *Vivre Sa Vie* (1962) and jump cuts between an Israeli storyteller, a refugee from Vienna, and a mother and her daughter among others. I wasn't interested in the representation of 'minorities'. Although most of the characters are culturally mixed, I sought to express a timelessness through the mainly monochrome images. I reworked Jewishness as a cool world of atypical faces. The setting is ambiguous, jumping from a retro 1950s to a punky 1980s, restless, rootless storytelling. Each scenario is a tableau vivant, reframing, re-visioning Jewish women in the world, on the streets, in cafes. In the 1980s subjectivity and cultural identity were being debated but not defined; *Rootless Cosmopolitans* (1989) found a voice for my practice, channelling arthouse cinema to write faces and stories large on a screen.

During the First Gulf War I went to Tel Aviv with the intention of making a film about Israeli leftists, artists and rebels: Ethiopian, Iraqi, Yemeni and Indian Jews and anyone with whom I could get an introduction via my Israeli friends in London. I went there for a year and documented many conversations and interviews on video, which I later edited together as *Talk Israel* (1994). I ended up with a collection of interviews and landscapes, street scenes and still-lives – hours of footage I wanted to make into a documentary. I didn't want to speak for Palestinians, or make a film about the war, or the intifada; I wanted to show Israeli culture as I encountered it, to show how Israelis speak and think, to portray the kinds of conversations people were having. I gleaned stories and backstories while working out my relationship to the political situation. As a non-Israeli Jew I was stimulated by being in Israel, and by the extraordinary sight of a multicultural Jewish state, and also horrified by the occupation and the general intransigence. I reconciled these feelings in a film that cut stories together which showed a spectrum of Israelis of different cultural origins talking about their own notions of self-determination. My film work is characterised by a desire to tell stories from a place that isn't prescribed, to reframe existing narratives, and to find the agency of my own voice and that of others in parallel.

Figure 3. Francesca Souza in *Rootless Cosmopolitans*, and in *The New World*.

In both *Rootless* and *The New World*, I use the same non-actor, Francesca Souza, to represent a Jewish character who isn't entirely European, and doesn't fit the stereotype. Souza is the rootless cosmopolitan, and the citizen of a new world; more than a representation, more than a metonym for something. She is a cosmopolitan film star.

While James' characters may have been born in the United States, they roam; they visit Asia Minor and Europe's major cities, settle in England, Florence or Paris and rarely return to the New World. They exhibit a nostalgia for something lost. Hemingway, James Baldwin and many twentieth-century writers and artists knew the wider world had to be experienced, and their reasons were often political or exilic. How we travel, and have always travelled, from the drug-fuelled trips of the beats and hippies, to social media's virtual spaces, there is a question of worlds, be they physical or mental, and these worlds are connected to stories that travel with the traveller. Karl Ove Knausgaard writes about a postmodern Norwegian author who draws a host of other worlds into the space of the page, and he dislikes Milan Kundera precisely because he stays entirely in the frame of Prague. Isabel Stengers writes of the cosmopolitical as an unknown, constituted by multiple different worlds and the articulations they might produce.[12] If the universe or cosmos is the totality of existence, how then does the personal and political play out across the borders of a globalised world? While riding in the Dublin Film Festival limo in the 1990s the driver told me she'd just dispatched film director Abel Ferrara to his hotel: 'He was drinking vodka in the back and asked if we could get him heroin and marijuana.' I was impressed that film directors could be that decadent, like twentieth-century writers or rock stars. The shamanistic, drug-fuelled journeying of poets and artists is a web of virtual travel before the Internet. As an experimental filmmaker process is key. Burroughs' cut-up films, Barbara Rubin's *Christmas on Earth* and Jack Smith's queer extravaganzas were all made while high; Dylan Thomas drank himself to death.

The experimental film is about process and engagement. The filmmaker serves as a prism, parsing the materials, which is in itself an intellectual cosmopolitanism. Questions of representation are not figurative, but are represented by intuition and thought. Drugs or alcohol reveal Dionysian, multivalent worlds thought through in the edit. Experiment is about language and conversation; it's convivial, deliberately marginal and transgressive. It is a mistake to consider Christopher Nolan's *Memento* (2000) experimental, and many young students, unaware of Maya Deren, Abigail Child or Sadie Benning's films, ignorant of Chantal Akerman's great revolution in bringing the margins into the mainframe, consider Nolan experimental. But *Memento* is just style. Nolan's fragmented narrative and neo-noir tonality mimic the intentionality of engagement that experiment requires. A moving-image practice has many levels and registers, experimental practice plays around with paradigm shifts. It's often the case that experimental filmmakers began as painters, and the layering of motif and form on the ground of the canvas underpins the way I work with film; there's a very deep engagement with the material which is akin to scientific experiment. A dense layering emerges from a range of media in conversation, the traces of music, poetry, art and architecture make up the work to build a transmedial, fragmented cross-pollination. Maya Deren wrote of the vertical poetry that drove her work; P. Adams Sitney called this kind of film visionary, where the layers interact with each other and these multiple worlds and idioms produce new vernaculars. Experimental film is about language; it frames, reconsiders and plays with the semiotics, signs and idioms of all the media it works with, and is perpetually in conversation.

Figure 4. Frame grab from *Radio* (2011).

In New York the discovery of a vibrant multiculture and an engagement with the vernaculars and idioms of the city reveal themselves in the colours, textures and tones of the film footage I collected and the voices I encountered there. *Radio* (2011) mixes these conversations and tones, parses the lyrical tonalities and makes them into a story. Akerman's *News From Home* (1977) takes the lyrical tonalities of New York's streets and cars (shot by filmmaker and cinematographer Babette Mangolte) and overlays them with her letters from her mother. A homesickness pervades the film; the maternal link is distant, epistolary and poetic. The city is the backdrop to a story of diaspora, of homecomings and leaving home. Exhilarated by the underground scene, its music, poetry and film, I made *Cactus Babylon* (1995–6) after a brief period at a reform rabbinical school in London, where I had hoped to deepen my understanding of Jewishness; I failed and went instead to New York. In *Cactus* I overlay a backdrop of streets, traffic and passers-by with questions about what home is. Friends spoke about their feelings of loss and displacement coupled with a longing for an abstract, cosmopolitan idea of home, which the city fulfilled. If my own cosmopolitanism was about running away from a home I didn't feel at home in, then anywhere could be home for a while, and exile and alienation were replaced by new voices, and their different, American rhythms and inflections. When I left New York these tones resonated; finding myself back in the UK on an artist residency in Devon, I reworked the US footage, remixing New York in an English village. Actually it wasn't an ordinary village. I was at Dartington Hall, which had an excellent art school, and a constant flow of visiting artists from all over the world. I was a dreaming, virtual traveller in England working in a New York vernacular, and processed the memories and the footage that turned into concise, nuanced films that uncovered a way to speak more subjectively, mixing fact, fiction, sound and image in the process. I was reading Chris Kraus' *I Love Dick,* a mish-mash of a diary-novel which surfed across genre and ventured into a new kind of feminist subjectivity that was new and great for me.[13] I was beginning to understand that citizenship of the world might involve more, not less interiority. Working in solitude, my cosmopolitanism was becoming somewhat theoretical, yet linked to the visiting artists who came to Devon with new ideas that were vibrant and exciting.[14] My own studio practice consisted of reading, playing music, writing and assembling film clips. Cheap video-editing technology, the Internet and experience created expanded spaces to think about framing and understanding the world of past, present and future. Could the tenses coexist as parallel universes, places, voices?

Radio and *The New World* are twenty-first century films that mine both biographical detail and the accelerated change of the moment to build complex narratives that serve as a barometer, for myself and my self in the world. Figure 5 was shot at the beach near Jaffa, where Palestinian and Jewish families gather with friends and family to enjoy elaborate meals by the sea. These picnics illustrate the collision of ancient and modern, where Jews and Arabs from many cultural backgrounds exist communally, and share the same space. My work discusses the co-existence of culture and daily life. Rory Stewart, writing of Bruce Chatwin's travelogue/novel *The Songlines* notes that:

> Scraps of academic research, lines of poetry, epiphanies on desert tracks, fragments of ancient lore; references to Muslim pilgrims, Indian monks, Lapland legends, modern Florida, Elizabethan plays; reflections on Stone-Age humans, nomadic tribes, and ancient myths, are combined to suggest that humans are forged and defined by two things – 'the beast in the dark' and 'the nomadic instinct'.[15]

Figure 5. Frame grab from *Radio* (2011).

Figure 6. Bobby draws a genealogical map in *Cactus Babylon*, New York City (1995).

These crossings of genre and narrative musing Stewart finds in Chatwin's text operate in my own film work as research and practice: a reading and thinking that result in audio-visual patterns that can be read and analysed. One (research) feeds the other (thinking), and this experience – of travelling, of reading – is worked into the structure of *Radio* and *The New World,* where found footage and documentation archives the moments I parse, juggle and play around with. The elements that will eventually become films are borrowed and remixed from a common heritage whose borders are endlessly fluid. This practice allows an epistemological field for abstract play with text, sound and image, and also with cinema itself. The fragments of twentieth-century films are a cultural commons Kenneth Goldsmith understands as our collective inheritance from which we should and must borrow and cite.[16] Other elements in these films include video diaries, music and other materials, and the borrowings are thrown into the same pot, their borders non-existent, overlapping. In this way a dialogue is created between the personal and collective narrative. Citation plays a cosmopolitical role in historiography, recontextualising an original, or foregrounding that which has been overlooked. A narrative overdubbed with anomalous sounds, cities jammed together, cut-up conversations and citations, produced *The New World* (2014) which ostensibly proposes a first-person, yet voices a polyphonic kaleidoscope. A cosmopolitan vision I only glimpsed decades ago, draws on dystopia and dreams to channel a wider world, leaping freely in time and space: a leap of faith. The film plays with questions of Jewish, transnational, feminist identity in flux, and of a nostalgia for a lost modernism: the broken technologies of the past, the off-kilter, the marginal modernism of memory which Svetlana Boym identifies as the off-modern.[17]

The film speaks of women protagonists who seek a role in a global world yet struggle to find a transnational rhythm within the accelerated change and neo-patriarchal formations of the twenty-first century. Reappraising the twentieth century through cinema and literature the film presents the cosmopolitan as perpetually fluid, in constant motion, and above all intersectional. The older, ageing, twenty-first-century woman is a scholar who takes available resources and reconfigures them, like making rugs from rags. The film itself posits a Venn diagram's shape to sketch a new world where characters and places intersect and overlap. All my completed films, shot over three decades in New York, London, Paris, Cairo, Morocco and Tel Aviv and many other locations, explore the fluidity of historical identity and the fragmentary nature of memory. I evoke the traveller as a feminist adventurer who enacts Jewish nomadism as a restless protagonist who ventriloquises several voices and registers, rhizomatic rather than rootless, evoking a world where memory and myth link, think and overlap. A nomadism of necessity rather than of privilege, almost random, dependent on either friendship or more often, on work, and cheap flights.

Rosi Braidotti writes, '[t]he cultural mutations, which I call "the cultural cartography"' are, she says, 'what is happening to bodies, identities, belongings, in a world that is technologically mediated, ethnically mixed and changing very fast in all sort of ways'.[18] She suggests a nomadic citizenship that disconnects nationality from ethnicity, to create a flexible subjectivity. *The New World* is about a post-national uncertainty that proposes the gendered protagonist, 'she' as vulnerable and struggling with what can't be seen in the film: the male gaze. She is looking out and she also looks at the future, the past, home and of the world, on the threshold of something that is in formation, becoming. The sexuality of my protagonists is ambiguous because they're presented as neutral but there is rarely a male in the frame; these women present contradiction and uncertainty as the norm. What Braidotti describes as 'a process of abandoning identity and entering in the construction of subjectivity, subjectivity being per definition transversal, collective' is happening in the way the film cuts between voices, time and place, to construct an image that is not graven but inscribed as if on a scroll that is continuous, becoming.

I map a Derridean new cartography that seeks a place of refuge but not roots. Braidotti's cultural mapping surfs the flux of things, and Beck's 'ambivalences in a milieu of blurring differentiations and cultural contradictions'[19] construct a map for a feminist cinematic ontology. *The New World* ends with the protagonist claiming we need 'a new password' as the image shows a ship sailing upriver. This journey is not about a salmon swimming upriver to spawn, but one that has no idea of a destination, that has no true north. The ship has run backwards at another point in the film, its direction is uncertain. The 'zombie apocalypse' envisaged in the film is the paranoid shadow of a new language emerging: a subjective Esperanto that enables a new configuration of home, of orientation as metaphor. *Cactus Babylon* explores both home and orientation through interviews and exchanges with New Yorkers. An Italian American talks about the sense of an Italian origin that imbues her daily American life; a relative of mine draws our family tree which covers several continents.

Kwame Anthony Appiah writes that Judaism had travelled to every continent without an evangelical motive, and of the vexed contrast between nationalism and cosmopolitanism. He describes a centuries-old cross-pollination to invoke questions of choice between 'mother or motherland' when the cosmopolitan is faced with war.[20] War is the cosmopolitan's stumbling block, the Israel/Palestine conflict, and the multiplying civil wars in the world loom large and larger in my work: a shadow of a doubt, a *noir*-ish uncertainty. This weighty ambivalence is evident in Chantal Akerman's films that address identity in Paris, Brussels, Tel Aviv or New York through a prism that refuses binaries or fixed positions, which Akerman herself relates to the idolatry of commercial film and capitalism. She echoes Levinas' insistence on facing the Other: her lens is facing her subject and her subject faces her. Helene Cixous famously advocates blowing up the language of patriarchy in *The Laugh of the Medusa* but language is the law.[21] Akerman takes the law into her own hands. For Jacques Derrida legal questions are irrelevant in the cosmopolitan quest for a place of refuge, mapping instead the possibility of a future cartography. 'Where have we received the image of cosmopolitanism from? *And what is happening to it?,*' Derrida asks.[22] The disturbance at the heart of my films, a sense of loss, of trauma, and of unbelonging, comes from this quest for a cosmopolitanism hidden in the binaries of conflict; I can imagine myself a citizen of the world, but it is a troubled and unstable world. The *noir*ish tonalities in many of my films, particularly *Radio* (2011) reveal a dystopian shadow in imagining utopian futures. In the nineteenth and twentieth centuries, Ellis Island was a conduit for the songs, stories, recipes, superstitions and values of the old world. New York was one of the great cosmopolitan centres in the mid to late twentieth century. But in New York people speak English. Its cosmopolitanism isn't multilingual, it's assimilative. Derrida's French secular cosmopolitanism refutes ethnic or religious difference in favour of republicanism. In Britain, we're not citizens but subjects, and assimilation is almost impossible. Better then to become a citizen of the world again, to eschew roots. My film practice is not only without borders but also jumps around in time and space, a rhizomatic rootless dialogue with the world. The process of reading, travelling, talking and thinking allows me to voice ambivalence, explore nuance, while warning of a possible world to come that is dystopian and menacing. By mixing *noir* with comedy, aphorism with documentary, my films attempt to address subjectivity Jewishly, that is, from the margins.

The cosmopolitan's world is wide and varied. In sharp contrast to the parochial or national, we are not bound to the land; we have no stake in it. (Israel of course is the grand exception). I started making films in the twentieth century and now I'm in the twenty-first trying to make sense of identity in all its facets: gender, culture, nature, citizenship. My work resists nationalism but my films don't believe in solutions. They're deeply pessimistic, full of aphorism and wry melancholic humour. Isn't this so Jewish, twentieth-century Jewish? The cosmopolitan is a twentieth-century figure: complex, multivalent, entertaining layers of language and paradoxical ideas. The cosmopolitan tries to embody multiculture in a cosmopolitical journey towards citizenship of a new world through dialogue and exchange. In a twenty-first-century context this seems naïve, absurd, lacking irony; cosmopolitanism nurtures progress and imagines hope because of a refusal to let go of the optimism of modernism.

In Mohsin Hamid's book *How To Get Filthy Rich in Rising Asia* the fictional protagonist reads 'breathtakingly boring foreign novels' in order to 'understand distant lands that because of globalisation are increasingly affecting life in your own'.[23] The writer Karl Ove Knausgaard has given up fictional characters in his novels altogether, and Elena Ferrante hides her true identity in order to have the freedom to write her own life. I have given up national identity beyond the fact that I have a British passport, but London isn't a backdrop for my particular subjectivity as Norway and Naples are the fabric into which Knausgaard and Ferrante inscribe themselves. The detail of daily life in London has no poetic resonance. As a city it cannot stand for anything metonymically, whereas New York's streets offer a cosmopolitan palette that can easily cut in Cairo, or Paris or Tel Aviv. My films reinscribe a lyrical cartography that cannot assimilate the grim Dickensian detail of London. The redbrick apartment building I grew up in just doesn't work on film, and the green of London's parks evokes Constable or Gainsborough, the weather unsuited to my interior aesthetic that crash edits one city with another. My recent films quote more and more from world literature, and I use the voice of others to assemble a collage of myself too, juxtaposing one anomaly with another, a cut-up that reveals surprising truths. I suppose I'm riffing on assimilation, or is it an unwillingness to be too 'niche' as the margins are described these days?

Working on my PhD on experimental film and feminism, I found I was reading novels, not theory, to find my way, because politics and philosophy are embedded in stories and always have been. The world as represented by social media is in a state of frenzied cross-referencing, tweets and assertions. Filmic cosmopolitanism moves toward the what-if's of self that spring from a perplexed sense of home. From the puritans to the Zionists, settlement has its price. As Phillip Roth remarks in *Operation Shylock*, Zionism, having restored the Jews to health and geographical unity in Israel, 'has tragically ruined its own health and must now accede to vigorous Diasporism'.[24] Ossification, tradition and orthodoxy emanate from the land and its borders, and the rhizome with its subterranean networks and links is the better structure for flux.

Albert Memmi, a Tunisian Jew, wrote that his ambiguous relation to identity emerged from the sense that he was 'a sort of half-breed of colonization', understanding everyone because he belonged completely to no one.[25] For those of us making films which try to understand the politics of our subjectivity, these positions are often called into the equation, an attempt to make sense of unbelonging. But the traditional nomad operates as part of a tribal system that has to do with survival. It would be impossible in this century to call myself 'a nomad' or simply a 'Jew' or a 'woman' and continue to make complex work. Experimental film demands a perpetual motion, a journeying into uncertainty, or it dies. In *The Songlines*, Bruce Chatwin proposes the idea that all indigenous peoples have been nomadic, thus their connection to the land is fluid, intuiting the earth or the sea, narrating their journeying.[26] I reimagine a cosmopolitanism open to discourse, intuiting a course. My films seek a password to cities of refuge in a world of *ecriture feminine* as we write ourselves into our multi-faceted and visionary perception. *The New World* envisions and reclaims many links to the old. In her book *Kartography,* Kamila Shamsie writes of Eratosthenes as 'the grandfather of cartography' who was the first to make a distinction between scientific and literary mapping, where Homer's *Odyssey* and sailors' accounts served as valid maps, and Shamsie applies this to Karachi's landmarks and stories which serve as signs, less about moving from one point to another than a means to 'hear the heartbeat of a place'.[27] History and memory diverge in a space of ludic and intuitive motives in *The New World* seeking the heartbeat of place and space. Experiment works from the margins, as do those who imagine a better world that cannot lie or sell itself for empty slogans. *The New World* represents a journey through a practice that intersects questions of identity, culture, history and gender; but these are embedded or submerged, reflecting the nuance that subjectivity requires in transforming autobiography into autofiction as self-inscription.

Notes

1. James, *Portrait of a Lady,* 204.
2. We were barely a family. My mother and I would travel together while my brother was in boarding school. My first trip abroad, around 1963, was to the former Yugoslavia.
3. Cixous, "Namesakes – No!," 1–5.
4. Beck, *Cosmopolitan Vision,* 1–4.
5. Bordowitz, "Programme Director's letter for Low-Residency MFA."
6. Stalin saw intellectuals who opposed patriotism as rootless cosmopolitans and this term is understood to be a euphemism for Jews during the Soviet purges.
7. Oz and Oz-Salzberger, *Jews and Words,* 15.
8. Benjamin, *Arcades Project.*
9. Eiland and McLaughlin, *Arcades Project,* xi.
10. Children's television at the time showed several adaptations of her diary, and often she was portrayed as a prim, middle-class English girl. Even then, in the 1960s, this perplexed me: she was assimilated!
11. Shamsie, *Broken Verses,* 144.
12. Stengers, "The Cosmopolitical Proposal," 994–1003.
13. Kraus, *I Love Dick.*
14. D.J. Spooky, a.k.a. Paul Miller, came with his remixes and mash-ups that were a revelation for me in using media in an unorthodox way.
15. Stewart "Walking with Chatwin."
16. Cottrell and Goldsmith in *Uncreative Writing: Managing Language in the Digital Age* explain how we already cite, and perhaps our references are so deeply ingrained it would be bolder to refuse to cite, to consider borrowing or appropriation as a collective commons.
17. Boym, "Nostaligic Technology."
18. Interview with Rosi Braidotti.
19. Beck, *Cosmopolitan Vision,* 5.
20. Appiah, *Ethics of Identity,* 239.
21. Cixous, *Laugh of the Medusa.*
22. Derrida, *Cosmopolitanism and Forgiveness,* 3.
23. Hamid. *How to Get Filthy Rich in Rising Asia,* 17.
24. Roth, *Operation Shylock,* 44.
25. Memmi, *Dominated Man,* 49.
26. Chatwin, *The Songlines,* 272.
27. Shamsie, *Kartography,* 180.

References

Appiah, Kevin Anthony. *The Ethics of Identity*. Princeton, NJ: Princeton University Press, 2005.
Beck, Ulrich. *The Cosmopolitan Vision*. Translated by Ciaran Cronin. Cambridge: Polity Press, 2006.
Benjamin, Walter. *The Arcades Project*. Edited by Rolf Tiedemann and translated by Howard Eiland and Kevin McLaughlin. New York: Belknap Press, 2002.
Bordowitz, Greg. "Programme Director's Letter for Low-Reisdency MFA." School of Art Institute of Chicago. http://www.saic.edu/academics/graduatedegrees/lowresmfa/letterfromtheprogramdirector/
Boym, Svetlana. "Nostalgic Technology: Notes for an Off-Modern Manifesto." http://www.svetlanaboym.com/manifesto.htm
Braidotti, Rosi. "On Nomadism." European Alternatives. http://euroalter.com/2010/on-nomadism-interview-with-rosi-braidotti
Cactus Babylon. Directed by Ruth Novaczek, 1995.
Chatwin, Bruce. *The Songlines*. London: Vintage, 1998.
Cheap Philosophy. Directed by Ruth Novaczek, 1994.
Christmas on Earth. Directed by Barbara Rubin, 1963.
Cixous, Hélène. "The Laugh of the Medusa. Translated by Keith Cohen and Paula Cohen." *Signs* 4, no. 1 (1976): 875–893.
Cixous, Hélène. *"Namesakes – No!" In Portrait of Jacques Derrida as a Young Jewish Saint, translated by Beverley Bie Brahim*. New York: Columbia University Press, 2004.
Cottrell, Robert C., and Kenneth Goldsmith. *Uncreative Writing: Managing Language in the Digital Age*. New York: Columbia University Press, 2011.
Derrida, Jacques. *On Cosmopolitanism and Forgiveness*. London: Routledge, 2001.
Eiland, Howard, and Kevin McLaughlin, trans. *The Arcades Project*. Cambridge, MA: The Belknap Press, 2002.
Hamid, Mohsin. *How to Get Filthy Rich in Rising Asia*. Hamish Hamilton, 2013.
James, Henry. *The Portrait of a Lady*. New York: Norton, 1995.
Kraus, Chris. *I Love Dick*. Los Angeles: Semiotext(e) Native Agents, 2006.
Memento. Directed by Christopher Nolan. Hollywood, CA: Newmarket Films, 2000.
Memmi, Albert. *Dominated Man: Notes Towards a Portrait*. Orion, 1968.
News from Home. Directed by Chantal Akerman, 1977.
Oz, Amos, and Fania Oz-Salzberger. *Jews and Words*. New Haven, London: Yale University Press, 2012.
Radio. Directed by Ruth Novaczek, 2011.
Rootless Cosmopolitans. Directed by Ruth Novaczek, 1989.
Roth, Phillip. *Operation Shylock*. London: Cape, 1993.
Shamsie, Kamila. *Broken Verses*. Boston, MA: Houghton Miflin Harcourt, 2005.
Shamsie, Kamila. *Kartography*. London: Bloomsbury, 2002.
Stengers, Isabelle. "The Cosmopolitical Proposal." In *Making Things Public: Atmospheres of Democracy*, edited by Bruno Latour and Peter Weibel. Cambridge, Mass: MIT Press, 2005.
Stewart, Rory. "Walking with Chatwin." NYR Daily Blog, 25 June 2012. *The New York Review of Books*. http://www.nybooks.com/daily/2012/06/25/
Talk Israel. Directed by Ruth Novaczek, 1994.
Tea Leaf. Directed by Ruth Novaczek, 1983.
The New World. Directed by Ruth Novaczek, 2014.

Maximalism as a Cosmopolitan strategy in the art of Ruth Novaczek and Doug Fishbone

Rachel S. Garfield

ABSTRACT
This article looks at the work of the experimental filmmaker Ruth Novaczek and the artist Doug Fishbone to think through the relationship between the cosmopolitan imagination, Jewishness and the visual arts. The author suggests through her analysis of their artwork that both artists proffer a cosmopolitan subject that arises out of their Jewish subjectivity. The author does this in different ways, discussing the artworks both in their various forms as well as the subject matter within the films. The author thinks through two recent publications on the cosmopolitan and art by Marsha Merskimmon and Nikos Papastergiadis to discuss what is at stake in the cosmopolitan in relation to the two artist case studies. Central to her argument is a maximalist tendency that goes against the usual current paradigmatic trend of the 'long look' that was first articulated by the influential André Bazin as more real than the dialectical editing techniques argued (and performed) by Sergei Eisenstein. But neither is she arguing for a return to Eisenstein. Maximalism, as offered by the work of these artists, signifies an excessive overloading that allows the viewer to insert themselves into the narrative of the work through the editing, the collage and in the density of the range of the material. Finally, the author brings the formal discussion into dialogue with the explicit meaning developed by the artwork. Each of these artists proffer an unstable subject that is profoundly formed out of their Jewish and Diasporic subjectivity. This arises not just out of the formal structural scaffolding of the work but in terms of the subject matter within the work. They both explicitly use Jewish cultural references as normative navigational tools in the work and as a way of forming their cultural worlds. These references range from dialogues of Jewish characters in cinema, to Jewish jokes and use of Yiddish or Hebrew. Importantly Jewish religion or ritual is absent. For both of these artists the Holocaust is a backdrop but not as way to valorise a victim status, but as a way to reach out to a wider humanity and to understand its legacies. This is done through multi-positionality and the questioning of what a 'home' might be outside of an attachment to a nation-state or a singular geographic location and embracing that estrangement. In sum, the author argues that the work offers a reiterative provisionality as a refusal to judge or to know the world; instead there is an attempt to incorporate its complexities and range into the vision of the work, challenging the viewer to identify what is at stake in the work and in the subject.

I will be looking at the artworks by Ruth Novaczek and Doug Fishbone in order to pose the question of how art can reconstitute the subject and what possibilities this offers for re-imagining the cosmopolitan. I will discuss theories of the cosmopolitan as they form through the artwork, first setting out the context briefly in art theory through which I analyse these works. Ruth Novaczek and Doug Fishbone are brought into focus here due to their use of collage that offers an alternative paradigm to the prevalent trend in much lens-based art of neo-minimalist tropes such as Sam Taylor Wood or Bill Viola, to name just two high-profile examples. This alternative is what I will identify as maximalist, and one that I will delineate through the case studies themselves. The aim is not to bring these artists into direct contrast but for each to exist as parallel examples of the aesthetic that I am proposing. Most mainstream narrative film uses the shot/reverse-shot sequence to establish a visual trajectory that informs the viewer of the relationships and the direction that the narrative is taking. In artists' film, this has given way to the use of a series of long shots as the central paradigm that slows down the classic mainstream trajectory. This long-shot trope, I suggest, establishes a focus of linear singularity. By contrast both artists I focus on here, in their own ways, use collage as a means to invoke a world-view that encompasses a multivalent vision in a single sweep of thinking, that is, within a single passage of video or artwork. The interlinking of images in a way that is fragmented, overlapping and non-linear is particular and it is this particular formal device that I will be analysing as a feature of the cosmopolitan in the case studies.

In order to do this I must first introduce the main body of recent writing that approaches the idea of the cosmopolitan in art in the UK, which is the contribution by the art historian Marsha Merskimmon and the theorist Nikos Papastergiadis. They both posit the cosmopolitan as important ground that artists have identified and taken on. I am an artist and my own field of study is art. It is this that gives rise to the aims and interests here. In order to look at how the cosmopolitan subject can offer insights through the artwork I must first look briefly and therefore broadly at the way explorations into subjectivity have been characterised in the prevalent debates in recent decades in art specifically. These of course are informed by broader discussion on the cosmopolitan but the scope of this paper requires that I focus on Merskimmon and Papastergiadis.

Key art critics, particularly those clustered around the influential *October* journal [1], have declared since the 1990s that exploring identity in art is narcissistic and that personal narrative is self-serving.[2] These claims have effectively marginalised work that uses the 'self' in the arts that is exemplified by Ruth Novaczek's oeuvre, which has been given relatively little critical attention and not had the visibility that her peers whose work does not deal with identity have had. In many cases I would concur with their argument that a focus on personal narrative or the self as a conduit for affirming identity is in many ways problematic.[3] The issue at stake is to ask what purpose art serves. The criticism that marginalised this kind of work was exactly that it is conservative as opposed to avant-garde – as the art historian Benjamin Buchloh stated in the aforementioned discussion within the Art journal, *October*:

> I'm not sure that the project is to critique identity.[4] I'm not sure that's the project of some of these artists. They would much rather be associated with a project of affirming and constructing identity. The articulation of the work is an act of empowerment, of conscription, of consolidating identity.[5]

It was this discussion that proffered a turning away from focusing on one's own cultural identity in mainstream art circles within a climate in the art world that art was to critique society rather than conserve tradition. I would agree that the work of personal narrative that Buchloh refers to here does not aim to rethink subjectivity in a complex world, but serves to assert the subject's special qualities because of the history of marginalisation and victimhood as an ethnic insiderist manoeuvre. However, not all work exploring identity has this feature. The work I am championing does not. Instead it uses a heterogeneous approach to narrative and identity through a maximalist aesthetic. Maximalism offers a complex subjectivity that I will explain through the case studies. The complexity that the work constitutes could be seen as the difference between an impulse to 'find oneself' compared with the impulse to question why identity might matter and how this can open up possibilities for the future. Novaczek's *Rootless Cosmopolitans* is an example of this as she posits Jewish identity through the question *What is a Jew?* at the opening the film, not as statement of fact. Furthermore, the film refuses to give a singular answer, instead delivering a wide range of possible narratives that all revolve around the question posed at the beginning of the film.

To situate cosmopolitanism and Jewish identity together may be problematic, even after Kwame Anthony Appiah's important contribution to the idea of rooted cosmopolitanism. Jewish cosmopolitanism implies the foregrounding of the culture as the identity of origin, which in turn may seem borne out of a need to hold on to the nostalgic desire to belong to a cohesive community. I have long argued for a relationship to culture as being citational and against the tendency towards nostalgia or imagined cohesion in relation to identity politics that seem particularly prevalent in relation to Jewish artists. Certainly in curatorial choices if not the artists' own, there is a domination of the impulse to either celebrate Jewishness that can be seen through examples of many Jewish museums[6] or to mine one's history for roots or atrocities, Judy Chicago and Susan Hiller being prominent examples.[7] I would go so far as to say that the desire for wholeness and restitution from a victim past is often the driver of Jewish work rather than the seemingly existential isolation of the cosmopolitan ideal of the 'citizen of the world'.[8] The overwhelming majority of artists who are Jewish choose not to make Jewish identity figure in their working practice in any way. Even when they do disavow intentionality, which in itself declares a hegemonic trope of disinterested internationalist uniformity, that is actually a Euro-American aesthetic.[9] There are of course notable exceptions such as the aforementioned Susan Hiller or Judy Chicago, but these are exceptions which prove the rule, for neither made 'Jewish work' until they were established in their reputation and for both these artists, the 'Jewish work' is the most conservative in concept of their respective oeuvres. So the apparently existing dilemma is whether to make celebratory Jewish work or work that buries any visibility of Jewishness at all.[10] I consider this a reductive binary and a lost opportunity to rethink a more radical Jewish subjectivity through the visual imagination. Doug Fishbone and Ruth Novaczek's work offer such a radical Jewish subjectivity through a multivalent collage that gives form to the complexities of negotiating a Jewish lived reality.

My focus and emphasis here is not to argue for a redefinition of cosmopolitanism but to find a language to talk about the subject in art. I also do not aim to privilege the 'theory' in order to use the art as examples of the theoretical positions, but instead to analyse the art for what it can offer to inspire and expand our understanding of subjectivity. I will demonstrate that Doug Fishbone and Ruth Novaczek find a way to make work that is infused with questions of cultural identity (in this case Jewish) while suggesting a position that has no truck with ethnic insiderist tendencies of re-inscribing difference as a special case. I will argue that their work creates an equalising force of chains of equivalence that the cosmopolitan demands and that I will argue for in these artworks: a cosmopolitan outlook not so much grounded in particularity but having a citational relational tension with it.

With this in mind, I would situate Natan Sznaider as an important voice in my argument as someone who discusses the relationship between universalism and particularism as being 'a co-existing pair'. In *Memories of Europe: Cosmopolitanism and its Others*, Daniel Levy and Natan Sznaider argue that we should be talking about cosmopolitisation as a process rather than cosmopolitanism as a noun. They suggest that we should be articulating an on-going and incomplete process rather than using the ahistoricity and fixity of the noun. Both artists I write about suggest Jewishness as an incomplete process. Furthermore both artists celebrate the Jewishness as an on-going process through the maximalist methodology of overloading imagery that doesn't cohere. Fishbone, for example, montages multiple still images gleaned from the Internet back to back. Sometimes the images make sense and sometimes not, the viewing process being one of moving between the images in a way that doesn't offer a seamless denouement. The lack of ending or linear narrative drive is analogous to what Levy and Sznaider is proposing. It is cosmopolitisation in action through the video.

Cosmopolitisation would acknowledge, they argue, that the central plank of cosmopolitanism, that is European Enlightenment, continues to exclude and particularise (the former resulting from the latter). They argue for cosmopolitisation as a way of ousting the parochialism of Europe.[11] In this spirit I would consider Jewish cosmopolitanism not so much as 'rooted', but more of the relationship of an on-going dialectic. Both artists' work offer a response in formal terms to the criticism of Levy and Sznaider and possibly to the idea of a local (that is, European) cosmopolitanism. For Novaczek, the device of taking sound and image apart so that the viewer cannot tell how the cultural references relate to each is a process that the viewer takes part in, by trying to make sense of the disjuncture and in the case of Fishbone, the same device used differently, as well as the incoherent sequences of images the disjunction between the narrative and image the viewer partakes in the process through trying to make sense of the way the visuals lend meaning to the narration.

In sum, I will argue that suturing these two notions – of Jewish and Cosmopolitan — together may offer, through a dialectical relationship, a way out of the impasse many find themselves in, of a desire to belong to a single or singular community, however one perceives that to be at the same time as positioning oneself through the ethical position of being part of a world community.

In *Contemporary Art and The Cosmopolitan Imagination,* Marsha Merskimmon makes her case for art and a cosmopolitan vision as a reinvigorating force in art: 'It is my contention that a cosmopolitan imagination is key to engendering a global sense of ethical and political responsibility at the level of the subject.'[12] Throughout her book she identifies the cosmopolitan as exemplified through a nomadic art practice that situates oneself at home or enables one to make a home in any location, moving home from 'a fixed site to negotiable situation'[13], and does this in various ways using a range of examples throughout the book. Merksimmon reclaims and links the terms nomadism and cosmopolitanism, terms that have both been linked historically as a slur towards Jews. Her linkage is thus not surprising. The sedentary life in the Enlightenment was identified with the development of cultural and artistic sophistication and Jews were considered as nomads and therefore lacking in substance. Thus the term has gone from a nineteenth-century insult borne out of the Enlightenment ideology of progress, where the nomad is seen to be less developed than the sedentary communities of Europe, to a contemporary metaphorical figure that represents our epoch of global travel and internationalism in the Global North at least. Like the nomad, the cosmopolitan is also a term that has undergone a process of recuperation: from the nineteenth-century attack on the Jew (and its Stalinist resurrection), the perceived unbelonging of Jews and 'rootless cosmopolitanism', to the reconfiguration of the 'nomad' by important political and cultural theorists Chantal Mouffe, Rosie Braidotti and Iain Chambers. For Merskimmon the artist as nomad, making a home wherever she shows, is the key plank of her book.

What is at stake for me in this article and why I champion the artists Ruth Novaczek and Doug Fishbone, in the ways that I am describing throughout this article, particularly later through the second half where I describe the work in detail, is that their work offers a completely different example of what cosmopolitan art could be that is in opposition to Merskimmon's popular argument for the nomadic artist. Both artists work with the idea of the global within the imagery and the textual narratives of their work, not in following a nomadic lifestyle themselves. The work thus operates on a metaphorical and analogous level rather than the literal methodology that much of the work within Merskimmon's book follows. Within the context of the art world or academia the nomadic subject is a figure of privilege that excises the politics of lived relations, which endows it with both specificity and urgency.[14] In art, it does this in a way that through symbolic or poetic gestures elevates metaphor and glosses over an often-brutal reality. The emergence and on-going popularity of the artist Francis Alÿs for example is a testament to the prevalence and popularity of the nomadic as a beacon in art for a cosmopolitan ideal.[15]

The other writer within the recent interest in the cosmopolitan and art is Nicos Papastergiadis, who, in *Cosmopolitanism and Culture*, offers a slightly different emphasis and engagement with the trope of the cosmopolitan and what is at stake and much closer to the outlook of Novaczek and Fishbone, who are locally grounded and globally oriented.

> Although globalization is increasingly identified as a threat, it is equally clear that the desire to stage an open conversation between the local and the global has emerged as a core aim among artists. This broad expression of aesthetic cosmopolitanism is evident in a range of locally grounded and globally oriented artistic tendencies.[16]

What is at stake for me in the formulation of the artist as globetrotter engaged in the business of biennale exhibiting is a good example of how class is conveniently put aside in assumptions about the conditions of cultural identity. In any event, the artist who gets to travel the world belongs to a privileged class of artist who doesn't make herself at home by investment and engagement in the places of exhibition but instead stays a few days here or there or a few months/weeks here or there in a residency supported by a network of grants and bursaries supported mostly by national interests and sometimes by wealthy philanthropy. In other words, I would argue that this is a form of cultural colonisation and soft power closely tied to the neoliberal ideals: (much like the criticism of Cosmopolitanism itself that has been argued as a privileged paradigm for the globetrotting Westerner). These artists are also a tiny minority: most artists work under precarious local conditions to support themselves and their practice. The trope of the cosmopolitan artist through the representation of a sense of the global (making work about the wars that happen elsewhere or the poverty and so forth) is not the same as the subject position that the artist themselves may inhabit. There is a slippage here between the abstract and concrete conditions of the artist in the global world.

It is in these definitions that my own outlook emerges through the choices of art practice to call up within this purview. My own examples exemplify a rebuttal of the pervasive cinematic trope that requires big teams, big budgets (in artistic terms) and the need to travel to shoot what is 'elsewhere'. They offer an alternative to expensive installations that require fabricators and a team of technicians. Instead Ruth Novaczek and Doug Fishbone work with lo-fi imagery that is accessible without a budget on equipment that is generally affordable.[17]

Finally I would suggest that in usual discussions of so-called issue-based work, and certainly in my own experience of discussing my own video work in public, content tends to override form in analysis generally. I will argue here that one constitutes the other in a relationship that is hard to disentangle but important to consider equally.

I will also argue that the importance of work that questions form as well as content allows for agency of the viewer through the imagination and slippage of repetition and parallel editing. Both the artists that I consider eschew visual narrative structure in favour of a re-invented parallel editing. According to Mary Ann Doane, there are three types of editing in early cinema, each of which creates its own drama.[18] The first is shot followed by reverse shot, as described earlier, using repetition to create narrative coherence. The second is the chase, popularised through comedy and thrillers, which serves to re-inscribe linear time. The third is parallel editing which creates a jump in space and time, implying that two events occur simultaneously. Parallel editing, unlike the classic shot/reverse shot, is editing where there is no linear accumulation of meaning, but instead a disjunctive range of shots that fold in a leap of time or space creating meaning in a different way. While the chase edit 'aggregates regularity' and creates normality, parallel editing creates suspense through desire and fear, which, according to Janet Harbord, 'displaces the temporal logic of film, creating a simultaneity that requires the spectator to insert herself into the relationship between images, to forge connections'.[19] Parallel editing is essentially a kind of montage that can offer an effect of collage as it venerates contingency like no other cinematic form. It is an edit that has a gap in meaning through its contingent incoherence. In this way it privileges heterogeneity rather than singularity as an equalising force that works as a powerful metaphor for the cosmopolitan in ways that I will explore through the case studies.

Ruth Novaczek (b. 1956) is a filmmaker who emerged in the 1980s out of the famous film department of the then St Martins in central London. Doug Fishbone (b. 1969) is a younger artist who did his MA at Goldsmiths London, graduating in 2003 Novaczek has generally screened at film festivals and Fishbone exhibited in galleries, however there is some crossover.

Ruth Novaczek uses video, working with montage through parallel editing, and Doug Fishbone uses Internet-derived stills but choreographing them through repetition and collage. The disjunction that collage and montage affords allows for the interplay between the rational observation, analysis and affect or excess where repetition opens up a possibility for a re-interpretation by the viewer. Both artists play with this trope in slightly different ways, but for both artists the effects of heterogeneous imagery is fundamental to their building of subjectivity in the work. It is in the equalising sweep of this heterogeneity that the cosmopolitanisation is evoked. Heterogeneity as it is offered through the work of both artists evokes a sense of incompleteness and a dialectic as proposed by Levy and Sznaider, although importantly both artists were developing this work before the suggestions of these sociologies and as such can make claims to constituting these ideas through their art.

Collage has been posited as a Diasporic concern by Kobena Mercer drawing on the African-American writer Ralph Ellison, registering inequality through 'sharp breaks, leaps in consciousness, distortions, paradoxes, reversals, telescoping of time, and surreal blending of styles, values, hopes and dreams'.[20] Ellison notably developed this technique from Romare Bearden's projected photomontages. Mercer suggests that the disjunctions in the imagery across the collages and photomontages cut (as they are themselves cut) through the meanings of Blackness (and the power of those meanings) as it traverses the twentieth century through different assignations from 'Negro' to 'coloured' to 'Black'. The cut then stands as witness to 'the dialectical flux of historical becoming'.[21] In this way, montage and collage could be seen to be of particular interest to artists working in the Diaspora. While the focus on the subject matter of art that is dealing with war and global power politics is associated with what might be called a cosmopolitan turn, my own claims and arguments are more to do with the ways in which the subject emerges and re-emerges in the world through art as a cosmopolitising effect.

Novaczek's oeuvre draws from the New American Cinema and the Second World War American filmmaking tradition, which is humanist in sentiment and believed in the integrity of the lo-fi aesthetic and the vision of the artist to express modern life from the streets. Her work is cosmopolitan and proudly Diasporic. 'I am from the Diaspora,' she actually states in one of her films in response to a cab driver asking her where she is from. Many of the filmic devices that Novaczek employs lend themselves to this reading: fragmentation, collage, composition and multiple voices. Each of these devices gives the viewing subject the means to take on what the cosmopolitan offers. As an inversion of Merskimmon's thesis, Novaczek doesn't take her rootedness to the world but brings the world to her (and us): a more outward-looking approach to the cosmopolitan. Although I'm focusing on *Rootless Cosmopolitans*, any one of her films could be analysed from a cosmopolitan point of view.

The film is made with a lo-fi aesthetic. Amongst filmmakers there is often a pragmatic reason for the aesthetic decision. This lo-fi aesthetic is also framed as an authentically driven camerawork that foregrounds experience as the focus of the filmmaker as she is filming the world. However, while in keeping in some ways with this ethos of the New American Cinema through her approach to camerawork and its views on the authentic experience, Novaczek's work also departs from it in her critiques of the authentic subject in films such as *Philosopher Queen* (1994), funded by the Arts Council, where she parades a range of different 'selves' in front of the camera in a panoply of undecideability. There is no stability in the subject in *Philosopher Queen*, which is more in keeping and possibly prefigures in its own way the work of younger artists such as Nikki S. Lee or Oreet Ashery, or indeed my own. Novaczek also departs from the post-war thrust in her self-conscious and self-reflexive borrowing of their 'authentic' language of shooting place. Her focus on Americana and its impact on post-Second World War British Jewish sensibility through cinema and the novel is particularly pertinent to a contemporary awareness of history and subjectivity.

All that sits alongside the way her camerawork and filmic structure creates a subject who is a citizen of world through multiple images of places that are not site specific and while evocative, cannot be identified, but repeat in a way that overloads the senses. This is not a construction of a singular subject but a shifting subject, provisionally constituted through many contingent possibilities that gives the film a global context, but one that is not specified nor specific and therefore cosmopolitan in its lack of identifiable originating location. The works are always moving, with camerawork that feels like it is not able to finish or finesse anything because her subjects are never in one place long enough to do so, 'always running towards something' as Novaczek states in *Rootless Cosmopolitans*.

'What is a Jew?' is the question that begins the film of *Rootless Cosmopolitans*. This is not a narrative film. As a response to the opening question the film offers an episodic set of vignettes: of women in the city, who suggest some kind of female equivalent of the urbane Woody Allen and their interior world. The narrator introduces two women as friends. The film very quickly moves to a conversation between these women that draws an equivalence between blacks and Jews and questions of who looks Jewish and who looks black. The contradictions are cited by the protagonists – of identification across the two groups – the identification of Jews with whiteness and the antisemitism of Farakhan. The ease of the discussion in the film between black and Jewish women in itself sets up a counter narrative to the cited identification. The narrator is a minor player in the sound as multiple voices begin to tell their stories. 'Lily's mother Marcelle. They weren't exactly a chicken soup kind of family.' She is sitting in a car smoking, while the voiceover tells this story of her family. 'She comes from a travelling family. Jews they live here then the borders change,' all the while the subject is silently smoking and talking. 'I came here in '39. I just earned a living.' The subject speaks but the voice is disconnected from the image of her smoking and talking and walking with her daughter in the street. Lily, the subject, then moves back to the existential questions, talking about accepting her Jewishness and what it means. Moving from the existential to the personal and back again – in this way the everyday and history are intertwined. The multiple voices, disconnected from the image, make equivalences between people and peoples. In a later passage the subject tells the story of her grandmother getting elocution lessons and the image shifts between two elderly women: a European-dressed woman and a woman in a white hijab. The narrative could apply to either of them and thus confounds assumptions of community, belonging and identity at the very moment that it identifies it.

Novaczek's 'always running towards something' can offer another way of thinking about the cosmopolitan, and here I will return to Papastergiadis who is clear not to focus on art that dwells on cross-cultural issues nor even on the processes of structural global interfacing, both of which I would add instrumentalises the methodologies and forms of art-making, but art that 'is concerned more with the proposition that the process of world making is a radical act of the cosmopolitan imaginary'.[22] He uses in part the idea of the *stoa*, which is just such a place that Novaczek visualises in her work, as an integral part of the envisioning of ancient Greek cosmopolitanism that was less formal or permanent than the *oikos* (home) and more intimate than the *agora* (public space) and less formal than the *bouleuterion* (Parliament). 'I imagine the *stoa* as a spatial metaphor for the emergence of critical consciousness within the transnational public sphere. It is a space for criticality without the formal requirements of political deliberation and sociality without the duty of domestication.'[23] In the passage that follows in Novaczek's film, the idea of 'world making' happens in a sphere that is both as intimate as it is public. Importantly the camerawork and narrative incorporates the oscillation between those two states and it is this that conjures up for me exactly the moment of the *stoa* that Papastergiadis delineates as the metaphorical place of the cosmopolitan.

Rootless Cosmopolitans (Figures 1 and 2) is shot in black and white, in fragmented moments of urban images. Most of the film uses voiceover to comment and explain. It also adds a surreal quality, undermining any sense of naturalism, implying a structuralist approach to the subject: 'She is here because of this context' kind of structuralism. The film brings past and present together, interweaving longing to belong but questioning to whom and to where. The form of the film is broken, fragmented; the image and the footage is purposefully

Figure 1. Ruth Novaczek, *Rootless Cosmopolitans*, 1991, 16 mm, permission of the artist.

Figure 2. Ruth Novaczek, *Rootless Cosmopolitans*, 1990, 16 mm, permission of the artist.

degraded. The disjunction between sound and image in some passages makes sure that the viewer cannot be sure who is talking and who isn't. This device of undecideability impedes possible judgement of the viewer for the filmic subject, equalising the subjects who speak. Furthermore, this work also has a temporal dislocation. The temporal is evoked through the black-and-white film stock, the vintage clothes and in the allusion to post-Second World War street documentary by artists, such as Helen Leavitt, who were committed to exploring the everyday of the pavement. These indicate nostalgia for the modern moment while the voiceover and 'cheesy' music signify a self-reflexive critique of that nostalgia.

In the second passage of the film the mood shifts from the conversations about Identity to a montage of disjointed images: 'In my dreams I'm a traveller but in my dreams I'm a Jew. In my life I'm running so much I can't see myself and I wonder where I'm running to. To orange trees or prison. Between Diaspora and Zion.' The images in this passage shift in a close succession of edits from a woman sleeping to a Middle Eastern building façade, to images overlaid and the moving of fragments of a passport; a wrought-iron gate; a shop window then sand dunes, a ship at sea, a train, urban scenes, a woman running, jackboots marching, a shield of David drawn in chalk on the pavement, orange trees, a woman walking. This is a fast edit with klezmer music in the background cranking up the tension, to be brought back to earth with the voiceover. Whereas the cosmopolitanism of the nineteenth-century Zionists envisioned a Europeanisation of the intelligentsia in Zion, Novaczek's work forms an affinity with postcolonial debates, with Blacks, Asians and Sephardi Jews, arguing against the over-determination of these categories through the visual in the pulling apart of image from voice and through the undecideability of these categories in her visual composition of subjectivity. There is no asymmetry between 'East' or 'West' in this vision: nothing that tells the viewer what is East or West nor who is black or white and particularly not where the Jew fits into any of these categories that melt into each other in Novaczek's films. Everyone is mucking in together.

I would suggest that in terms of form, this is a quintessentially cosmopolitan passage in a film that explores the theme. It is a vision of multiples, multiple places, multiple voices and visions. The composition is tight so that the context is impossible to read. In other words, all context is made by the juxtaposition of images and the further juxtaposition of the music and the voiceover. Through the fast edits and the disaggregation of sound and image, *Rootless Cosmopolitans* questions these geographical and cultural hierarchies: here the Jew has no originating location. The continual close-ups ensure that the film is both particular and non-specific. Or, looking at it through Szneider and Levy, the viewer experiences the processes of cosmopolitisation in the build-up of imagery and the dialectic between the universal and particular in the tight frame versus the multiple montage within each passage. They seem to take in sweeps worldly impressions coupled with specific faces that read as human. The lack of site-specific context defies the idea of provenance. The pavement could be London. It could be New York – but it might not be. The film also posits multiple viewpoints. For example, in this montage, there is an image of a woman in a white raincoat running in the distance. She is being seen through railings. She is both a minute figure in the distance and in the centre of the shot. This recurs a couple of times, but so does another shot that is looking down at the camerawoman's feet as she walks across the floor. These are simultaneously overlaid as with the other shots enumerated above – all happening at once in a destabilising gesture that asks the viewer to try and make sense of these floating signifiers that coalesce in an experiential world, only to 'run towards' more fleeting images of a different order in the following sequence. In the undecideability of the context and geographical location and in the sweep of the world through its maximalist and multivalent takes, this work offers a cosmopolitan imaginary.

Suddenly there is another shift in tempo. 'When I have difficulty knowing where I'm running to I would go and see my cousin.' The cousin is seen here sitting by some lupins in a garden, then with a group of people where she is telling a traditional fable, then to a passage where the narrator and Lily Klein meet at a café by accident and discover a connection: a romantic relationship is implied. Thus the film travels from the global to the domestic, from the existential to the specific – and from communal, formal interactions to an intimate relationship. In this way no relationship, no interaction is privileged. Novaczek prefaces this work that it is about Jews, but destabilises the term even as she speaks it, which I would argue is also an equalising gesture that interconnects the citizens of the world. So this film offers critiques of nationalism; of the whiteness of Jews and their exclusivity; of rootedness as an aspiration and the cosmopolitan figure.

Doug Fishbone works with the idea of the collage and the disjunctions between image and voice to create the gaps and maximalist overload that Novaczek does through parallel editing. Whereas Novaczek's work emerges out of the tradition of experimental film, Doug Fishbone is situated within the art world and would consider his work gallery art.[24] He is a younger artist who has emerged in the early twenty-first century, graduating MFA in 2004. He uses a range of deflationary devices to destabilise the power relations between the viewer and subject that cuts across the idea of hierarchies and place-making.

> To grasp the dynamic of cultural cosmopolitanism we may need not only to consider the big shifts and wide networks of global change but also to ponder over how little commonality is now necessary before people find a connection with others.[25]

Fishbone is interested in the possibilities of a subject that cannot be pinned down nor contained which he constitutes through a world constructed through mediated imagery and 'shaggy dog' stories. His subjects have no authenticity nor specificity beyond the internet-derived imagery, but yet create believable and recognisable personas that reach across geographical specificity because of the global reach of the internet and demonstrate how profoundly cosmopolitanising this reach is. Between 2003 and 2005 Fishbone made a group of works that combined a voiceover and a vast plethora of still images corralled from the internet. The world Fishbone creates is one that is hermetically sealed within its confines and also, like Novaczek, operates within the schema of the *stoa* in its somewhat cavalier approach to the subject. The subject here is constituted through the smoke and mirrors of mediated imagery that stretch modes of acceptability collapsing judgement: no one in this world can take for granted her place in the world nor attack anyone else's idea of place in the world. It is provisional – that is, ever-changing, depending on the word and image juxtaposition at any given time that itself never stops moving. This lack of stasis demonstrates the processes of cosmopolitanisation.

In terms of visible Jewishness, Fishbone creates composites made of images of stereotypes of Jews, the *magen david* (shield of David) symbol, Hebrew words, photographs of the *Shtetl* (Jewish village) or Israeli soldiers and Jewish celebrities. He juxtaposes these with images of pornography, 'trailer trash', animals smoking, the hammer and sickle and other symbols of ideology. This is not the elevated Jewish subject of the dominant paradigm in Jewish art, which follows an immersive lament for a past of loss and atrocity. It is somewhat abject. There is no pure subject in Fishbone's vision but the opposite of the elevation of ethnic insiderism: a deflationary Jewishness of the everyday dilemmas and problems.

These are short works, each between 10 and 20 minutes long, and each has a similar format that involves an American East Coast voice philosophising on life. The voice narrates over the still images in his films, as a riff on the stand-up comic, telling seemingly disconnected anecdotes, jokes and asides. He also performs live. The tales told conjure a neighbourly breeze-shooting kind of effect replete with puns, platitudes and 'common sense' laden misapprehension of the complexities of the world. There is constant juxtaposition between the images that come and go and the story told by the narrator, clashing against the mundane drone of the voice that stretches modes of acceptability. The meanings created by the contrasting images and the narrative are problematic and challenging but too fast to reflect on, or even make sense of in a single screening. This is in direct contrast to the 'long look' type of film that commits the viewer to contemplative reflection on the image slowly and beautifully unfolding. In the 'long look' the point of slow is to help the viewer see the beautiful in the normal and the everyday: the tasteful of the long look versus the tasteless of Fishbone. The narrator, usually in cinema, is the voice of authority. In Fishbone's work the narrator becomes the trickster playing the imbecilic man of the people in order to undermine the power of that very figure. Using the seeming randomness of internet image searches (although these are carefully ordered), Fishbone creates a world with no apparent logic external to the tale he weaves and like Novaczek, this work is lo-fi and deflationary. However, unlike Novaczek, Fishbone's work is firmly anti-humanist in its ethos, situating the subject as formed through mediation and absent from the centre stage of his own construct. He does this culturally through the images of shtetls, Chagall paintings, stereotypes of Jews, Klezmer music and snippets of Yiddish. That there is no certainty seems to be the main point at stake in the world of Fishbone's making (Figure 3). However, it is not individual images that create the overall meaning in the work but the maximalist overloading and the humour built up through the absurdities of the juxtapositions throughout the works. These absurdities delineate the contemporary dissolution of division between global and local, national and international, us and them as an everyday and on-going practice.[26]

Figure 3. Doug Fishbone, Religion (2008). Digital Giclee Print; size: A2 (59.4 cm x 42.0 cm), permission of the artist.

One of the most interesting claims of the work is to question entitlement through a temporal inversion. It is striking that the works make a call to being out-of-time. 'What if what we think now turns out to be as silly in the future as our past seems to us today?,' the voiceover asks, also asking if the woolly mammoth knew what it was called by humans or if the Incas knew what period they were living in. He does this to make the point that we can never be safe in our assumptions of ourselves or of our understanding of the world. Fishbone thereby questions the supremacy of the contemporary, the embeddness of key assumptions of subjectivity and our place within it. I see this as a profoundly cosmopolitan device.

In the first film, *The Ugly American* (2003), there is no redemption, just a relentless Lenny Bruce-inspired alienation and self-hatred. While the works are explicitly Jewish, the work naturalises the Jewish voice and fuses it with an imbecilic, working-class, homespun voice narrating lines such as 'then there's that nursery rhyme, I'm sure you know it. "Corn on the cob Paul Pott pie, dirty fat slob, were all gonna die". You see life is a bit of a gamble and to be honest with you the dice have never seemed to go my way.' Then he talks of his mother, who was an alcoholic, then his abuse by the priest, then 'but sometimes I wonder, what with all that recovered memory therapy', then a picture of Freud, stopping for a mere moment before continuing to talk about wanting to live in the country. The explicitly Jewish references interweave with all other imagery in a way that deflates any special status of any kind. It is a collage – all that is available is to contemplate the whole composite piece in its entirety, losing the detail. For example, in this film he asks the viewer 'Can you see anything hidden?', showing an elephant with six legs, then the IMF insignia that shifts to contain an image of an antisemitic stereotype of a Jew. His tactics are shock tactics: he does not self-exoticise nor explain Jewishness in his work. Central to the piece is that he doesn't make the Jewish references key to the meaning of the piece either. In *The Ugly American* he takes the viewer into a world that he considers normal, with its mere smattering of Jewish references, yet a world that is not directed at a 'Jewish' audience but an assumed predominantly non-Jewish art world.

The fast-moving imagery equalises through visual overload. The work also equalises class by mixing folding imbecilities into philosophical references and allusions. This overlap between different viewing publics is created through the wacky humour and through shock; Fishbone creates a crossover through the idea of eccentricity and imbecility as the new normal.

In *Towards a Common Understanding* the film begins with various images of fish, then a diver swimming beside the fish in his wetsuit. Finally a bikini-clad woman appears, then another giving way to an porn image of a woman, on her back, holding open the lips of her vagina. The narration over this display is, 'My dad used to say, statistics are like bikinis. What they reveal is interesting but what they conceal is essential.' The porn image is viewed just at the utterance of the word 'essential', quickly giving way to a censored sign. The film goes on to talk about how we need to give order to the world all the while the film is ripping through images of war, The Bomb, Einstein. However the message is actually irrelevant, signalled by the contrast between the highly charged and deliberately provocative motifs. The message that is eventually delivered is a platitude: we are all different. The message is thus revealed as irrelevant with the lack of message being the point. The platitude is also a deflationary tactic that situates the artist against what he is setting up: the narrator is not the seer that is the usual voice, but instead is an equaliser that intersects with the viewer, forcing the viewers to think about the limits of their morals.

Much of the imagery is also objectionable and the juxtapositions are shocking through his use of pornography, 'trailer trash', animals smoking, people with extreme disabilities and other absurdist internet obsessions all 'mashed up' together with symbols of Jewish identification, political beliefs (such as the hammer and sickle) and Israeli figureheads. There is no hierarchy or differentiation and the flatness itself shocks – shocks us out of any liberal ideal of a genteel comfort zone in cosmopolitanism or a middle-class nomad. All amounts to little in the end as it collapses through the continuing overload. The accumulation of information is so much that the effect is of a build-up of these fragments into a reeling sense of undecideability as the viewer struggles to construct some kind of overall meaning. Through the characters' ignorance and parochialism he sees the world and while judgements are made, they are annulled by the fluidity and contingency with which he makes those judgements and moves on because he never really understands what is at stake. This is the projection, the delusional fantasy of a putative YouTube subject – the obsessive, distrustful but authoritarian conspiracy theorist scouring the net for clues that offer no conclusive answer and no real self-reflection. Maybe somehow the superficiality of this subjectivity offers possibilities for cosmopolitanisation through its fluidity and ephemerality of identification (Figure 4).

Figure 4. Doug Fishbone, Religion (2008). Digital Giclee Print; size: A2 (59.4 cm × 42.0 cm), permission of the artist.

So, importantly, Fishbone does not elevate Jewishness. The normalisation of Jewishness acknowledges that this is merely one ethnicity amongst many and that it is not special nor more worthy and certainly not fixed. The aim in using the stereotype and the collision of brutal imagery is as an absurdist Dada-esque device. The work of Fishbone situates itself through cosmopolitan ideals, it could be said, through the tactic of deflating all that he represents: the Jewish, the educated, the middle-class subject. He does this as an equalising manoeuvre of absurdist ignorance. Neither education nor riches release one from prejudice and bigotry in this worldview. No one has the right to laugh at others, nor judge. The critique is present through the juxtaposition and contradictions of the imagery and narrative and the images from one another.

Which brings me to the heart of my claim that my own recuperation of the term 'cosmopolitanism' aims not to make the contentious issue of belonging 'all right' through referencing the nomadic, nor to elevate the home as a site of safety (for it may well be a site of ambivalence, claustrophobia or threat, especially for women), but to hold on to the discomfort of *not* belonging as a radical possibility for subjectivity, to normalise the expectation that the subject is always an incomplete project but that incompleteness is a condition of being. Home can never represent total comfort and 'belonging' is an impossible if necessary aim.

Novaczek and Fishbone in very different ways situate an incomplete subject of provisionality and discomfort in their work. Neither of these artists make a home anywhere, but seem to engage in the emotional processes of being unsettled. In this way they posit a contingent subject that is incomplete, analogous to Levy and Sznaider. As art, its incompleteness, however, is replete with possibility for the viewer through the cinematic experience, thus taking it to another level. Novaczek's example is humanist and offers the possibility of redemption through the cosmopolitan and relations with others, while Fishbone's vision is post-humanist and seemingly profoundly non-redemptive. However I would argue that the redemption offered is one that is pulled from the equality of the squalid worldview – equality from below. Despite their differences what both artists have in common is a presentation of a subject mired in reiterative provisionality as a positive force that offers a way of being in the world through the celebration of the disparate, the disjunctive and the composite as a new normal. This new normal borne out of a maximalist tendency of contingency and flux that is, I would argue, the condition of a Diasporic identity, rather than the nomadic homing, can offer a model for the contemporary cosmopolitan ideal.

Notes

1. *October* is a journal of Art History, Theory and Criticism.
2. Krauss, "Video: The Structure of Narcissism," 50–64.
3. Garfield, "Towards a Re-articulation," 99–108.
4. Adorno, *Aesthetic Theory* and Debord, *The Society of the Spectacle* are two key texts that inform the idea of art as critique that has been the prevalent force for many decades in art. In addition, many Modern forms of art, such as Dada, have established a critical manifesto in the earlier parts of the twentieth century. Finally, the idea of an avant-garde in art, which is much discussed and commonplace in relation to modernism, particularly assumes a critique on previous art.
5. Buchloh, "The Politics of the Signifier," 7. See also Garfield, "Towards a Re-Articulation of Cultural Identity," 99–108.
6. Such as *From Generation to Generation*, http://www.jewishmuseum.org.uk/generation, or *Golem*, http://www.jmberlin.de/main/EN/01-Exhibitions/02-Special-Exhibitions/2016/

golem.phpNormal Kleeblatt, curator at the New York Jewish Museum is a notable exception, with a number of groundbreaking and critical exhibitions about contemporary Jewish and Other identities, such as *Too Jewish? Challenging Traditional Identities* (1996).
7. Judy Chicago, a prominent pioneering feminist artist, has this on her website explaining her "Jewish themes:" "As a result of the investigation of their Jewish heritage that Chicago and Woodman undertook during the Holocaust Project, Chicago became interested in Jewish themes. Since then, she has created a number of works, including a series of prints based on a recent translation of the Song of Songs along with a number of Judaic ritual objects. These include designs for tallit bags; a unique matzoh cover celebrating the women associated with Passover; and a personal Haggadah for use by the Seder group that she and Woodman have participated in for over twenty years." http://www.judychicago.com/gallery/jewish-themes/jt-artwork/
8. Bohm-Duchen and Grodzinski, *Rubies and Rebels*.
9. Garfield, "Playing With History," 320–39.
10. Baskind, *Jewish Artists and the Bible*. I would consider the particularism of the Bible, as in Baskind's book, as part of the dilemma of mining one's particularity for celebratory purposes. The issue of the absence of Bible stories in Western art is to do with the importance of Greek mythology as the ideal of Western civilisation in opposition to the Hebraic, as outlined by Arnold, *Culture and Anarchy*.
11. Levy and Sznaider, "Memories of Europe," 160.
12. Merskimmon, *The Cosmopolitan Imagination*, 7–8.
13. Ibid., 64.
14. Ahmed, *Strange Encounters*, 80.
15. Cheyette and Marcus, *Modernity, Culture and "The Jew."* Cheyette and Marcus use the same argument with regard to "the Jew" as the paradigmatic other in modernity. "The Jew" as paradigm elides real Jews.
16. Papastergiadis, *Cosmopolitanism and Culture*, 9.
17. Fishbone later worked with a Nollywood director as an actor in a bone fide Nollywood film entitled *Elmina* (2010) but launched the film at Tate Britain (as well as the director launching the film in the usual Nollywood cinema distribution).
18. Doane, *The Emergence of Cinematic Time*, 187–94.
19. Harbord, *Rethinking Film Studies*, 72.
20. Mercer, *Cosmopolitan Modernisms*, 125.
21. Ibid., 126.
22. Papastergiadis, *Cosmopolitanism and Culture*, 91.
23. Ibid., 92.
24. This distinction is complicated, as Novaczek did her practice degree at Central St Martins.
25. Papastergiadis, *Cosmopolitanism and Culture*, 89.
26. Beck and Sznaider, "Unpacking Cosmopolitanism," 383.

Disclosure statement

No potential conflict of interest was reported by the author.

References

Adorno, Theodor W. *Aesthetic Theory*. Minneapolis, MN: University of Minnesota Press, 1998.
Ahmed, Sarah. *Strange Encounters: Embodied Others in Post-Coloniality*. London: Routledge, 2000.
Arnold, Matthew. *Culture and Anarchy*. Oxford: Oxford University Press, 2009.
Baskind, Samantha. *Jewish Artists and the Bible in 20th Century America*. Hong Kong: Penn State University Press, 2014.
Beck, Ulricke, and Natan Sznaider. "Unpacking Cosmopolitanism for the Social Sciences: A Research Agenda." *The British Journal of Sociology* 61 (2010): 381–403.
Bohm-Duchen, M., and Vera Grodzinski. *Rubies and Rebels: Jewish Female Identity in Contemporary British Art*. London: Lund Humphries, 1996.
Buchloh, Benjamin, Hal Foster, Silvia Kolbowski, Rosalind Krauss, and Miwon Kwon. "The Politics of the Signifier: A Conversation on the Whitney Biennial." *October* 66 (1993): 3–27. Cambridge: MIT Press, 1993.
Debord, Guy. *The Society of the Spectacle*. Kalamazoo: Black and Red, 2000.
Chambers, Iain. "Unrealized Democracy and a Posthumanist Art." In *Democracy Unrealized: Documenta 11, Platform 1*, edited by O Enwezor, 169–178. Ostfildern-Ruit: Hatje Cantz, 2002.
Cheyette, Bryan, and Laura Marcus. *Modernity, Culture and "The Jew"*. Cambridge: Polity Press, 1998.
Doane, Mary Ann. *The Emergence of Cinematic Time*. Cambridge, Mass.: Harvard University Press, 2002.
Garfield, Rachel. "Towards a Re-articulation of Cultural Identity: Problematizing the Jewish Subject in Art." *Third Text* 20, no. 1 (2006): 99–108.
Garfield, Rachel. "Playing with History: Jewish Subjectivity in Contemporary Lens-based Art." In *Routledge Companion to Contemporary Jewish Cultures*, edited by Nadia Valman and Laurence Roth, 46–59. London and New York: Routledge, 2015.
Harbord, Janet. *The Evolution of Film: Rethinking Film Studies*. Cambridge: Polity Press, 2007.
Krauss, Rosalind. "Video: The Structure of Narcissism." *October 1* (1976) 50–64. Cambridge: MIT Press.
Kwame, Anthony Appiah. *Cosmopolitanism: Ethics in a World of Strangers*. New York: W.W. Norton, 2006.
Mercer, Kobena. *Cosmopolitan Modernisms*. London: Iniva and MIT Press, 2005.
Meskimmon, Marsha. *Contemporary Art and The Cosmopolitan Imagination*. London: Routledge, 2010.
Mouffe, Chantalle. "For a Politics of Nomadic Identity." In *Travellers' Tales: Narratives of Home and Displacement*, edited by G Robertson et al., 102–110. London: Routledge, 1994.
Papastergiadis, Nicos. *Cosmopolitanism and Culture*. Cambridge: Polity Press, 2012.
Sznaider, Natan, and David Levy. "Memories of Europe: Cosmopolitanism and its Others." *Cosmopolitanism in Europe*, edited by Chris Rumford, 158–177. Liverpool: Liverpool University Press, 2007.

Index

Note: Page numbers in **bold** type refer to tables
Page numbers in *italic* type refer to figures

Aaronovich, D. 163
Abraham 21, 22
Abschiebung (Vertlib) 151
Achcar, G. 63
Adelson, L. 152
Adorno, T. 30–31, 62, 71, 72, 73, 207n43
Akerman, C. 186, 189
Alexander, J. 90–91
All Russians Love Birch Trees (Grjasnowa) 144–145, 150–157, *158*
Alÿs, F. 197
American Jewish Joint Distribution Committee (JDC) 135
American Revolution 39, 40, 41
Améry, J. 98
ancestors, and ghosts 117–120
Ancient Judaism (Weber) 22
Anderson, B. 66, 112, 115–116, 117, 120, 121, 124
Antichrist, The (Roth) 48
Antigone (Sophocles) 119
Antiquity, social modalities 38
Appiah, K. A. 146, 147, 189, 195
Arcades Project (Benjamin) 182–183
Arendt, H. 5, 61, 62, 73, 98, 99, 101, 107, 147, 148, 150, 157
Arnold, M. 85
Aron, R. 10
Asher, H. 75n42
Ashkenazi Jews 132, 133, 136, 137
At Home in Exile (Wolfe) 145, 148
At the Mind's Limits (Améry) 98
Austria, and national identity 166
Auto-Emancipation (Pinsker) 21

Babi Yar 68
bad universalism 2
Badiou, A. 10
Bagno, O., and Bodemann, Y. M. 151
Bankier, D. 66
Baron, I. 121, 122
Bauer, B., debate with Marx 6–8, 10, 63, 65–66, 70

Baum group 68
Bauman, Z. 99
Bebel, A. 8, 65
Beck, U. 3, 9, 30, 60, 146, 173, 181, 189
Behemoth (Neumann) 71
Belilios, E. R. 132–133
Belinsky, V. 97
Benhabib, S. 29, 73, 98, 146, 147
Benjamin, W. 120, 148, 182
Benner, E. 63
Bentwich, N. 88
Bhabha, H. 146
Birnbaum, P. 63, 65
Bisky, L. 169
Black Book: The Nazi Crime Against the Jewish People 69
Blair, A. (Tony) 120
Blatman, D., and Poznanski, R. 67–68
Bloodlands (Snyder) 99
Bodemann, Y. M., and Bagno, O. 151
Book of Job as a Greek Tragedy, The (Kallen) 86
Bordowitz, G. 181
Bouretz, P. 32
Bourne, R. 88, 91
Boyarin, D., and Boyarin, J. 82
Braidotti, R. 197
Break, The (Rühle-Gerstel) 100–103, 105
Breckenridge, C., *et al.* 81–82, 90
British Empire 130, 137
Brod, M. 24
Brody 50–51
Broken Glass Park (Bronsky) 151
Bronsky, A. 151
Brumlik, M. 145
Brun, C., and Fábos, A. 122
Brussels 172, 173
Buchloh, B. 194–195
Büchner, G. 174
Buddhism 33
Bunyan, A. 163–178

INDEX

Butler, J. 56
Buxbaum, D 137

Cactus Babylon (1995–1996) 186, *187*, 189
Calhoun, C. 114
Calvin, J. 39
Chamberlain, H. S. 22–23
Chambers, I. 197
Chatterjee, P. 115–116
Chatwin, B. 186, 190
Cheah, P. 112, 114–115, 116, 117, 119, 120, 121, 122, 124
Cheap Philosophy (1992) 181, *182*
Chernilo, D. 60
Cheyette, B., and Marcus, L. 208n15
Chicago, J. 195
China 136, 137, 140
China Light & Power Company (CLP) 136
Chirot, D., and Reid, A. 112
Christianity 81, 85, 86
citizenship tests 125
Civil Sphere, The (Alexander) 4
Cixous, H. 180, 181, 189
Closs Stephens, A. 112, 113, 120–121, 122
collage 198–199, 203
Communism 95; National Socialism and the Jews 96–100
Communist Manifesto, The (Marx and Engels) 8
communities, paranational 123, 151–152
Contemporary Art and The Cosmopolitan Imagination (Merksimmon) 196
cosmopolitan memory 147–150
Cosmopolitan Vision, The (Beck) 3, 30
Cosmopolitanism and Culture (Papastergiadis) 197
Cousin, G. 13n40
Cristaudo, W. 29–45
Critique of the Gotha Programme (Marx) 72
cultural nation 166
Culture and Anarchy (Arnold) 85
Cynicism 29

Darkness at Noon (Koestler) 100, 103–105
Darwin, C. 85–86
Davies, W. D. 24
Declaration of Independence 39
Dee, J. 17
Delanty, G. 29, 30, 114
Delitzsch, F. 23–24
Democracy in America (Tocqueville) 11
Deren, M. 185
Derrida, J. 61–62, 115, 118, 119, 121, 157, 189
Dewey, J. 88, 91
Dialactic of Enlightenment (Horkheimer and Adorno) 72
Die Europäischen Nationen (Rosenstock-Huessy) 36
Diestel, J. 137, 138
Dische, I. 151

displacement 49
Disraeli, B. 132
diversity 81–82
Doane, M. A. 198
Döblin, A. 54
Drowned and the Saved, The (Levi) 105
Durkheim, E. 2

Ehrenburg, I. 69, 99
Eichmann in Jerusalem (Arendt) 147
Eisenberg, S. 139
Eisenman, P. 121
Elias, H. 140
Ellison, R. 198–199
emancipation 2, 3, 4, 5, 6, 7, 8, 9, 11, 18
Emperor's Tomb, The (Roth) 54
Engels, F. 64
English Revolution 37, 38, 39, 40
Enlightenment 196
Enzensberger, H. M. 149
Erasmus 17
Erfahrungsraum 79, 83
Essential Outsiders (Reid and Chirot) 112–113, 115, 116, 118, 119, 121, 123, 124
ethics 32, 33
ethnic cleansing 114
European Commission 167, 170, 171
European Courier, The (Menasse) 163–164
European Parliament (EP) 169, 170
European Union (EU) 164, 165; bureaucrats 165–169, 170; elites 169, 172; Nobel Prize 171; post-national 166, 167, 170; Soviet Union 171
Euroscepticism 163
Eurozone crisis 167
exile, notion 124
Extraordinary Memory of Rosa Masur, The (Rabinowich) 151

Fábos, A., and Brun, C. 122
Fairbank, J. K. 130
Fascism 114
Feldt, J. E. 79–94, 113, 114, 116, 118, 120
Ferrante, E. 190
Fichte, J. G. 19
film, experimental 185, 203
Fine, R. D. 1–15, 30, 65, 80
First Opium War (1839–1842) 130–131
Fischer, L. 8, 65
Fischer, R. 67
Fishbone, D. 193–209
Flight Without End (Roth) 56
Foundations of the Nineteenth Century (Chamberlain) 22–23
Frank, T. 49
Frankfurt School 71
Frankfurter Zeitung 47, 53
French Enlightenment and the Jews (Hertzberg) 4
French Revolution 2, 36, 37, 40, 62, 70, 98

INDEX

Friedlander, S. 67
Full Count of the Times (Rosenstock-Huessy) 38

Galut 25
Garfield, R. S. 122, 193–209
Geiger, A. 84
Geisler, B. 150
Gelbin, C. S. 95–111, 146
Geras, N. 74n26
German Idealism 115
German Ideology, The (Marx) 63
Germany: and national identity 166; national interest 167; paternalism 172; reunification 166
Giant in Chains, The (Broder) 171–172
Gildemeister, O. 23
Gilman, S. L. 16–28, 146
globalization 17
Goethe, J. W. von 20, 34
Goldziher, I. 21–22
good universalism 2
Gorelik, L. 151
Great Purge 97, 103
Greene, D. 84
Grégoire, H. 17, 19, 63
Gregory VII, Pope 37, 40
Grossman, D. 56
Guenon, R. 23
Gypsies 20

Habsburg Empire 46, 54
Hacohen, M. 51, 54
Hall, S. 129, 132, 134, 140
Hamburger, A. 139
Hamid, M. 190
Hannema, F. 57n2
Hansen, D. T. 91
Harbord, J. 198
Hardoon, S. A. 131, 132
hauntology 115, 116
Hebrew Bible 87, 88
Hegel, G. W. F. 13n19
Heidegger, M. 24
Heilsgeschichte 42
Held, D. 61, 114
Hellenism 85
Henry IV, Holy Roman Emperor 37
Herder, J. G. 18–19, 22
Hertzberg, A. 4
Herzfeld, M. 121
Hess, M. 81, 82
Hessian Courier (Büchner) 174
Hillier, S. 195
Hinduism 33
Hinterland (Zaimoglu) 152
History of Mankind (Ratzel) 23
Hitler, A. 24, 97, 98, 99, 105, 108, 109, 116
Hoffmann, J. 99
Hofmann, M. 48

Holocaust 9, 10, 121, 151, 152, 153, 154, 155, 156, 157, 158, 165, 166; Jewishness 145, 148, 149
Holocaust and Memory in the Global Age (Sznaider and Levy) 149
Holton, R. J. 90
Holy Family, The (Marx and Engels) 7
home, and homeland 120–124
Hong Kong 129–143; Jewish Community Centre 130; Jewish history 130–135; post-1997 life 138–141; schools 140; twentieth century Jewish life 135–138
Horkheimer, M. 62, 71, 72, 73
Horthy, M. 49
hospitality 119
How To Get Filthy Rich in Rising Asia (Hamid) 190
Hughes, J. 50–51
Huguenots 39, 40
Human Condition, The (Arendt) 147
Human Rights 148, 149, 157, 158
Human Rights and Memory (Sznaider and Levy) 149
humanist universalism 3
Hungary 48–49, 167–168
Hurwitz, H. 88

I Love Dick (Kraus) 186
Ideas for A Philosophy of the History of Mankind (Herder) 18–19, 20
identity, national 166, 181, 190
illiberal multiculturalism 54
imagined community, nation 112, 114, 115, 116, 120–121, 124
In the Cross of Reality (Rosenstock-Huessy) 36, 38
Ingram, J. 61
internationalism 96–97, 101
Iranian Revolution 42
Islam 33, 38
Islamism 42
Israel 10

James, H. 179, 184
Jerusalem (Mendelssohn) 82
Jewish Anti-Fascist Committee (JAC) 69
Jewish Benevolent Society 135
Jewish Community Centre (Hong Kong) 139
Jewish Memory and the Cosmopolitan Order (Sznaider) 144, 146–147, 149, 150, 157
Jews and Modern Capitalism, The (Sombart) 22
Johannine Christianity 35, 42
Judeo-Bolshevik myth 49
Judicial Uncertainty of a Marriage, The (Grjasnowa) 158
Jüdische Merckwürdigkeiten (Schudt) 20
Judt, T. 50
Jung, C. G. 24

Kadoorie, E. 133
Kadoorie, L. 134, 135, 136

INDEX

Kadoorie, M. 136
Kaldor, M. 114
Kallen, H. M. 123
Kaminer, W. 151
Kant, I. 2, 19–20, 29, 35, 62, 82, 98, 119, 154
Kantian cosmopolitanism, history and Jews 80–81
Keun, I. 56
Knausgaard, K. O. 184, 190
Koestler, A. 100, 101, 103–105
Kohl, H. 167
Korea 117, 118
Koselleck, R. 79
Kristallnacht 67
Kwon, H. 112, 113, 116, 117, 118, 119, 120, 122, 124

Lamprecht, J. F. 17
Langeswieche, D. 63–64
Laquer, W. 163
Last Days of Europe, The (Broder) 164
Lazaroms, I. J. 46–59, 121, 122, 125
Lenin, V. I. 64
Levi, P. 105, 136
Levy, D., and Sznaider, N. 196, 198, 202, 207
liberalism, and nationalism 62, 63
Libeskind, D. 121
Like a Tear in the Ocean (Sperber) 106–108
Littler, M. 159n28
Löwith, K. 8
Luther, M. 39
Luxemburg, R. 8, 64–65, 66, 72, 73, 124

Maccabean, The 88
Mann, K. 66
Marcus, L., and Cheyette, B. 208n15
Marshall Plan 165
Marx, K. 21, 41, 61, 62; debate with Bauer 63, 65–66, 70; early nationalism critique 62–64
Mass Psychology of Fascism, The (Reich) 103
Mein Kampf (Hitler) 24, 97
melting pot metaphor 88–89
Memento (2000) 185
Memmi, A. 190
Memories of Europe (Levy and Sznaider) 196
memory 147–150
Mendelssohn, M. 5–6, 11, 81, 82, 145
Meng, M. 150
Menorah Journal, The 88
Menorah Society 84, 86
Mercer, K. 198, 199
Merkel, A. 167
Merksimmon, M. 194, 196–197, 199
Mignolo, W. 123
Mikhoels, S 69
minoritarian modernity 90
Modernity and the Holocaust (Bauman) 99
Monroe, K. 68
Mouffe, C. 197
multiculturalism, illiberal 54
Multidirectional Memories (Rothberg) 99

Münzenberg, W. 106
My White Nights (Gorelik) 151

narrative, personal 194–195
Nathan, M. 134–135
national identity 166, 181, 190
national interest: concept 166–167; Germany 167
national sovereignty, concept 168
nationalism, Marx 62–64
Nazis, antisemitism 66–68, 71
Nazism: Communism and the Jews 96–100; and Stalinism 98–100, 102, 105, 106, 108, 109
Netanyahu, B. 145
Neumann, F. 71
Neusner, J. 24
New American Cinema 199
New World, The (2014) 184, 186, 188, 189, 190–191
News From Home (1977) 186
Nietzsche, F. 35
Niewyk, D. 66
Nolan, C. 185
Nolte, E. 98–99
nomad 196, 197
Novaczek, R. 179–192, 193–209
Nussbaum, M. 146, 147

October 194
Ohel Leah Synagogue 130, 134, 137, 138, 139, 140
On Cosmopolitanism (Derrida) 118
On the Jewish Question (Marx) 7, 8, 64
Open Society and its Enemies, The (Popper) 51
opium trade 130–131
Origin of Species, The (Darwin) 85–86
Origins of Totalitarianism (Arendt) 98, 99, 107
Oser, A. 140
Out of Revolution (Rosenstock-Huessy) 36
Oz, A., and Oz-Salzberger, F. 182

Papal revolution 37
Papastergiadis, N. 194, 197, 200
parallel editing 198, 203
paranational communities 123, 151–152
Paris 53, 54
particularism 3, 4, 11, 148; and universalism 146, 150
Paul, St 30
Peirce, C. S. 86
Penslar, D. 18, 53
perception 181
Perpetual Peace (Kant) 98, 154
personal narrative 194–195
Philosopher Queen (1994) 199
Philosophy of Money (Simmel) 21
photomontages 199
Pianko, N. 83
Pinchuk, B. -C. 68
Pinsker, L. 21
Plesch, D. 75n43
Pol Pot 98

INDEX

political nation 166
Popper, K. 51
Portrait of a Lady, The (James) 179
post-universalism 33
Poznanski, R., and Blatman, D. 67-68
Pragmatism 88
prejudice 2
Private History of Pereginus Proteus (Wirland) 18
proletarian universalism 2
Puritanism 39, 40, 41, 42

Rabinowich, J. 151
Radetzky March, The (Roth) 54
Radio (2011) 186, *187*, 189
Ratzel, F. 23
redemption 207
redemptive cosmopolitanism 49-53, 150
Reform Judaism 84, 88
Reformation 37, 38, 39
Reich, W. 103
Reid, A., and Chirot, D. 112
Reifenberg, B. 53, 54
Renaissance 37
Renan, E. 23
Republic of Letters 51
ressentiment 11
revolutionary socialism, mid-nineteenth century 6-9
Roma 61
Romanticism 115
Römhild, R. 152
rooted cosmopolitanism 146
Rootless Cosmopolitans (1989) 183, 184, 195, 199-203
rootlessness 164, 179
Rosenstock-Huessy, E. 36-38
Roth, J. 2, 121-122
Rothberg, M. 99
Rühle-Gerstel, A. 100-103, 104, 105
Russia 42
Russian Revolution 36, 37, 40

San Juan Jr., E. 129
Sartre, J. P. 11
Sassoon, D. 130-131
Sassoon, E. D. 131, 132
Sayce, A. H. 26n29
Schäuble, W. 172
Schlosser, J. G. 19
Schmidt, S. 84
Schopenhauer, A. 35
Schudt, J. J. 20
Schulz, B. 150, 158
Schulz, M. 165, 171
Second International 61, 71
self-assertion, Jewish 88
self-centredness 7
self-criticism, European 9
Self-Fulfilling Prophecy (Neusner) 24

Sephardic Jews 132-133, 134, 136, 137, 146
Shamsie, K. 191
Simmel, G. 21
Simon, L. 88
Sinn, H.-W. 172
Sino-Japanese War (1930s & 1940s) 135
Sinti 61
Slánský, R. 108
Slezkine, Y. 81
Smith, C. T. 132
Snyder, T. 75n42, 99
socialism, revolutionary 6-9
Socialist Response to Antisemitism in Imperial Germany, The (Fischer) 8
sociological cosmopolitanism, and diversity 81-82
Sombart, W. 22
Songlines, The (Chatwin) 186, 187, 190
Soviet Union: antisemitism 68-70; communism and the Jews 95-111; and European Union 171
Spectral Nationality (Cheah) 112-113
spectrality 115
Spectre of Comparisons, The (Anderson) 115
Spencer, P. 60-78, 124
Sperber, M. 106-108
Stalin, J. 64, 68, 69, 180
Stanislawski, M. 85
Star of Redemption, The (Rosenzweig) 31-36
Stengers, I. 184
stoa 200, 203
Stoetzler, M. 74n6
Stoicism 29
Sutherland, C. 112-128

Taberner, S. 144-162
Talk Israel (1994) 183
Taoism 33
Tea Leaf (1983) 183
Tentzel, W. E. 20
Theological Letters (Herder) 19
Third International 61, 71, 96, 97, 104
Titoism 108
Tocqueville, A. de 11
totalitarianism 98, 99
Towards a Common Understanding (2005) 205-206
Traverso, E. 64
Treaty of Westphalia (1648) 61
Trotsky, L. 66, 96, 100, 102

Ugly American, The (2003) 205
United Jewish Congregation 137-138
United Kingdom Independence Party (UKIP) 119
United States of America (USA) 170; hegemony 41; Immigration Act (1924) 49
United States of Europe 172, 179
Universal Declaration of Human Rights (UDHR) 39

INDEX

universalism: Enlightenment 4–6; and particularism 146, 150; post- 33; two faces 1–4
uprootedness 49, 56
usury 4, 5, 19

Vertlib, V. 151
victim ideology 10
Vieten, U. 18
Voegelin, E. 36
Voltaire 6
von Dohm, C. 4, 5, 6

Wagenseil, J. C. 20
Wahrmund, A. 23
Wandering Jews, The (Roth) 53
Weber, M. 22
Weininger, O. 103
Weltbürger 17
Wieland, C. M. 17–18
Wilhelm Meister's Apprenticeship (Goethe) 20

Wilson, W. 39–40
Wissenschaft der Judenthums (WdJ) 84
Wolfe, A. 145, 147, 148
World Congress of Writers 48
world making 200
world risk society 146
world-building 147
writers, and exile 50

Yad Vashem 150, 156
Yugoslavia 108

Zaimoglu, F. 152
Zangwill, I. 88
Zhdanov, A. 97
Zhou, X. 129–143
Zinoviev, G. 104
Zionism 10, 16, 25, 69, 82, 84–85, 88, 113, 121, 122, 190
Zweig, S. 2, 48, 52, 55, 56
Zwischenstationen (Vertlib) 151